The Childhood Emotional Pattern and Human Hostility

Leon J. Saul, M.D.

Emeritus Professor of Psychiatry,
Medical School of the University of Pennsylvania

Honorary Staff, Institute of the Pennsylvania Hospital

Emeritus Training Analyst,
Philadelphia Psychoanalytic Institute

Emeritus Chief Psychiatric Consultant,
Swarthmore College

Dean, The Philadelphia Academy of Psychoanalysis

VNR VAN NOSTRAND REINHOLD COMPANY
NEW YORK CINCINNATI ATLANTA DALLAS SAN FRANCISCO
LONDON TORONTO MELBOURNE

Van Nostrand Reinhold Company Regional Offices:
New York Cincinnati Atlanta Dallas San Francisco

Van Nostrand Reinhold Company International Offices:
London Toronto Melbourne

Library of Congress Catalog Card Number: 80-10904
ISBN: 0-442-23993-9

Manufactured in the United States of America

Published by Van Nostrand Reinhold Company
135 West 50th Street, New York, N.Y. 10020

Published simultaneously in Canada by Van Nostrand Reinhold Ltd.

15 14 13 12 11 10 9 8 7 6 5 4 3 2 1

Library of Congress Cataloging in Publication Data

Saul, Leon Joseph, 1901–
The childhood emotional pattern and human hostility.

Bibliography: p.
Includes index.
1. Hostility (Psychology)–Etiology. 2. Violence–Psychological aspects. 3. Personality in children.
I. Title. [DNLM: 1. Emotions–In infancy and childhood. 2. Hostility. BF575.H6 S256c]
BF575.H6S28 155.4'18 80-10904
ISBN 0-442-23993-9

To the children
and grandchildren

Preface

The purpose of this book is to explore what the new emerging science of psychodynamics can contribute to the study of man's hostility to his fellow man, and to call the attention of the relevant sciences and of intelligent men and women everywhere to this most important and urgent danger to mankind. The great strides that are being made in the understanding of human nature and behavior rarely make headlines. But the dream of man maturing fully and living peacefully with his fellow man is now as much within our reach *theoretically* as is the dream of space travel. What was unthinkable yesterday becomes tomorrow's reality.

The essentials of what makes criminals and great men, what makes the loftiest achievements of the human spirit, and what makes the destruction, chaos, and unutterable bestiality and misery of crime, tyranny, and war—these essentials now are known. To *apply* such knowledge is a vast, almost inconceivably difficult task in human engineering, but it is only a practical task, and it is mankind's greatest challenge.

LEON J. SAUL, M.D.

Acknowledgments

It is a pleasure to thank Dr. Jerome Barkow, Dalhousie University, for Chapter 16, which is largely based on his work supported by the H. F. Guggenheim Foundation; Dr. Sarah Blaffer-Hrdy, Harvard University, for her comments on the ethology of hostility; Drs. Solveig and Charles Wenar, Ohio State University, for their assistance with Chapter 18; Dr. Ward Goodenaugh and Dr. Robert Harding of the department of anthropology, University of Pennsylvania, for their advice and guidance; Dr. Milton L. Miller, for help in obtaining needed data; Dr. Silas Warner, who provided some of the clinical material; Susan (Mrs. Vernon) Bender, my peerless secretary and assistant, without whom this book could not have been written; and June Strickland, librarian of the Institute of the Pennsylvania Hospital, for her prompt, ever willing, and indispensable help in providing books, articles, and references. Thanks of a special kind are due my wife for her patience and support throughout.

Thanks also to Harper and Row publishers for permission to include Chapter 17, which is based upon the author's *Bases of Human Behavior,* first published by J. B. Lippincott (1951) and reissued by Greenwood Press (1972).

Certain of the other chapters contain material that originally appeared in technical journals and in previous books by the author, and for permission to publish these thanks to *The Psychoanalytic Quarterly, The Proceedings of the American Philosophical Society,* and *The American Journal of Psychiatry.*

ACKNOWLEDGMENTS

Contents

Section I
Perspective and Preliminary Considerations

We remain on the surface so long as we treat only of memories and ideas. The only valuable things in the psychic life are, rather, the emotions. All psychic powers are significant only through their fitness to awaken emotions.

Sigmund Freud, *Delusion and Dream*

1
The Problem

He that is slow to anger is better then the mighty; and he that ruleth his spirit than he that taketh a city.

Proverbs 15:32

The less pressure of hostility a person is under, the less the need for controlling it.

In an exchange of open letters between Albert Einstein and Sigmund Freud on "Why War?" the great physicist wrote: "How is it possible that the mass of the people permits itself to become aroused to the point of insanity and eventual self-sacrifice [in war]? . . . the answer can only be: man has in him the need to hate and to destroy. . . is it possible to so guide the psychological development of man that it becomes resistant to the psychoses of hate and destruction?"

* * * *

War, although the most extreme and widespread expression of human hostility, is only one form that hostility takes. Man's hostility to man is expressed in every conceivable way, from mild gossip to murder; in crime, both individual and organized; through "irrational hostile acting out" by individuals and by some political and even so-called religious groups; and in the common social inconsiderateness and meanness of everyday life. Hostility that is repressed rather than directly acted out can manifest itself in neurotic symptoms such as psychosomatic conditions, hysteria, anxiety, phobias, and compulsions. When strong enough, hostility can break down the orderly operation of the mind, including the sense of reality, causing psychoses such as severe depression (in which the hostility is directed to the self and may result in suicide) and paranoia (in which the hostility is perceived as coming from others, and may lead to delusions of being attacked, and therefore to murder). Hostility also appears as masochism, that is, self-defeat and self-injury, including self-ruinous addictions. The more mature a person is, and the better adjusted, the less pressure of hostility he is under.*

Man far surpasses all other animals in his powers of speech and intellect, but also in the extent of his brutality to his own kind. Because of it, the human race may destroy itself—by pollution, overpopulation, atomic blast or otherwise, in some combination.

How can we understand this hostility and destructiveness, which causes all humans such deep and widespread suffering and constitutes mankind's central problem? This book is a clinical study of the *psychodynamics of hostility*, which is a vitally important aspect of the central problem if only because it suggests possibilities for prevention and a better life for humanity.

* * * *

Man lives through the same life cycle as do all other animals—conception by sexual reproduction, birth, childhood, adolescence, maturity, senescence, and death. He shares with other animals a method of adaptation to his world by use of the flight-fight reaction, that is, responding to every threat, frustration, or irritation by physiological arousal to escape it or to attack and destroy it. The flight response is apt to be associated with feelings of fear, and the fight-and-destroy response with feelings of anger and hostility.

Yet there are significant differences between man and other animals.

The first difference is quantitative: man matures so slowly that he is dependent upon his parents for twenty or more years, much longer than are other animal young. Secondly, he has a greater capacity for learning. The third is a huge qualitative difference: unlike other animal species, man does not live so much by instinctual, automatic reflexes, drives, and reactions in the wild. He lives centrally and preponderantly in societies, almost exclusively in close, indeed intimate, interrelations with his own species. Some city dwellers may spend their entire existence without experiencing unaltered nature.

---

*We freely use "he," "him," or "his" in the generic sense of "he or she," etc.

Human societies, ranging from small primitive tribes to great modern industrial nations, have provided their members with protection against dangers from nature, such as man-eating beasts and the elements. Societies have made possible the specialization from which science and art have evolved. Medicine, as part of science, now offers protection against many hitherto fatal diseases, and meteorology offers some protection, if only by forewarning, against irresistible forces of nature, such as great storms.

But living within a society, whatever securities it provides, is also a strain on any animal. Man's animal impulses, urges, motivations, and reactions, whether or not released in action in nature, generate fantasies. Certain talented persons shape these fantasies into works of science and of art—that is, culture. But because man lives in a society and in a civilization and culture* formed by society, these animal urges and reactions create emotional pressures that also produce the mental aberrations remarked above: neuroses, psychoses, and criminal, violent, and destructive behavior—mostly the effects of a combination of flight by regression and of fight as repressed or expressed hostility. These mental and emotional illnesses, including crime, threaten the existence of society and the security of its members. The greatest threat to human social cooperation is the fight part of man's fight–flight reaction in the form of sadism and violence to his fellow humans. The sex drive, although hard to control, does not, like hostile impulses, directly cause damage, maiming, and death, but only jealousy and confusion of relationships including parenthood. Such emotional forces as envy and jealousy and also the dependent love needs and narcissism are threats to individuals and society insofar as they arouse the fight–flight response.

To protect the existence of individuals and of society, religions, customs, and laws, written and unwritten, have evolved; courts and police have been formed to control the most blatant of man's hostile, destructive acts, his criminal behavior. The mass demand for help with emotional suffering demonstrates the extent of these disorders (in all of which the fight–flight response is an element). But as Thoreau said, "a thousand strike at the branches for one who strikes at the root. . . ." It is to Freud's everlasting credit that he "went for the root," which turned out to be so deep as to be unconscious. Civilizations,

*"Civilization" is used to mean a human society in which generally the conscious or unconscious goal of the individual members is to be "civil" (considerate) to each other. "Culture" is used to mean the activities within such a society that help the well-being and happiness of its individual members, especially through creative activity, interest or appreciation in crafts, art of all forms, and knowledge in all areas—physical, mental and emotional.

cultures, and national characteristics influence the personalities that grow up within them; but these ideologies are themselves created by the individuals who compose these societies. ("Whether it be a work of art or a significant scientific achievement, that which is great and noble comes from the solitary personality."—Albert Einstein)

A beginning analysis of the ancient conflict between love and hate, which is the essence of the problem of understanding and reducing man's hostility to man (which causes more suffering and death than all other diseases combined), lies in discerning the components of both the pro-human and the anti-human emotional forces, in order to increase the former and reduce the latter.

Some *pro-human* forces are:

1. The animal instinct toward *social cooperation* (on which the first and most authoritative biological work still is, I believe, Warder Allee's *Cooperation Among Animals*).

2. Elements of *parental love*, especially maternal love for the young, which is seen throughout the animal kingdom, especially in the mammals, and to which the young respond with a capacity to love that continues throughout their lives.

3. *Sexual love*, but with qualifications and limitations because in man the sex urge is readily separated from love and is readily fused with hostility, so that instead of dependable caring love we also see rape and hostile sexual attacks.

4. *Identification* or perhaps only *sympathetic identification*. Conscious identification is a "feeling with" another person; it is harder to be cruel to someone if you realize how he feels. Not much is known as yet about identification, but we know it can be pro- or anti-human. For example, a man's father had been overtly cruel to his mother. The man grew up identifying with his father and gradually became as cruel to his own wife as his father had been to his mother, and in the same ways.

5. *Humility*, which seems to increase the capacity for understanding, sympathy, and identification.

6. A strong *conscience*, a mark of "character" and morality, which is usually a check on hostility. But if the adult was properly reared with love, respect, and understanding, he carries less hostility that requires checking.

7. *Receptive-dependent love needs* toward another person, which lessen the hostility one might feel toward him. It is less easy to

feel hate and rage toward someone whose love and help you want.

8. *Maturity*. The more mature a person is, the more secure and sympathetic he is—"only the strong can be gentle."

Turning to *anti-human* forces in the mind, we note that:

1. These forces seem to vary enormously from men of genuine good will and peace to callous, brutal sadists and murderers. Compare, for example, St. Francis, Thomas Jefferson, and Abraham Lincoln with Caligula and Hitler. Such wide individual variations in the strength of the anti-human forces suggest that they are not entirely the result of genes.

2. One possible factor in the anti-human trends is *xenophobia,* about which little is known psychodynamically. Perhaps this fear of strangers and hostility to them is part of the fight–flight reaction, or only a lack of identification with the unknown. Xenophobia may be an instinctive protective response to what is unknown and therefore potentially dangerous. Also, it is easier to respond to with paranoid projection, that is, to feel one's own hostility as though it came from the unknown.

3. What has been called *narcissism* and includes self-love, egocentricity, egotism, conceit, vanity, arrogance, and contemptousness (contrasting with sympathetic identification and mature "object interest"), is often associated with hostility and seems to facilitate it.

> All sensible people know that vanity is the most devastating, the most universal and the most ineradicable of the passions that afflict the soul of man, and it is only vanity that makes him deny its power. Time can assuage the pangs of love, but only death can still the anguish of wounded vanity . . . . it is vanity that makes man support his abominable lot. (Somerset Maugham)

4. As one possible element among others in this anti-human trend, *carnivorism* must be considered. Man is an omnivore, that is, in part a meat eater. In nature the carnivores such as the great cats (lions, tigers, etc.) or the predatory birds (eagles, owls, etc.) have instinctual mechanisms to kill and eat their prey, but the prey is not normally their own species. There is at present no solid evidence that such instincts of carnivores in the wild exist in humans or operate regularly in man's relations with his own kind.

5. As to an *instinct of aggression,* of hostility and destructiveness of man to his own species, the preponderant evidence seems to support ethologist Richard Leakey, who sees man's cruelty and killing of his own kind as a reaction that is mostly conditioned, rather than a constant innate instinct, as described by Konrad Lorenz, for example, in a species of fish like the piranha. Cogent clinical evidence for Leakey's view derives from the fact that we can regularly trace an individual human's hostile behavior to the precise conditioning forces in his childhood emotional pattern.

6. One factor in hostility that is definitely observable (and was first studied scientifically by Walter Cannon) is the adaptive reaction we have mentioned, the *physiological arousal for flight or fight* with which every animal responds to danger, threat, frustration, or irritation—the automatic, reflex arousal of the body for the emergency effort to escape or destroy. In humans this is mostly a form of *reaction*, not an identifiable, continually operating instinctual force. There is so much cruelty and violence in the world that we tend to think, statistically, that hostility must be an instinct that is intrinsic to human nature. But this is not established. The fight–flight reaction is sensitive in the extreme, making hair-trigger hostility. If this reaction is kept aroused for a sufficiently long consistent period of time in childhood, it tends to become a constant trend in the personality, often erotized, that is, fused with sexual satisfaction, making sadism or at least violence-proneness. But this trend is conditioned, not genetic; as noted above, it is regularly possibly to trace it back in analytic therapy to the precise conditioning patterns of childhood.

However, such firmly established and conclusive clinical evidence does not invalidate additional causes. There is now a slowly expanding literature on hostility between humans. Perhaps the necessity of rearing children with repression of hostility creates in those so reared a distaste for the study of it. Perhaps this is why students of hostility have so readily fallen into the old "either–or, nature-or-nurture" way of thinking, and have added to the confusion by using the term "aggression" to mean hostility (see definition of hostility, Chapter 2, p. 17).

In reality, there are many causal factors at play: hostility may be caused by conditioning factors such as faulty childrearing, but this may not be the *sole* cause. Possibly human hostility may also be determined to some extent by an innate drive, as Konrad Lorenz describes in piranhas and other species. Both Leakey and Lorenz may be describing true causal factors, both *nature* and *nurture* in some way.

Dr. Sarah Blaffer-Hrdy, although unable to contribute a full chapter to this book on the ethology of hostility, has written the following, drawn from her special field of expertise. It should be noted that the observations are limited to certain species of primates except for certain baboons, langurs, gorillas and chimpanzees.

> Although "crime," "sadism," and "war" almost by definition must be considered uniquely human, murder by individuals or groups is, if not common, at least routine in the natural world. Murder of adult animals by other adults has been observed among wild rhesus macaques in the Himalayan foothills, savanna baboons in East Africa, and hanuman langurs. Murder is also known to occur among caged *Macaca fascicularis* (the "longtailed" or "crab-eating macaque"). Murder has been reported on the basis of incompletely witnessed events among wild mountain gorillas and wild chimpanzees. On the basis of current evidence, there appear to be two chief contexts in which murder occurs; both involve competition, either competition between males for access to females or competition between females or between males over disputes involving rank in dominance hierarchies. Since rank is typically related to access to resources, etc., I count such disputes as related to competition.
>
> In the natural world, then, competition for resources or mating opportunities is nearly universal, and such aggression and murder as listed above occurred as outgrowths of this competition. Since the individuals engaged stand to gain by winning in such disputes (i.e., to gain increased access to resources, etc.), such behavior must be regarded as "adaptive" rather than pathological . . . however, because conspecific adults are more or less evenly matched, aggressors risk serious retaliatory damage. The greater vulnerability of immature animals is probably one reason why infanticide is the most common form of murder among animals. The ways in which an infanticidal animal gains are complex.*†

---

*Described at length in "Infanticide Among Animals: A Review, Classification and Examination of the Implications for the Reproductive Strategies of Females," to be published by the *Journal of Ethology and Sociobiology.*

†Anthropologist Jerome Barkow points out that: "Only in the past 10,000 years have we been farmers–for several million years before that we were hunters and foragers. Quite possibly the lower frustration of hunter-gatherer childhood and life reflects our ethological heritage. We evolved as hunter-gatherers and our psychodynamics reflect that adaptation."

Even the slight listing of the pro- and anti-human tendencies given above must make use of the contributions of physiology and ethology, to say nothing of all the other fields of study of human behavior. It is obvious that more thorough knowledge must be interdisciplinary, whether research by one person or by interdisciplinary teams. This may have to wait for the next generation of clinicians and behavioral scientists.* Today, however, analytic psychotherapy is able to describe in detail one important causal factor: The source of hostility that stems from faulty childrearing. This source can be corrected, if only by prevention.

The connections of the most common emotional forces seen clinically, which cause individuals the most difficulties in their ordinary lives, can be organized in a simple, comprehensive theory.

There are the *progressive* trends in the personality, which probably reflect in some part the biological tendency to social cooperation seen throughout the animal kingdom as well as the forces of growth and maturing (physical, emotional, and intellectual), including the capacity to love. These are trends toward responsibility, productivity, and independence and giving love (RPI).

On the other hand, there are the *regressive* trends, which are usually less conscious and which include the fight–flight reaction. The fight part causes (1) hostility, rage, hate, and destructiveness; the flight part causes intensification of (2) the tendencies to return to the passive receptive dependence and needs for love of the adolescent, child, infant, or even fetus (PRD), which usually cause (3) feelings of inferiority that are reacted against with exaggerations of (4) the narcissism, egotism, vanity. And there are (5) the sexual urges, which are intensified by both the fight and flight reactions and normally also express the progressive, maturing trends of the personality. The regressive tendencies are largely unacceptable by parents and society and therefore by self, and hence are largely unconscious.

We note in passing that these basic dynamics are in every human personality—in the husband, the wife, and the child; in teacher and student; in the accused, the judge, and the jury; in the patient and

*The most comprehensive contribution the author knows to date is: Edward O. Wilson (1975): *Sociobiology, the New Synthesis*, Cambridge, Mass.: Belknap Press of Harvard University Press, pp. 242–255. This volume provides an exhaustive bibliography as a bridge to the literature.

the analyst, no matter how well and thoroughly analyzed. Of course the amounts, proportions, and interrelationships of these emotional forces are highly individual. Small wonder that interpersonal relationships are so intricate. The analytic therapist who lets himself become personally involved in the least with his patient damages the patient and also himself. Psychotherapy requires the strictest adherence to a purely professional attitude with no thought of involvement whatever, sexually, financially, or socially. *Primum non nocere*—the first duty above all is to do no harm. In fact, the whole of morality, ethics, and law comes down at bottom to doing no harm to others or to self. It has been said in many ways: "Love thy neighbor as thyself"; the Golden Rule—"Whatsoever ye would that men should do to you, do ye even so to them, for this is the law and the prophets." Sex cannot be evil in itself but only if it injures someone. This is also true for dependence, vanity, and everything else. The basic evil is only hostility to human beings—everything, all evil, all crime, the source of all man-made suffering, traces ultimately to some form of human hostility.

Stimulation of the fight-flight reaction can come, in whole or in part, from any immediate situation, from a personal circumstance reenforced by socioeconomic conditions (those who have never known anything but cruelty usually grow up acting with cruelty toward others), and prevailing ideologies, for example, that to be physically violent (mugging and killing) is tough and masculine.

But the threat, frustration, or irritation need not be *external* to stimulate the fight-flight reaction in immediate self-defense; they can also be *internal* through the enormous *conditionability* of the immature human mind. The experiences during the most formative years of childhood, from conception to age about six, shape in the child emotional patterns of reaction to those close to him and responsible for him. As he grows up, these emotional patterns are felt (transferred) toward other persons in his current life. Moreover, these patterns of feelings toward others continue relatively unchanged for the individual's entire life. If a child is accorded love, respect, and understanding during his 0 to 6 by his parents or substitutes, then as an adult he will give others love, respect and understanding, and will be a loving, considerate, responsible person of good will. Contrariwise, if he is treated with such threats, frustrations, and hostility as to keep his fight-flight reaction aroused during this period of early childhood, he will continue to see the world in this way and to expect such treatment from others when he is an adult; his fight–flight reaction will continue to be aroused; he will be neurotic or psychotic, or a sadist or murderer, reflecting his early treatment.

Given today's knowledge, we can conclude with reasonable certainty that *one element in man's hostility to his fellows lies in each person's reactions to his experiences during his earliest childhood, especially from 0 to 6*—"As the tree is inclined, so was the twig bent."*

* * * *

Of course, as in all human behavior, whether the violence is acted out, by either individuals or organized groups, depends upon the internal status of each person's dynamics of violence interacting with the external situation, which tends either to suppress or stimulate such hostile acting out. If the childhood emotional patterns of a large enough part of the national population tend toward violence, then given suitable current external conditions—historical, philosophical, physical, socioeconomic, psychological, political, and so on—such a trend, for example, as Nazism, could again be aroused nationally in any country. Regardless of external conditions, there are always persons who have been so treated during their 0 to 6 that they react with childhood emotional patterns containing strong drives to egotism, power, cruelty, and killing; they form a reservoir of violence-prone personalities in every population. Like attracts like; individuals with similar dynamics form more or less homogeneous groups, and these groups sooner or later constitute organized crime and violence-prone cultish, political, and other organizations.

Such persons, in the course of their lives, cause more harm to others than good, and many innocent people suffer at their hands. The innocent victims and society at large would be healthier and happier if those prone to hostile acting out had never existed, or if they were eliminated from society. But such a solution raises many moral and practical questions: Who would make the final evaluations? Is it morally right to eliminate those who pose a hostile threat to humanity, like a social cancer, when we know their behavior has been mostly determined by their unconscious reactions to the traumatic

*For technical studies by a variety of methods establishing this, see Chapter 18.

ways in which they were reared as small children, before they were six or seven?

It is easy to understand why God would advise the primitive tribes and cities of more than 3000 years ago to be fruitful and multiply (Genesis 9:1)–they were fighting each other and required ample population, especially males, to fight for survival. But today we do not need more cannon fodder. Our crying need is not for *more* people but *better* people, that is, individuals who are more mature, rational, loving, and cooperative.

Quality, not *quantity,* of population is what the whole world of humanity needs desperately in order to survive and make a better life with less man-made suffering for endangered mankind. Quality means, essentially, men and women of maturity, a condition achieved by the quality of love, understanding, and respect accorded every child from 0 to 6 by those close to it and responsible for it. There is, moreover, an optimal density of population for all animal forms, including humans. As important as optimal density within the family unit is density of population in community and nation. Congestion is an important factor in causing violent hostile aggressive behavior, as we see in our cities and nations today.

We conclude that a child reared with love, understanding, and respect will grow into an adult who can in turn give love to others and be a good, constructive spouse, parent, and citizen. If reared with deprivation, depreciation, domination, or other forms of hostility, through omission or commission, the child becomes hostile to his own kind, for it was his own kind who caused his early suffering. He burns with inner hostility, which causes suffering for both himself and others. The repressed flight into psychological regression and the fight expressed in hostile behavior (or urges to it) produce the whole gamut of psychopathology that fills our jails, mental hospitals, and therapists' offices. If we had one generation of children properly reared with love, respect, and understanding, we should see a marked decrease in man's hostility to man, in crime and cruelty. The path to maturity leads away from misery and destruction toward the dictates of religion, education, and rational common sense–toward cooperation and love and a better life for all.

* * * *

The author's clinical observations during his years of practice have concentrated on psychodynamics; thus this book deals only with the modern psychodynamic approach to hostility.*

Not until the turn of the century did knowledge of man's mental and emotional life begin to become a part of science. Previously, such insights had been evident in folk wisdom and in the works of philosophers, writers, or others with the special gift of understanding people, the "menschenkenners." Psychiatry was chiefly descriptive, and psychology, too, was little concerned with the deepest feelings and motivations. There were exceptional individuals, but few followed them. Kraepelin, in the 1890's, introduced a system of classification of the psychoses as seen in the mental hospitals, but he had little or no interest in the emotional elements that might have caused the psychoses. In his office Freud saw neurotics, not the insane or psychotics. His great contribution depended chiefly upon his ability to listen to patients sympathetically and patiently, not deriding them but taking seriously what they were trying to tell him, and searching for causes. Through unremitting study, Freud won for science systematic knowledge of the neuroses. Everyone has something of the neurotic in his makeup; so Freud's investigations led to an understanding of the general population. The study of neuroses led to a comprehension of the total personality. Investigation of emotional and mental disorders led to an understanding of how healthy maturity develops.

---

*It would be beyond our scope to include any list of man's manifold hostilities to man. One general principle should be noted, however: Every situation involving social change gives hostile personalities the opportunity to vent their hostility. The most dangerous conflict between groups today is that between the United States and the USSR. The most dangerous revolution today is the Industrial Revolution, still intensely active. (Although labor has begun to solve some worldwide problems, the place of women in industry is far from solved.)

Problems of great complexity are far from solved, for example, the disposal of hazardous industrial wastes. Such wastes pollute the entire planet, mortally endangering all human and animal life. A great chemical company that has been manufacturing millions of tons of such toxic oil is only now, after 50 years, beginning to recognize its danger, and neither the company nor the government knows how to dispose of it. People are slow to recognize danger to others when their own livelihood and financial profit are at stake. It is easy for their hostility to leak out along with the mortal poisons when it becomes a financial advantage to ignore the danger. The dire danger of industrial poisons is intimately interrelated with the other major threats to mankind, a fundamental cause of pollution being overpopulation.

At this writing, according to the Population Reference Bureau, one million people are being added to the world's population every five days.

The discovery of unconscious processes stimulated research in all the behavioral sciences; independent discoveries in these fields have added enormously to knowledge of the human mind. Two of these discoveries were made by physiologists. Pavlov, a contemporary of Freud, explored the process of "conditioning." Walter Cannon described the mobilization for fight or flight as an emergency reaction to any threat or frustration—and it is also probably a fundamental biological mechanism of adaptation.

Freud did not become sufficiently acquainted with the contributions of Pavlov and Cannon to see the relationship of their work with his own. Studies of conditioning have been carried on chiefly by experimental psychologists who have also investigated field, learning, and gestalt theories, all with direct significance for the understanding of man. Psychologists have expanded our knowledge of "imprinting," first described by animal ethologist Konrad Lorenz. Ethologists and social scientists are contributing to our insights, as are criminologists and cultural anthropologists.

A new basic science is emerging, still embryonic but soundly based upon all the psychological sciences, operating as they do with different methodologies: reconstructive, longitudinal, cross-cultural, experimental, etc. (see Chapter 18). This is the science of psychodynamics. It is already able to describe the nature of the personality and the emotional life, its healthy development to maturity, and the forces that impair and distort such healthy development and functioning. It holds the key to health and disease of the personality, and thus to the well-being of society. The science of psychodynamics discerns the sources of man's hostility to man and how it can be preventively reduced. It makes clear why many people struggle to love each other but cannot, and emphasizes the truth of the adage: if we had one generation of properly reared children, we might approach Utopia itself.

2
What Hostility Is

The threat to the survival of the human species by an astronomical accident is negligible. Man is now reasonably secure against the elements. Floods, earthquakes, volcanic eruptions, and tidal waves are by their very nature sporadic local catastrophes and not general threats to mankind. Today, famine need no longer be a threat because we have the resources, technology, and manpower to produce ample food for the present population of the world, and we can contain the population, which left unchecked would glut the earth.

Modern medicine has made such enormous strides that, although important problems remain, even infectious diseases no longer are a major threat to humanity. Man is still endangered by heart disease, cancer, and the degenerative diseases, but breakthroughs in knowledge and reduction of these diseases are likely to come soon.

There is only one dire threat to mankind today, and that is from man himself. The readiness of human beings to be hostile to each other is by far the greatest problem of mankind—a fatal danger to our species for the imaginable future. The child, as it matures and goes through life, is more in danger from other persons than from any other source. It takes no vast marshaling of facts to establish this. Examples of hostility on a gross scale are everywhere—tyrannical rule, by the right or by the left, which persists in many countries of the world; the fact that modern nations squander countless sums and resources on mobilization for global destruction, reminiscent of lemmings rushing to their own death in the sea; rates of violent crime, divorce, spouse and child abuse mounting to staggering dimensions. But the fact that man's brutality to man has bloodied every page of history and continues to do so does not mean that it is basic to human nature and, as such, inevitable. A close look at man's behavior reveals that it has all the earmarks, not of nature, but of sickness, of psychopathology.

* * * *

Let us begin our investigation of man's hostility with a working definition of the term. As a point of departure, we can say that hostility is the tendency of an organism to do something injurious and harmful to another living organism or to itself.

The dictionary tells us that the word "aggression," often used interchangeably with hostility, has a Latin origin, *ad:* toward, *gradere:* to move. This movement toward need not be destructive; indeed, we can see how it would be desirable, for example, to be aggressive in the pursuit of constructive goals, such as developing better methods of agriculture or getting a much-needed dam constructed. Herein lies the telling contrast with the notion of hostility. Coming from the Latin word for enemy, *hostis,* hostility has none of the ambiguity implicit in aggression; it is always destructive, or at least aimed at destructive ends. Furthermore, unlike the word "aggression," which is a term descriptive of behavior, "hostility" is a psychological term primarily denoting attitude, feeling, and motivation. As such, it can properly be described dynamically: for example, as conscious or unconscious, as repressed, suppressed, or expressed, as active or passive. In contrast, to speak of "repressed aggression" strains the term, while the notion of "passive aggression" is a paradox if not a semantic and conceptual monstrosity. The term "aggression" probably came into English usage from the French, in which, as well as in German, it does have a connotation of attack and destructiveness, which makes it ambiguous for scientific use. To attack a problem can be constructive, not destructive.

As a technical definition we might hazard the following: hostility is a motivating force—a conscious or unconscious impulse, tendency, intent, or reaction—aimed at injuring or destroying some object, animate or inanimate. In humans, hostility is usually accompanied by some shade of the feeling or emotion of anger and hate.

Hostility can take almost limitless forms, can be used for every sort of purpose, and can range in intensity from a glance or a breath of gossip to vindictiveness, violence, brutality, and murder. Hostility is the essential evil in man. It is fundamental and constantly present as a central link in psychodynamics. If one knows the *causes* of hostility and their *effects,* then one knows most of that individual's psychopathology and much of his total personality. All symptoms (always excepting physically caused ones, with which this book is not concerned) can be arranged on a scale of diminishing restraint grading from psychosomatic effects and conversion hysteria, in which the hostility is most inhibited and internal, through the classic neuroses with their anxieties, compulsions, and depressions, through the psychoses with extensive projections and other distortions of reality, to the most overt acting-out range, wherein the hostility is turned masochistically against the self or criminally and even sadistically against others.

Hostility, if it causes psychosomatic, neurotic, or nonviolent psychotic symptoms, or if it is expressed masochistically against the self, causes suffering to the individual and to those close to him but does not menace society. But when hostility takes the form of direct acting out, it breeds violence, crime, and senseless torment and destruction of innocent victims, even children.

Man has always considered it important to understand the motives by which he lives, loves, and hates. (As Plato wrote, "The unexamined life is not worth living.") But today, with the capacity for total destruction in his hands, man's ability to understand himself and to use that understanding for the prevention of violence is crucial to his very survival. Each individual is activated by strong asocial and antisocial motivations, as well as by social ones. Only by understanding these two sets of motives can we maximize those that are pro-human and reduce the anti-human. All this seems clear enough, but there are those who resist understanding it nonetheless. Emotions are complex and difficult to discern at best, but discussions of hostility and its role in problems involving motivations of, for example, dependency, sex, vanity, and envy arouse in most people such passionate feelings that detachment in comprehending this subject is rare indeed. In societies of bees and termites we recognize specialized members: the queen as the reproductive machine, the drones, the workers, the soldiers. But human beings as far as we know are all equal in their basic goals and desires, that is, to use a broad term, in their "instincts." For human societies to work or even exist, some sacrifice of "instinct" is necessary. The major instincts that must be sacrificed to some degree for social living can be summarized with some of their interrelations: Starting with the fight–flight reaction, the first emotional force that must be controlled is hostility. Other forces manifesting the flight response as fixation or regression are the passive dependent love needs and one form of them as narcissism, that is, vanity, conceit, needs for adulation; and sex, which can express both parts of the fight-flight.

Many people would like to believe, and therefore do believe, that hostility is inherited and therefore should be dismissed as something about which nothing, at least for the present, can be done. Others believe, falsely, that hostility is strength, that without it men and women would be left defenseless in a world all too ready to attack and exploit the weak. Others resist the study of hostility just from the tendency of mankind to resist any new idea. The great William Harvey feared to make known what is now accepted as a commonplace fact—the circulation of the blood: "I not only fear injury to myself from the envy of a few, but I tremble lest I have mankind at large for my enemies, so much does wont and custom become second nature. Doctrine once sown strikes deeply at its root and respect for antiquity influences all men. Still the die is cast and my trust is in the love of truth and the candor of cultivated minds."

Besides such general reasons for shunning the problem of hostility, there are others more individual and deep-seated. Some people balk at accepting hostility as a psychological force because of resistance to recognizing hostile reactions within themselves. An acquaintance of mine, hearing of this study, reacted unsympathetically. Because he was basically a man of good will, his reaction aroused my curiosity. He was one of those people whose hostilities were overinhibited when he was a child, and as a result he had always felt that he lacked the capacity of self-defense even for proper purposes. In shunning this unpleasant conflict within himself, he maintained that the less said about hostility the better.

The guilt that an individual feels for his own known hostile reactions and deeds also may impair objective understanding. The reason for this is that the feeling of guilt carries with it conscience reactions and a need for punishment. It is not uncommon to see patients who truly feel that they do not deserve to be cured. This need for suffering, this masochism, is so widespread that it often extends to feelings about society in general, with a resulting attitude, usually unconscious, that mankind deserves its miseries and should not and cannot be helped toward a better life.

This resistance to facing and dealing with the central issue of man's hostility is nowhere more striking than in the writings of Freud. He began his study of the neuroses with his perceptions of the sexual drives. Although hostility is mentioned in the case histories, it was not until eight years before his death (at 83) that Freud articulated any theoretical formulation of "unerotized aggression" (that is, hostility without sexual, sensual, or sensuous feelings). At this late point in his life he was unable to give it the detail clinical attention that he had earlier devoted to the libidinal impulses. However, Freud expanded his instinct theory into a broad dualistic view of life as fundamentally an interplay between the forces of creativity (Eros) and the forces of destruction and death (Thanatos). What is interesting to us here is not the specific content of Freud's theory, but rather the astonishment with which he acknowledges having overlooked the "tendency toward aggression," which he remarked constituted "the most powerful obstacle to culture." In *Civilization and Its Discontents* he wrote:

> I know that we have always had before our eyes manifestations of the destruction instinct fused with erotism, directed outwards and inwards in sadism and masochism, but I can no longer understand how we could have overlooked the universality of non-erotic aggression and destruction and could have omitted to give it its due significance in our interpretation of life . . . . I can remember my own defensive attitude when the idea of an instinct of destruction first made its appearance in psychoanalytic literature and how long it took until I accepted it. That others should have shown the same resistance, and still show it, surprises me less. Those who love fairy tales do not like it when people speak of the innate tendencies of mankind toward aggression, destruction, and, in addition, cruelty.

But obviously the nature of tendencies can and should be studied—for the sake of our own survival. We can begin by asking: Is hostility a drive, an innate tendency, or is it a reaction? Or if neither, then what?

3
Hostility and Biological Adaptation

If we observe an individual member of any species—a goldfish, an elephant, a mosquito, a python, or a man—we see the effort to survive and thereby the life cycle. Whatever the vicissitudes of individual experience, the basic plan is always the same. First, there is sexual conception; then birth and infancy and development to maturity; then reproduction, with some care or provision for the young, then decline; and finally death. This cycle of life fulfills a fundamental biological force that operates within all of us. Any attempt to deviate from it, or any failure in fulfilling it, brings difficulty and pain. We all strive to live out our lives until we die of "natural causes," postponed as long as possible.

From an astronomical point of view, man is, in essence, not very much. On this tiny planet, within one of perhaps ten million solar systems, there has developed a combination of molecules in a jelly-like substance, about 85 percent water, called a colloidal suspension. One form of colloid we know as living matter or *protoplasm*. The earth's surface teems with this substance; man is only one form of it, of the biological life on this planet.

Why, millions of years ago, did this protoplasm take human form? There is no verifiable answer. But we do know how it has survived. This has been accomplished through its capacity to adapt to the changing conditions of life on this planet. The dinosaur, with its pea-sized brain and huge clumsy lumbering body, did not survive; the ant, with its complex and sophisticated social organization, has existed far longer than man. But the fact that the human race exists today does not mean that it will automatically continue to survive. And most of us, for ourselves and our children and grandchildren, would not relish participation in its extinction.

It seems clear that all forms of life use at least two major mechanisms of adaptation: social cooperation and the fight–flight reflex.

The eminent biologist Warder C. Allee found that cooperation serves animals not only as a protection, but also as an aid to development. Allee's lifetime studies revealed that the organism living in association with others increases in size, swiftness, and the ability to recover from damage more quickly than those animals that are isolated. Isolated animals prove much more susceptible to poisons and retardation, and tend to suffer more often from hunger and the attacks of other animals.

It is Allee's conclusion that "no free living animal is solitary throughout his life history," and that the tendency of animals to aggregate is a primitive, unconscious drive. On its higher levels, these aggregations attain refinements of organization. We are all familiar with the advanced social life of bees, ants, and termites, with the way elephants gather in herds, wolves in packs, fish in schools, birds in flocks, and so on. The features of both leadership and class orders are found among animal organizations. Just as there is the queen-worker-drone order among bees, there is the somewhat despotic peck order among hens and other species confined domestically by man in societies. Each hen can peck those lower in the order than herself but must submit to pecks from those higher. Similarly, among lizards, there is a nip order. And the same type of domination–submission order is found in other species as well.

Social cooperation is also enhanced by various types of communication found throughout animal organizations. Mating calls, for example, exist in almost all forms of life. Bees dance in a certain way to inform their fellow hive-dwellers when and where honey can be found. Certain types of birds are signaled toward migration by leader-birds.

In human societies, we find greater complexity, but a similar tendency to communicate, to group, and to organize. It is only through social living and sharing that man, like other animals, has been able to protect himself and thus assure his continued survival. But so far as is now known, there is one crucial difference that distinguishes human organization from animal groupings: only among human beings have organization and aggregation been used not only for protection from other animals but also for large-scale attack on and destruction of their own kind. "One species of animal may destroy another," Allee wrote in *Cooperation Among Animals*, "and individuals may kill other individuals, but *group* struggles to the death between members of the same species, such as occur in human warfare, can hardly be found among non-human animals."

Why is this so? Why are such constant features as war and mass murder found in human societies but not on such a scale among any other species? This is the single most important question confronting us as human beings.

One aspect of the many forms of man's hostility to man is understandable if it is seen as a symptom of a *mechanism of adaptation run rampant*. If you were alone in the wilderness and were set upon by a predatory animal, your life would depend largely upon the speed and effectiveness of your automatic fight and flight reflexes. These reflexes, so essential to man's survival in the cave and jungle, continue on through a sort of biological lag into our present modes of living, which are, of course, almost exclusively in social settings, remote from wild animals. These reflexes may be compared to other basically normal mechanisms of the body that also overshoot themselves. For instance, note the way in which body temperature rises to combat infections. It does so without any conscious directive on the part of the individual; you get an infection (a sore throat, say), and this biological defense against disease simply rises automatically. But it may outstrip its controls, climbing to 106°, 107°, 108°F, and thus kill the individual before it kills the microorganisms against which it went into action. Similarly, the membranes of the nose and bronchial tubes swell and secrete juices in order to defend the body against irritants we breathe in. But frequently they go too far in attempting to shut out dust, fumes, pollens, and the like, and hay fever or asthma may result. When severe enough, asthma may clog the bronchial tubes and cause death.

Observing animals closely, we find that certain biological changes take place when danger threatens. Typical are the famous experiments conducted by physiologist Walter Cannon in 1928 and confirmed by many others since. Cannon, working in the early days of X-ray, mixed a little barium with a goose's food to make it opaque, and then watched the stomach's reactions through a fluoroscope as the bird digested its meals under different conditions. The regular peristaltic movements of the esophagus were grossly disturbed by threats of danger such as a barking dog. Following this experiment, Cannon tested a variety of animals, including humans; for example, students before an important examination or before playing in a football game. Functional abnormalities showed up repeatedly whenever the animal was under stress. When threatened, the body's whole machinery goes into high gear: the blood flows from the viscera to the muscles, the heart pounds with greater force and increased speed, breathing is more rapid, the liver pours extra sugar as fuel into the blood, adrenalin levels increase, and so on. In this way the entire physiology prepares for extra action.

Exploring states of fear and rage in detail, Cannon found that, faced with any threat, frustration, or irritation, the animal becomes physiologically aroused for maximum effort—ready to forestall, to fight and destroy, or to flee and escape the antagonist. It is important to emphasize that while the two activities of fighting and fleeing appear quite different, inwardly the basic physiological preparations for them are essentially the same. The particular *direction* the resulting activity takes stems from the circumstances prevailing outside the animal, combined with his own inner needs, perception, and judgment. The carnivorous tiger, for instance, is more often aroused to *fight* when he senses danger or the nearness of edible prey. The vegetarian rabbit, on the other hand, is aroused to *flee* when dangerous carnivores enter his territory. In the main, the rabbit's flight reaction is aroused mostly for defense, whereas the tiger's fight response is mobilized for attack. Fight and flight thus represent two outcomes of a single physiological adaptive reaction for specific effort. The one that prevails in action is largely a matter of expediency dictated by the mind. If, for example, a mosquito attacks, you have no hesitation in striking to kill it. But if a swarm of hornets came at you, you would probably use your aroused energies for flight, which you would doubtless find yourself doing automatically without consciously thinking about it.

4
The Fight-Flight Reflex and Psychological Adaptation

The fight–flight adaptive mechanism must have been vital for man in the earlier, more physically dangerous times of cave and jungle; it is still valuable in primitive situations where instant automatic mobilization for fight or flight can make the difference between life and death. But in the complex, cooperative, civilized living of today, with involved moral, emotional, and intellectual standards, this mechanism, when misunderstood and unrestrained, is apt to outstrip its controls and be destructive to others and to oneself.

Until fairly recently, aroused and courageous people could put an ocean safely between themselves and oppression, intolerance, and want. There were in our land new frontiers; rich, arable soil could be had for the tilling. Those who wished to do so could lose themselves among the lonely hills; and isolation from mundane problems could be sought and found in the wilderness. But today, as in the rest of the world, people who are frustrated, those who are under stress, and even those who are in real political, social, or economic danger are barred by circumstances and by the absence of unpopulated open spaces from actual physical, geographical flight and can only seek refuge in psychological flight. Our sparsely populated frontiers are gone.

Psychological flight takes many different forms, which we can arrange into four main groups: sublimation and fantasy; use of drugs and intoxicants; withdrawal states; and regressions. These groups do not represent discrete categories. Rather, there is much overlapping in the behavior described for each.

It is quite normal and sometimes constructive for an individual under stress to seek refuge by unconsciously returning (regressing) to mental, emotional, and biological states such as he experienced earlier in his life. This may be achieved in recreation, play, rest, or sleep. Some individuals, on the other hand, find that by throwing themselves totally into their work they gain escape from emotional strain. Others escape into fantasy, either through daydreaming or through creative expressions of their own or those of others readily accessible in fiction, films, drama, and the other forms of art and amusement. The artist, like the scientist, handles his fantasies creatively, and he can combine an element of escape with responsible productivity to give others pleasure and to make his way in the world. The normal healthy person, if he does not use his fantasies professionally like the artist and the scientist, is apt to take them in small doses, as needed, and he is probably all the better for them. There is nothing harmful in these activities of fantasy unless the flight is extreme and prolonged, in which case there may be a serious threat to the emotional health of the individual. For example, clinical experience reveals that early schizophrenia not infrequently begins with escapes from responsibility into addiction to movies and television. Problems may also arise if hostility enters as a destructive element, as in the case of a game that becomes a gambling racket.

Intoxicants and drugs tempt the sorely pressed with promise of quick surcease from the burdens of life. Many who feel assailed by hardships from without and by emotional tensions from within, find the relief experienced through tobacco, alcohol, and drugs to be irresistible. Unfortunately, the blessing is mixed: the element of fight, the hostility, usually enters in, turned against the self. The addict seeks escape in vain. Eventually physical dissolution comes, often preceded by emotional disruption.

Withdrawal states are a third form of escape. An extreme example of this is catatonia, a severe manifestation seen in schizophrenia. The patient is practically immobile and responds not at all to his surroundings and to other persons. If his arm, leg, head, or entire body is placed in a certain position, he will maintain it without change for prolonged periods.

A less severe form of withdrawal involves the giving up of all or nearly all responsibility. This may result from quite evident outside pressures or from stresses and strains from within. Often the trend to withdraw is very strong because of early traumatic influences that occurred years before, when the adult was a growing young child.

In such cases only slight pressures are enough to throw the individual into flight. For example, a seemingly responsible and industrious man begins to be unable to discharge his duties or pursue his regular routines. We learn that as a child he was severely overprotected. Although he has been able to make a go of life on his own thus far, he has done so under inner protest and with a persistent undercurrent of longing to return to the old responsibility-free days of childhood when he was entirely dependent upon his parents and had no one dependent upon him. No very hard knocks are needed to initiate the flight reaction in such an individual. The psychological flight here may be expressed mostly in behavior or be accompanied by changes, more or less extreme, in mood, such as depression or apathy.

For example: James was subjected to excessive overprotection during childhood, permitted to do almost nothing for himself without someone taking over and doing it for him, as though he were still a helpless baby, but he managed to fight his way free and assert a measure of independence. He married, had three children and built a successful manufacturing business. To all appearances he was stably adjusted. But he was skating on thin ice. Suddenly, his partner withdrew from the business, deciding to retire to another city. James had depended upon this man, not only for the role he played in conducting the business, but, more than he realized, emotionally. In fact, James never suspected how much he relied on his partner, and the loss of the emotional support precipitated a withdrawal. He could no longer concentrate on work, and after a while he had almost insuperable difficulty just getting up mornings. He witnessed with dismay the beginning of the ruin of his business and with it the loss of his family's security. He saw all this, but he was powerless to do anything by will power alone to get himself to discharge his responsibilities. His mind and body simply withdrew; they refused to function. He was anxious rather than depressed. He was frightened, for this dangerous withdrawal seemed as much out of his conscious control as would be a raging fever in pneumonia. James was helpless to reverse this course of deterioration.

Withdrawal also plays an obvious part in most cases of depression, wherein the individual is apt to feel his frustrations as so severe that life is no longer worthwhile. He loses interest in people and the outside world. Often physiological functions reflect this retreat by responding with a kind of clamping down of action—including constipation and diminished appetite for food and for sexual pleasure. The typical depression is a crystal-clear example of psychological flight combined with fight in the form of pent-up rage, which may be vented on the person himself, in the extreme as suicide.

A fourth form of flight is regression. It has been found that various kinds of emotional disorders, whether occasioned by inner tensions or outer pressures or some combination of both, are in large part returns to disturbed patterns of behavior that the individual had in infancy or childhood. Of course, this is seen in everyone to some degree. Just as many children, when they are injured physically or in their feelings, suck their thumbs or console themselves with sweets, so, too, when they are in trouble as adults they also turn to sweets, food, drink, or smoking, as substitute mothers. Some frightened children seek help by being overly dependent and submissive; many adults do the same. And most adults turn back to the form of fight–flight reaction that served them in childhood. A man may have learned mature ways of handling conflicts, but if in his childhood he met every irritation with attack or with a sit-down strike of regression to passivity, sufficient pressure and threats may revive this pattern in him, and he may destroy his marriage and career by his fight and flight.

The pressures that occasion a regression may be caused by an internal conflict that was initiated in childhood but which does not emerge until years later. Bill is a typical case. His mother was a high-powered and dynamic woman who was admired for her outstanding social and community activites. His father was an alert, energetic, and successful businessman. Exposure to these parents imbued Bill not only with a drive to be successful, but also with an image of himself as a superior being, the son of superior parents. This kernel of vanity was fed directly by his parents' adoration of him. They projected upon him their own needs for superiority. And Bill, growing up in this laudatory emotional atmosphere, naturally absorbed their feelings and early developed an unusually strong image of himself as a superior individual.

In addition to this "narcissism," this vanity, egotism, and need for admiration, there was another trend that persisted with equal strength in Bill, namely, an excessive dependence on his parents. At the same time that they were adoring and attentive, his parents were also overly anxious and protective about his every activity, and any sign of growing independence was met with resistance. Too fondly they continued to see him as a child, hung onto him, clipped his wings. It was all not too far from being perfectly normal in intention; it was just too strong in the degree of its expression. Bill partly identified with his strong parents but was also overly tempted to lean upon them because of their strength.

Not until he reached adolescence did Bill become definitely and acutely aware that something was very wrong. He could not define it, but only sensed that he was a little different from the other boys. At the core of the problem were his strong dependent love needs toward his parents and his feelings of being restricted by them in conflict with his needs for independence, strength, and prestige, as represented by them. But he was not consciously aware of all this. All Bill knew was that he felt weak and inferior to other boys, and to girls, too. Because of the narcissistic core in his personality, he found these new feelings to be confusing. His self-image was hurt and threatened by this strange sense of weakness and inadequacy.

Bill reacted with inner rage, but what appeared on the surface was the flight part of the reflex mechanism. He became increasingly withdrawn until he was so regressed that he could no longer continue school. Before long, his competitiveness, the inevitable concomitant of his egotism, was defeated by seeing others going ahead while he was doing nothing and getting nowhere. The final blow to his already shaken self-image came from being forced to recognize that something was seriously wrong with him mentally and emotionally. Bill was by this time 20 years old; after all these years of thinking of himself as superior and of being treated that way, he could not tolerate the thought of existence as an inferior, as a failure. He was not conscious of what was going on within himself and naturally felt that nothing could be done to correct it. Bill felt hopeless and began experiencing suicidal impulses.

Regression, as essentially the flight part of the fight–flight reaction, is probably an essential element in all emotional disturbances. In phobias, for example, a person may undergo states of feeling similar to the insecurities characteristic of the small child when left alone. Typically, the phobic loses these fears when another person is with him, just as a small child's anxiety is allayed by the presence of a parent or other trusted relative or friend. Hysterical behavior, such as uncontrolled weeping, laughter, temper, and the like, is usually intelligible when viewed as a regression to the behavior of the child. The same connection is seen in those mercurial individuals who amaze us with their radical shifts of mood, behaving like uninhibited children who are devastated by trifles one moment but delighted by other trifles the next. In a compulsion neurosis, such as excessive hand-washing, excessive care about dress, or the obsessive need to count everything, the abnormal behavior often derives from training in cleanliness, manners, arithmetic, and so on. An adult may express the child's obedience to its parents through compulsive symptoms, while at the same time betraying his defiance by making a caricature of conscientiousness and conformity in general by gross exaggeration. "You force me to wash my hands—all right, I'll wash them for four hours—see how you like that!"

Perversions also reflect psychological flight through regression. In the case of perversions, this usually means a return to the sexual play or fantasies of childhood, such as erotic fantasies in boys who play with the clothes of the females of the family. Many people who have a neurotic or a psychopathic personality show quite frankly behavior in which reason and mature judgment are all too much at the mercy of the emotions, as was the case early in life when the young child's ego, with its grasp of reality, was still relatively undeveloped. In psychoses, of course, the regression is deeper, for example, more like the feeling and thinking of a child less than two years old, and involves more disorder of the ego. Delusions of grandeur, for instance, bear a striking resemblance to childhood indulgence in make-believe. The hallucinations of schizophrenia become comprehensible as a return to preverbal thinking in images, still utilized by us all in our dreams.

Thus withdrawals and regressions are fundamental to the production of all the disorders that we recognize as perversions, addictions, psychoses, neuroses, and infantile behavior. And this form of flight is important in psychosomatic conditions also, where the wish to escape is not satisfied in reality but causes disturbances in the physiology. For example, studies of persons with peptic ulcers suggest that in some cases the structural damage results from the individual's constant exposure to stressful situations from which he wishes, but is unable, to extricate himself. Biologically this reaction to emotional stress manifests itself as a disturbance in the functioning of the stomach (hyperactivity and hyperacidity) which in turn renders that organ more susceptible to injury. Other studies have shown that emotional forces also play a role in essential hypertension. It would seem that persons who force themselves to carry weighty responsibilities while struggling against powerful longings to withdraw and flee from such burdens, develop high blood pressure partially for this reason.

In all the emotional conditions that we have been discussing, regardless of how prominent the element of flight, there is always present at the same time the other side of the automatic adaptive mechanism, that is, the enormously powerful fight reaction. Thus hostility is inextricably fused to all forms of withdrawal: depression, manic episodes, hysteria, phobia, compulsion, perversion, addiction, paranoia, schizophrenia, psychosomatic disorder, and the rest.

Interestingly enough, psychiatry first explored and then continued to focus primarily on flight syndromes. Freud studied and described regression in detail, but, as we have noted, only toward the end of his long life did he turn his attention to the importance of the fight aspect, that is, man's hostility. But although he did come to recognize the portentous implications for humanity of "unerotized aggression," even today, hostile drives have not been fully worked through clinically, theoretically, or in the practical training of analysts. Thus hostility remains less stressed, less clarified, less understood, and certainly not yet adequately appreciated for its fateful power. Always a cause, result, or concomitant of regression, hostility deserves at least parity of concern with libidinal impulses. In fact it is correct to emphasize that fight–flight reaction is inevitably an essential link in the dynamics of all emotional disorders, that is, of all psychopathology.

Unlike flight, actual fight is all too available an option to modern man, and because of the awesome weaponry he can summon to serve this goal, it poses a far greater threat to survival. At one end of the scale it is expressed overtly as destructive aggression; at the other, it is expressed in a masked, overcompensatory form under the guise of justice, righteousness, and love. It can be acted out, within or outside the law, by individuals acting on their own, by unorganized crowds or mobs, or by highly organized gangs or armies. It finds easy expression in crime, delinquency, oppression, rebellion, and warfare, the prevalence of which serves as an index of how widespread the problem is.

In the United States, for example, more than nine million crimes are committed annually.* In 1977 there were more than 18,000

**World Almanac* (1979), New York: N.E.A. Association.

homicides, 59,800 forcible rapes, 484,903 cases of aggravated assault, 2,852,212 burglaries, and 5,554,355 larcenies. Alcoholics, in whom both the escape and the destructiveness are obvious, now number in the millions. Neurotics add another five to 20 million, and there are well over two million psychotics. Of course, there is some overlap in these statistics, but it is nevertheless clear that the numbers of persons in these categories run into the tens of millions and include a sizable percentage of our population—probably a majority. The wars of the generation now in advanced chronological maturity killed more than 22 million and injured more than 35 million. This does not include the "undeclared" and continuing conflicts around the world. Lesser, but no less pertinent, evidence of the fight reflex may be found in divorce statistics and in the increase in child and spouse abuse. According to a 1978 study by the National Institute of Mental Health, nearly two million American children are stabbed, shot, kicked, bitten, punched, or hit with an object each year—by one of their own parents. All figures of this kind relating to war, crime, divorce, and battered wives and children, however, only serve as crude guides to the overt expressions of hostility. Not reflected here are the myriad emotional problems involving covert or indirect expressions of hostility that is aimed at others or, masochistically, at the self. In 1975 alone there were more than 25,000 suicides in this country, and we averaged 50,000 fatalities a year in automobile accidents. And how many children and adults were injured psychologically by their own hostility or the hostility of others?

To answer this last question with a single example: there are more than one-half million illegitimate births per year, according to the U.S. Census Bureau; half of these births are to teen-age mothers. In the past decade the average age of girls giving birth to illegimate babies in Salvation Army homes has declined from 17 to 15. Fourteen and 13 year olds are not uncommon, with some mothers as young as 11. These girls, themselves still children, would surely not have become pregnant unless they had serious emotional problems with one or both parents, problems involving intense hostility that masochistically injures themselves. The tragedy is really borne by the babies, however. Even children raised in reasonably stable homes with reasonably mature parents who love one another can grow up with emotional problems that spell suffering, but these illigitimate babies with immature, emotionally disordered, half-grown mothers, do not have a chance. Enough is known today about the results of faulty childrearing by emotionally disordered single mothers, or by a home lacking the devotion of a steady, loving father, to say that the vast majority of these children are doomed to neurosis, psychosis, drugs, and hostile, criminal acting-out behavior, which will make society and themselves miserable. Doubtless it is they who will bear the next generation of illegitimate babies. For such babies, assuredly the Greeks were right: it were better not to have been born, for they are born to lives of torment.

5
Psychodynamic Sources of Hostility

We have met the enemy and they are us.
Pogo

Begin with an individual, and before you know it you find that you have created a type; begin with a type, and you find that you have created–nothing. That is because we are all queer fish, queerer behind our faces and voices than we want anyone to know or than we know ourselves.
F. Scott Fitzgerald

We have listed some results of hostility when this biological mechanism of adaptation, this fight–flight reaction, overshoots itself. The question then arises: Why does this once invaluable mechanism, now become so damaging, threatening our very survival, continue to exist with such force? Is it like the vermiform appendix, an anatomic hangover, no longer useful to our intestinal tract, only of value to surgeons who remove it when it is infected?

The answer is at once simple and complex. There is no scientific evidence to surely establish that hostility per se (except as the mechanism of adaptation we have described) is inherited. Nor is there evidence that any other form of neurosis is carried in the genes. Individual differences in temperament are doubtless inherited to some extent, just as there are differences in body build and coloring. A glance around any hospital nursery shows the newborn to be of all shapes and sizes, and of varying motility and tenseness and responses to cuddling. But there is only meager and uncertain evidence for heredity being of any appreciable weight in the etiology of emotional disorders (other than, possibly, some forms of psychosis). Hostility cannot simply be passed off as something we inherit and hence can do nothing about. On the other hand, excessive hostility is regularly found to be a disease of personality, transmittable from person to person and from group to group, and, basically, by contact from parents to children, from generation to generation.

It is true that from earliest recorded history we read of tribes, cities, and nations attacking others, stealing lands and movable wealth, taking as many slaves as they wished for cheap labor and for sexual purposes and killing off all the rest to eliminate competition and the risks of retaliation. Then the fear of being themselves looted, pillaged, raped, murdered, and enslaved by other nations led to constantly expanding frontiers. Rome pushed her boundaries farther and farther for all these reasons: to take the riches and to impose her peace.

And yet not every man in every nation yearned for aggressive pillage and murder; not all rulers were cruel tyrants. The hostility involved in robbing, murdering, and enslaving is not necessarily a general human characteristic, but rather an attribute of certain personalities. It is a matter of how readily corruptible the individual is. Indeed, if the major motivating forces in each of us could develop normally, without damaging interference or coercion from the outside, the result would be friendly, social cooperation. Only when this development is disturbed during the earliest formative years of infancy and childhood, by active mismanagement or by gross neglect (whether unconscious and well-meaning or conscious and willful), does the fight–flight reaction, with its resulting hostility, burgeon in full strength.

In contrast to the absence of evidence for hereditary factors in determining the intensity and status of hostility in different persons, the clinical experience of dynamic phychiatry with children and adults repeatedly emphasizes the significance of conditioning influences and their basic importance in causing vulnerabilities to external stresses and emotional disorders. (We are, of course, referring exclusively to physiologically healthy organisms and not to those suffering the effects of physical or chemical damage, deformity, or impairment of the brain, glandular system, or other parts of the body; also excluded from our discussion are those having gross congenital developmental defects and severe schizophrenic or manic-depressive psychoses.)

In some of Howard Liddell's most notable experiments at the Cornell animal farm he observed twin kids, one of which Liddell isolated from its mother and placed alone in a room that was identical to the one in which its mother and sibling remained. A few simple events were made to occur simultaneously in both rooms. For example, lights were flashed on and off, and sudden sounds were made—nothing harmful. The kid that was allowed to remain with its mother became alarmed, rushed to its mother, and clung to her; it soon felt reassured, and managed to adapt to the situation. The kid that was isolated from its mother panicked at the flashing lights and sudden sounds, but had no one to turn to for security. When this kid was reunited with its mother after a while, it revealed an incapacity to be mothered and reassured. The basic but delicate instinctual relationship, that elemental feeling normally existing between mother and child, had been disrupted. And the ramifications of this upset are enormous. The kid who could not get into the feelings of being mothered by its own mother also showed a striking inability to get into good feelings with any other animals. The relationship of the mother to its offspring serves as the model and pattern for future relationships. When this interplay of feelings with its mother is disrupted, the young cannot form future relationships with others in a normal way. The kid that had been isolated became, in essence, at the least asocial or antisocial, and, at most, psychotic.

Ethologists have referred to this initial need of an offspring to cling to its mother as *imprinting*. In his revealing experiments, Eckhardt Hess prevented ducklings from attaching their dependent love needs to their mother within the period of maximum imprinting, which in ducks is the first few days after hatching. The ducklings grew up unable forever after to relate to other ducks, socially or sexually.

Interference with the normal process of imprinting in humans too seems to lead to disastrous consequences. Rene Spitz produced a remarkable documentary film called *Grief—A Peril of Infancy*. It showed illegitimate babies with their own mothers. The children seemed to be happy and thriving despite the often shabby, poverty-stricken environments in which they lived. At age five months the children were placed in a foundling home where the architectural and interior decorative facilities were excellent. The building was beautiful, and the children were guaranteed a perfect diet and the best medical care. The physical surroundings were obviously far better than the homes from which the babies had come. But in the foundling home there was no real mothering–no maternal love or consistent attention, affection, or play. With all the right food, medical attention, and lovely surroundings, the babies wilted. Some twisted up as though suffering from a terrible disease of the nerves and muscles. Others became lethargic and apathetic. All lost weight, and as many as 20 percent deteriorated until they died. These children failed to thrive, and some died because of ruptured imprinting or because their dependent love needs were starved. Yes, humans do indeed die of broken hearts.

The normal growth and development of the child that does not imprint properly or relate properly to its mother or substitute in the first hours, days, weeks, and months of life is seriously jeopardized. But this is also true for every child that grows up without a loving and secure image of its mother and father (or substitutes). The child's enormous plasticity and capacity for training, its tremendous conditionability, is certainly one of the most outstanding characteristics of human beings. And the child we once were lives on in us all.

The infant normally craves love and security. If these needs are met by its mother whenever she appears, the child will come to associate the mother with feelings of satisfaction, love, and security and carry that image during her absences. But if the appearance of the mother is associated with neglect or rejection, or with overprotection and domination, or any other form of hostility, the child will become conditioned to this response. That is, the child will come to expect bad treatment from its mother and will respond with fear and resentment, holding an image of the mother as frustrating and threatening. The fight–flight adaptive mechanism will be mobilized. As noted earlier, this is the primitive response of all animals to any and every threat to living out the life cycle. This is true whether the irritant, hurt, or danger comes from outside the organism or from within it, whether it is physical or psychological. The small child is in no position either to fight or to flee, and this situation of living and growing up under parental abuse that can neither be escaped nor destroyed, and that comes from a person upon whom the child is utterly dependent, generates chronic fear and rage. If it occurs before the child can talk and can comprehend what is going on, then the emotional damage is all the more dire. If the parent also loves the child, then the hostility usually causes guilt; and the child's primitive impulses to destroy the person upon whom he is so helplessly dependent typically create anxiety. The guilt and anxiety usually increase the child's clinging to the mother, who generally resents this and becomes even more rejecting, setting up a vicious circle. Thus a pattern of disordered feelings toward the mother is formed in the small child. The problem with a child who has been conditioned in this unfortunate way is that this deranged emotional pattern tends to spread to people other than its mother. And so it constitutes a core of psychopathology.

Studies of sheep have helped us to understand how this phenomenon of conditioning and this "spread" of conditioned responses works. In one study, a sheep is brought repeatedly into a building where it undergoes a harmless but distressing experimental situation. After a time it reacts not only against the specific situation, but also against the experimenter, the building as a whole, and even the adjacent fields. If the sheep is regularly kept in a nearby field, it is found to isolate itself from other sheep, to be hostile when approached by man or sheep, and to try frequently to escape. Its antagonism to the experimental situation spreads to the animal's entire environmental surroundings and results in seriously disturbed personal relations with humans and with other sheep. This parallels what happens to the child subjected to early mistreatment. It reacts at first just against the parents, but then its resentment spreads to other individuals and often even to society itself.

The human mind is powered by (1) the biological processes of the body, (2) the effects of childhood conditioning, and (3) adaptive reactions to external circumstances. The extent to which the various motivations are subject to influence is mostly a result of man's very long childhood as compared with the young of other species. This slow maturing gives him vast advantages over other animals, but it also exposes him to greater dangers. Each person's drives and reactions are patterned by his first experiences and training and are given their main directions by the character and behavior of those who became the individual's first models. And, in general, the earlier the conditioning, the more potent its effects are, and the more likely it is that these effects will persist unchanged for life (i.e., the more emotionally disordered the adult will be).

The child reacts to other persons, as we all do, by object relations (wanting dependence, love, sex, guidance, and so on from the other person) and also by identification (by being like the other person). A child needs a parent but also becomes like the parent.

Each person has a certain picture of the world, of other people, of values, of himself. It is part of the way he understands reality, part of his conscious ego. Underlying this view, in the unconscious depths of his mind, is another picture that conforms more or less closely to the way things were first seen in childhood. What the individual's senses and his intellect tell him about reality are actually colored, if not grossly distorted, by composite images formed by his very early experiences. When the treatment of the infant and young child by those closest to him and responsible for him helps his development to emotional maturity, it increases his natural capacity for responsibility, productivity, independence, love, and a clear sense of reality. It is these vital qualities that will develop the individual's capacity for social cooperation and happy mating and parenting. But when conditioning influences impair the emotional development, disordered childhood reactions establish patterns that tend to persist as sources of irritation, frustration, and anxiety, and therefore, through the fight–flight reaction, regression and hostility.

The mind is made up of reason, conscience, and animal impulses, which together act out the inner drama of our life, with our consciousness as the audience.

Grouped together under the term *ego* are: (1) consciousness with the powers of perception through the five senses, including the grasp of both outer reality and inner needs and urges; (2) the integrative powers of memory, reason, and the like; and (3) the executive functions of will, repression, control, and decision. The ego is the conscious and most flexible part of the personality. It plans and coordinates action, is the essence of what we call "I," the self, and acts as the great organ of adaptation to living with people. Without consciousness and its functions, as in a coma, the individual is helpless, only a vegetative organism.

The term *superego* includes those controls, models, and dictates that "stand over" the ego, and includes all the effects of training, all the ideals and standards imbibed from the family, personal experience, and cultural custom. It includes the conscience, the core of which is formed during the earliest weeks, months, and years of life. This core, though a powerful and enduring feature of the personality, is not static and entirely unalterable. Some changes in the effects of early conditioning result from the very process of living; others can be brought about through psychodynamic treatment. The nucleus of the superego is probably the innate biological tendency of the mature organism toward social cooperation. Added to this are the effects of those who rear the infant and young child, the main characters in the drama of its early life. Because this core of the superego is formed so early, it usually remains to a large extent automatic and unconscious and therefore much more powerful and much less reasonable than we prefer to think. This tendency of repeated actions and reactions to become automatic and often unconscious serves the principle of conservation of psychic energy, by which many everyday experiences are rendered automatic responses. For example, at first there is a considerable conscious struggle in learning to ride a horse, or a bicycle, or to drive a stick-shift car; but in time we do so automatically. In time our hands, feet, and eyes and whole bodies become perfectly coordinated without conscious thought on our part.

The animal impulses that develop out of the chemistry and physiology of our bodies are called the *id*, denoting their more impersonal nature. Drives for food, sex, love, mating, dependence, parenthood, competition, and the like involve the whole organism and are reflected in the mind. Our awareness of other drives fades out as these drives descend to lower "levels" of the nervous system. For example, we are not conscious of the reflexes that maintain our muscle tone, operate our liver, or contract our pupils against bright light. Thus the psychological, what is or can become conscious, merges into the subpsychological. (See Chapter 17.) It should be emphasized that mature drives, as well as infantile ones, are in part id. For example, mature sexual mating and parental drives are mature id impulses, as are the drives toward social living, which are probably related to them. These drives are discernible in all mammalian species, with rare if any exceptions, and in most other species as well.

The major motivational forces in the mind are rather limited in number. The endless variety of individual personalities, problems, and symptoms results from different combinations of these few powerful underlying motivations. They can be listed in shorthand form as: (1) dependence and the drive to independence; (2) needs to receive and to give love; (3) sex drives; (4) inferiority and egotism (narcissism); (5) competitiveness; (6) superego reactions.

The most common reactions to disturbances of these basic motivations are: (1) fear and anxiety; (2) fight–flight: exaggerated hostility and guilt with withdrawal and regression; (3) disordered sexual feelings; (4) inferiority feelings; (5) a distorted sense of reality. These motivations and reactions combine in various degrees and proportions to produce the vast array of personalities, forms of psychopathology, and symptoms that are manifested throughout suffering human kind.

The basic motivations, although discrete forces, are intimately interrelated with one another. The infant is utterly helpless at birth and completely dependent upon its parents for survival. This dependence is distinguishable from but closely connected with its needs for their love. If such dependence and receptive needs for love become too strong, as they are apt to in overprotected, deprived, or otherwise mistreated children, they regularly give rise to feelings of inferiority. As the child grows, it comes to feel ashamed of being overly dependent on others. The resultant feelings of inferiority intensify egotism, vanity, envy, and competitiveness. The weakness causes shame, and the concomitant hostility causes guilt; both guilt and shame are reactions of the superego, which includes the conscience and standards.

Sexual feelings may be disordered directly by excessive repression or by overstimulation during childhood. And anxiety may be cultivated in the child by an overanxious parent, just as by any persisting threat to the child. These are essentially the effects of something wrong in the superego, that is, in the reactions that the individual has taken over from the parent and from the mores of society. Disturbance in the sense of reality is also a symptom rather than a force, but it is of special importance. All emotional disorders represent an excessive persistence of or regression to disordered childhood emotional patterns. The disorders may be classified as either *internal* or *reactive* to stress upon emotional vulnerabilities in these patterns of childhood.

The major sources of hostility are the results of disturbances in the normal maturing of these motivations. In the next chapter we will trace in some detail how disorders of the motivational forces lead to mobilization of the fight–flight mechanism and so to psychological expressions of hostility.

Section II
Clinical and Theoretical

A theory is the more impressive the greater the simplicity of its premises is, the more different kinds of things it relates, and the more extended is its area of applicability . . . . classical thermodynamics . . . is the only physical theory of universal content concerning which I am convinced that, within the framework of the applicability of its basic concepts, it will never be overthrown. . . .

Albert Einstein

6
Hostility as Disease—A Symptom of Disordered Motivations

Men of intemperate minds cannot be free—their passions forge their fetters.
Edmund Burke

If any psychiatrist today considers "mental illness" a misnomer because illness can only denote a physical disability, then he fails to understand the elementary psychodynamics of mental illness. Even physical disorders are today thought of as processes rather than in terms of a single cause and effect.

In physical medicine, no one would deny that pulmonary tuberculosis is a disease of the lung. Its "cause," its pathogenic agent, long a mystery, is now known to be the tubercle bacillus, also called the Koch bacillus after its discoverer, Robert Koch. When invaded by this bacillus, the body reacts with low-grade fever and fatigue that slow the person down; as the lung becomes congested and destroyed, the body reacts with cough, which raises sputum and eventually blood. However, some victims die, whereas others do not, and most people at autopsy, whatever the cause of death, are found to have some scarring of their lungs which suggests a tubercular infection long overcome, at some time in the distant past.

We have mentioned that, just as the nose and bronchi overreact to certain pollens, dust, or other allergenic substances in individuals with hay fever or asthma, so the fight–flight reaction, if overly aroused in childhood, can overreact to frustrations and threats in adult life. For example, Bertha, aged 45, was so supersensitive to the least hint of rejection that she was always anxious, depressed, and weeping. She always felt that "This is just like my father—he didn't love me, and this rejection is still another proof that I am unlovable." Here the "cause" of emotional illness was not a bacillus but was just as real: a rejecting father. Instead of arousing a fever and increasing white cells in the blood, the rejection by her father kept Bertha's fight–flight response aroused, creating in her constant tension from chronic anger and an urge to give up trying, to withdraw. Thus disorders of mental and emotional functioning are just as much diseases as are disorders of bodily functioning: the "causes" and *processes* are emotional, psychological, instead of physical.

The quantitative aspect is important in emotional disease just as it is in physical disease, the difference between health and disorder in both being mostly a matter of degree. We are all still in part the children we once were. If the child had a good, easy, happy relationship with those close to him and responsible for him and continues these good relationships with others, he matures with emotional health. If the child was made unhappy and afraid, he develops inner problems and does not mature adequately. A little anxiety in our lives can be shrugged off or even act as a stimulant; but when anxiety becomes severe enough, it can incapacitate us. Just as a slight fever is only mildly distressing, but a high fever can kill, so a high degree of deprivation of love can lead an individual to depression and can kill by suicide, either directly or indirectly. Often the emotional disease consists of internally caused excesses of hostility in reaction to abuses by omission or commission during the earliest days, weeks, months, and years of life, the 0 to 6. "Vicious circles" are characteristic of the emotional life; dependence can cause anger, which can cause guilt and anxiety, which in turn causes further retreat into childish dependence, and so on.

It follows that human hostility can be viewed as a form of disease, as *part of a disease process*, susceptible to scientific methods of therapy and of research into understanding it, treating it, and preventing it. Psychoanalysis and psychodynamic therapy have developed out of medicine; analytic therapeutic techniques, when mastered, can penetrate deeply and accurately into the human mind. Just as science has conquered smallpox and greatly reduced such childhood diseases as diphtheria, so what we learn through psychodynamic therapy has the potential of reducing man's hostility to man, appalling as is the vastness of the task.

The central importance of the child's dependence upon the parents and the exceedingly long period of that dependence (as compared with other species) is a basic factor in the development of neurotic disorders. There is probably always in the adult some of the child's emotional dependence, but what is important is *how much* of this persists and how it is dealt with. One of the most striking features in the development of the human personality and mind is the interplay of *progressive* and *regressive* forces. The progressive forces involve the organism's maturation from parasitic dependence upon the mother toward independence in caring for itself, and the capability of caring for others. This progressive trend is always in conflict with an opposite, regressive tendency of the individual to retreat from later, more mature patterns back toward earlier, less developed ones–from responsible, productive independence (RPI) back to the passive, receptive dependence (PRD) of early childhood.

The child's drive toward independence from the parents is a basic force in the young of all species. At birth, the infant begins to breathe for itself. Before long it can take in solid food by mouth instead of being dependent on the mother's milk. With strength and coordination it begins to walk and do things for itself. With curiosity it learns about the world and develops judgment. Then finally, when full size is reached, the energies toward growth and independence overflow into responsible activities of sex, mating, parenthood, and social productivity. From being parasitic, the individual becomes parental. It is this capacity for self-reliance and for the care of self and others that gives the mature adult his relative independence, his strength, his sense of security. And only with this kind of independence comes real social maturity–interdependence.

In conflict with this progressive drive is the tendency to be *fixated* at or to *regress* to childish dependence. The drives to maturity must conquer the pleasures of being babied. Sometimes it is overprotection that impedes growth to self-reliance; sometimes, on the other hand, being forced to independence prematurely causes an aversion to it. Either way, parents who interfere too strongly with the normal progressive development make an adult who, however powerful physically and intellectually, still craves a support for which he never outgrew the need. Such cravings, of course, can rarely be gratified in life. Few adults get from mates, colleagues, or friends the treatment they had or wanted to have as children from their parents. Also, because the underlying needs to be dependent are usually in sharp contrast with the wish to be mature, they are apt to cause an inner sense of frustration and of weakness and inadequacy, which, in turn, insults the self-esteem and leads to reactions of rage.

HOSTILITY FROM DISORDERED INDEPENDENCE

For example, Charles, a young student, became so hostile that he was unable to get along with his professors or classmates. He began to have ideas that everyone was against him. This led him to a break with his girlfriend, whom he had been dating regularly for more than a year. He became so upset that he had to leave college. He managed to find a job, but soon discovered that his old troubles persisted. It turned out that for as long as he could remember he had been much pampered by his mother and older sister. Charles's parents had been divorced, and the two women centered all their interest and attention on him. They praised his slightest achievements and cushioned his every hurt, "killing him with kindness." Thus, when the time came for him to move away from home and go to college, he felt that he could not exist without them and was angered when they insisted that he try. Moreover, his exaggerated dependence made him feel inferior to his contemporaries, and this enraged him because of envy, competitiveness, and the threat it posed to his self-esteem. While he was away from home, Charles's fight–flight reaction was kept constantly aroused by the frustration of his desires for dependence on his mother and sister and by his unconscious protest against having to be independent and to assume responsibilities, even the minor ones of a student. His hostility was forcing him into paranoia; that is, he projected his own mounting rage onto others, not appreciating its intensity but feeling that others were hostile toward himself. At the end of his sophomore year Charles had a psychotic break and spent a year in a mental hospital.

Paul presents a contrast to Charles, showing what can happen when the hostility arising from feelings of excessive dependence is turned outward against others. The dynamics in this vignette sketches a little more of the interrelationships of all the major motivational forces, suggesting how disorders of the basic motivations lead to psychopathological expressions of hostility.

Paul, 21 years old, was referred for psychiatric treatment while under indictment for burglary. He was the youngest son of a well-to-do, middle-class family. He was attractive, of superior intelligence, and in excellent physical condition. His father held a responsible position in a large manufacturing company. His brother, two years older, was working. His sister, six years older, was stably married. The mother took care of the home, which was comfortably appointed and desirably located. The family history was psychiatrically negative on the father's side, but with a suicide and also a few nervous breakdowns on the mother's side. Paul's developmental history as reported by his parents was normal and uneventful throughout the pregnancy and early years except for finickiness about food and temper tantrums. In contrast to this infantile behavior was an almost compulsive desire to be stronger than his brother. This exaggerated competitive demand to be strong, later to be tough, turned out to be also a reaction against his exaggerated needs for dependence, which made him feel weak.

Paul was dismissed from one high school after another because of unruliness, drinking, and exposing himself to girls. The discipline of a series of military academies failed to socialize his behavior. He nevertheless somehow succeeded in finishing high school and in being accepted by a college, but was again expelled on the same charges of unruliness, drinking, and indecent exposure. During his psychiatric treatment Paul denied these charges, with the exception of admitting to some instances of rebellion against authority. He would either deny the dismissals from school outright, or he would claim that they were due to low grades. Actually his conversation, work, and I. Q. tests all showed him to be of superior intelligence.

Paul's difficulties repeated themselves according to their stereotyped pattern in his job, his relationships with girls, and all of his social encounters. His life was, so to speak, lived for him by unconscious forces, which he could not perceive, understand, or control. Thus in the jobs that he was occasionally able to get, he would be insubordinate and rebellious while at the same time demanding higher wages, thus assuring his dismissal. His pattern toward a date was to pick a fight with the girl and then refrain from any gesture of reconciliation. This behavior was designed to prove his independence of her. So prominent was the denial of the dependent element in the relationship that, although he would provoke the quarrel, he considered that any friendly step on his part would be a show of weakness.

Paul's behavior in general social relations showed the same pattern: bravado and toughness as a front to hide from himself and the world his core of softness and weakness, his exaggerated dependence upon others for shelter and subsistence. Thus in place of constructive work of value to himself and to others, at school or in his jobs, Paul overslept, overate, drank to excess, gambled, stole, and in general defied all authority. At the same time he was supported by his family, whom he practically blackmailed by his behavior. Sexually, he did not love, but only peeped and exhibited himself.

Such delinquent behavior netted him a court record of four arrests in the five years prior to his coming for psychiatric treatment. The various charges included indecent exposure, larceny, disorderly conduct (peeping in windows), and burglary. He was seen by the court psychiatrist, who made a diagnosis of "psychopathic personality—not committable as insane or feebleminded." The prognosis being very poor for any improvement without radical changes in his personality, he was given a choice between jail and psychiatric treatment during parole. (Of course, psychotherapy cannot directly change anyone, but can only help a person to change himself.) He chose treatment. However it later came out that his soft dependent core actually yearned for the irresponsible life of jail, where he could be entirely dependent, supported without effort, and secure, but still seeing himself as the tough guy he longed to be.

Throughout the analysis, Paul never mentioned his perversions, exhibitionism, and peeping, and much of what he did tell was probably colored by his imagination. At one point rather early in treatment he was frank enough to say that he could not face his own soul, that he would go only so far and no further. Nevertheless he did cooperate rather well in free-associating, and thus revealed the problems that his pride and fear resisted seeing but that deep down he timidly wanted to face and solve.

In practically everything he said or did, the soft–tough conflict was apparent. The affectations of his appearance (broad belts, garish shirts, heavy shoes), the swagger, the jaunty cigarette always dangling, the sophisticated air, were all quite transparent. Beneath this veneer was the attractive smile and naive, even sweet expression of a little boy, frightened and appealing. So, too, in the analysis the defiant delinquent toughness was only a front for what showed clearly beneath—namely, the soft core, the never outgrown, fixated, infantile passive, receptive dependent needs.

These attitudes, in their common, typical conflict, were traceable back to his infancy in an amost unaltered pattern. His overly strong wish to be dependent caused him to feel weak and inferior in comparison with other men. This, in turn, impelled him to prove that he was the opposite, that is, strong and independent. But he did not realize that the sense of weakness came from his childish receptive dependence, and that his unconscious denial by the veneer of toughness betokened a wish for strength that could only be achieved by independence and responsibility. Thus he was in a constant confused muddle and struggle to satisfy these conflicting desires–to be as dependent and receptive as a child, and yet also to feel like a man. His mother, when questioned as to Paul's earliest behavior in infancy, said that from before he was a year old and until he was about five years of age, he had recurrent temper tantrums. These episodes of rage would be terminated only when his mother picked him up and carried and rocked him. In this way Paul not only vented his anger, but also dominated his mother in getting her to indulge his receptive dependent demands. Moreover, said his mother, from the time of his very earliest activity, he showed an intense desire to be stronger than his older brother. His dependent need made him feel weak in comparison with his brother, and he tried constantly to prove he was stronger.

During treatment it was no surprise when Paul said that he always feared only two things: to be humiliated by a woman and to meet a man in his own field. He could not stand competition with a man if there was a chance of losing. Therefore, he would never compete with his brother or, transferring this pattern, with other boys, in the common fields of scholarship, sports, and, later, business. (He once lost at squash before a small audience and became so furious that he barely restrained himself from attacking his victorious opponent physically, and he never played the game again.) So instead of competing normally in the natural pursuits, Paul tried to make himself expert "on his own turf," in gambling, drinking, and stealing–that is, in fields in which his brother and classmates would not follow him. Thus the trend toward criminality developed out of the need to show his toughness and superiority which combined with his own hostility, he felt he could not show in normal competition because of his infantile, receptive dependent demands. The surface show of strength masked a flight away from independence and responsibility.

The early finickiness about food showed the same earmark and persisted into adulthood: he tyrannized his family, especially his mother, by eating only when and what he pleased. This trend was connected with his later drinking, which he regarded not as a pleasurable indulgence and escape but as another exhibition of toughness.

This receptive dependent conflict was clear in relation to Paul's family. Coupled with extreme demands upon his mother and rage at the slightest thwarting, was a feeling that he could not stand to receive anything from her. Similarly he demanded money from his father (whom he preferred to his mother), and yet he could hardly stand to accept it. He preferred stealing to financial dependence on his father. He could not endure indebtedness to anyone and never expressed gratitude to anyone for anything. Toward his brother, beneath the active competition, was an intense envy of any attention the brother received; that is, he competed with his brother both progressively for strength (independence and responsibility) and regressively for dependence and receiving. This regressive trend filled him with a bitter hatred of women, because, as his mother was supported in all ways by his father, he saw women as people who can be supported and can be frankly receptive—something he could never admit his craving to be. He had no interest in a girlfriend except, as mentioned earlier, in trying to show his strength by denying his dependence on her.

Outside of the family the conflict repeated itself with precision. In school and at work Paul asserted his independence, but only in order to demand privileges and escape responsibilities. Gambling was thrilling because of the anticipation of easy money—and he had little to lose, for he used other people's money. Horse racing provided the same daydreams plus the thrill of identifying with the competing horses. In stealing and holdups, too, Paul could play the strong, dominant man and yet get something for nothing, without feeling inferior, dependent, and obligated. Eventually, however, this came to involve not only risk, but initiative, when he landed a job with an underworld gang. He was hired to drive trucks, which at first had great appeal. But then came the problems of competing with other men and the responsibility and danger. So Paul never got deeply involved with organized crime, but just hovered on the edge of the underworld.

In the sexual sphere his reactions were no different. Paul would pick up girls as a show of masculinity. He never mentioned the exhibitionism and peeping in the analysis because it was too patently infantile, too close to the soft core. His typical mechanism was again demonstrated by the circumstances of his last arrest. The police were summoned because Paul was seen peeping in some windows. When he was apprehended he admitted to attempted burglary, but not to peeping. He could boast of criminality to deny a sexual perversion, in an attempt to hide the soft core by what seemed to him a more masculine front. Perversions are infantile fixations, childish impulses that have not been outgrown. Unable to take masculine responsibility for a woman, he peeped as a substitute for it. His sexual perversions were in essence manifestations of the same conflict that was so apparent elsewhere in his life.

Paul's feelings of inferiority and failure to compete, together with his conflicting needs for dependence and independence, filled him with rage and defiance, and this persistently hostile, hateful, angry attitude made him constantly guilty and fearful of retaliation. Much of the bravado was itself a denial of his fears. He dared not relax. No wonder then that he ran away from home, from school, from jobs, where his emotions made human contacts so painful. It is also not surprising that he even welcomed the idea of prison, where he need not compete, where his conscience could be appeased, and where he could indulge his desires to be dependent and yet maintain a self-image of toughness. Paul shows the dynamics of a common type of criminal. That attraction to prison was the reason for his laconic, detached, schizoid attitude when the judge threatened him with commitment for life. Paul reported that when he heard the judge say that, he could hardly keep from laughing in his face.

HOSTILITY FROM DISORDERED LOVE NEEDS

Dependence and needs for love are not identical but are closely intertwined. The child's needs for physical care must be distinguished from his demands for attention and coddling. For the child, feeling loved is the guarantee of the care and protection that assure survival. Being loved is the libidinal accompaniment of dependence. Adults with mature needs for love fulfill them by giving responsible love and by being loved in return. But they are reconciled to the fact that no one ever receives all the love that he wants. Persons in whom childish needs for love remain too strong may be incapable of this realistic adaptation to experience and thus go to desperate extremes to get attention directly without recognizing that no adult can get all of the kind of love he wanted as a small, helpless child, and that even if he could, other adults also want it, and there are not enough individuals willing or even able to give it. Such realization that the deepest childish love needs cannot be satisfied is one of the great lessons of maturing, and is best learned early in adult life.

The roots of such cravings go deep into infancy. Sometimes the inherent needs for love were disturbed in chilhood by being threatened, frustrated, or otherwise injured; sometimes they were overindulged; sometimes the behavior necessary to get love is warped by excessive demands on the part of the parents. For example, one patient, a personable young man, was reared to get love only by being entirely submissive to a tyrannical father. He grew up with this submissiveness, but hated himself for thus thwarting his masculine, normally assertive, independent drives. He went through life feeling that he must always be submissive, yet inwardly he raged against this. Another man only got approval from his father through outstanding accomplishments almost beyond his abilities. He always was driven but never satisfied, and in such a rage because of this that he could not love, became addicted to drugs and alcohol, and overworked himself to early death.

People grow up unconsciously feeling that they can get love only if they behave as they had to behave in childhood to win it from their parents. Thus the force of the hunger for love causes other patterns of behavior to so shape themselves as to gratify it. This powerful need can give rise to a variety of emotional problems not only by molding these other motivations but also through abnormalities in itself of kind and degree.

Some people, although they are independent in their judgment and actions, and betray no need to lean upon others, are yet tormented by cravings for love that are so intense as to be insatiable. Normally as the child grows to maturity, there is a gradual diminution in the intensity of the need to receive love and an increase in the enjoyment of giving love. Deprivation and overindulgence are two of the common errors of upbringing that disturb the normal give–get balance. If the emotional diet in childhood is too rich or too poor, then the appetite for love later in life is exaggerated or otherwise disordered. And where excessive submissiveness or overgoodness or overachievement is the price of love, many try to force the love by distortions of such behavior.

Cravings for love, like other emotional forces, are more or less readily displaced and redirected away from the parents to other people. When they are excessive and disordered, they may form the nucleus of an addiction. In such cases, the cravings are tenaciously fixed onto other persons (often as infatuations), or onto objects, such as food (as in bulimia) or money (as in avarice) or alcohol or other drugs, in blind, vain attempts to satiate childhood needs for love, with an admixture of hostility from the frustration, and an effort to escape the frustration and strain.

Betty, a capable young executive, had the intelligence and good looks to set her well on the road to success. But instead of being happy, she was hostile and chronically depressed. At the office she made no close friends among women, while outside the office she established the most intense attachments to men. Repeatedly she would fall so all-absorbingly in love that she would become almost unable to work; yet these affairs invariably ended in violent quarrels. As a child Betty never received adequate love from her mother, who was too busy with her very active social life to give much attention to her daughter. Desperately, Betty turned to her father. Though she clung to him, he was not around enough to satisfy her needs because his work required much traveling. As a substitute for himself and his love, Betty's father offered her gifts as compensation. Now that she was grown, Betty could not feel comfortable with members of her own sex, nor could her young male friends match her father's gifts. Because of her excessive demands, she would lose her boyfriends and then become furious at everyone. At times she became depressed to the point of suicide.

Like exaggerated needs for dependence, the child's desires for love, through their very intensification by fear, frustration, spoiling, and other faults in upbringing, cannot be gratified in adult life. Who can give any of us what we wanted so exorbitantly as small children? Inevitably thwarted, the love needs form a source of constant frustration, which leads to a sense of hopelessness and failure, to all varieties of neurotic symptoms, and always to rage.

Alice, a 15-year-old girl, is currently at a rehabilitation institution for juvenile delinquents. She has been there for about a year. At the age of 13 she was arrested and charged with disorderly conduct, resisting arrest, assault and battery on an officer, and damage to city property. Just six months prior to this incident she was arrested and charged with assault with intent to kill—for serving poison to her mother. Alice denied this charge, saying that some Draino accidentally fell into her mother's coffee cup, and that she didn't mean it to happen. Alice has been known to the courts almost since her birth because of recurrent custody problems.

Her parents are both heavy drinkers who have constantly been involved in illicit sexual relationships with a grotesque constituency of paramours. Alice has three brothers: Robert is a year older than she and is now at a juvenile correctional facility because of generally incorrigible and criminal behavior; Steven, a year younger than Alice, now lives in a foster home; Michael, three years old, born of one of the mother's extramarital relationships, lives at home.

Alice's parents have a long history of separations and reconciliations; the mother has moved many different times with the children, usually to new neighborhoods. When the family is together, the mother and father drink excessively and fight most of the time. Alice's earliest memory is of her mother and father fighting. Alice recalls that she and her brothers, Robert and Steven, were always trying to push the father away to prevent his pummeling their mother with his powerful fists. Alice reported that she had frequent fights with these two brothers, and that when they would make up they would all agree, "Let's love each other and not be like Mother and Father."

Because of the drinking and the paramours, the children were left alone a great deal and were usually dirty, ill-nourished, poorly clothed, inadequately supervised, and in various other ways severely neglected. For a few years, until she was about 10 or 11, Alice used to wait up at night for her mother to come home. She would stagger in drunk, and Alice would make her some food and put her to bed. She would carefully tuck her mother in so that she wouldn't, in her stupor, fall onto the floor. The mother is large and husky, and sometimes when drunk she would mercilessly beat her daughter. Alice says she never fought back because she felt her mother did not know what she was doing, and that it wasn't right to hit her.

The father deserted the family when Alice was 10. The mother moved to a tough neighborhood, where the children had to learn to fight to protect themselves. Quickly they mastered the necessary skills for survival. The mother got a job as a barmaid, but was soon dismissed because of her drinking. To get money the children took to stealing. They were caught and placed in a detention center.

Alice kept running away, always returning to her mother only to find her completely wrapped up in one or another lover.

Alice was placed in two successive foster homes. In the first placement, she became demanding of attention through negative behavior. Unable to live within the limits of a normal home environment, she was stubbornly defiant and unable to accept directions from figures of authority. When agitated, as she was much of the time, she would listen to no one and would refuse to take responsibility for her own feelings and behavior.

In the second home she did receive some of the attention she demanded, but it was not enough for Alice, and of course the sense of deprivation and anger were built into her childhood emotional pattern. Her school situation deteriorated during this period. She developed no peer relationships and fought with everyone, including teachers who opposed her insistence on having her own way. She seemed a spoiled, demanding child with a violent temper. Just as she had run away from the detention center, so too she fled these foster homes, always returning to her mother. Alice wanted desperately for her mother to become a devoted, caring parent, but such a change in the mother might have had slight effect because Alice's sense of deprivation, rejection, and rage were by now intrinsic to her childhood pattern.

When she was 11 Alice became pregnant for the first time. She claims that she yielded sexually because a boy threatened to hurt her if she didn't have intercourse with him. Alice became pregnant but aborted by going with her brothers to a vacant lot where she convinced them to jump up and down on her abdomen. A year later Alice was raped by one of her mother's boyfriends. Again she became pregnant, but this time she had a spontaneous miscarriage (fortunately for the baby).

A year later Alice was charged with attempting to kill her mother by poisoning. She was adjudicated delinquent and committed to a correctional facility for juveniles. While there she discovered that she was pregnant. Alice again acted out her impulses by becoming abusive to the staff, generally hostile toward the other inmates, and excessively demanding of all who came in contact with her. Finally she succeeded in running away. She returned to live with her mother and was allowed to stay there. Not long after returning home Alice prematurely delivered a baby boy, and it was during her hospital stay that she resumed her outbursts of violence. The baby, underweight, remained hospitalized for two months, after which time he was discharged to Alice and her mother. They both refused placement for the baby. In fact, Alice threatened suicide if either she or her baby were placed. (It is hard enough for a baby born into a relatively stable marriage and home to mature into a reasonably normal happy adult. Is there any greater crime than to bring an innocent baby into such a situation in which it is doomed to severe mental and emotional illness, including almost surely some form of criminality? The world needs more quality, not quantity of population.)

Although officially she returned to live with her mother, Alice spent extended periods away from home. While her mother seemed only superficially concerned, she refused to keep custody of Alice and the baby if this continued. Nevertheless, the girl persisted in her periodic disappearances, and her mother finally filed a police report. Soon thereafter Alice tried to commit suicide by taking an overdose of pills. When she returned home, she claimed that she had been staying with a boy and that she tried suicide because he had thrown her out. At that point, Alice's mother requested that her daughter be placed. Alice became distraught, insisting that she remain with her baby. She convinced her mother that she would kill herself, and the woman finally changed her mind and agreed to allow Alice and the baby to remain with her. Three months later the baby was found dead, having fallen from a second story window. Alice was accused of killing him, and she was then placed in a youth detention center. After a homicide investigation, the death was ruled accidental, as there was insufficient evidence to prove otherwise. While at the center, Alice continued to get into fights with the other girls and to physically abuse the supervisor. She was easily provoked and showed a complete lack of control over her temper.

Clearly, Alice is lonely and still longs for a positive relationship with her rejecting mother, but could no longer tolerate it even if her mother, by some miracle, could now offer it. Alice is an insecure, inadequate youngster with irresistible needs to act out her hostility and violence. She tries to deny her feelings of rejection and the realistic anticipation of rejection in response to her behavior, which at times camouflages her deep-rooted needs for love. These needs are exaggerated and disordered by the fact that Alice never received satisfaction of them from her parents or substitutes. Although she still yearns deeply for her mother's love and attention, her feeling for her mother as a rejecting, punitive, and destructive person is now so deeply part of her childhood pattern that Alice could not change even if her mother did.

Alice's evasiveness, cunning, and hostile acting out not only vent her rage, from frustration of her love needs and from her inferiority feelings, but are also in some part methods of compensation that bring her attention, recognition, and, in ways distorted by repression, forms of acceptance by other people. During her most recent psychiatric interview it was noted that Alice's thinking is becoming increasingly paranoid. She is daily becoming more demanding and more absorbed in fantasy. All frustrations and threats stimulate the fight–flight reaction with its hostility. Alice had more than her share of frustrations and fears; and with such conditioning, almost from birth and so consistent, the chances of her changing or outgrowing these pathological childhood patterns through any form of therapy are negligible. The twig has been too severely bent for the tree ever to be straightened.

HOSTILITY FROM INFERIORITY FEELINGS

Another powerful source of hostility, partially discussed in the case of Paul, is inferiority feelings and the drive for power. In most cases this begins with the little child's feelings of weakness in comparison with his parents. Normally this is balanced in the child by the assurance that, though smaller, he is essentially like his parents and in time will grow up to become their equal. Assuming there is no disturbance in development, the child will pass through adolescence and reach his full powers as an adult. He will reach adequate maturity through outgrowing the childhood motivations and reactions (discussed in Chapter 5) and reach identification with the mature members of his family, friends, and co-workers. The sense of independence, self-reliance, and security and other satisfactions gained through the mature use of his adult powers will yield more enjoyment and pleasure than the earlier self-centered pleasures of the child's helplessness, weakness, and impotence.

If an individual has been reared in such a way that he retains into adulthood too much of the attitudes of childhood, he will continue to feel like the child, small, dominated, and inferior. In such a person the pattern of still feeling like a child in a world of adults continues. In reaction against this he is apt to be driven to prove his worth, to demonstrate all sorts of compensations and overcompensations—or else he may give up the struggle altogether. Like all disturbances in development, this is felt by the individual, although not understood by him, as a serious threat to self-esteem and perhaps even survival, and thus stimulates his fight–flight reaction with its feelings of rage, hostility, and impulses to violence.

Sometimes the need for prestige in reaction to the sense of inferiority is directly fostered by the parents: a child may be conditioned to expect their love only when he achieves outside recognition. Much of the competitiveness between adults has its roots in the early inculcation and prolonged striving for good grades, athletic distinction, or popularity. Such a basis for the parental giving or withholding of affection intensifies the inevitable envy and competition between brothers and sisters and also the frequent rivalry inherent in a child's relations with a parent, usually of the same sex. Of course, a certain amount of competition is useful in growth, but when childish competitiveness is prolonged or exaggerated, it is apt to cause ceaseless, compulsive striving and bitter envy. Obviously this will damage good feelings and good relations within the family and generate outside hatreds, which usually persist through later life.

Adults crippled by their failure to outgrow inflated demands for prestige usually become filled with envy and chronic hostility. And it is this emotional force that underlies the struggle to keep up with the Joneses, to beat out the other fellow. Strength and teamwork are disrupted by ubiquitous battling for personal status. Such vanity and exaggerated needs for recognition, prestige, and esteem are a corrupting influence on healthy human values, on the system of ideals that allows men to live together in communities. Although it takes a little imagination to see it, the survival and happiness of a society depend on how much each member contributes, not upon how much each member takes out.

A superior young man in his late twenties, handsome, brilliant, capable, was accepted for an excellent position in a large company. There was no reason for him not to feel completely confident in the job, yet he felt anxious about holding his own with the other bright young men there. The night before he began work, he had a dream that depicted with dramatic clarity a portion of his dynamics:

"I am riding an unusually powerful motorcycle down a broad highway. There are many other fellows, maybe a hundred, on similar machines riding with me. It turns out to be a race. I know that I have to win and I am in the lead. Then the road becomes rough, no longer paved, and I cannot keep up the pace. The road becomes nothing but mud and ruts and I can no longer ride the motorcycle over it. But I have to keep in the lead, so I just push the cycle forward with my legs, with my feet on the ground. Finally I cross the finish line ahead of all the others."

This manifest dream shows the competitiveness in the patient's personality, but not the hostility or guilt, both of which come out in his life mostly as accident-proneness: smashing up his automobile, sometimes several times in a week; injuring his knee in sports; and other minor injuries in everyday life. The sports he chose to enjoy were all life-endangering, such as mountain climbing. In addition, he would make himself miserable over a girl. Without going into the details of this patient's dynamics, we make the point here that extreme competitiveness caused self-injurious behavior. In his new job, if he were to concentrate his superior abilities on his own tasks and hold a live-and-let-live attitude toward his collegues, he would unquestionably progress brilliantly. But should he keep the competitiveness portrayed in his dream, he would be apt to antagonize others, disrupt the organization, make his own life strenuous, and endanger his own security, success, and well-being.

Closely related to the needs for prestige and status is the drive for power. Before his sense of reality is fully developed, the infant is said to go through what has been called "a stage of ominipotence." When the infant's needs are satisfied as soon as they arise and in an almost automatic fashion, the responsive parents appear at first to be mere extensions of the baby's wishes, cries, or gestures. This period, if unduly prolonged, may condition the child to the feeling that if he only wants something it will automatically materialize.

Power is the individual's great assurance that his needs can be satisifed no matter what. Whether an adult seeks power in order to make a constructive contribution to humanity or seeks it only to satisfy his own inner personal desires is a test of emotional security and maturity. Drives for power can take many forms—muscular prowess, sexual potency, the ability to compel obedience from others, sheer physical domination over another. The important issue is how this power is used. It can be directed toward mature and humanely beneficial purposes associated with protecting and providing for the family and community, regardless of how broadly this latter term is meant. Or, at the other end of the spectrum, it can be utilized for selfish, infantile purposes of exploitation and brutality.

At the core of both excessive power drives and exaggerated demands for prestige are usually feelings of inferiority, which in greater or lesser degree seem to harass a huge number of people in our civilization. Disguises for these feelings are often unsuccessful; it takes no particularly astute observer to recognize that beneath most inflated egos lie inferiority and insecurity. Put generally, feelings of inferiority usually result from actual emotional inferiorities that are representative of failures of parts of the individual to develop adequately to emotional maturity. Desires for power, a sense of inferiority, egocentricity, failure of feeling human sympathy—these are cardinal characteristics of the hostile mind. They are most obvious in the ruthless spouse and parent, the political tyrant, the merciless criminal. All these people share a deficiency in identification with other individuals (that is, an inability to feel and empathize with others as human beings like themselves); they react to others only as bodies, as objects of their own hostile and frequently sadistic lusts.

The various distorting forces that warp the maturing of the infant or child for life may be subtle, or they may come into the open as direct cruelty and even violence, from parents or others. Whatever the nature of the hostility—overprotection, neglect, inconsistent training, excessive ideals, debased standards, seductiveness, exploitation, beating and battering—whether stemming from the parents' misguided "love" or from conscious sadism, the result is some form of crippling of the child's emotional life, as we have seen in the case of Alice. The impairment may be in any or all parts of the personality. It may be primarily a reaction of the id (for example, excessive dependence upon one or the other or both parents), or it may lie in a disorder of the superego (e.g., in guilt, in harshness of conscience, in false standards, in imposition of ideals that are so high as to be impossible of fulfillment, or in deficient conscience). Simply the lack of good loving persons with whom to identify during the earliest years of childhood can also be a cause of emotional crippling, for it may result in a poor sense of reality and poor control over the impulses. These reactions of the child to the way it is treated by the parents and to its identification with them become traits of the child's personality and as such form the foundation for its reactions to other persons. This childhood emotional pattern of response, once formed, persists for life. As always in psychopathology, all is a question of degree, a question of the intensity of the emotional forces and the balance that results among all of them from their interactions.

Whatever the specific nature of the personality deformity, the resulting sense of inferiority is usually reacted against violently. It is an intolerable internal irritant and a threat to the individual's security. It is so widespread a problem that it would be impossible to list briefly all the ways in which different individuals react to their feelings of inferiority. All the reactions, however, regardless of the specific form they assume because of the frustrations and threats, inevitably have one powerful element in common: hostility.

A person feels a nameless, indefinable inferiority, which he may not fully recognize himself. He cannot come to grips with its sources. He may try to change, but the core of his personality is actually unknown to him and is probably so fixed that, without analytic treatment or unusual experiences, he is unable to do anything about it. He feels vaguely threatened but he cannot change, he cannot flee, and he cannot fight the threat itself. He is blind to his inner unknown assailant, and the result is what has been aptly termed "impotent rage." Irritated and threatened from within, the individual generates a constant pressure of rage and hostility that can come out against the strong, who he bitterly envies, or against the weak, who remind him of his own inferiority. To the world he may be the very image of every success. But, like the fictional Richard Corey, while we scrape for bread, he may go home one fine night and put a bullet through his head. Or he may do himself in by alcohol or drugs or overwork.

Douglas has spent nine of the last 10 years in a federal penitentiary. He is now 28 years old and serving a sentence for manslaughter. Four years ago, while confined to a maximum security cell, he attempted suicide. This uncontrollably hostile young man is the youngest of five brothers, three of whom are now serving terms in prison for various crimes of violence. The fourth brother was killed two years ago, while on parole, in a shoot-out in a local bar. Douglas's earliest memory is of the police coming to arrest his oldest brother. When his parents refused to admit the officers, they broke down the door. The father viciously attacked the police, who nevertheless succeeded in seizing the boy.

In describing his early years, Douglas rather mournfully notes that he always felt rejected and ignored by his father, whom he believes had always favored his other brothers. In all he says about his family it is clear that Douglas has never had a relationship of loyalty and trust with either his parents or any of his brothers. His mother unfairly beat Douglas with a stick several times a week. There were numerous fights between Douglas and his father, especially when the father was drunk, which was often, as he had a serious drinking problem. Douglas, even as a very young boy, knew that his father saw other women and that his mother saw other men. In fact, his mother would become exceedingly promiscuous whenever Douglas's father was away in prison. And this, too, was not an infrequent occurrence. There is little evidence of family loyalty or love.

Douglas was a severe disciplinary problem in school and was repeatedly suspended for misbehavior (mostly for fighting with classmates). He recalls being tauntingly called "jailbird" by the other students because of his father's and brothers' prison records. Douglas dropped out of school when he was 16 and soon thereafter was arrested for aggravated assault and battery. He had viciously attacked a black man in a movie theater because, as he later explained to the judge, "I didn't like his looks." This seemed to Douglas to be an adequate motive, even though he almost killed his victim.

Apparently blacks are a chief target of Douglas's hostility. Now in prison, he struggles with only modest success to control his hatred of them. When asked about his feelings toward blacks, he replied that he just hates them "in general—the way they act, the way they treat other people, the way they control the prisons. Why they rape us white people! I'd like to kill 'em, kill 'em all!" Black prisoners are not his only target. He claims all the officers and guards in the prison treat him unfairly. Douglas believes they are jealous of his ability to control the other inmates—the white ones. He detests the prison personnel because he feels they should keep the black prisoners segregated from the white ones.

Not surprisingly, Douglas describes pervasive feelings of being inferior and of being exploited by others who are hostile to him (as his parents were). Vicious, powerful, and narcissistic hostility is his only defense. He is frustrated, enraged, and depressed about the future, and seems constantly perplexed by the enormous difficulty he experiences in controlling his behavior. Because of his irresistible tendency to project the responsibility for his actions onto others, he cannot come to any real understanding of his own motivations.

In Douglas we can see a young man who was severely traumatized by his hostile, disloyal, rejecting parents. His experience of not being valued by his parents and often beaten by them resulted in excessive feelings of inferiority and worthlessness and expectations of physical attack. His overcompensatory attempts to deny these feelings display hostile, dominating, and violent behavior, which is also partly retaliation against his parents and partly identification with them. He has a pathological quantity and intensity of hostile feelings and an equally pathological lack of control over his behavior.

It is because of the high proportion of individuals filled with feelings of inferiority and with reactions to it of pride, power-seeking, and hostility that we have so many of this world's problems. What engenders so much of the anxiety, pain, and suffering between nations, within nations, in families, in business, in labor and political organizations, and even in professional societies is the pride and hate that drive men who think they know better than other men, the men who ruthlessly impose their will with little capacity for sympathetic understanding. Yet, despite their power, these men are usually emotional cripples who have failed to develop a mature capacity to give and to receive love. *The person who shows exaggerated egotism, need for power, and above all, hostility is suffering from serious emotional disease. He is psychopathological, and it is of immense practical importance that this be recognized.*

* * * *

HOSTILITY AS PRODUCT OF THE SUPEREGO

The superego, of which the conscience is a part, is largely a product of conditioning. Essentially it is a precipitate of parental feelings, training, and attitudes that have clustered about the nucleus of the individual's natural instinct toward social living. As we noted earlier, this instinct for social cooperation is a common feature seen throughout the animal kingdom. The conscience of most children is formed chiefly from the parent's training and attitudes, through conditioned obedience and through imitation of and identification with the parents.

The attitudes and behavior of the parents, because of the very long period of childhood and therefore conditioning, become impressed on the child's mind and persist in memory all through life. This becomes a vital and powerful element of his personality, both as a child and as an adult. With growth, this superego, this composite of memories and feelings toward his parents and identifications with them, is in turn transferred or projected onto others. This projection assumes the form of expectations on the part of the individual that others will react and respond to him much as his parents did.

This does not, however, take only a verbal, conscious form. Its compelling power goes far deeper—into the unconscious. There is evidence to suggest that before we learn language our thinking is predominantly through pictures. We return to this form of visual thinking nightly in our dreams. Apparently the young child forms images in his mind of those persons toward whom he had his first strong feelings. These images are formed as composites, wherein the varied behavior of the key emotional figures is telescoped together. Such *imagos* comprise and mold the conscience and the person's pattern of attitudes and feelings toward others throughout life. The child who has been reared with love tends to see others as loving; the one (like Douglas) who has been brutally treated expects such treatment from others and behaves as though all people were his enemies. If the parents caused guilt in the child, then imagos will be formed that at once threaten punishment and offer love. And if the training was inconsistent, the result will be conflicting imagos that cause serious confusion in the mind of the child and later of the adult.

For example, a mother filched from her husband extra allowance money for her son, who knew of this. As an adult he felt he could indulge himself, even illicitly, but felt painfully inferior and guilty toward his father and toward other honest, hard-working men. He struggled between indulging himself illegally as his mother had done and being the responsible worker and family man his father was.

It is in the family that the emotional patterns of outlook, feeling, reaction, and behavior (which will form the core of the superego) are shaped. The rest of the personality matures as the body grows, but this core will be altered little in the course of an ordinary life. The conditioning begins at birth and possibly, to some extent, even before that. In general, the younger the organism, the more sensitive it is to emotional influences and the more easily its personality can be damaged.

For example, John, whose father had been harsh and dominating from the very beginning, was so sensitized to this treatment that he reacted to everyone who had the least position or even air of authority with a submissive attitude which, inwardly, the more mature part of him could not bear and which enraged him.

His father's image so ruled him that he would even become anxious in the presence of a friendly conductor on the train. As a grown man, John would spend weeks mortally dreading a business trip to Europe solely because he knew he would have to face the authority of the customs officers. He viewed every authority figure with suspicion and hostility. It became increasingly difficult for him even to leave his apartment every morning because he knew he would have to pass by the traffic cop on the corner. To give in had once been too painful, too total a yielding of his will; but to fight it meant to him identification with those above him, and to his unconscious this meant that he himself would have to become the dictatorial, controlling type of person he despised in his father.

Dependent, receptive wishes for love can be made too strong by excessive overindulgence during childhood. An individual who was raised in this way may feel in his adult relationships that he is toward others too much like the child he was toward his parents, that he too much lives only to please others, only to win love and approval. Understandably this gives rise to a general sense of weakness, which in turn generates feelings of envy and rage toward the stronger. But because he has always been lovingly treated, this individual dares not admit to these feelings of hostility. He controls them and is in reality a kind and considerate person. His hostility may be perceived as coming from others (paranoid projection) or it may be acted out against himself (masochism), often because of guilt.

* * * *

SEX, ANXIETY, AND HOSTILITY

It has long been believed that social cooperation can arise as an extension of sexual-familial relations. According to Allee: "The more closely knit societies arose from some sort of simple aggregation, frequently . . . of the familial pattern." Sex and family feeling is perhaps one expression of the underlying tendency of protoplasm to preserve and expand itself.

Sex involves and is involved in both sensuality and love. Sensuality derives from various bodily erotic zones (e.g., lips, mouth, skin, and breasts), normally contributing to and culminating in genital sensations and orgasm. Thus sex is a physiological mechanism. But it also has a psychological content—normally, love. However, any strong feeling can be erotized to some degree, and sex can serve the purpose of expressing and draining a variety of feelings. In the mature adult, sex is an expression of love and the mating impulses, and motivates marriage and children. In persons who have not matured sufficiently, however, sex, like other biological drives, can be misdirected and misused. For example, it may be used only for childlike play, for making money, or solely for the purpose of satisfying narcissistic needs for attention and admiration.

Obviously every sexual act, to be mature, need not be for the deliberate and exclusive purpose of procreation; but in maturity, sex eventually becomes part of or operates in a setting of love for others. The person who continues to use sex *only* as childish play and as nothing else, who fails to fuse it with love, does not fulfill his adult sexual role in life. The result is usually emptiness, loneliness, frustration, pain, and guilt, all of which combine to cause hostility. Conversely, if overinhibited or denied all expression, sex can become a major source of anguish and anger.

There are also minor sources of hostility in sexual feelings themselves. This is true when sex is used as the chief pathway for releasing the body's surplus energy and emotional tensions. For example, one young male patient had such a passion for his girlfriend that he became more and more possessive and jealous. As time went on, Fred attempted to attack physically any other boy who made even the most innocent gesture of attention toward her. He was only a step away from paranoid jealousy, having already begun to hint at delusions about her unfaithfulness. Fred had been severely deprived emotionally during childhood. His father had been cruel, and his mother had merely tolerated him. Thus he grew up with intensified longings for parental love and with especial hatred toward his mother for denying him. Subsequently these feelings were transferred to his girlfriend. She meant everything he had desired and never received from a woman throughout childhood. And there also lurked within him, unconsciously, impulses to revenge himself on her as a substitute for his depriving mother. The fight–flight reaction was provoked day after day, year after year, by this sense of deprivation. Sex meant to him not love, but selfish demands and hate and attack. Because he had been led by his mother to see all women as beings who would surely reject him, his sex life was obstructed, and, because of this, he burned with hostility that he could neither understand nor handle. Only by resolving his childhood pattern of internal frustration could he avoid using his relationship to the opposite sex as a means of satisfying his childish needs for love and revenge. Instead of making love to a girl, he made hate. He hurt every girl he became close to.

* * * *

FEAR AND ANXIETY

In psychiatric usage, *fear* is described as an emotional reaction to a danger that is external and obviously real. For instance, it is reasonable to fear a mad dog if one is near you and growling threateningly, with ears flat back. *Anxiety*, however, is a term used to describe feelings of fear that are experienced when no good external reason for them is perceivable, as in the various phobias. Generally speaking, fear is rational, whereas anxiety is not.

However, this distinction breaks down as soon as the reason for the seemingly irrational, neurotic anxiety is understood. The man who fears heights usually does so because, looking down from them, he feels impelled to hurl himself to injury or death. Thus the danger is to him thoroughly real: but it is labeled irrational and unreal because it lies within the man's own motivations, within his often unconscious, self-destructive impulse to jump. The more we probe the reasons for neurotic anxiety, the more we find that there does in fact exist a danger from inner urges that is as real and intelligible as an external threat.

What is this inner danger? Studies made of children during wartime bombing raids on London give some illuminating insights into this question. Anna Freud and Dorothy Burlingham found that small children who felt secure with their parents, and whose parents did not show excessive fear, did not betray signs of fear themselves even in dangerous situations. But if the parent panicked, the child did also. The experimental studies of Liddell, which we mentioned earlier, demonstrate the same principle in animals. You will recall that the twin kid that was separated from its mother broke down under stress, whereas the one that remained with its mother did not.

In contrast to these studies in situations of real danger let us look at a child who is in physically safe circumstances but develops intense neurotic anxiety. Usually such a child is filled with angry impulses, which he is desperately afraid will come out (directly or indirectly). Perhaps they will emerge in the form of forbidden activities and thereby bring down upon him harsh parental punishment. The dreams of children reflect clearly how they struggle with their own forbidden urges to hostile behavior and with their reactions of guilt. Usually in their nightmares, just as in the nightmares of adults, the dangerous animals, witches, bogeymen, and robbers are representations or "projections" of their own destructiveness. They may also be the effects of guilt and consequent tendencies to self-punishment. Guilt stems predominantly, if not exclusively, from hostility, although this may not always be obvious at first glance. Guilt for, say, sexual transgression is often found to be actually guilt for hurting someone through disloyalty or defiance, or because sex has the meaning to that person of attack or exploitation. But if a child is raised in a sexually repressive atmosphere, it is likely that he can never freely indulge his sexual desires thereafter without guilt even if no hostility is involved.

Hostility and anxiety are close in the mind. This is in part because of the remarkable unconscious mental mechanism of "projection," which causes an individual's own inner hostility to appear to come from outside himself. It is then this externally generated threat that arouses fears. This is clearly seen in nightmares and delusions of persecution in paranoids. The intimacy of fear and hostility should not be surprising in view of the fact that they have common physiological roots in the fight–flight reaction.

The point is emphasized here because the realtionship between these forces is not simply a matter of fear causing hostility. It is certaintly true that fear arouses hostility—to flee or to destroy the danger. But so, too, time and again, anxieties are found to be produced by hostility. If you do something hostile, injurious to another, you expect retaliation (simple "retaliation fear"). But also you may feel guilty and that you deserve punishment to expiate your hostile act. Thus, some frustration, irritation, or even real danger makes the child angry and enraged. If this hostility is directed against those who rear him, or toward siblings or others in his environment against whom he cannot freely vent his anger, then because of fear of retaliation or of guilt, love, or training, or any combination of these, the hostility must be held in check, controlled, repressed. It is then experienced as anxiety. The patterns thus formed in childhood are then followed, in the main, for life, waxing and waning with the vicissitudes of experience.

* * * *

HOSTILITY AND SENSE OF REALITY

The adult's projections of his imagos and of his reactions to them may distort his concepts not only of individuals, but also of groups, the social scene, nations, and international forces. In fact, it is easier for the unconscious to emerge in relation to large and unfamiliar groups. Contact with actual people who can be seen and spoken with provides the sense of reality that is often sufficient to correct the distortions caused by the imagos. But nations, for instance, cannot be known in this concrete way, and they tend therefore to be thought of as abstractions. Consequently, they and the leaders who determine their policies are fitted more readily into childhood symbols, imagos and stereotypes.

Some demagogues and politicians understand this well, although they might express it in other terms. Each person has in his mind something of a bogeyman, either the direct imago of a punishing parent or else a dream creature, which has been formed out of his guilt and his own repressed hostile feelings. Witches and devils and other dangerous creatures of fantasy are usually, as mentioned earlier, projections of the person's own hostility.

There may also be a complementary figure because imagos are often split. One male patient loved his very dominating father and in part even enjoyed being under his control because this relieved him of the responsibility of having to make his own independent decisions. At the same time his masculine pride rebelled, and unconsciously he hated the subservience his father imposed, and longed to strike out against him. This patient solved the conflict by always having two men in his life—one whom he could love and another whom he hated.

This so-called splitting of the imago as a solution to the conflict between love and dependence on the one hand and hate on the other reflects the dualism of a god and a devil. It rests on the fact that it is a very difficult emotional situation for anyone to hate a person whom he also loves and on whom he is dependent. If only that person were two, it would be possible to vent both feelings. The origin and appeal of many secular and religious ideologies is that they formulate simple solutions for just such conflicts. Similarly, demagogues paint pictures that conform to our different imagos and, by so doing, are able to stir up infantile patterns and direct reservoirs of childhood hostility one way or another against all sorts of groups, with little regard for reality. In fact, the less reality there is to offer correction, the easier it is to manipulate the imagos and direct the hostility.

Another aspect of domination by such imagos is people's own tendency not to face the reality of "personality" in other human beings (to say nothing of animals). This is partly a form of failure of object relations and of identification, and it underlies all sorts of group prejudices. The individual members of a particular race or group are not seen as human beings like oneself, as having similar strivings and feelings, as loving their mates and children, and as struggling as best they can with the same problems all humans face. Instead, the tendency is to amalgamate all the individuals in the group and then apply a label to them, which is typically a fantasied caricature representing the individual's own repressed feelings. Thus a person might try to get rid of his own feelings of inferiority by attributing them to minority groups or to others who are in positions of lesser social or economic status. For example, an individual who loathes his own feelings of deprivation and failure may vent his hatred on the poor, whom he sees as representing these feelings. In similar fashion a person's hostile impulses can be projected onto Wall Street, unions, or political candidates—just as they were onto witches not so long ago. Projection is a convenient mechanism for it allows the individual to feel: "I am good and virtuous—the inferiority, evil, malevolence, hostility is not in me. No it is there, in him; that is where to seek it, see it, and attack it."

How the mechanism of projection operates is seen with great frankness and clarity in dreams. The night before coming for analytic treatment, one patient dreamed that he opened the door to the basement of his house, saw a big, murderous man below in the darkness, and then slammed the door shut in terror. A woman dreamed that she was chased through an underground tunnel by a man with a knife. Another man, also in reaction to coming for treatment, dreamed that he was exploring underground passages when he came upon an armed intruder whom he attacked and tried to kill in self-defense. Sometimes the malign creature is not a person but a monster, a gang, or the representation of some nation or other group; and sometimes the hostility appears as a force of nature, such as a storm, flood, or earthquake, or as a free-floating vague terror. Associations showed that in these dreams the cellar and underground passages were symbols of the patients' unconscious, the depths of the mind. There the dreamers saw their own murderous impulses in the threatening figures. The figures, although formed by their own fantasies during sleep, were not recognized by the dreamers as parts of themselves, but appeared to be entirely alien. There was no insight into their being the dreamers' own hostility or guilt and, hence, no conscious sense of identification with them, no empathy or sympathy, and it was therefore possible to release unbridled hostility against them as not part of oneself but as dangerous alien beings.

It is this same mechanism that makes possible many human brutalities in everyday life. A person sees as alien, feared, and hated those individuals or groups upon whom he projects his own alien, feared impulses. What he cannot face in himself, he sees while asleep in the fantasied figures of his dreams, and while awake in those with whom he fails to identify. Prejudice is therefore a confession; intolerance announces something intolerable within. This is the essential dynamics of prejudice and superstition, and the basis for a fascination with stories and dramas that offer us ready-made fantasied figures for our projections.

Not all superstitions have to be hostile and fearsome. We are sorry to read in Kipling's *Puck of Pooks Hill* that the little people, the fairies, gnomes, leprechauns, and others, have left England.

Helen is a young suburban matron who has come to the psychiatrist because of a physical symptom (recurrent and severe headaches) that she and her regular physician suspect of having a large emotional component. Helen is secure in her relationships with her husband and children, and she enjoys considerable financial security as well. She is not aware of feeling prejudice of any sort, and thinks of herself as being entirely liberal and loving. Despite her conscious thoughts and humanitarian behavior, her dreams clearly revealed, to her utter surprise, unmistakable expressions of racial intolerance.

Helen has a strong tendency to envy and depreciate others. She becomes tense out of a sense of competition whenever she is with anyone whom she can view as an equal or a superior. Often this evaluation has no basis in reality. For example, she will think that some other woman is better dressed, wealthier, a better tennis player, or more socially acceptable when in fact none of this may be true.

Apparently this proclivity of Helen's is derived largely from feelings of inferiority and envy toward an older brother. He was clearly favored in the family all through childhood simply because he was a boy. Coupled with this was the father's persistently negative attitude toward Helen and his marked lack of parental interest in her. Thus Helen grew up feeling like an inadequate, unaccepted, and dominated child. The result was an intense need for acceptance coupled with virulent competitiveness and envy toward the favored brother.

What a paradox! Here is a woman of uncommon intelligence with considerable mental and physical attractiveness, with wealth and social position, and yet she feels herself to be grossly inferior. All her energies are aimed at achieving acceptance. In short, Helen was born at the top of the social and economic ladder, but, because of the disturbed emotional relationship with her parents, she has the psychology of a disadvantaged social climber.

Her sense of hurt pride along with feelings of rejection, envy, and frustration supply a chronic source of rage and hostility. There was never any possibility of expressing these feelings openly during childhood, and they were strongly inhibited, especially those toward her father. He was already so tense and irritable that any expression of hostility toward him only further exacerbated his negative criticism and rejection of Helen, with added risk, in childhood, of corporal punishment. All her relationships with people outside her family reflect this childhood pattern within it, and as such persistently generate feelings of tension and hostility. It is partly for this reason that she always felt so much more comfortable with those she could readily recognize as being inferior to herself. Unconsciously she always tried to get into a position where she could be unquestionably superior. That is, she manipulated herself into situations wherein she could identify with her father and assume the parental role. Hence her recurrent dreams about blacks and Jews, Catholics, and various individuals of what she sees as lesser social status. Yet part of Helen's personality feels more comfortable with those she considers social inferiors, and this contributes to her image of herself as being liberal in outlook. In addition she feels a certain amount of identification with individuals in these groups because they represent the underdog to her. This feeling of inferiority and of herself being an underdog was generated in her childhood mostly by her father and continued as a pattern in her adult life.

Why, then, if Helen prefers being in a superior position, and if she identifies with those she sees as socially inferior, does she harbor these unconscious prejudices? The answer is that Helen also identifies with her parents. She could never, as we said, rebel against them openly, and her repressed hostility generated constant anxiety during childhood. This led her to rather extreme perfectionism—hoping and striving always to win their love and attention by being perfect in their eyes. Therefore, she could never accept her own identification with those she saw as inferiors. In fact, Helen feared and hated this identification and therefore hated all those who reminded her of how inferior and inadequate she herself felt. Further, to identify with the underdog is to feel like one, and this consists at bottom in feeling as the rejected, guilty, and inferior child feels toward its parents, and having its self-image.

Of course, fearing and wishing to destroy the stranger who is really the stranger within ourselves is not the only mechanism operating here. No doubt there is often some element of biological suspiciousness toward the unfamiliar, which all animals seem to show to some extent. But the mechanism of projection, because of early repression, seems to be rather specific for human beings and central in the emotional, irrational roots of prejudice. Its fateful significance, moreover, lies in its *distortion of reality to fit the emotional needs* and in its impairment of the adult capacity for cooperation, which is the very foundation of the human family and society and of human security.

* * * *

External factors may also produce hostility, although it is doubtful whether they are frequently the basic source. Even in those societies where anger and hate are encouraged as a social characteristic, early training must be given in order to ensure the successful inculcation of these qualities. For instance, anthropologist Margaret Mead contrasted the Arapesh of New Guinea with the Mundugumor. The latter are violent, hateful, and cannibalistic, whereas among the former such hostile behavior is rare and regarded as pathological. Dr. Mead ascribed some of the differences between these cultural groups to the way each raised its children. The Arapesh are kind to theirs, and responsibility for all the young members of the tribe is shared by several individual families. Each child, therefore, is brought up with many parents besides his own. If he has trouble with his real father, mother, or siblings, he has a whole series of other families to turn to. Therefore the intense emotional relationships characteristically found in the immediate nuclear family are diluted, and he learns from infancy on to feel secure with many people. The Mundugumor, on the other hand, treat the child from birth in a manner consciously designed to arouse his rage. For example, the infant is typically pulled half-suckled from the breast, and the behavior of his parents and other adults encourages him to vent his anger freely in action. The purpose seems to be to make him a fiercer hunter and warrior.

Civilizations, cultures, and national characteristics thus influence the personalities that grow up within them, but are self-perpetuating through the individuals who compose them. It is to be expected that some stimulate more hostility in childrearing, and some less. Some encourage hostility in the adults while others inhibit it. Anthropologist Ashley Montagu states (in a personal communication) that: "Among gather-hunting peoples living today, such as the Tasaday of Mindanao, the Yamis of Orchid Island off the coast of Taiwan, the Pygmies of the Ituri Forest, the Eskimo of the Arctic Circle and others, there is absolutely no sense of territoriality. As one would expect, some peoples are territorial, some only indifferently so, and others not at all."

Also, "The Pygmies of the Ituri Forest, the Tasaday of Mindanao, the Lapps, the Hadza of Tanzania, the Ifaluk of the Pacific, the Eskimo, the Todas of southern India, the Tahitians and other peoples have managed to avoid the alleged 'internal urge to fight.' "

Closer to home we often see how frustrations engendered by poor housing and education, by illness and poverty, tend to brutalize human beings. Clearly it is urgent to find solutions to these problems; but it must at the same time be noted that history has not shown that brutality and hostility are reactions to material circumstance alone. Great leaders and despots alike have come from shacks as well as palaces, slums as well as well-groomed suburbs. Semi-starvation, chronic disease, or relative well-being provide only one factor in shaping personality. Emotional reactions to people in adult life continue and repeat the emotional reactions to people that were formed in the earliest years of childhood. It is the emotional relations of the earliest days, weeks, months, and years, these conditioning interpersonal relations to members of the nuclear family, that are the great, predominant factor in the development of the hostile mind. External factors serve to bring out the hostility by affecting these childhood patterns and existing specific emotional vulnerabilities. Thus an unsuspecting rebuff, however mild, to an adult who was rejected as a child, or even a hint of command in one's voice when speaking to an individual who was overly dominated in childhood, may cause an astonishing flare-up of seemingly inappropriate rage.

7
Hostility and Personality

The history of man's hostility begins with the history of man. The earliest known picture drawn by prehistoric man is that of men killing one another. In the very first chapter of the Bible we find murder (from sibling rivalry?): "And Cain talked with Abel his brother; and it came to pass when they were in the field that Cain rose up against Abel and slew him." Probably parallel with this kind of individual act of violence, and possibly in defense against it, the bonds of society developed. Then religion, law, and morality developed, but this did not put an end to violence. Indeed, if anything, man's coming together in communities in part extended his destructiveness, for now entire tribes and city-states could attack each other. The individual was no longer restricted to one-to-one combat. Today nations and teams of nations fight counterparts of differing political, economic, and social ideologies, and perhaps at some time in the future interplanetary war will be possible, as depicted in science fiction.

Hostility persists and in fact is supported on a grand scale, but there has been some *slight* change in moral emphasis, in how the human personality handles this destructive potential. The feeling that wars will get you something (food, shelter, land, glory) has shifted slightly to a feeling that wars will only help you to defend something (home, family, country, and way of life). At least today excuses must be advanced for warring—a nation can no longer go to war frankly and exclusively for fun and gain. Is it then unreasonable to hope that if excessive hostility can be recognized as an adaptive mechanism that is today as vestigial and useless as the appendix, some progress toward peaceful cooperation will be at least possible?

The place to diminish hostility is at one of its main sources of transmission—within the family pattern. But to accomplish this, the dynamics of hostility must be isolated, studied, and understood. The expression of hostility by the adult personality is determined not only by the intensity of the feeling but also by the ways in which it is handled.

In the technical language of psychiatry, the hostility, arising in various forms and intensities and in combination with other motivations from the id (the biological source of impulses), is handled by the superego (the conscience with its nucleus of biosocial cooperativeness plus early, and to some extent later, conditioning) and the ego (the intellect, reason, memory, the conscious "higher" faculties). The ego and superego can accept the individual's hostility and permit or even encourage its expression, or they can control, transform or prevent it. To do the latter, that is, to prevent an individual from unrestrained acting out of impulses, mechanisms of defense are used. (Technically these defenses are mostly unconscious and can be distinguished from mechanisms of conscious control, but for our purposes we need not separate them.) We pass them from a consideration of the sources and characteristics of hostility to an examination of its controls and status relative to the rest of the personality.

The many and varied manifestations of hostility can be grouped to fit into three major categories. This grouping depends mostly upon how freely the individual, in his ego and his conscience, can consciously and unconsciously accept and act out his hostile impulses. Hence the categories are organized to describe behavior ranging from full criminality, through varying forms and degrees of repression, to transformations of the destructive hostility into socially constructive activity. In other words, the groups chart behavior ranging from direct and open hostile actions against other individuals and against society, through more or less inhibited, disguised hostility toward other individuals, to actual social constructiveness. We identify these groups as (1) antisocial, (2) private, and (3) social.

Antisocial behavior toward other individuals and society is a broad category covering three principal mechanisms for handling hostility: the criminal, the criminoid, and the neurotic criminal. The criminal mechanism is characterized by the fact that the hostility is accepted by the person, in his ego and conscience, sometimes even with pride in it, and is deliberately acted out with little or no restraint in antisocial form. The criminoid mechanism is characterized by the fact that the hostility is not fully accepted by the person, who defends himself against acting it out directly in antisocial form, but who is willing to act it out indirectly, within the confines of the law, so that however hostile and immoral and destructive, it is not illegal. The neurotic criminal mechanism is characterized by the fact that although the person indulges in direct or indirect hostile, antisocial behavior, he does not fully accept it and punishes himself for it in various ways, the whole pattern operating unconsciously.

The second category includes what we may call the private dynamics of handling hostility. The basic mechanisms in this category are: the neurotic character, classic neurosis, and psychosomatic disorder. The mechanism of the neurotic character is distinguished by the fact that the hostility, inadequately repressed, is only little acted out antisocially, but causes suffering to the individual himself and to those involved with him personally. An example of this would be the self-destructiveness observed in "losers" such as alcoholics and compulsive gamblers. The classic neurosis is characterized by the fact that the hostility, repressed successfully in behavior, produces specific symptoms for the sufferer (such as anxiety, phobias, hysterical mood swings, compulsions, and the like) and also makes life miserable for his intimates. The psychosomatic mechanism is marked by the absence of a direct expression of the hostility toward others. The person remains calm and gentle while seething inside, his hostility affecting only his own physiology, causing, for example, headaches, stomach or bowel disorders, or elevated blood pressure.

The third category of behavior describes the social handling of hostility. The fundamental mechanism involved here is that of "sublimation," which is characterized by the fact that the hostility is used constructively for the welfare of individuals and society. Overcompensation might be included in this category.

All of these dynamics, as seen in clinical practice, are summarized in the chart. It shows the three major categories and the seven principal dynamic mechanisms involved in handling hostility. The term and category "criminoid" are new, but their usefulness will become clear in the next chapter, where they are discussed in some detail. The first four groups, from left to right, reflect an attempt to separate the types of persons sometimes lumped together under the wastebasket label of "psychopathic personality." This is so broad a term

HOSTILODYNAMIC MECHANISMS Form, direction, and status of hostilities as seen in clinical categories. All of these dynamics probably exist in some degree and proportion in everyone, always mixed with others. They may be: (1) latent, (2) reactive, (3) character traits, regular or occasional.

HOSTILITY EXPRESSED	ANTISOCIAL			PRIVATE			SOCIAL
	A. TOWARD OTHER INDIVIDUALS AND SOCIETY			B. TOWARD OTHER INDIVIDUALS BUT NOT AGAINST SOCIETY		C. WITHIN SELF	D. USED CONSTRUCTIVELY TOWARD OTHERS AND SOCIETY
	1. CRIMINAL	2. CRIMINOID	3. NEUROTIC CRIMINAL	4. NEUROTIC CHARACTER	5. CLASSIC NEUROSIS	6. PSYCHOSOMATIC DISORDER	7. SUBLIMATION
Sound, reality-sense, integration, and control. ↑ EGO ↓ (NEUROTIC Range, levels)	Hostility is accepted and deliberately acted out in antisocial form.	Hostility is defended against in direct, antisocial form but acted out indirectly and within the law.	Hostility is acted out in direct antisocial form but defenses cause self-induced suffering.	Hostility, defended against and repressed, is acted out in indirect, distorted form toward other individuals (but not antisocially) and with self-induced suffering.	Hostility, defended against and repressed, generates neurotic symptoms, indirectly affecting other individuals but not in an antisocial way.	Hostility, defended against and generally repressed, produces physical symptoms, not acted out directly or indirectly against other individuals or society.	Hostility, direct or transformed, is used for welfare of others and society.
Marked distortion by emotional forces of reality-sense, integration, and control. (PSYCHOTIC Range, levels)	PSYCHOTIC EQUIVALENTS						

More toward others, antisocial ←	*Hostility Directed*	→ Less toward others, more social
Less mature, social, effective ←	*Superego*	→ More mature, social, effective
Accepts hostile impulses, behavior ←	*Ego*	→ Rejects hostile impulses, behavior

that it can be misleading and ambiguous, since it may range from an innocuous eccentric to a brutal murderer.

We all have some of these dynamics so that the heading under which an individual is placed is quantitative; it depends on how intensively and predominantly one or more of these mechanisms operates in his emotional makeup and behavior. Such differentiations are deep ones because of the fundamental importance of hostility in all psychopathology, in all personalities, and in everyday human affairs. Hostility occupies a place in psychological processes that is quite analogous to that of heat in physical processes. All mechanical processes generate heat. All emotional friction generates hostility. Hence, just as thermodynamics is a fundamental branch of physics, so the dynamics of hostility is a fundamental branch of psychiatry and can properly be called *hostilodynamics.*

How the hostility is handled, that is, the extent to which each of the above mechanisms is used in the personality, depends upon (1) the intensity of the hostility and (2) the maturity and health of the rest of the id, ego, and superego. If the hostility grossly distorts the sense of reality and behavior, but if the person nevertheless remains adequately responsible for himself and others, the result is a *psychotic character.* If, as in more extreme cases, the perception of reality and the processes of reason are so excessively distorted that the person is incapable of taking care of himself, then the result is psychosis. But insofar as psychosis is only an extreme form of neurosis with much greater loss of control and distortion of the sense of reality, it reveals no basically new mechanisms for the handling of hostility. The fundamental feature is the relative weakness of the ego in coping with motivations from id and superego, so that the person's feelings can distort his ego functioning, including his thinking and sense of reality, and even lead to frank delusions and hallucinations, or to total disruption of reason. Extremely psychotic persons are, just because of this, usually easy to recognize. However, in the milder cases the person may exercise considerable influence in society for long periods without being recognized as psychotic. Many individuals distort only that portion of reality that serves directly the purpose of rationalizng their hostility (e.g., to excuse prejudice). (The extremes of frank psychosis are excluded from our discussion insofar as there may be a toxic cause for them.)

Of course, as just noted, no one individual handles all of his hostilities exclusively in the manner described for each category. These are listed as sharp divisions, whereas in reality people regularly show mixtures of these mechanisms in their behavior. If a large series of actual cases were arranged in order, they would form a continuous spectrum grading from one extreme to the other. Nevertheless, just as the seven separate colors can be perceived as such in the solar spectrum (e.g., the rainbow, although the whole is a continuum), so these seven major categories can be differentiated by the *predominance* of one or another mechanism for handling the hostility.

In discussing any of these mechanisms a very important factor must be identified, that is, the extent to which the motivation is mostly internal or reactive. A quiet social person who is by no means given to criminal acts, can generate such rage under certain external conditions that he loses control of himself, bypasses his judgment and standards, and commits acts that are seemingly out of character. Examples of this would be what are commonly called "crimes of passion." Under sufficient external pressure, especially if it bears on his particular emotional vulnerabilities, the most stable individual can break down (or break out) into hostile behavior. On the other hand, many persons in satisfactory life circumstances are sadists who indulge, without any apparent external provocation, in cruel behavior out of internal motivations. Thus in every category the hostility and the way it is handled, that is, the hostilodynamic mechanism, may appear (1) latent, (2) reactive to unusual external stress, or (3) a character trait (emerging occasionally or regularly without discernible provocation).

It is possible for a person to shift, temporarily at least, from one mechanism to another. But how easily the latent hostility can be aroused in him and how far he acts it out depend chiefly upon his basic character, that is, upon his childhood emotional pattern. Under the influence of physical or emotional hardships or temptations, or under the sway of demagoguery, there is an increasing chance that the conscience will be lulled or bribed, or that the grasp of reality will weaken and hostility break through, or that neuroses or psychoses will develop.

Our chief concern will not be with these mechanisms as evoked by traumatic external events and acted out in brief, transient episodes. Rather our attention will be directed more to persons who show them as part of an accustomed way of life, as permanent character traits, which are mostly determined by the childhood emotional pattern.

The distinction between private and antisocial hostility reflects a contrast that is frequently observed in everyday experience. Many people treat their own families very differently from the way they treat other individuals, other groups, and society at large. A man may be a criminal killer and involved in all sorts of illegalities and still be kind to his wife and children. Conversely, another man may be a constructive figure in his occupation and in the community and yet be a sadistic tyrant in his home, doing to his wife and children what he would be jailed for if he tried to do it to anyone else.

In psychoses, the tendency to regress to childhood patterns is strong enough to derange the perceptive, integrative, and executive functions of the ego. As noted earlier, in some of the milder forms of psychosis the individual may even manage to get by quite well in society. History records many examples of such psychotic individuals. Because they were plausible enough in certain areas, they were able to become fringe cult or political leaders. By their very intensity and extremism they could arouse emotional resonance in others. In magnified form, these men expressed personality tendencies that were latent in their followers, who therfore accepted their leadership. The public became aware of this extremism in pseudoreligious cults in 1978 when Jim Jones accumulated a following of two or three thousand, and revealed his paranoia by leading over nine hundred of them to mass murder and suicide. Such intensity also finds expression in books, making them successful by this emotional impact.

The same hate, rage, and impulse to attack may come out in the criminal in direct murder. In the depressed patient it may manifest itself in overwhelming self-reproach and even suicide. Psychosomatically, it may find expression in an epileptic attack or some other severe illness.

It may even show up disguised as pleasure. This exercise of a function for pleasure rather than for survival is called *erotization.* Franz Alexander, in his *Fundamentals of Psychoanalysis,* sees it as an expression of surplus energy not needed by the organism for growth, propagation, or maintaining a livelihood. Muscular powers are used for enjoyment in sport. People eat because they like it as well as for calories. Similarly, some people fight, or create fights, because they enjoy them. This is seen in varying degrees throughout history. In the Roman circuses condemned men and women were turned loose among wild beasts to be torn to pieces for the pleasure of the audience. Among some tribes of American Indians, fighting was frankly a form of play—spoken of rather like a football game, with its pageantry and dash under the bright sun and blue sky—and as such, a source of enjoyment. Even today, war is not wholly a means to an end. Furthermore, little children play war for fun; adults relish the brutality of boxing and prizefighting; dramas of violence and brutality today often become instant box-office successes because of the enormous following that violence attracts.

There is a tendency for any strong emotion to be connected with sexual feelings, that is, to become "erotized." All during life every person has sex hormones circulating in his bloodstream and, especially during maturity, is under constant sexual pressure. This pressure is reflected subjectively in the mind, which fills with sexual impulses and fantasies that are more or less repressed, disguised, or elaborated. A prime function of the mind is integration. It naturally integrates the sex drives and feelings with other motivating forces. Because of the pervasiveness of the sexual feelings, they can easily mix with hostility, the other great drive and source of man's fantasies.

One of the most sinister features of hostility is this ready fusion with sexual feelings. Hostility can be aroused by sexual feelings and it can arouse sexual feelings. Sadism, which is far more widespread than is recognized, means pleasure, including full sexual responses, derived through inflicting cruelty. Sadists reach orgasm only by causing pain to another. Here sex expresses hate and violence, not love. Such persons can enjoy sexual satisfaction through every form of cruelty.

The treatment of the Albigenses by Montfort, of the heretics by the Inquisition, of the Jews by Hitler, afford a few examples from history of the pleasures some individuals take in pillage, violence, cruelty, and killing. Man has gotten sexual pleasure from the worst tortures he can fantasy. Caillou observes (whether accurately or not, I do not know): "The tiger will kill only when he's hungry, and the lion only when he's disturbed. The elephant won't harm you unless you're fool enough to go between him and his females, and even the crocodile will let you swim if his larder is full. But the leopard . . . for the sheer enjoyment of killing, just for the pleasure of it . . . kills because he likes it. There's only one other animal that does that . . . and that's man." Gregory Zilboorg noted, in his *Psychology of Criminal Acts,* that some murderers experience multiple orgasms during the deed. So do some soldiers when shooting an enemy or when in extreme danger of being shot themselves, as for instance aviators, flying over flak. Certain persons get their sexual satisfaction out of being threatened, beaten, or otherwise badly treated. In this sexual *masochism,* the need to be punished or the repressed hostility turned against the self is erotized and becomes an essential component of gratification.

Before proceeding to a detailed look at each of the dynamic mechanisms for handling hostility, let us summarize the variables involved:

1. The inherited, genetically determined force of certain impulses and reactions or the capacity for them.
2. The early conditioning, which by stimulating hostility determines the dynamics of its intensity in the id.
3. The proportional strengths of the disordered infantile patterns versus the mature motivations.
4. The different forces in the childhood emotional pattern that keep the hostility going, such as continuing rage for mistreatment in early childhood during 0 to 6, frustrated infantile demands for love or prestige, and so on.
5. The direction and degree of fixation of the hostility on certain imagos and its transferability to other persons.
6. The degree to which the hostility is accepted in its different forms and directions by the ego and the superego.
7. Whether the superego (which includes the conscience) operates in advance or with constant effectiveness, or whether it permits acting out and then brings down punishment later, if at all.
8. The extent to which the conscious ego accepts the restrictions of the superego or to which it feels justified in accepting the hostility with or without later punishment.

All of this will be made concrete and more readily comprehensible in the following chapters through discussion and examples of each of the categories.

We will start with the strongest and most freely expressed hostility and grade to that which is most repressed, inhibited, and sublimated.

8 Antisocial Mechanisms

The literature devoted to the psychodynamic sources of criminality is still relatively meager, although now rapidly expanding. The older theories that criminality is congenital and hereditary can be given little credence because the facts offered to support such theories are totally inadequate. And while it is certainly conceivable that physical, developmental defects in the brain itself may result in every kind of emotional aberration and misbehavior, including uncontrolled criminal behavior, these cases are not the ones that concern us here, and any theory as to congenital or hereditary factors producing such functional effects in the healthy, intact organism still carries the burden of proving itself.

There is growing evidence that the child who develops into a criminal character either has been subjected to gross mistreatment during his early years (0 to 6) or has been provided with a model for this kind of behavior by one or both parents or by others with whom he was closely involved emotionally. Without this background, even strong influences toward criminality usually fail. For instance, in so-called high crime areas the accepted social standard among a child's playmates frequently involves direct participation in juvenile gangsterism. If a child does not accept this neighborhood ideology and join in with the gang, he not only may be ostracized and despised, but his actual physical safety may be threatened. Nevertheless, not every child in such a crime area becomes a delinquent and later a criminal. If the family influence on the child has been stable and healthy enough, despite all group pressures and threats of retaliation, he will not accept criminal patterns of behavior, or, even if he does so at the time, he soon outgrows them. So, too, in later life, a man or woman under extreme external pressure and in spite of every temptation may never behave in a criminal fashion because this is too foreign to his personality. The twig must have been bent in childhood in the direction of overt hostility and crime for the tree to be so inclined.

We call criminal the kind of person whose makeup is such that he accepts his hostile feelings against other human beings as part of his accustomed behavior and is willing deliberately to act out these feelings. He may injure other people through crimes against their property, such as theft, or through crimes against their person, such as assault. The career criminal may show no impairment in his sense of reality or intelligence, but the mature restraints of identification, empathy, social feeling, and a normal conscience do not seriously hamper his overt hostile behavior.

Throughout our discussion we treat crime in the sense of injury to life and the living, particularly human life and human living. By injury we mean not only bodily damage, mild or severe, but anything that impairs development and adjustment, individual liberty and happiness. An injury is thus considered criminal if widespread perpetration of it would cause mental or emotional injury or suffering, or would threaten the foundations and functions of society. It should be noted that this definition is basically independent of any laws or customs that may or may not exist in a particular community. In fact, if the laws injure human life and living, then the laws themselves may be termed criminal. This would hold true even for a savage community like the Mundugumor, mentioned previously, wherein the mores are described as involving free acceptance of a relatively large amount of hostility in violent behavior. In this society the noncriminal citizen is the exception and the eccentric. But the prevailing custom of hostility is criminal and immature on a biological, psychodynamic scale of maturity.

Of course not every inconvenience that someone imposes upon us need be called a crime: essentially we are seeking the quality that can be isolated and properly described as criminal. This quality seems to be an inner, psychological one, a mechanism that conceivably can and perhaps does exist to some perceptible extent in everyone. Its essence is an individual's acceptance in his ego of sufficient hostility for him to act it out with relative freedom for selfish personal purposes against other human beings, regardless of the damage he causes them and their happiness.

An analogy with illness may clarify the use of the term "quality." If a person has a slight transient sniffle, he is not considered by himself or others to be sick. If he has a tiny splinter in his finger, he does not call it an injury. But while these are mild, perhaps even negligible conditions, still their essential quality is harm to the organism. In like manner you would not label a relatively minor offense, such as maliciously slighting a person's name or trampling a corner of a neighbor's lawn, a crime. Nevertheless, such an act, however negligible in quantity, may in its quality be criminal, and if extreme enough it would be so recognized by everyone.

This formula naturally must be used with caution. Human behavior is difficult to judge. Usually it is essential to know the person's motives. Suppose someone injures, even kills, another for purposes of self-defense. If the main motivation is mature, and life-preservative for himself, his family, or country, if the act is not done out of egoistic malevolence, then it lacks the essential quality of criminality. The purpose of an act may even be constructive though the means used may take a hostile form. For instance, the policeman who shoots a killer solely to defend society and its members is not acting criminally; but if he commits the same act out of personal motives, such as thrill, revenge, or self-aggrandizement, then psychologically the act itself is criminal despite its socially good results. Because of the rampant immaturity in the world, peace must usually be maintained through force, and, unfortunately, men all too often use the authority of law as a mask for their own criminal mechanisms. Criminality is also seen among individuals who commit crimes more for emotional satisfaction than for material gain and economic security.

Thus to understand the hostilodynamic mechanism in a given person and circumstance, not only the act itself but its purpose in the mind of the doer as well as his internal feelings in the doing of it must be considered; for crime is basically motivational, psychological. This distinction is seen repeatedly in fiction. The hero presumably kills "more in sorrow than in anger"; and he is able to do so only because he feels that it is for some worthy, necessary purpose, such as protecting the heroine or defending his country. The villain, however, freely accepts cruelty as a means to achieve selfish ends. Often, in fact, he is portrayed as deriving his chief satisfactions from the evil act itself.

Happily for human welfare, the majority of people do not find such hostile impulses acceptable to their consciences or their conscious judgment. The well-being of society rests on the capacity of individuals to control and sublimate hostility. But, for that reason, no society is or can ever be entirely safe, secure, and stable, until hostility is reduced in the childhood patterns of its constituents, through proper rearing of its children.

Every person has been in situations where, impelled by anger, he has nevertheless not felt free to satisfy his hostile impulse and has restrained himself. This is *suppression*, or conscious control, which is exerted by the ego. Many of us, too, have been trained from infancy to restrain or even reject such impulses entirely. These impulses then become unthinkable and are checked before they can even reach consciousness. Such automatic, unconscious *repression* is powered by the superego rather than by the ego. Impulses thus blocked from direct expression may seek other paths and may produce or contribute to neurotic, psychotic, or psychosomatic symptoms instead of criminal behavior. More about this later.

It was perhaps Freud's main discovery that most of what goes on in our minds is remote from awareness. Most feelings, reactions, and thoughts are not conscious. Any form of analytic, psychodynamic therapy depends as a first step upon insight into the major elements of the interplay of motivations, reactions, and feelings. This is accomplished by a somewhat laborious process of fitting together childhood emotional patterns, personal history, and patterns of present life with the patterns of free association and the interpretation of dreams and of earliest memories. Most of this information must come from the patient himself, for the same forces that keep the main dynamics unconscious (shame, guilt, anxiety, and the like) naturally resist attempts to make them conscious. Therefore, this can only be accomplished in persons with relatively strong therapeutic urges, that is, in individuals who are strongly motivated to reveal themselves because of sincere wishes to relieve their psychic suffering. It is these persons who come for help to the private practitioner. Usually these people have considerable maturity and intelligence; they are well motivated to reopen their emotional development and are usually gratified with the insights gained into themselves. (For the techniques of obtaining such insight, see L. J. Saul, *The Childhood Emotional Pattern and Psychodynamic Therapy*.)

Antisocial persons usually do not have any such wholesome therapeutic urge. They do not come voluntarily for help. Like Mary, the subject of our first vignette, they are already in the throes of the legal system and are ordered by the court, however sympathetically, to have an interview with a doctor, whose speciality they do not understand. The psychiatrist is typically seen as an authority toward whom they are conditioned to feel suspicion and hatred, and to whom it is unsafe to reveal anything about oneself. Therefore it is difficult or impossible to elicit, in the time available, the first memories, free associations, dreams with associations—that is, all the paths to the dynamics we want to understand. This situation limits the vividness of the following vignettes. We are able to present enough analytic material to see that there has been gross abuse in early childhood and that this is cause for the current dynamics; but we are unable to present enough of the unconscious emotional data to convey a sufficiently deep feeling to the reader. The good analyst, as Freud said, "Feels his way into the patient's emotional life." But that takes time and much desire on the patient's part, both of which are lacking in most of these persons seen only a few times and only at the behest of the courts, not of the individuals themselves.

In private practice the goal for effective therapy is to understand quickly and in detail, using all the tools we have mentioned (first memories, dreams, history, life pattern, and so on) the patient's childhood emotional pattern of interaction with those close to it and responsible for it, especially from conception to age about six. *We also want to see, in detail, how extensively and intensively this childhood pattern is affecting the patient's present-day life. It is the operation in the adult of this childhood emotional pattern that is (as we have said in earlier chapters) the basic cause of psychosomatic, neurotic, and psychotic symptoms, and of acting out against oneself and others, that is, the basic cause of all psychopathology, including criminality, in the physically healthy organism.*

In the following vignettes we can indicate this, but not demonstrate it in full detail. We tried to obtain clear convincing cases from the FBI and the courts, but found very little interest on their part in the basic psychodynamic causes of antisocial behavior. Nevertheless, we have seen and read enough that fits perfectly with our experience with private patients to state with confidence that patterns of antisocial behavior, as of all psychopathology, are formed by abuses in the rearing of children. This is as certain as the laws of gravity, but if you are cautious, consider it as only a theory to be tested, realizing that it is the most important theory for humanity in the world today. Humans, because of their hostility to one another and themselves, may yet annihilate us all.

* * * *

HOSTILITY EXPRESSED TOWARD OTHER INDIVIDUALS

Criminal Behavior

Some of the key dynamic mechanisms involved in criminality (see chart on page 81) are seen in the following two individuals.

Mary, a teen-ager from a depressed urban area, is presently being kept at a center for delinquent girls as the result of her involvement with a gang of girls in the murder of another teen-ager. Mary is thought to be the gang member actually responsible for the stabbing that occurred. Mary's story is that she and several friends were walking down the street after a dance when they met the victim, who was with a male companion and another girl. Someone in the gang bet the victim that she could not beat up Mary. The group then egged the two girls on, but Mary claims that she tried, unsuccessfully, to walk away several times. Finally she agreed to fight the victim, and in the ensuing scuffle managed to pull the other girl's coat over her head. Mary says that she then felt something wet and realized that it was blood. Mary denies having stabbed her.

Mary's family consists of her mother and an older brother, Lester. The children's father, whose whereabouts are unknown, never played any role in their lives and was never married to their mother. He was, by all available reports, an irresponsible and sadistic individual. Mary's mother, like her daughter, was illegitimate. During her childhood she was subjected consistently to violence, being savagely beaten and abused regularly. The mother's mother (Mary's grandmother) was finally put in prison for child abuse. Mary's brother, who is now in jail serving time for armed robbery and aggravated assault, was an overactive and wild child. Mary's mother was determined not to have another child like him; so from the time of her daughter's birth, the mother says she was very controlling and protective toward Mary. She constantly checked up on her to make sure she was not doing anything wrong, and she repeatedly warned Mary about an endless variety of things that might conceivably go awry.

Mary's earliest memory (eloquently depicting an essential aspect of her emotional life, her emotional alienation from human relations) is of standing in her crib all alone at night crying. No one came to her although she and her mother lived in the same room, suggesting that Mary had no good relation with her mother and therefore with anyone at all. At first Mary reacted to her mother by being quiet and obedient and by preferring to be alone. She would play for hours on end with pots and pans or the one doll that she had. After a while, when she was three or four years old, her mother tried to get her to play with other young children, but Mary seemed disinterested (which confirmed the impression that her childhood pattern contained no good relationship with anyone). Consequently, she daydreamed a lot and would say very little. Mary's lack of responsiveness made her mother angry, but she did not know how to punish her daughter except to berate her. Because the mother had been so brutally treated as a child herself, she vowed "never to lay a hand on Mary. No matter what!" Her anger at the child, however, did show through, although whether or not she did in fact strike her we do not know.

When it came time for Mary to attend kindergarten she refused to go. Her mother then started a pattern that was to last to the present, that is, she bribed her daughter into going. Although they were on relief and had severely limited financial resources, the mother sacrificed spending anything on herself and Lester and instead bought things for Mary. A pretty new dress got her into kindergarten. Mary received toys, clothes, candy, and the like almost on demand, while her mother and brother were literally in rags and often in a rage.

In her early school years Mary made a quiet and marginal adjustment. She did average work but alienated, as her first memory revealed, had great difficulty relating to her peers, who increasingly excluded her. Most of her teachers felt sorry for this neat, clean, sad little girl who seemed so out of step with the other children. Mary gradually developed a stubbornness at school against trying anything new or doing anything she did not wish to do. Only by bribes and promises could teachers break through her resistance. When Mary complained to her mother about anything going wrong at school, her mother would reassure the girl by always blaming the teacher or the other children (which conceivably risked starting a pattern of paranoia). She frequently told Mary that they would soon be moving out of their neighborhood into a better one where people would act nicer to her. Because her mother had made a show of protectiveness toward Mary, as did some of her teachers, the children frequently teased her and called her deprecating names. When Mary felt upset by this, her mother would keep her out of school for a few days.

By the time she was in fourth grade, Mary became slightly more outgoing and went through the initial stages of developing a few friendships with peers. However, her mother was highly critical of the children Mary chose and did not allow her daughter to see them outside of school. Mary gradually developed a double life, whereby she would see whomever she wanted to and not disclose it to her mother. Of course, no one perceived that Mary was unconsciously trying to save herself by making such human contact as she was capable of, with other unconsciously hostile, withdrawn children like herself. By the sixth grade she was openly lying to her mother about where she went and with whom. By the seventh grade Mary's behavior at school began to deteriorate rapidly. This heretofore quiet, stubborn, and uninvolved youngster became defiant and rude to her teachers, using profanity and threats of violence. She terrorized and physically beat up younger children to make them turn over their lunch money to her. Before long, she developed her own gang to aid her in this (thereby achieving the only kind of human relations possible for her). Her mother was called to school repeatedly, but usually she denied the possibility of Mary's misbehaving. Typically she would blame the teachers or other students for picking on her daughter, whom she saw as a quiet, innocent, persecuted, and misunderstood little girl. One day at school Mary shattered the angelic image that her mother struggled to maintain when she viciously attacked an elderly teacher who was reprimanding her. So many students witnessed this attack and testified against Mary that her mother was forced to recognize that her daughter had serious behavior problems.

Mary was suspended and assigned to a special school for disciplinary problems. Her mother became irritated at both the school system and Mary, whom she started punishing by not allowing her out after school or during the weekend. Mary was not about to be made a prisoner (and isolated from all human relationships, which might have precipitated a psychosis, as breaking a last libidinal tie is apt to do). She countered her mother's punitive measures by sneaking out of the second floor window. She joined a street gang that fought other gangs, shoplifted, snatched purses, and mugged elderly people. Mary was speedy of foot and clever enough not to be arrested in these gang activities until the fight in which she allegedly stabbed another girl to death.

For all her hostility, Mary seems timid and fearful of her environment and expresses concern over abandonment and over her own self-image. She feels isolated and afraid of the power of others. The world, to her, is basically hostile, following her early pattern toward her mother and brother. She is highly dependent on her mother, and is unable to express her feelings freely, suppressing much of her hostility because of this dependency. In the past this hostility had been channeled through gang activities. Mary has expressed the feeling that her mother is not her real mother, or she would treat her better. Mary gives the impression that she is trying to deny that her mother was often enraged at her and in fact often beat her.

Regarding the murder for which she is now in custody, as might be expected from a childhood emotional pattern devoid of good personal relationships, Mary feels no sorrow or remorse. She hated the deceased girl, who was known by her peers to be sneaky and deceitful. Mary had a particular loathing for the victim because the latter was more successful than Mary in presenting an innocent facade while at the same time stealing, using drugs, and being excessively promiscuous. Mary was envious and jealous of this girl and detested her for having succeeded where she had failed.

This case shows clearly some of the limitations of available information and therefore our deficiencies in knowledge of the dynamics. It is rare to see violence and murder in an individual if there has been no violence whatever in childhood. We know Mary was hostile to her mother, but the reasons for this hostility are not entirely clear, beyond the absence of any positive relationship. We have insufficient information on how her mother, who had herself been so brutally treated in childhood, actually felt and behaved toward her daughter. There must have been something in her mother's feelings and behavior (perhaps only the lack of love for Mary, who got no love from any other sources during her 0 to 6) to which Mary reacted with such hostility, and probably some example of violence that Mary followed in the stabbing.

Our next subject, George, was not the kind of person in whom you would expect to find the criminal mechanism. Nevertheless, from a psychological point of view, he was a killer.

George was a high-powered business executive, smooth and charming in appearance and manner, and successful in public life. Privately, however, he was coldly hostile to his wife while at the same time professing to be madly in love and full of admiration for her. In his office he was calm in exterior appearance: at home he was usually agitated and sometimes violent. More than once he had deliberately destroyed expensive possessions that his wife valued. George sought psychiatric treatment because he found himself methodically planning to kill his wife.

As usual, his personality characteristics were traced to specific warping influences during childhood. His father had been much preoccupied with his own affairs and remote emotionally from the mother and children except for one daughter, toward whom he showed blatant favoritism. George's mother was an unstable woman of violent temper and hates. She was free with family beatings and on one occasion inflicted rather serious injury upon one of the children in the neighborhood. It is not known whether or not she fought with the father physically, for when George was not yet six his mother left, abandoning the family. The father remarried soon thereafter; his second marriage was also of short duration.

George was not conscious of any hostility against his father or his preferred younger sister. All of his conscious hostility was turned against his image of his mother, though he had no concrete conscious memory of her. He could not recall what she looked like, how she acted or dressed, or even any specific incident about her. What remained in his mind was the image of a person whom he blamed for all the unhappiness and frustration of his childhood. Whether or not his father directly encouraged such feelings, this image of his mother became the object of his every resentment. Perhaps her mistreatment of him started before he could talk, and therefore lived in his feelings but did not permeate to his conscious memory. He grew up with few friends, continuing toward other persons the emotional remoteness that he experienced from his father and took over himself as a defense against his painful feelings, especially those toward his mother.

The only person with whom he had the least warm, emotional relationship was his younger sister, whom he both loved and envied. No one can develop properly nor can most people even continue to exist without having at least one reasonably good human relationship (see the case of Mary, preceding). In all probability, this affection for his sister saved George from severe mental disorder. It became the model for such friendly rapport as he was capable of in his adult life. The patterns of kindliness, which this relationship contained, repeated themselves toward his children and served to protect them from his otherwise nearly uncontrollable hostile impulses.

What in his wife's emotional makeup led her to marry him need not concern us here beyond her appreciation of his fine surface qualities plus identification with him and a masochistic attraction to danger, which grew out of her own disturbed childhood. His feelings toward her repeated at first the profound longing for a good mother, continued from the earliest years of his life. But, of course, in an adult this longing was far too primitive and infantile to be satisfied in reality. It was not the kind of need to love and be loved that is appropriate in maturity; rather, his feelings contained all the intensity of the demands of the infant or very small child upon its mother. This quality alone foredoomed them to frustration. Thwarted in his needs, he soon felt toward his wife the same disappointment he had felt as a child toward his mother—along with his old pattern of implacable rage. And his mother, with her beatings, provided the model for venting hostility through actual physical violence.

Meanwhile, a neurotic mechanism of hostility also showed in his overanxiety about his children. On rare occasions he might lose control and strike one, but then would feel guilt and remorse. Although jealous and resentful of them at times, following the pattern toward his younger sister, he could not, without inner conflict, take out his hostilities upon them, probably because of identification with them as well as such good feelings as were in the pattern toward his sister. He repressed these feelings, but under their pressure he developed a sense of anxiety about the children. He felt that they were in danger, but he did not realize that the danger lay in his own motivations, his own hostilities to them. (The insufficient material available suggested that this pattern repeated that toward his envied but still loved younger sister.)

By contrast, much of the hostility toward his wife became conscious, permitted by his ego and superego. Having unconsciously placed his wife in the role of his mother, he now felt free to revenge upon her his mother's beatings and desertion of him as a child. George planned his wife's murder precisely and repeatedly, never aware that this was following his pattern of feelings toward his mother in childhood. This conscious acceptance of hostility and the willingness to act upon it is the criminal mechanism. Although his wife died a natural death, and he never carried out his designs against her, this man was psychologically, in his intent, a criminal in that he had murderous impulses that his ego and superego permitted him to act out.

George's infantile impulses did not discriminate between his mother and his wife. This failure is probably much more common in criminals than is generally believed and explains those superficially bewildering incidents that appear from time to time in the newspapers, the totally unprovoked, apparently motiveless assaults and murders. An example of this was the case of two men in their early twenties who assaulted and beat to death a harmless, middle-aged man whom they had never seen before and who was not even worth robbing. The status and intensity of the hostility in these two young men, regardless of who or what shaped it during their formative years, was now such that it could be taken out on almost anyone, even a complete stranger. This "displacement" to other objects is a basic characteristic of hostility—this "spread" to other persons, animals, or even inanimate objects of the child's revengeful, murderous hatred of whoever abused him during his helpless early life.

Criminoid Behavior

Ugly and antihuman as is the frank criminal, there is another type of personality that can be equally, if not at times more, sinister: the criminoid. This type complements the criminal and makes organized crime possible. Criminoid behavior is so widespread that we might consider it a characteristic of our times. Although this type of person stays within the letter of the law, his way of living, his decisions, his social and political attitudes reflect his hostility to mankind and his subtle destructiveness to individuals and to society and its cooperative goals.

The overt criminal is relatively direct about his antisocial hostility. But the criminoid, in contrast, does nothing openly for which he could be charged in the courts. His hostility, although acted out, is masked and disguised as legal and proper. Indeed, he may appear to himself and to a large part of the community as a model citizen, "an honorable man." What we are describing by the term "criminoid" is again a psychodynamic mechanism, a way of dealing with hostile impulses. This mechanism, like all the others, may play only a minor role in a personality, or it may be of such proportional strength as to dominate it. It, too, may be latent, or reactive to unusual stress, or a character trait, occasional or permanent.

At one end of the criminoid range is behavior that is so close to the directly criminal that it is transitional between these two types. This would be exemplified by the man whose inner restraints and defenses are such that he cannot himself kill anyone but can arrange for another to commit such an act. At the opposite extreme are minor manipulations that are within the law, injure no single person directly, and are often valued as being "smart." A United States senator was exposed in flagrant criminal dealings, but his constituents expressed faith in him. The dual conscience of some businessmen has frequently been described–he who would never peronally harm the poor widow and her children but as a business matter will foreclose their mortgage to his own profit. Similarly, several decades ago it was not uncommon economic practice to exploit immigrant workers through forcing them to rent poorly constructed company houses and to buy goods, often inferior, priced and sold by company stores. Labor unions, as they have grown in power, also have tolerated forms of blackmail and racketeering.

Overt criminality is generally all too evident as such, and neurotic behavior is increasingly attracted recognition. But criminoid behavior, masked and camouflaged as it is, more easily eludes notice and has not been defined and brought into focus. However, when it is widespread, it usually is quickly recognized as corruption. Its ability to elude investigation is probably related to the fact that the criminoid mechanism permeates so many of our attitudes. We tend to avoid thinking of accepted criminoid activity in moral terms. "Oh, don't be naive, that's done every day–politics (or business, labor, or human nature) is like that," we say. In the statistical sense of average, criminoid behavior may even be "normal." But just because it is normal to get dental caries, does not mean that these conditions are any less a disease or problem. They are not normal in the sense of healthy. In fact, the acceptance of the criminoid individual as normal makes him an even more serious threat to our society.

Let us now look at who some criminoids are. In politics there are the demagogues and hate-mongers, those leaders and groups who seek gain by manipulating and exploiting individual hostilities. Usually they are extremists (right or left) who try to discredit and paralyze the moderates, and bring on overt violence for their own benefit. There often seems to be an appalling affinity between politics and criminoid behavior. The public official who uses his cloak of authority to protect underworld activities in exchange for various kinds of gratuities is a routine fixture on the political scene. But corrupt politicians are not alone in this kind of acting out. Hundreds of thousands, if not millions, of apparently stable men and women avidly support demagogues advocating violence and hatred, if some reasonable rationalizations can be found to do so. Pressure groups out to serve their own ends act upon government to secure their goals regardless of the welfare of others. Such behavior may be normal in the sense of average in the political and economic life of society. But our measuring rod for a society is psychological and biological, not statistical. It is a scale of emotional maturity derived from observing the contrast between the egocentric, hostility-prone attitudes of the mistreated infant and the responsible givingness of the adult of good will.

Criminoid dynamics may be prominent in the lives of many persons without conscious recognition of the behavior by those persons or the people involved with them. Few people may aid criminoids with a view to doing harm deliberately and maliciously; most people simply do not know any better, and some even think of themselves as being quite virtuous.

So diverse are the manifestations of the criminoid dynamics that no single example is adequately representative. The case of Steve, a young man of high caliber, must suffice. He was quite mature in his capacity for love and sympathy and would not knowingly hurt anyone in any way. Steve had the common dynamics of feelings of inferiority as a result of overprotection by his mother during childhood. Insecure in his masculinity, he believed in all good faith that a young man of any virility should prove himself by, as he said, "getting women." Being attractive and highly motivated sexually, he seduced, lived with, and then abandoned many girls, causing some of them serious unhappiness, if not permanent harm. Yet Steve was only doing what he thought was expected of a "real man." Only when he learned the nature of maturity and saw realistically what he had been doing, was he able to find less criminoid, more adult modes of expressing his masculinity.

In our society a great many people understand democracy and freedom to be a license for grabbing something away from the unwitting next person, despite the cost to the other. This is done under the admirable guise of pursuing success. But success is not a purely egocentric matter, If it were, the very biosocial foundation of society would be dangerously undermined and probably destroyed, as it yet may be. True success is a value given for a value received; it is measured by constructiveness, by contributing to the well-being and happiness of others. Success in any field is measured by the excellence of the person's responsible contribution, what he has given to others, be it for their safety, their entertainment, their knowledge, or the advance of the human spirit. The tiny infant is, in its very nature, egocentric, even parasitic, for its primary task is its own development; but as we develop, society is our sole means of security against impersonal forces of nature. Our health, pleasure, and survival are made possible only by society through the contributions of each member giving a value for a value.

When an individual's self-love is too strong, it may lead him into criminoid behavior, however righteous he may seem to himself in his own self-image. Through his impatience for personal success he may sacrifice the very rewards for which he burns himself out. More hostility is then aroused, and this hostility (as does all hostility), in turn, seeks some person or group to hate—a scapegoat. Demagogues rise to power by offering objects for this hate. Rationalizations are readily found. And thus the criminoid mechanism becomes widespread.

Not all criminoids are important leaders; for example, Joan, a small-town woman, was raised in a modest, middle-class family, and at 18 married the town "catch," the only son of a well-to-do real-estate broker. The young man, unlike his father and wife, was not aggressive about work. His chief ambition was to write a history of the area in which they lived. Thus Carl preferred poring over the early settlers' records to buying and selling property for his contemporaries. At first his wife was content with her marriage. The business continued to thrive under her father-in-law's direction, and the income from it and Joan's position in the town satisfied her needs to be first and favored.

Then, however, the general economy of the country slowed down dramatically, Carl's father died, and the business was in danger of going under. Carl forsook his career as a historian and devoted himself unflaggingly to the business in an effort to maintain financial security for his family and, beyond this, to satisfy his wife's needs for social prestige. It was an uphill fight. Increasingly frustrated by lack of money and success, Joan began to ridicule and blame her husband to his friends behind his back, meanwhile showing him a contempt and coldness that gradually undermined his stamina and his self-respect. Mounting but repressed retaliatory rage at his wife made Carl anxious and depressed, and he began to drink and to neglect the children. Tensions in the home increased, and Carl drank more and more heavily. In desperation he attempted suicide. Now his wife rejected him totally. His reputation was ruined. He had no one to turn to. Carl was not sufficiently mature to handle matters, and soon afterward he developed mild schizophrenic symptoms. The worsening situation led to temporary committment to a state hospital.

Joan, far from standing by Carl when he needed her and when she could have helped to save him and thus have kept a father for her children, was glad to be rid of him and to be free to pursue her ambitions unhampered. As the economy improved, Joan advanced in a store where she had found a position, and after some years she became assistant to the manager. The children had a difficult time, for the relief of the tension between their parents was gained at the price of losing their father, who had been their chief emotional support and their only model for good human relationships. Joan was callously indifferent to them. She entrusted their care to what hired help she could find, and, when this failed, she would often lock them in separate rooms, tying the youngest to a chair or putting him on a leash to keep him out of mischief. Both children developed nightmares and a variety of behavior problems that signified the inevitable arousal of their fight–flight reactions with excessive hostility, irrational fear, and consequent warping of their development.

Joan's relationship to society was similar in feeling. Though desirous of respect in the community and charming on the surface in her business and social relations, she inwardly despised all those who were beneath her socially, while, true to type, she fawned upon those whom she saw as stepping stones for herself. Where she worked she tacitly encouraged certain excessively harsh and unethical practices, and in the community she strove to keep minority groups off all local committees. Once after having had a few cocktails at a party she revealed that she believed blacks, Catholics, and Jews should be deported wholesale or else exterminated.

On the whole, however, this woman's actual behavior would not be considered criminal, and most of her intimates would not have considered her antisocial. She could quite righteously justify her actions. The hostility behind them was, for the most part, indirect. The fact that it helped to ruin the lives of her husband and her children was considered only a family matter. Her civic attitudes were considered her own business. Joan's behavior was not illegal, and no one could criticize her without being accused of meddling in purely private affairs.

But her criminoid nature is obvious, and the lack of neurosis (in the narrower sense of specific symptoms) probably shows best in the fact that she could not only behave the way she did but could do so without accumulating any effective feelings of guilt. If she had had more of a conscience, more internal checks, she could not have acted out her hostilities to such an extent, even in this indirect form. So much guilt would have built up that Joan would have been forced into some type of emotional or psychosomatic disturbance. The hostility, like heat or water under pressure, would have been forced into other paths.

Other families have broken up during periods of severe economic distress; other women have been forced to work under conditions less than optimum for their children. Also, the kinds of prejudices (though perhaps not the intensity) that Joan held are not unusual, especially in towns where class lines are rigidly drawn. But this woman did not merely reflect the attitudes of a family or group, nor did all members of her group accept such attitudes or behave as she did.

Criminoid groups are analogous to crime areas. We have already noted that a certain percentage of boys in crime areas do not go along with the gangs. Joan's social group might have provided the temptation, opportunity, and encouragement for some of the criminoid behavior in which she indulged. But there must have been something in her own motivations that led her to the particular patterns with which she handled her hostilities. In brief outline, these inner motivations and the early influences that shaped them were as follows.

Joan's mother had also been a beautiful girl, without education but deeply ambitious "to amount to something," as she incessantly proclaimed. Disappointed in her marriage, she had never really wanted children, but when Joan was born, she was determined that this child should realize all the goals she herself had not achieved. Increasingly neglected by her husband, she drilled her daughter in dress and deportment, and took domestic jobs so that her child might have voice and piano lessons. But she did not give Joan the two great essentials: unselfish love and respect for the child's own personality.

The father also resented the child, seeing her as an emotional and financial drain.

As the child was shaped, so the woman became. Following the pattern of her own and her mother's reactions to her father, Joan felt only contempt for men, and her fine social manners covered the hatred and rebellion she felt against the depriving, dominating mother who had imposed these manners upon her.

It is a general fact that an adult behaves toward others in later life according to two chief responses to his parents: (1) he identifies with the parent and acts as the parent did during his childhood; and (2) he reacts toward other people with the same feelings he had toward his parents as objects. Usually, probably always, there is some mixture of these two; that is, there are simultaneously *identification* with, and *object relations* to, the parent.

Joan, identifying with her mother, tended to treat her husband and children as her mother had treated her father and herself. She turned away from her husband when he failed to live up to her expectations, and she neglected her children (as her mother had neglected her) for the pursuit of the goals her mother had instilled within her. But Joan also harbored feelings of revenge against her parents and, in retaliation, lived out toward her husband the hate and rejection she had felt toward her father and mother. Her capacity to love, to feel good will toward others, was crippled by this lifelong, repressed resentment for the lack of love and understanding during her childhood and for the disregard of her own personality under the imposition of her mother's ambitions. Beneath her surface conformity there burned to a pathological extent constant and intense hostility.

Why did these hostilities not come out more openly? Probably because there had not been a model for naked cruelty and violence in Joan's upbringing to enable her to indulge in this behavior directly herself. She was raised to be a perfect lady,. and her parents were always models of correct behavior. Instead, the pent-up feelings were forced into other channels, perhaps no less harmful, but not as overt. Viruses are such tiny organisms that they cannot be seen under the usual microscope, as bacteria can. Yet the viruses can produce in our bodies just as serious diseases as the relatively large bacteria. Indeed, just because they are so small, they elude direct study and hence are today the more dangerous enemy of man. Like these viruses, the hostility that finds expression in criminoid form through masked interpersonal and group cruelties may achieve ends just as destructive as frank criminality, which, like bacteria, is open for all to see.

As our previous example suggests, the home is a fertile setting for criminoid behavior. Married couples who suffer at each other's hands have little choice but divorce (however, in one state a wife has prosecuted her husband for rape). They must ask themselves: Is divorce preferable to the current marital unhappiness? But in seeking a divorce, is one or the other partner simply following a logical procedure to relieve suffering, or is the divorce action a subtle form of cruelty toward the spouse, a criminoid act?

A young man, Bob, marries and accepts all the devotion of his wife, Stella, who holds a job to support him through college while also bearing and caring for two children and running the home. Stella makes Bob and the children her whole life. She does everything she can to further her husband's career, including remaining cheerful in the face of his numerous weekends away and his late evenings at the office. She serves dinner at six for the children and again at nine for her virtuous husband, who works so hard for his family. But one day, after twelve years of marriage, Bob announces that he has for the past five years been seeing other women and no longer loves Stella. Stella is devastated. Her entire reason for existence and her identity have been destroyed.

This situation is seen so frequently as to be typical. In some cases the husband simply leaves and gets an apartment for himself, eventually asking for a divorce. Sometimes, out of her own need for self-respect and her frustrated love turned to hate, the wife will want the divorce, choosing an uncertain future over a humiliating life of financial dependence upon a man who has rejected her. But while she slaved over the years for her husband's schooling, training, and success, she has had no time to train herself for making her own way in the world. And of course the children involved in such marital dramas are always injured by divorce.

In the specific case of Bob and Stella, is the husband criminoid? Bob had been more or less an outcast in his own family when he was a child. His father was cold and rejecting to Bob, his sister, and their mother, but indulgent of himself. He brought his mistresses into the home and was unnecessarily cruel to Bob's mother. There was not overt physical violence other than spankings, but it was enough to make Bob look for excuses to use his fists. Bob's hostility came out only indirectly in adulthood, primarily toward his wife, typically following the pattern of his father's flagrant hostility toward Bob's mother. This hostility superseded and apparently counteracted most of Bob's ability to love.

Immediately after separation from Stella, he started living with a younger woman whom at first he described as having everything his wife lacked. But four years later he still showed no inclination to marry her, and she was beginning to vent a biting sarcasm upon him. The injury Bob caused his innocent children and Stella, his faithful hardworking wife, who had earned for him his schooling, can be considered criminoid. If he continues to make himself miserable at the hands of his present mistress or subsequent women, then his self-punishment would indicate that Bob's dynamics are those of the neurotic criminoid who acts out his hostilities but also acts out punishment of himself for doing so. (Of course, wives walk out on their husbands, but less often because their financial and psychological security is normally so different. The man has usually been raised from birth with the expectation of a career, and family life is truly for him "a thing apart," while "it is the woman's whole existence.")

Neurotic Criminal Behavior

As we have pointed out, the differences among the various hostilodynamic mechanisms are based not only upon the form and intensity of the hostility and its mixture with other motivations, but also on how the hostility is handled by the ego and superego. In the neurotic criminal, to whom we now turn our attention, hostile, antisocial impulses break through into behavior, but they do so only against strong opposition from the individual's judgment and conscience. These ego and superego influences operate in various ways, two of which deserve special mention here.

In one type of case, the inner reaction from the superego is quite thoroughly repressed and is not conscious. The ego consciously accepts the antisocial impulses, and the individual appears to himself and to others as an unalloyed criminal character. Ostensibly, he approves of this in himself and in his acts; but meanwhile his conscience, though it operates without his awareness, has grown more and more powerful, grinding silently but no less effectively. This is the sort of criminal who repeatedly gets caught or otherwise manages to bring suffering on himself; this is someone who—like Lady Macbeth—can freely plan and initiate murder, apparently with the most complete determination and no conflict at all, but after the deed finds himself shaken with guilt, which may be quite unconscious and brings about self-punishment, even self-destruction.

Andy exemplifies this kind of neurotic criminal. He was the first child born to a fortyish, middle-class salesman and his young wife. The father was a large, husky, aggressive, talkative man who had completed college and was ambitious to achieve financial success. He enjoyed people and parties, but his alcohol consumption gradually increased until it became a serious problem. His temper was short and could easily be triggered, especially when he was drinking. Andy's mother, who appeared to be a sweet, immature, and insecure woman, had felt that her problems would be solved by her marriage to this older, seemingly secure, and knowledgeable man. She had finished high school and worked as a salesgirl in a department store. She had a beautiful, enchanting face, which tended to mask her basic immaturity or turn it into sex appeal. She had never felt close to her parents and craved physical affection.

Andy's mother was 29 when Andy was born, and it was a totally perplexing experience for her to be a mother—not at all like having a doll to play with. From the start things did not seem to go right with Andy. Breast feeding did not work, and he did not do well on the bottle either. He seemed to cry all the time, and his mother never could figure out what to do to quiet him. She even tried spanking him before he was a year old, but this only made him cry more vigorously. Andy's father was away traveling on his job much of the time and so could offer little help. When he was home he was irritated by his wife's yelling and complaining about Andy, who was crying.

Although Andy's mother really did not want any more children, her husband convinced her that having another might make Andy happy. So Lisa was born when Andy was three. She did seem like a different baby. She loved her bottle, never cried much, and slept regularly and well. Andy remained difficult. (It is not unusual for the first child to be difficult, and the second not; but the reverse is also seen.)

Andy's earliest memories show a kind of bleakness. He early sensed that Lisa was the favored child. He was frequently punished, but she never was. He quickly learned that both parents were moody and unpredictable. Some days almost everything he did was wrong, and his mother would scream at him and slap him. She repeatedly let him know that he was a bad boy who would never amount to much. His father gradually realized how unfair his wife's treatment of Andy was, and he would bitterly reprimand her for it. This meant that Andy might have this argument between his parents used against him because his mother would wait until the father was on the road and then she would beat the boy, seeking revenge for his having turned her husband against her. Her treatment of Andy became increasingly cruel as time went on. One day when he was five, he got his new pants dirty while playing outdoors. Her punishment was to fill the bathtub with cold water and have him lie in it for half an hour with his clothes on. Andy was too frightened of his mother at this point to even report this incident to his father. By now he knew better than to incur her wrath by having his father stand up for him.

By the time he entered school, Andy was subdued and submissive. Remarkably, he also was very bright and never had any difficulty with schoolwork. Although his grades were usually good, Andy seemed to spend a lot of time daydreaming. Also he failed to make any friends at all. He read a great deal, especially science fiction books. His parents continued to get along poorly, and an unplanned daughter was born when Andy was seven.

By the fourth grade, Andy's teachers felt that psychological tests should be ordered because of the boy's atypical behavior. The results were that:

> Andy is a cooperative nine-year-old boy who was overly serious in his approach to the tests. He is a very methodical worker, and throughout the testing period there were many evidences of compulsivity and overcontrol. He tried desperately to work to the best of his ability. However, he had to be reassured and praised constantly. He criticized his productions and was unduly disturbed over any failures. He appeared eager to please, and in fact went to extremes to gain acceptance and praise from the examiner. Personality and projective test results indicate that Andy has a very poor self-concept and that he feels extremely discouraged in the home situation, where he thinks he is receiving little warmth and understanding. In order to satisfy some of his needs, Andy has resorted to much fantasizing. He also has a great amount of hostility,

which he turns inward. He has many feelings of isolation and helplessness in his present situation, and these are coupled with feelings of inferiority and inadequacy. Andy thinks things are hopeless and he feels frustrated.

It was recommended that Andy and his parents accept a referral to a child guidance clinic. The father wanted to go, but because he was away from home so much, he was not able to arrange it. His wife, on the other hand, felt guilty and angry and refused to go for professional help. She felt it would just make her feel worse.

By the time Andy reached the sixth grade, his overt behavior had seriously deteriorated. He started smoking cigarettes and stealing money at home and at school. His parents were separated by now, and he lived with his two sisters and his father. Since the father still had to travel for his job, he hired a series of housekeepers to care for the children. These women were ineffectual when it came to Andy and he regularly took advantage of them. By the eighth grade, when he was 14, he had been suspended several times from school. He joined forces with a group of young hoodlums from another school (probably because he, like Mary, could only relate to people with whom he identified as unconsciously hostile like himself), and they formed a gang. They terrorized many local neighborhoods, and their activities became well-known to the police. Seldom, however, were any of the boys actually caught. They were clever thieves and muggers who constantly moved to new locations. Andy's father tried everything to get the boy to stop his criminal acting out. But neither reason nor threats nor even severe punishment, including physical beatings, had any effect on Andy. He would promise to change but never did. (Probably also, like Mary, he could not leave the only kind of person with whom he could identify without risking mental breakdown.)

Psychiatric treatment was tried when Andy was 15 and on probation with the juvenile authorities. By this time he had started using drugs. In psychiatric interviews, Andy would be pleasant and agreeable if he were talking about what he wanted to discuss—which was mainly drugs or his anti-establishment feelings, these being his hostilities toward his parents transferred to "the establishment." However, any attempt at insight or the facing of realities would result in his walking out or yelling at the psychiatrist in an abusive fashion. Once Andy filched the psychiatrist's prescription pad and forged his name to obtain barbiturates. This young man had been sent for treatment, but he had no motivation of his own for it, no desire to change in any way, and therefore he did not.

His father was remarried by now to a kindly woman who had been widowed and had four children of her own. She genuinely tried to understand and help Andy, but he rejected outright all her overtures. If she even asked him to pick up his clothes, which he typically left on the floor of his room, he would shout tirades of abuse at her and stomp out of the house with clenched fists. The woman lived in daily fear that Andy would get one of her children started on drugs. It was finally decided that because of his uncontrollable use of drugs it would be impossible for Andy to continue in out-patient psychotherapy and that he could no longer remain at home. His family was given the option of committing him to either a correctional institution for juvenile delinquents or the adolescent unit of a state psychiatric hospital. They chose the hospital. Andy failed to use the drug rehabilitation program effectively and instead made the hospital the base of continuance of his drug use.

After he had been at the hospital for six months, Andy hung himself in his room. He had harbored a deep and abiding hatred of himself, though you would not readily have known this when you first spoke with him. On the surface he seemed bright, friendly, and alert, and he had many fascinating ideas. These had to do especially with how society should be restructured so the "bad guys" would not be on top and the "good guys" squashed under their heels. Who were these bad guys? Well, they were the ones who ran things, like parents, teachers, doctors, lawyers, politicians, policemen—in fact, maybe all adults, all authorities. The good guys, naturally, were the kids who wanted their freedom and independence to be themselves, to do their own thing, and to build a better world. So far his theme did not sound too different from that proffered by many idealistic young people who turn their rebellion from their parents to the establishment. Andy's hostility reached such intensity that it solidified into a hatred that forced him to strike out against society in the form of stealing, mugging, fighting, drug abuse, and the like. But at the same time that he engaged in these criminal activities, Andy's internal checks were operating and causing unconscious conflicts for him. More and more his conscience directed his hostilities toward himself. In the three months prior to his suicide, Andy's intake of drugs increased dramatically, and it is rather surprising that he didn't kill himself in this way. His hostilities against himself, originating in his conscience and standards, (i.e., in his superego as guilt), were so intense that they had to be vented somehow. His superego reflected them back upon himself. We never learned exactly why or how this was—probably some of his parents' training to social behavior, almost from birth, took effect silently under his hostile defiance.

In a second type of neurotic criminal the superego forces are more conscious although, as in the unwilling alcoholic, they are not sufficiently powerful to alter or control the patterns of the individual's behavior. His ego judges him harshly; he knows that he does not conform to his own or society's standards, and he may even seek psychiatric treatment in an effort to change. But meanwhile, his guilt and need for punishment are great. Tim, an accountant in his early thirties who came for treatment after serving a prison term for embezzlement, was just such a neurotic criminal. He was a family man with a wife and two children, a kindly husband and father who enjoyed his home.

Personable, with high intelligence and a quick wit, Tim had no difficulty in inspiring confidence and obtaining excellent positions. He always gravitated to rather high-level jobs in which he was responsible for considerable sums of money. For a while Tim would function with complete reliability, but soon after establishing himself he would begin to devise clever methods of embezzlement. These schemes would succeed for a while, but then, inevitably, he would find himself on the brink of discovery. In desperation he would struggle to hide his acts; Tim would plead with his wife and friends to help him raise funds to cover what he had taken. Swearing that this was the last time he would do such a thing, he was so convincing, so pitiable, so desperately anxious to save himself and his family from disgrace, that he repeatedly succeeded in extracting sufficient funds from others to cover what he had stolen. This was his recurring pattern, his "fate neurosis"; and while Tim struggled heroically to free himself from its compulsion, the power of his childhood emotional pattern was such that he found himself repeating it against his will, again and again. Because he did not accept his criminal motivations but fought against and was tormented by these childish residues, his most prominent dynamics were those of the neurotic criminal.

Tim had been one of those children who are unwanted from the moment of conception. His parents' marriage forever hovered on the brink of divorce. Tim's mother and father lived together in a state of armed truce, hostile to each other and escaping from each other into outside interests as much as possible. It was in this hostile, ungiving, unloving world of his childhood that Tim learned to manipulate others. It was only through wit, charm, and cajolery that he could achieve any attention and emotional satisfaction. The starving man finds food as best as he can; the emotionally starved child struggles for love as best he can.

Many a child tries to stay his emotional hunger by consuming candy. Often he cannot refrain from filching it. Others crave such inadequate substitutes for love as toys or money, and such children, even when grown, are frequently unable to keep themselves from secretly appropriating these items. Tim's father sometimes gave him pennies, dimes, and nickels. This was not done in a setting of interested love and understanding, but rather in place of it. Nevertheless, so little attention did Tim get from his father that these gifts provided thrilling moments for him. He would literally dream about the small change, and, when it was not forthcoming, he gradually learned how to remove it from his father's clothes without being detected. This kind of history is sometimes found in compulsive, usually masochistic, gamblers. Some criminal types, however, feel too humiliated by being grudged the small change their parents give them, and reject this activity in favor of stealing.

Soon his whole interplay of emotions began to cluster around this pilfering. Getting the small change came to represent not only the love and concern he wanted from his parents, but also, by using it to treat his friends, the means for buying love. Through this act he also expressed the hatred against his parents that was engendered by their rejection of him, and by his behavior he courted punishment for this acting out of his hatred. This tendency for self-punishment was not conscious to him as a child or as an adult. Even as a grown man Tim was unable to face the pain of acknowledging to himself how unwanted he had been and still felt. All he was ever aware of both then and earlier was a sense of impending doom, of some unknown sword of Damocles hanging over him by a hair. This latent guilt and need for punishment, no weaker (indeed probably stronger) because not conscious, provided yet another motive for his thefts. Each time he stole and was not caught he felt a greater reassurance, seeing in his escape the proof that fate, so often seen in the image of the parents, had not after all really abandoned him.

Thus his neurotic criminal behavior came to express emotions too powerful for him to resist. This caused a true psychological addiction to embezzling, which in others is frequently fixed on food, tobacco, gambling, alcohol, or drugs, and in which the hostility to self and others is typically silent and unconscious. In adult life Tim struggled against this. He was not, like the criminoid character, able to control the direct acting out of his antisocial impulses; but unlike the true criminal, he could not embrace and make a career out of them. His defenses were not strong enough to prevent the acting out of his warped, childhood emotional patterns, but they were strong enough to see to it that he punished himself with poignant suffering.

In alcoholism, the hostility is usually unconscious except in those who become violent when under the influence and know it. Guilt is apt to be strong, even though not strong enough to control the drinking. The delicate balance of forces, as is generally known, might be expressed as "I am guilty because I drink, and I drink because I am guilty," or "I drink because I am lonely," often without realizing that "I am lonely and deserted by others because I drink."

There are no doubt many psychodynamics of gambling: gamblers who were severely neglected as children are often attracted by trying to "beat the odds." For one who feels unloved, the unconscious fantasy sometimes is, "Although I am rejected, still I might be the one in a hundred who wins." Unfortunately, unconscious guilt usually assures punishment by losing, as well as the inevitable setup of the games to profit "the house."

Overeating, too, whatever substitute gratification it might provide, vents unconscious guilt by eventual cardiovascular, gastrointestinal, glandular, or other physical disorder, usually accompanied by repulsive obesity.

9
Private Mechanisms

For a long time the term "constitutional psychopathic inferiority" was used as a catch-all label for behavior disorders that would not fit the other diagnostic categories. With increasing knowledge of the effects of early conditioning experiences and with the realization that there was no valid evidence to support the term "constitutional," that part of the label was dropped. As many of these individuals came to be treated psychodynamically, it was recognized that they were motivated by precisely the same kinds of emotional dynamics that in other persons produced physical and psychological symptoms. Here, however, the neurosis was expressed more in patterns of behavior than in psychosomatic or neurotic symptoms. Hence the term "neurotic character" or "neurotic personality" came into use.

HOSTILITY EXPRESSED TOWARD OTHER INDIVIDUALS BUT NOT AGAINST SOCIETY

Neurotic Character

As we have noted, infantile impulses persist in everyone to some degree. If they have been patterned by basically good relationships, and if they blend with mature motivations, then they cause no difficulty. On the other hand, if they have been so distorted by faulty early conditioning that the person suffered too much emotionally as infant and child, or if they have been so intensified that the mature development is hampered or warped, then they will disturb some aspect of the individual's functioning. The neurotic character differs from the criminal, the criminoid, and the neurotic criminal in that he defends himself against his infantile hostile impulses in such fashion that, though acted out, they appear only in indirect, disguised form. Essentially he suffers from a private neurosis in which the underlying hostility is repressed and causes mostly self-induced punishment, although like all emotional disorders it affects intimates and anyone close to the person; it is hard to live with a person tormented by anxiety, phobias, compulsions, or unpredictable or aberrant behavior.

The example we shall present shows an underlying personality structure similar to that of Tim, one of the neurotic criminals described previously. The two histories, however, contrast in certain important details, which illustrate the specific quantitative role that early influences play in the choice of outcome.

Alex, an ambitious, highly intelligent young man, had lost his mother through death before he reached the age of one year. His father hired a nurse to care for him, and himself gave the boy very little attention or companionship. Meanwhile the nurse answered any childish misbehavior by reminding the growing child that she was not his mother but was being paid for taking care of him and would leave if he did not act as he should. The combined rejection by both nurse and father filled Alex with anxiety and resentment. Although in childhood, while the ego is weak, feeling is usually almost synonymous with action, this boy strove to repress all retaliative behavior because, vaguely or even unconsciously, he desperately feared total abandonment.

Why was Alex able to develop effective enough psychological defenses against his anger, induced by such treatment, to prevent him from acting out his hostile tendencies in the form of criminal behavior? There were two primary reasons: In the first place, in spite of the faulty upbringing the father and nurse did have considerable affection for the child. Alex's father loved his small son after the fashion of so many busy, self-centered men who find too little time to translate their interest into a real experience for a child. The nurse, too, notwithstanding her terrifying threats to leave, actually stayed on faithfully for many years and grew truly fond of Alex. In the second place, as we have mentioned, this boy was so insecure that he dared not put into action his real resentful feelings. Any hostile behavior that would verge in the direction of the criminal was checked by love and by fear. Alex dared not act in any antisocial way for fear of losing what little emotional support he had, and also he repressed hostile impulses toward those he loved and was loved by to some degree.

When a person hates those he also loves, or whose love he wants, guilt is probably inevitable. Two mechanisms can be distinguished here. One involves hostility originating from the id, which is pent up and turned against the self, presumably by the superego, the effect of all one's training. The other mechanism involves hostility to the self, which originates in the superego—one's conscience blaming oneself, and causing guilt, for past deeds or current wishes. In Alex this meant that pent-up anger toward his father and nurse was largely turned against himself. And the inevitable guilt for his hostility then made him feel that he deserved to be rejected and that he was in reality just as bad as his father and nurse suspected. These motivations of hostility and guilt added important dynamics. In the emotional life *the punishment fits the source*—that is, punishment takes the form of whatever caused the anger. In this case the source or cause was rejection; it caused anger, which caused guilt; the guilt led to a desire for punishment, and this fitted the specific form of being rejected, which led Alex unconsciously to provoke rejection—a truly neurotic and vicious cycle.

As we all do, Alex grew up to expect from other adults the treatment he had received from those nearest him in childhood. He would enter into a friendship yearning for the loving attention he had sought in vain since birth. But soon he would feel that the other person (like his father and nurse) was not really interested in him and did not understand him. Then his underlying feelings of deprivation would ignite his anger. This appeared mostly in subtle reproaches against his friend, such as tacitly making him feel that he did not quite live up to expectations. The hostility toward himself came out by continuing these reproaches in such a way that the friend would lose patience with him. He thus provoked rejection and reestablished the childhood pattern. When this occurred, Alex would complain to a new confidant about his disillusionment with and betrayal by the former friend. This complaining to another was the nearest he ever came to expressing any direct hostility to anyone other than himself.

Occasionally as he went through the cycle, Alex would in fact get himself so rejected in spite of conscious efforts to avoid it that the relationship would break off entirely. Usually, however, he would be able to continue a precarious rapport, at least for a while, with the new confidant. And so the relationships of his adult life were of the same tenuous, ambivalent nature as his feelings toward his father and nurse in childhood, and he continued to live as an adult in the same fear of rejection in which he passed his childhood.

This childhood pattern of turning from one to another repeated itself with friends in school and in a whole series of jobs. It also repeated itself with girls. He did marry, but in spite of every attempt to preserve the relationship, his wife grew wholly intolerant of Alex's petty and constantly fretful pattern of provocativeness as it emerged toward her. In the end she divorced him. With his ego-saving capacity for projection he convinced himself and also some others that the entire fault for the dissolution of the marriage lay with his wife. Alex complained of her inability to have sufficiently deep interest in him (the same complaints he had of his father and nurse).

In Alex hostility was rarely expressed in a direct way. For the most part it caused guilt and was turned against himself to harm his own life by making him feel and actually become rejected and isolated, deprived of good, warm feelings for and from other persons. His behavior shows the mechanism of the neurotic character because, although he was consciously striving to get along with others in close gratifying relationships, his adult life was unconsciously lived for him by the child within himself. Alex was conditioned to his pattern of behavior during his earliest years. This childhood emotional pattern eventuated *in the way he lived* rather than in specific psychological or physical symptoms, as is the case with the classic neuroses. But, on the other hand, we must note that all symptoms are manifestations of a disorder of the personality; they are symptoms of disordered dynamics.

The term "neurotic," taken in its broadest meaning, refers to any emotionally caused disorder resulting from influences during childhood that block and warp full development. According to this definition all the hostilodynamic mechanisms (except perhaps some instances of sublimation) would be considered various forms of neurotic disturbance. On the other hand, the word "neurosis," when used in a restricted sense, applies only to certain symptoms and combinations of them (that is, psychological syndromes), especially those designated as hysteria, phobias, and compulsion neurosis. These are the ones that were first intensively studied and elucidated by Freud. The now well-known mechanism of neurotic symptom formation is the disguised return from repression of strong, mostly infantile, emotional forces.

Because of the individual's mature drives and adult standards, training, and conscience, these infantile forces are controlled and denied direct expression. But such unrelieved tensions affect the normal mature thought, behavior, vegetative functioning, and even sensory perception; that is, they cause disorders of feelings, thought, and behavior and the formation of symptoms. If the forces of maturity and restraint are inadequate and cannot master or offset (repress) the infantile motivations, then we see the dynamics of criminal acting out, impulse-ridden behavior, certain perversions, masochism, and similar deficiencies of mature social controls. This is not neurosis in the classic and narrow sense of repression by conscience and reemergence of the repressed infantile impulses as hysterical or compulsive symptoms, but it is neurosis in the broad sense of the same disturbed psychic forces being at work that result from the persistence of disordered childhood patterns.

Classic Neurosis

To illustrate the dynamics of hostility in classic neurosis, we have selected a simple, relatively common type of case and, for variety, one where there is a strong reactive element. That is, in the following vignette, an external life situation has intensified the emotions to the point of their producing symptoms.

A mentally and physically attractive young woman, Dee, complained of anxiety that was without content; that is, she did not know what she felt anxious about. She lived in a state of constant fear and felt only that this might portend some evil about to befall her family. She was married and had one child. The anxiety, it turned out, had developed in the course of pregnancy and became much more severe when Dee left the small town in which she was raised and came with her husband and new baby to live in the large city to which his work brought him. Dee's anxiety now had mounted to the point where she was quite unable to enjoy anything in her life, and she began to fear that she was headed for a nervous breakdown.

The salient feature of her childhood was overprotection since her birth. Her parents had seen to it that everything was done for her; even as she grew older, her life had been a playtime with practically no responsibility. Both her father and mother were leading citizens in the town, and wherever their daughter went, she was welcomed and treated with deference. Dee knew "everyone," and "everyone" knew and accepted her.

When she married, however, a very common difficulty arose. Shortly after the baby was born, her husband was promoted and transferred. The only life Dee had known had been her entirely dependent, protected play-relationship to her parents and to the community in which she grew up. Now she was suddenly removed from this to become, far away, just one of millions. Naturally her husband could not provide all the emotional support that she had left behind. It was a rude awakening for the girl to find that he was not father, mother, and friends rolled into one but merely another person of her own generation who had to devote a great deal of time, energy, and interest to his job and even had to travel and be away from home for a week at a time.

Not only was Dee's emotional intake suddenly diminished from a flood to a trickle by the geographic move, but in addition, for the first time in her life, she had real responsibilities. Now she had a young baby with its insatiable demands for attention and its relentless interference with her indulgence of herself. In addition to the baby, there was also the house to run, the problems of shopping, cooking, cleaning, and getting help, to say nothing of the harassments of budget. In other words, her emotional *give–get balance* had shifted—less was coming in, much more was going out. Dee, although young and strong, felt like a little child abandoned by her parents, and, to make matters even more difficult, she had to be a parent herself while trying to adjust to a new community.

She reacted, as do all animal organisms, with the fight–flight response. She thought of running home to mother; but much as she wanted to, Dee could not accept this path of action, jeopardizing as it would her marriage and the security of a home for her child, and running counter as it did to her healthy drives to maturity. With the possibility of flight cut off, she felt trapped, and her anger mounted. However, the rage could not be expressed either; there was no pattern in her life for that. The anger pent up inside her was the danger she sensed; but she was by no means aware of her emotional situation as we have described it. Dee did not think of herself consciously as a dependent, overprotected child. Neither did she realize the strength of her anger protest against the responsibilities of husband, home, and baby, in a new, strange, and distant city.

Repressed hostility, usually with guilt, is perhaps the most common single cause of simple anxiety states (anxiety hysteria), although any emotional imbalance causes some anxiety. At times Dee occasionally lost her temper with her husband, but that was about all the hostility that ever came to the surface. She would have been horrified at the idea of having any resentment against her husband and her child. Thus her own unexpressed rage caused the threat of impending doom.

This is a typical neurotic mechanism. The hostility is defended against and repressed, and the individual does not behave violently or antisocially. But this hostility, which is apparently dismissed so effectively, does not simply dissipate and lose its power. It generates a neurotic symptom: in this case, simple anxiety. This anxiety is basically only a personal symptom, but it does affect those with whom the individual is intimate. An anxious wife, unable to enjoy her child and husband, feeling restricted in her activities, is not the easiest person to live with; the husband and the child both suffer. This indirect effect of a repressed motivation is partly what Freud called "the return of the repressed."

This type of case is seen so frequently that another characteristic feature is worth mentioning. The repressed hostility may return pointed inward against the person himself and, directly or through generating unconscious guilt, create urges for self-punishment. Usually the individual then reacts by denying himself relief from the very responsibilities that he protests against. For example, the husband or friends sense something of what is going on as, vaguely, does the young woman herself. They urge her to get some help with house and baby, to get out more, to get her life into balance. But typically, as in the case with Dee, the anxiety prevents this solution. She fears that if she is away, something will befall her child. And, by similar motivation and thinking, she cuts herself off from the normal satisfactions of recreation, attention, and emotional support, which friendly contacts might yield. She becomes caught in a vicious circle: frustration, which leads to anger, which leads to guilt, which leads again to frustration. This is another example of how the punishment fits the source.

* * * *

Throughout our discussion of human personality development, we have seen that man is a biological unit, and that when he is under stress, from either internal or external sources, his functioning is affected. Because he is a well-integrated unit, such stresses are reacted to by the entire organism. However, they disturb one area of functioning more than another in different persons. Insofar as the higher centers of the nervous system are affected, we see manifestations of abnormal perception, thought, feeling, or behavior, or any combination of these. And insofar as the autonomic nervous system (which controls our viscera) is affected, we see disturbances in the vegetative organs, that is, psychosomatic symptoms. When disturbed emotionally, each individual reacts characteristically. One may burst out in a childish tantrum; another may be depressed; still another may develop pain in his stomach, an asthma attack, heart trouble, or a headache. Any and all combinations of reactions and symptoms can occur in a given person, in all areas of functioning, from the highest intellectual levels to the lowest. Even the fragility of certain cells of the blood, the lymphocytes, is reported to alter under stress, emotional or physical. (The most thorough studies of the effects of stress have been made by Hans Selye, to whose works the interested reader is referred.)

HOSTILITY EXPRESSED WITHIN THE SELF

Psychosomatic is commonly used in the broad sense to mean any physical symptoms in which emotions are of appreciable causal importance. At least three mechanisms can operate in the contributions of emotions to physical symptoms. In the first group are those symptoms that are dramatizations or symbolizations of emotionally charged ideas. An example would be Freud's famous one of the girl who repressed her guilt about making a misstep sexually but expressed it symbolically by dragging her foot. Such a mechanism is that of classic conversion hysteria, only rarely seen today in our country.

In the second mechanism a particular emotional need is expressed through a particular organ. Franz Alexander, in *Psychosomatic Medicine*, portrays a fairly well-established example of this: that of hunger for love being expressed through the stomach as hunger for food. This seems to derive from the child's nursing years when the intake of food is closely associated with the intake of love. Thereby these two hungers seem to become linked to each other through conditioning. Later in life, when the adult craves love, his stomach may react as though it were preparing to receive food. If the need for love is not satisfied, and the individual is angered, the anger, too, can affect the functioning of the stomach. The whole interplay of emotions, then, influences that organ system which chiefly expressed the need.

A third mechanism is that in which the symptom is simply *part* of the body's normal physiological reaction. When a person or animal is angered, there is regularly, as part of his fight–flight response, an increase in the rate and forcefulness of his heartbeat and an elevation of his blood pressure. These symptoms subside, along with the rest of the physiology, when the danger or irritant is past. In some cases, however, these cardiovascular symptoms are observed to occur without adequate external stimulation. In at least some of these cases, they are found to be reactions to threats that arise from within. The readying of the physiology for the exertion of fight or flight, of course, occurs regardless of whether the threat, irritation, or frustration is from outside or from within.

This physiological arousal can be observed to occur in full or, apparently and for not well-understood reasons, only in part. For example, an elevation of blood pressure may be seen, but few or no other signs of physiological overactivity appear. In such cases (of essential hypertension) preliminary studies suggest that these persons are usually in a state of constant anger, which, although near the surface, is typically well controlled so that their manner is pleasant and gentle.

This was the case with Tom, the oldest of six children. He had been spoiled and dominated by his mother, who also dominated Tom's physically strong father. When Tom was about ten years old, the family lost almost all its money, and fire destroyed its possessions. Because of the dire financial circumstances, Tom's mother forced the boy to get a job after school and on weekends. He reacted with bitterness to being thus prematurely forced to work and having to give up the parental indulgence that had characterized his earlier childhood.

Tom's mother was dominating and also overprotecting. She forbade sports as dangerous, and later she even refused to allow Tom to see girls other than those of his own religious faith, girls whom she personally selected. He envied the other boys who freely engaged in athletics and in dates with girls. Tom's mother set him the ideal of wealth and inspired him with excessive ambitions and great expectations. When the time came, she even forced Tom into marrying a girl of her own choosing.

Thus Tom's whole life, his work, his religion, his marriage, came to mean submission to his mother. He tried in vain for many years to escape or rebel against this now ingrained unconscious submissive attachment to his mother, but she was too powerful for him. At length, when he was in his midforties, Tom did divorce his wife, whom he had never loved, and then he tried plunging into a series of sexual affairs and alcoholism. At one point he even took a girl to the Orient in an unsuccessful effort to escape his fears and achieve sexual and emotional freedom. For Tom, drinking and illicit sex were symbols of defiance against convention, which symbolized his mother, as well as a means of escaping from the dependence and submissiveness imbued in him by her. However, his feelings of guilt and anxiety for his attempted licentious behavior soon mounted and forced him to abandon this rebellion. Tom's hypertension always increased markedly during these periods, in which anxiety frustrated his attempts at heterosexuality.

In an effort to escape the conflict with his controlling mother, Tom as a child turned to his father. However, the unconscious masculine competitiveness with his father was intense, encouraged as it was by his mother, who made Tom feel that he was much better than his father. Tom reported dreams of his mother undressing before him and of direct sexual advances toward her. Evidently she had been seductive as well as dominating, which increased Tom's rivalry with his father for her approval, wanting to show her that he was superior to his father in every way. This intensified his feelings of inferiority and of hostility to his father, and also his fear of him. The anxiety caused by this in turn drove Tom to further dependence upon his mother and to an anxious, submissive, masochistic attitude toward his father.

While it is true that on the surface his relations with men were less acutely disturbing than with women, the dependence and submissiveness toward them was even more intolerable than toward women. Always Tom yearned to rebel. This was most evident in his relationship with his boss. For example, Tom would take orders obediently and submissively, but then he would feel so rebellious and hostile as to be on the verge of attacking his boss physically. Tom claimed that he fought a desperate battle with himself against "bending the knee" to his boss. Not surprisingly, this was precisely the phrase he used in describing his submissiveness to his mother: "I was always bending the knee to her." His rage at his mother was conscious and at his boss partially so, although he knew almost nothing of the source of these feelings.

Besides his hostility from rebellion against his dependence and submissiveness, Tom would rage at not getting the passive receptive satisfaction he demanded, that is, at having to work hard and unremittingly as he had been trained to do by his mother so prematurely as a child, and thus never having been able to indulge his normal child's desires to be dependent on others. This rage also was never expressed directly; Tom was always quiet and gentlemanly. He dared not express his hostility for fear of losing the love of those around him, and he was trained to be the perfect gentleman. Tom would express his defiance privately in short-lived attempts at indulgence in a sexual affair and solitary drinking until feelings of anxiety and guilt overwhelmed him. We say "attempts" because his anxiety from sex meant for him rebellion against his mother and defiance of her impaired his sexual potency. He once got a girl to agree to go to a hotel with him, but his hand shook so that he was unable to sign the register. That precipitated his taking the same girl to the Orient in his unsuccessful attempt to be free sexually.

The continuing frustration of so many powerful feelings made Tom chronically pessimistic and anxious, and mildly depressed. He struggled against his own strong wishes to be passive, submissive, dependent—and was in a perpetual state of rebellion against these wishes, for his training, pride, and maturity demanded that he be independent and responsible. Although his hostility was successfully inhibited and found almost no direct outlet in behavior, it was not bound in an organized neurosis (e.g., paranoia, compulsion neurosis, or chronic alcoholism). Tom was unable to accept and satisfy either his flight into his passive dependent wishes or his fight as hostile defiance and rebellion. Consequently he was neither weak and dependent nor aggressively hostile. He was blocked in both directions. *He could not submit without rebellious rage or assert himself and rebel without intolerable guilt and anxiety*. During periods when either trend was temporarily more satisfied, Tom's blood pressure was notably lower (dropping from 190/110 to 145/90; we knew this from taking his pressure at every analytic session). Tom's hostility was defended against and repressed psychologically, but it affected his physiology.

This hostilodynamic mechanism of psychosomatic disorder (repressed feelings affecting the physiology in some part) seems to be ubiquitous. Who has never felt an anger within him make his heart pound, his color change, or his stomach and bowels tense up? Who has never noticed how often illness in himself and others occurs during periods of emotional stress? Hostility in one form or another seems to be of critical importance in many bodily conditions. Some epileptic attacks are apparently massive discharges of rage through muscular convulsions. Repressed hostility seems to play a role, at least in part, in certain cases of hyperthyroidism and diabetes and indeed to some extent (probably because of being part of the fight–flight reaction) in most, if not all, disturbances of the physiology that are caused by emotional strains. Here is a case of how it affected a patient suffering with a peptic ulcer. Of course it is only a question of whether emotions are one factor among others in any of these conditions.

Julie, a college student, was appealing, intelligent, and quick to gain insight into her problem. A flare-up of the ulcer from which she had suffered since she was 14 brought her for treatment. The story she poured out rapidly made clear that what was chiefly disturbing her was inner rage.

Her father, to whom she was deeply attached, had died when she was 13. His death necessitated the mother's obtaining a job in order to support her three children—the patient, a younger sister, and an older brother. When an opportunity was offered the mother back in the small town where she had been raised, she took the children there and began a new life. Thus, precipitously, Julie lost not only her favorite parent but also her close friends and her whole school environment, all of which it seems meant more to her than to the average girl because of tensions in her home with her mother. Now her relationship with her mother, never close, was severely strained. Julie's mother, through the loss of her husband and the emotional drain involved in suddenly having to earn a living, was herself under great stress. Frustrated, uprooted, and lonely, Julie became irritable and withdrawn—fight and flight.

At about the same time she also developed the stomach trouble. Her physical condition declined as her emotional situation worsened until she finally suffered a gastric hemorrhage. Julie was rushed to the hospital, where it was found that she had a peptic ulcer. Under strict medical supervision she improved. Her mother, meanwhile, was by now feeling more secure, and she could see that Julie was unable to make an adjustment in the new town. With the help of a scholarship fund, she decided to send Julie to boarding school. Here Julie became much happier and had no further trouble with her stomach until she left to go to college—a move that again meant leaving old friends and the security of established ties. Julie still felt ill at ease with her mother and was unable to talk over her personal problems at home. Her shyness made it difficult for the other students to get to know her. And so once again she was cut off from her dependent attachments. Her longings were frustrated and intensified, and the old reaction occurred—withdrawal, inner rage, and flare-up of the ulcer.

Needless to say, not all ulcers or other physical symptoms are caused by emotional factors alone. In this case, however, the evidence was strong for some emotional *element*; even such a small thing as a disappointing letter from her mother or mild rejection by a friend would precipitate abdominal pain.

Julie obtained marked relief after a few interviews with the psychiatrist, as she became rapidly aware of what was going on in her emotions, and she had a sympathetic, understanding, supportive listener. For the first time in her life she began to face frankly her deep-seated needs for love and dependence, and the hostility aroused in her by the frustration of these needs. She had not realized the amount of anger that was concealed beneath her sense of being lonely and shy. Directed mostly against her mother, it had been too full of conflict with love and dependence for Julie to face. As she began to become acquainted with these feelings, the conflict moved, as it were, from the physiological level up to the psychological. Instead of being reflected in her stomach, her problem became a matter of comprehensible emotional reactions that she could now understand, deal with, and begin to solve. The hostility, too, so long unacknowledged, could be faced as a psychological problem and as a force within herself that did no good and much harm. The hostility could be reduced by understanding its sources and shifting the attitudes that underlay them. This is not always achieved by insight alone, but may require systematic reconditioning by psychodynamic therapy to correct the childhood pattern. (See L. J. Saul, *The Childhood Emotional Pattern and Psychodynamic Therapy*.) Julie *worked through* the hostility to her mother; as it diminished over the years, the love between them increased.

In the following example we see the direct therapeutic use of the fight–flight reaction. A patient's hostility is central in every therapy.

Every threat, frustration, and irritation is reacted to by the fight–flight response; and an individual would not be in therapy if he were in perfect harmony with himself and his world. Thus knowledge of this fight–flight reaction can be directly useful in treatment, for it leads directly to its sources.

Ann, an intelligent woman of 50, came to my office complaining of tension. After obtaining her personal history, including her 0 to 6 and current life situation, I began to explore her immediate complaint, her tension.

ANALYST: You must have some idea of the reasons for your tension.
PATIENT: Yes, I guess I could say that I hate the way I live.
A: Would you be a little more specific? What is the worst thing that you hate in your life style?
P: My husband.
A: You hate him or the relationship?
P: I hate it that there is *no* relationship!
A: Is that correct? Or do you mean you don't get what you want from him?
P: Yes—more like that.
A: And what do you want?
P: I want love, companionship, communication.
A: And is there anything positive that upsets you?
P: Yes. I see what you are getting at . . . it is the *absence* of love, companionship, and communication and the *presence* of anger and instability. If you ask me what that means, I'd say unpredictability. I never know when the next explosion will come. Like this morning, as he left for the office, he suddenly turned to me in a rage: "You haven't had the car winterized yet!" When he comes in after work, I never know whether it will be quiet or an explosion. My husband has no reality, and therefore no consistency. It is such a relief when he is away on a business trip.
A: This anger at you about the car, is that a complaint that there is *no* relation or that he make demands?
P: Oh, the most extreme, endless, insatiable demands, in every area of life—for instance, demands that I fix his grapefruit, help him with his business matters.
A: Then is your complaint that there is no relation, or is this really an unbalanced give-get relation, you getting nothing of what you

want from him and his insatiable demands that make you feel you give much more than you want to give?

P: Yes, that's it. When I was a little girl we had a housekeeper I would complain to; she said, "That is good, to express your complaints. There's more room outside than in."

A: Then we should discuss how you can get more and give less, and how to deal with your fight–flight tension.

P: I can see now that it is what you call my fight–flight arousal that makes my tension. And the source is the imbalance in the give–get, and also the uncertainty, the inconsistency, and the hostility in my husband.

A: What can we do to relieve your own tension from your unbalanced give–get and your fight–flight?

P: Many years ago I tried getting what I wanted from another man. But it didn't work. He wanted to marry me, which I did not want. And anyway, it is too complicated. Today it would probably be a married man I would get involved with, and that is more than I can handle.

A: How about friends among women? And do you have useful activities?

P: That is what I gravitate to—being on the boards of things that interest me. And for the flight I think this last separation while he was away on the business trip was so successful. It was peaceful alone. I'll try for more of that. But what can I do with the fight part of the reaction, my anger. Would you suggest exercise?

A: By all means.

P: I like to swim and live near a pool. I also thought of jogging, which takes the least time, and I can do it easily and independently of others.

A: Great. Now you are thinking in terms of the components of your tension and what can be done about them. It will not be easy, but at least we know what you are trying to solve.

10
Social Mechanisms

[I have seen] the process [of stagnation and self-destruction] in my father; and I have never felt anything since. I learned soon to laugh at it; and I have laughed at everything since.

George Bernard Shaw, *Collected Letters*

The term *sublimation* was introduced by Freud to signify the transformation of crude, animalistic impulses into socially acceptable and useful drives.* As first used by him it applied chiefly to the libidinal impulses. For example, love, however physical its nucleus, can become the kind of love that is felt toward parent, child, country, humanity, and it can be expressed in literature and art. There is, of course, no reason why sublimation should be limited to libidinal impulses. Even direct hostility can be rerouted or transformed within the personality so that it motivates action devoted to the welfare of others. This can occur in a variety of ways.

Freely accepted, overt hostility can be used to attack social evils such as crime or tyranny; or it can be used in the defense of home and family. Here the destructive impulse may be retained in its original form and acted out, but its aim is pro-human and constructive. Albert Einstein, for example, who all his life avowedly detested the idea of war and violence, disappointed many organized pacifists when he refused to oppose war against Nazi Germany because he felt Nazism was something worse than war, and so joined the U.S. war effort.

*In his *Introduction to Psychoanalysis*: " . . . each individual who . . . enters the human community . . . sacrifices his instinct-satisfactions for the common good–they are . . . sublimated, i.e., diverted, to ends socially higher . . . ."

Second, the hostility may not be overt or expressed in an open fashion, but may be verbal and intellectual rather than physical. To distinguish it more clearly from our first example above, contrast the commando or police officer with such a crusader for human rights as Dorothea Lynde Dix. Though physically frail and ailing, she stumped the country, storming the citadels of authority with rousing speeches against those who maltreated the mentally ill. In like manner, Florence Nightingale was hostilely aggressive in battling for proper medical and nursing care for British soldiers. Another illustration of sublimation of hostility is the well-known dodge of giving little Willie, who is smashing the furniture, nails and wood and teaching him to hammer just as freely, but constructively instead of destructively.

Third, hostility that is unconscious and in no way evident may generate overcompensatory, sometimes excessive attitudes or acts of good will, which betray their source only when analyzed. This overcompensatory reaction may be quite successful; it is a mechanism that can contribute to much socially useful work and humanitarian activity.

Dynamically speaking, perhaps only the crusader mechanism represents true sublimation in the most precise sense. There is in the others some mixture of rationalization—that is, an ostensible (and often a good) reason masks the deeper motivations. This must be distinguished from true sublimation. For instance, conscious rationalization is a well known and frequently used mechanism in international affairs. There are countless examples throughout history of wars being rationalized by an attacker who consciously and deliberately devises reasons to justify his armed hostile aggression.

The following vignette illustrates a form of sublimation in which the hostility is coupled with a mature drive for responsibility. Martha, a young woman lawyer, was married and had two children. She could boast of an excellent private practice and was famous for her work among the poor. Not only did she extend them professional aid, but she often sacrificed much herself on their behalf, and sometimes much of her family. This drive stemmed in large part from a mature wish to use her own powers and fortunate position to improve the lot of others, especially the underprivileged. Reinforcing this, however, were a number of childish impulses, including a considerable amount of hostility.

Both the drive for responsibility and the feelings of hostility had their origins in her childhood. Martha had lost her mother when she was not quite six. This left her, an only girl, with her father and two small brothers; and the father soon came to use her all he could in the care of these younger children. About this she had mixed feelings; in part, she deeply resented the burden, but in part it gave her a sense of superiority. There was considerable hostility to the boys, not only because of having to care for them when she wanted to be free like other girls of her age, but also because of rivalry for the attention of her father, who she felt somewhat preferred the boys. Martha felt an intense need to be the first in her father's affection and to hold a favored place as the oldest child against the competition of her younger brothers. During the day she managed to put up a brave front, but at night, when she was alone, she would weep, look up at the stars in search of her mother and feel very small, needy, poor, and forlorn.

Two main mechanisms shaped themselves out of these childhood patterns during these years. First, there was an identification with people like herself who were burdened with responsibilities beyond their ability, people who struggled beyond their strength; second, she overcompensated for her competitive-resentful hostility against such weaklings as her brothers and her own weakness.

As these two dynamics developed, Martha did not dare show any anger toward her brothers or father for fear of losing her father's approval. As a defense she exaggerated her maternal feelings and behavior toward her brothers. Like herself, the boys were destitute of a giving mother, and so by identifying with them she was able to enjoy some of the help she gave, vicariously, as though it were interest and caring help that she herself received. But Martha could express some hostility very indirectly through her need to be superior and to keep the boys in tow. Thereby she gained considerable satisfaction.

In Martha's adult life both these patterns operated in a similar way. In helping the poor, as she had her brothers, she could prove herself secure, worthy of admiration, and well placed, and she could also satisfy her hostile impulses in an overcompensatory, kindly way through her role as a superior with authority. The total result was a constructive contribution to the welfare of others even though largely supported by sublimated hostility.

11
Hostility and Love

The most important human endeavor is the striving for morality in our actions. Our inner balance and even our very existence depend on it. Only morality in our actions can give beauty and dignity to life . . . . To make this a living force and bring it to clear consciousness is perhaps the foremost task of education.

Albert Einstein

Strengthening morality is not simply strengthening controls of immorality. The root lies in the abuses of children by omission or commission that disorder the child's development toward maturity and thereby stimulate the fight–flight reaction and intensify the immoral impulses. The child properly reared with love, respect, and understanding has few immoral tendencies that require controlling.

* * * *

A search for causes to explain man's propensity to injure and kill his own kind reveals many and diverse clues to his hostility. Some of these reasons seem to be fundamentally rational and reactive, as when a human community requires salt for survival and another community unyieldingly holds the entire supply of that necessity within a confined geographical area. In contrast to this example of realistic need, the reasons for propitiatory human sacrifices at seedtime are much less direct, involving as they do superstitions that seem to arise from still obscure sources in man's emotional life. Serious attempts to penetrate beyond superficial explanations for man's hostility always seem to return at bottom to the same identifying characteristic that gives mammals their name: the care and concern for their young, epitomized by the feeding breasts, the "mammae" of the nurturing, protecting mother.

This deeply instinctive, protective care and nurture seems to be what we experience as parental love. It is so strong that a parent may sacrifice his or her very life for the child and can barely face existence if the child should die. We also know from clinical experience that this powerful parental love is complemented by the child's even more powerful need *for* this love. And if it is not forthcoming, the child's whole emotional development to maturity is usually seriously warped. Unwanted, rejected, neglected, or abused, the child goes through its entire life with these now ingrained feelings. And these feelings, as we have already noted, are then reacted to with the fight–flight response, which generates inner rage and hate and also regression.

Why then do we not see the same hostility, acted out or not, in other mammals? The answer is that we probably do. Recent studies by ethologists suggest that those other mammals that have a long period of dependence upon parents do in fact display psychological problems and hostile behavior when something has gone awry in their nurturing and therefore in their normal growth to maturity. In her fascinating book *In the Shadow of Man,** ethologist Jane Goodall records her observations of chimpanzees and their society, which she studied closely in their natural setting in Tanzania for many years. Because some of her observations are directly relevant to our discussion at this point, they are presented here in some detail.

Merlin was a three-year-old male chimpanzee. After the death of his mother, Marina, he was for all intents and purposes adopted by his six-year-old sister Miff. Despite her attentions toward her brother, various deteriorating changes in his appearance and behavior began to appear, which sound remarkably similar to those changes described by Spitz in human infants separated from their mothers (see Chapter 5).

> Merlin became more emaciated, his eyes sank deeper into their sockets, his hair grew dull and stringy. He became increasingly lethargic and played less and less frequently with the other youngsters. Also in other ways his behavior began to change. [By the time] he was four years old Merlin was far more submissive than other youngsters of that age: constantly he approached adults to ingratiate himself. At the other end of the scale, Merlin was extra-

*From *In the Shadow of Man* by Jane van Lawick-Goodall. Copyright © 1971 by Hugo and Jane van Lawick-Goodall. Reprinted by permission of Houghton Mifflin Company.

> aggressive to other infants of his own age group. When Flint [another young male chimpanzee] approached to try to play, Merlin, although he sometimes merely crouched or turned his back, was equally likely to hit out aggressively . . . . As Merlin entered his sixth year his behavior was becoming rapidly more abnormal.

Before we draw any conclusions, we must note by way of comparison the behavior of another orphaned chimpanzee:

> Beatle lost her mother when she was about the same age as Merlin had been when Marina [his mother] died . . . . Beatle showed similar signs of depression to those shown by Merlin: she too became rather emaciated, she too played less and less frequently. At about the time when Merlin's behavior had begun to deteriorate even more, however, Beatle's began to improve . . . . Both of these infants had been deprived of the reassurance of the breast. Both initially showed gradually increasing depression. Then Merlin's condition declined, whereas Beatle's improved. Beatle was able to continue riding about on another chimpanzee after her mother's death . . . once she scrambled aboard she was again in close physical contact with a large chimpanzee—an individual who knew what to do in times of trouble, who would rush her to safety up a tree at the right time, who could run fast and swiftly carry them both to safety.
>
> Merlin, by contrast, had no haven of refuge after Marina's death. Miff was no more than a constant companion and was of little use to her brother in times of social excitement in the group. And so it seems possible that Merlin's troubles were principally psychological, that his terrible physical condition resulted more from a sense of social insecurity than from any nutritional deficiency.

Clearly, the cases of Merlin and Beatle represent examples of interruptions in the normal pattern of parental care and consequently in the normal growth of the offspring to maturity. Nevertheless, the key feature differentiating the two cases is a telling one. What enabled Beatle to improve from her deteriorated condition following her mother's death would seem to be that she was provided with an effective mother substitute. Merlin was not. Miff could not assuage Merlin's feelings of insecurity and provide him with the continued nurturing care that he needed in order to grow properly into maturity.

Jane Goodall has studied other chimpanzees who, although not orphans, show disturbed behavior similar to that of Merlin:

> Flint's prolonged infancy was possibly due to Flo's extreme age, to the fact that she no longer had the strength to battle with her somewhat obstreperous child . . . . as Flint grew older he had taken to hitting and biting his mother when she refused him the breast—and although Flo had sometimes retaliated, she had at the same time held the child very close, as if trying to reassure him even while she bit or cuffed him . . . . Flint was a bully to his old mother . . . . When his sibling Flame was born Flint threw the most terrible tantrums if Flo did not immediately permit him to climb into their communal bed. As the weeks went by Flint's behavior began increasingly to resemble that of an orphaned youngster: he started to decline invitations to play . . . he became noticeably listless and lethargic.
>
> What went wrong with Flint's upbringing? Had he as a small infant been "spoiled" by too much attention from his mother, sister and two big brothers? Whatever the reason for Flo's failure there can be no doubt that Flint, today, is a very abnormal juvenile.

The love of the mother for her child is not only a model for love but for maturity. The mother and her young, in humans and in other species, represent the essence of maturity and immaturity, respectively. The offspring begins life as a single cell. While within the womb, it is completely parasitic. At birth it must learn suddenly at least to breathe for itself, and soon thereafter must learn to swallow and take in food for itself. Gradually it gains the use of its senses and powers of locomotion, becoming less utterly dependent upon its mother. The mother represents the complement of this. The more parasitic the infant, the more giving must be the parent. The child sucks up energies, for its goal is its own growth and development. The mother pours out energies, for her goal is now to assure the best development of her offspring—not for any tangible return, not to fulfill her ambitions, not for personal gain, but for the child's own sake. This is the essential of true maternal love and the pattern for true paternal love as well. This feeling for the other, for his or her own sake, probably forms the core of all true love between the sexes and between friends. All strong feelings such as love, dependence, and hostility tend to become erotized, that is, mixed with sexual desires. Thus arise sadism and lust murders and also the great passionate romantic loves of history and fiction.

The unselfish love of the mother for her child is also at the bottom of those feelings between human beings that make society possible. Human beings are not the only creatures to form societies. In fact, many other species do to some extent. What specifically holds these species in societies is no doubt a combination of many motives; but one powerful force, as is evident from the study of human beings, lies in this capacity for love, which we see epitomized in the mother's relationship to her child. Identification with others as humans like ourselves probably has its source in this same love and is a component of it—in the mother's identification with her child and in the child's with its mother.

"Love thy neighbor" is an ideal of Western culture, an ideal that, as we all know to our sadness, is only partially achieved. Many people try to love but cannot. And when we come to examine why an individual is not able to love, we discover invariably that it is because he was not properly loved during the formative years of his childhood, that is, from conception to the age of about six or so. Perhaps he has not loved at all, perhaps he was loved not wisely but too well, but always something was wrong in the attitudes and feelings of the parents toward him during his tenderest years.

For example, Linda, 21 years old, was causing her parents much anguish because of her profligate sexual behavior and her repeated troubles with the law. Linda said she saw nothing wrong with it, but her parents could not reconcile themselves to her sexual affairs with several men, changing "lovers" every few weeks. They were shocked with her lecherous, reckless, and irresponsible way of life, her flouting of convention. At length she capitulated to her parents' insistence that she see a psychiatrist. Linda's attitude was simple: she pointed out that she did not yet want to get married and settle down, that she had strong sexual feelings, and that she did not see why she should not have her fun while she was young and free and bursting with desire. Convention, she said, was outdated and hopelessly irrelevant, and she saw much to recommend freedom. Linda was very direct and forthright and superficially happy in her self-indulgence.

At first Linda discussed her parents quite objectively; she said she loved them, but felt they simply did not understand life. As she described her growing up; however, her cool, dispassionate tone began to betray an underlying anger. She described her parents, especially her father, as being suspicious and impossibly strict in terms of standards of behavior. She said she felt under constant pressure from them and continually under the imposition of their ideas of what her life should be. Linda complained bitterly of their constant attempts to handpick her friends and her forms of recreation. While she lived at home, they demanded exact obedience as to the hours she came in at night, and they always insisted on detailed accounts of where she had been and with whom, and every detail of what she had done.

It soon became apparent that it was in self-defense that she had developed a fight–flight reaction; without it, she felt unconsciously she could not preserve the integrity, identity, and independence of her own personality. The rebellion, of course, was aimed—again unconsciously—at the very heart of her parents' wishes for her. Since they tried to compel her to a rigid "goodness," she sought a defiant pattern of "badness" as a outlet for her hostility in her fight to keep her individuality from being crushed.

The parents' protectiveness was doubtless born out of love for their child, although a fearful sort of love. All children need some guidance toward socialization, but Linda's parents did not *win her over* to what was good and reasonable through love and the "inevitability of gradualness"; rather, they sought to *impose* it upon her without sufficient respect for her personality. It did not take long in therapy for Linda to learn that the chief motivation for her unconventional way of life was an unconscious form of rebellion against this imposition of parental domination, a rebellion by which she asserted her independence and revenged herself on her parents. As Linda came to realize this, she also began to see that she was not yet a free adult, not yet emancipated from her childhood conflict with her overly controlling parents. She was still trapped in her childhood pattern, now not of submission but of the opposite, hostile rebellion. Once this became apparent to her, she saw that a way of life based on rebellious hostility would not be happy—that she was, in essence, destroying the very love and freedom she sought by misusing her sexual drive for an ulterior purpose of rebellious revenge. After a number of visits, Linda was able to admit her feelings of emptiness and loneliness in spite of all her free indulgence in sex and so-called love.

Parents who deeply desire their children's success in any form of endeavor usually have no conscious intention of using the children as pawns for their own dreams; usually they sincerely love their children and wish them happiness as they see it. As a result, the children usually have a basically sincere feeling of love for them in return and no conscious wish to hurt them.

Therefore, the hostility arising in children against parental impositions and deprivations typically brings considerable guilt. The guilt, in turn, creates a need on the children's part for self-punishment. The resulting rebellious behavior then serves two needs: both attack on the parents and punishment for the children themselves, sometimes even to the extent of running their lives. The whole process is often acted out quite unconsciously. In cases that are detected early enough, the untangling process is sometimes fairly rapid and easy, especially when the love overbalances the hate. Often the child's intellectual insight into the punishing behavior reveals it as only a weapon, and not a major personality trait. With this knowledge there may come enough freedom to permit new growth and fresh patterns. But if the pattern is deep-seated in the personality, systematic psychodynamic therapy will probably be indicated.

Love appears to be vital to happiness, but hostility and happiness appear to be discordant and incompatible, except, perhaps, in the rare case of overcompensatory reactions to unconscious hostility (see Chapter 10), wherein the hostility may indirectly generate socially useful work and acts of good will. But here, too, the individual is in jeopardy. Even a small amount of hostility can be threatening. This is seen in well-meaning, well-intentioned people who repress their hostilities and attempt to lead loving, generous lives of achievement. Without doubt this repression is far better for society as a whole than the criminal and criminoid acting out of hostility, but the nature of hostility is such that completely successful repression is probably not possible. Thus the good do indirectly what the bad do directly (with apologies to Plato): "The good dream what the wicked do." Some sacrifice of personal gratification of desires for dependence, sex, vanity, and hostility is necessary for society to hold together and for individual humans to live in society with a modicum of happiness.

The return of what is repressed is a general human phenomenon in which poetic justice sometimes operates with unerring precision, although often unfairly: we have noted that the punishment is regularly directed to the desire that is the source of the hostility. For example, Linda, the young girl just mentioned, did not explode openly at her parents. Instead, her underlying resentment came out indirectly in disorders of her social relations and sexual experiences, which were unwittingly used to hurt her parents, and which eventuated not only in breaking off treatment but in a lonely and unhappy life for herself, and in her apprehension by the police for prostitution and drug abuse. Thus she brought on herself a punishment consisting of stricter control than what she rebelled against.

A corollary to this is that the guilt that arises in the individual is not generated solely by unconscious impulses that never come through into action. On the contrary, in most cases the guilt is for actual behavior even though the hostile meaning of this behavior is not known to the person himself. This guilt for unconscious and indirect although actual hostile behavior causes tendencies to self-punishment. The form taken by the self-punishment is, of course, not accidental but specifically determined. As we noted earlier, the punishment fits the source; that is, the punishment regularly strikes the very desire that, being frustrated, generates the hostility.

David is a young man who was doted on and excessively indulged as an only child. He strives now for prestige, feels dissatisfied and enraged by his failure to gain all the esteem he desires, and out of envy hates others who achieve it. His punishment is in the form of defeating his own strivings, so that he goes down instead of up his ladder of success. Significantly enough, David reports having repeated dreams of climbing a cliff but slipping down into a mine shaft. Dreams are indeed, as Freud said, the royal road to the unconscious. In the dream our true motivations appear, although in disguised form, so that we must learn their language in order to understand them.

David's personal history showed him as a man who was defeating himself and, through anxieties about his health and work, driving himself toward failure by a self-punishing mechanism.

What was the crime that brought about his sense of guilt? David was charming, well-educated, and, at least on the surface, upright and conscientious. It seemed, however, that he had always been what he described as "too attractive to women." As a young man, David had been engaged several times but had always managed to break off these commitments on one pretext or another. Finally, with reluctance, he married a lovely girl. But almost from his wedding day he was disappointed and dissatisfied. Four children were born to the marriage, a situation that only served to irritate him further. He resented helping around the house, refused to assume any authority over the children, detested playing with them, and wouldn't hear of spending time with them when they were off from school on holiday. In fact, the only pleasure David seemed to enjoy during this period was a series of flirtations and philanderings with a string of women. Toward none of them did he form any real attachment. In due course, however, he met a woman who was extremely well-to-do, ~~and it seems~~ that her social position and wealth pleased his vanity and captivated him. He divorced his wife and married this new attraction. While he was consciously aware that he did not love his new wife and that he had never deeply loved his first wife, he placed all the blame upon them for his lack of happiness.

Superior as he was intellectually, David was completly unaware of the hostility in his life, which resulted chiefly from inner protest against any responsibilities and demands. He saw himself as considerate and thoughtful, and never imagined the load of guilt and resentment he carried because of hating to give any love and responsible effort in a relationship, although he demanded enormous quantities of attention and support for himself.

During treatment the source of David's hostility was uncovered, bit by bit. His mother had been a beautiful and vain woman who had asked nothing from him, her only son, but praise and flattery. Preening herself in front of him in pretty new dresses and jewels, she rewarded his admiration with kisses and then left him to babysitters and maids, to entertain himself while she went out. She was not malicious or mean apparently, but simply neglectful, careless, and childish. As her son grew, he began to dislike the emptiness of their relationship, but he repressed his hostility toward her and turned it inward on himself.

Because David had inherited her good looks and imbibed her charm, he was successful in attracting much more love and attention than he might otherwise have received. However, because of his inability to return love and interest, he was not successful in keeping it. This failure, of course, increased his unconscious hostility, which in turn built up more guilt, and eventually a trend to self-punishment. He brought punishment on himself by unconsciously provoking the real loss of love and feelings of responsibility from his wife and children and from other women, the very deprivations that in his childhood relationship with his mother had caused the trouble in the first place.

Generally speaking, it is better for society and hence for humanity for hostility to be repressed, but this alone is obviously no final, enduring answer for the individual or the race. The unconscious return of the hostility, the resulting guilt, the motivations to self-punishment, comprise a major mechanism by which a childhood emotional pattern comes into dynamic equilibrium and persists for life, casting a pall over the inner emotional atmosphere.

We have discussed the biopsychological nature of maternal love and its relationship to the normal growth of the child to maturity. Let us now turn our attention to the implications for society of love considered in a spiritual and human sense.

Science in the form of psychodynamics has come squarely face to face with humanity's great problems of good and evil, love and hate, and the origins of these forces; that is, what shapes, influences, and determines them. It was in the nineteenth century that science began to come to some systematic understanding of these forces, which, until then, had been almost solely the concern of religion, philosophy, and literature. However, much misunderstanding has been generated about the attitudes of psychiatry toward religion, in part because Freud's initial insights into the causes of emotional disorders concentrated at first on the importance of sexual motivations. He broadened the concept, as we have noted previously, far beyond sensuality, to cover love in its most sublimated forms, and, in fact, practically all positive feelings between people. However, many ignored this theory and misunderstood the sum total of his views as carnal pansexualism. This misapprehension, plus the vulgar misinterpretation of his descriptions of resolving repression as license to sensuality, resulted in a gross misconception of Freud and of psychoanalysis as antimoral, licentious, and anti-Christ.

The reality is precisely the opposite. In his personal life Freud was puritanically moral, untouched by any breath of gossip. So too were his scientific conclusions—namely, that the whole course of the libidinal development consists in outgrowing childish egocentricity and achieving the capacity for unselfish responsible love. This is the essence of his libido theory. Mental disorder, he said, is a matter of childish libidinal fixations that are caused by faulty upbringing during the earliest formative years; it is in essence the result of a failure to lose oneself sufficiently to be able to love another. (Matt. 10:39: ". . . he who loses his life for my sake will find it.")

The striking point is that this conclusion, which has been amply confirmed by later analysts of all "schools," is identical with that of the world's great religious leaders. Thus depth psychology, by a totally different route, came, millenia later, to the same "commandments" that Judeo-Christianity and other great religions have always held to: for a good life man must reduce his hostility and be able to love fully.

Yet on second thought this identity in the teachings of science and religion is not striking at all. For it signifies the confirmation, achieved through painstaking scientific work, of realities long divined and felt to be true by great prophets and the mass of the people. Moreover, this knowledge, together with discoveries of the biological drive toward cooperation within animal societies, allows us to say we have the beginnings of a scientific base for morality and ethics.

It is hardly necessary to state in detail how it is that dynamic psychiatry has reached this moral outcome, for all that has gone before in this book shows that the path from infantile egoism to relatively unselfish, responsible, and productive love is the path to emotional maturity. Put conversely, the failure to mature properly emotionally is the basic source of hostility and of deficient capacity to love. Excess of hate over love is a sign of emotional disorder, the result of warping in the emotional development.

In medical school the doctor learns that his task is to help make the bodily conditions such that the curative powers of nature can heal most effectively. "I only bandage, Nature cures," as Pares said. The physician's powers come essentially from going along with nature. The role of the doctor evolved in society as part of man's adaptation to nature. The doctor is himself part of nature's process of healing and prevention. This is undoubtedly why for so long religious leaders were called "healers." The underlying truth is that health of both mind and body, that is, full psychosomatic health, depends upon the harmonious development and operation of all the motivations and reactions, and anyone who helps people to the fundamentally proper ways of life in keeping with the deeper motivations of nature is thereby helping people to mental, bodily, and spiritual health. It is not only foolish to think of science and religion as being at loggerheads, but it is fundamentally untrue. The doctor and the "healer" have the same goal: the well-being of man. In this sense psychiatry is an instrument of religious feeling, of man's efforts to comprehend the forces of nature and the goals of mature living and to find his place in the universe.

Moreover, if the feeling of relationship to divinity does consist in part at least of a sense of closeness to and realization of nature's power and wisdom, and particularly of the forces that motivate mature behavior, then many diverse phenomena of religion and science become more intelligible. There is nothing new or revolutionary in this psychiatric approach except the specific importance of the mature drives, in contrast to the fight–flight response.

In clinical practice when psychodynamic treatment is successful, the development toward emotional maturity is unblocked and hence moves toward increasing energy, freedom, enjoyment of the mature responsible, productive, and independent drives, and the ability to love. This ability, this growth toward emotional maturity in compassion and understanding, seems properly designated as spiritual growth. And the sense and feeling of the mature motivations in relation to other persons and to the rest of nature seem to be one component at least of what we remark as spiritual and religious feeling.

Dostoevsky, despite his severe neurosis, seems to have had a spiritual quality and a religious sense that gave him an unusual sensitivity to motivation. His hypersensitivity resulted in all likelihood from the anguish of his own severe personal emotional disorders. Dostoevsky's interest in hate and suffering and his fight against them were coupled with painful longings to love and be loved, which probably stemmed largely from his father's cruelty toward him as a young boy. But it was not his neurotic problems that made possible his capacity for sustaining an intense interest in man and for producing his insightful contributions to literature. In his short story, "The Dream of a Ridiculous Man," he expressed the central issue of human experience simply and directly in words lifted from the Gospels (Matt. 19:19): "The chief thing is to love others like yourself, that's the great thing and that's everything; nothing else is wanted." He seems to have been one of those who saw it but did not succeed in achieving it.

Thus religious feeling seems related to a depth of and closeness to maturity of motivation. First, it involves humility, that is, a realistic consciousness of the self as only one tiny expression of the forces of nature, which underlie the whole universe and operate inexorably in all of us. Second, it involves the ability to love. Both of these characteristics demand a freeing of the mind from exaggerated or otherwise disordered infantile motivations and from hostility, and both result in the freeing of the creative forces within man.

Anyone who tries honestly to understand himself and others must realize that his ego perceives the interplay of motivations within his own mind, welling up from his own body and reacted to in accordance with his own early conditioning and his present situation in life. Each person's ego then perceives (as far as it is possible) these interactions in the forms specific to himself. If we could devise a modified and vastly more effective electroencephalograph, we could tune in to the other person's brain and experience in our own consciousness what he is experiencing in his. How humble this should make us—and how considerate.

Insofar as man's very survival depends on increasing knowledge that will diminish hate and increase love, science should welcome religion and certainly also education as allies in a world with few allies. It should make open and public the need for cooperation with education and religion. Science can only describe; by itself it can accomplish little toward aiding humanity in furthering the great goal of love. Science must make its knowledge known to those who can utilize it in leadership for progress toward the goal of love—and for such utilization religion has long had the organization and a shared objective.

12
Some Legal Considerations

I think we have to safeguard ourselves against people who are a menace to others quite apart from what may have motivated their deeds.

Albert Einstein

We must not make a scarecrow of the law
Setting it up to frighten the birds of prey,
And let it keep one shape, til custom make it
Their perch and not their terror.

William Shakespeare, *Measure for Measure*

"Ladies and gentlemen of the jury, the question we face here today is not whether John Doe committed the crime, but whether John Doe can be held *legally responsible* for this act." This question may reflect the clever dodge of a skillful defense attorney, or it may be an expression of considered and legitimate doubt as to an individual's culpability in the face of psychopathology. Regardless of the circumstances or sincerity motivating the inquiry, it points to a persistent problem in our courts of law.

From the larger perspective of general human concerns, criminal responsibility is, of course, only one aspect of the much larger problem of human personal responsibility. In part we are what we are because of our genes, our heredity. For this we cannot take much responsibility. In part also we are shaped by our early environment, especially that from birth to age about six, which has strongly conditioned us to certain patterns of thinking, feeling, and behavior. Hence a strong case can be made to show that our psychic lives are almost entirely predetermined and, so to speak, are lived for us. It has also been argued that our feeling of free will is only an illusion, a subjective sensation that gives us the feeling that we are making choices and decisions, whereas in actuality each choice and decision is predetermined by our makeup, our dynamics, interacting with our environment, as often becomes evident in retrospect. If this is true, then no one is really entirely responsible for his feeling, thinking, and behavior—neither the good man for being good, nor the vicious one for being cruel, an observation that Benjamin Franklin supported.

On the other hand, perhaps we do have at least some degree of free will, of personal responsibility. Certainly our lives, our society, our government, and our laws are based upon this assumption. If there is no responsibility for criminal or any other behavior, then we have chaos. Of course the whole problem of personal responsibility is a critical one, but we cannot disrupt our entire system of government, law, and society because it contains unresolved problems and difficulties; improvements must be developed as replacements before the present protections of society are discarded.

Statistics on crime have mounted steadily for decades—crimes against property and against persons (see Chapter 4, p 32). No longer can one leave his house, car, or bicycle unlocked in traditionally honest America. Honor students at our greatest universities cheat in many ways; a U.S. senator is known to have paid someone to write a paper for him while at college (cheating and stealing are so common as to be no longer deplored); West Point and the Air Force Academy have endured scandals. Shoplifting is an expensive epidemic; white-collar crime and organized crime are inestimable, as is tax evasion. Corruption in Congress and the highest levels of government is commonplace. Citizens can no longer walk safely in the streets of towns, cities, and cultural centers, not even in their own capital, Washington, D.C. Nor can one live safely on the campuses or environs of some of our greatest universities.

How can we reestablish personal responsibility for morality? "True human progress is based less on the inventive mind than on the conscience of men," Einstein said. We must learn much more about the conscience and how to form healthy, mature ones, as well as about the antisocial, anti-human impulses that need control, if society is to exist.

Clearly the problem of responsibility for criminal acts is far from solved; but as an initial step we should strive at least for a clarification of the basic concepts of mental illness and its relationship to this problem. The majority opinion in *McDonald vs. United States,* in speaking to the question of "whether a stated mental disease 'caused' the person to commit a given unlawful act or 'produced' that act," made the point that the question ought to be whether mental disease or defect "substantially affects mental or emotional processes and substantially impairs behavior controls."

Criminal behavior–murder, rape, assault, and the like–is not usually "caused" by mental disorder, as the term "cause" is generally used. The reasoning however tends to be: "He committed a criminal act; he is to some extent abnormal mentally; hence, this mental abnormality 'caused' the criminal act, either by intensifying the motivation for the act or by weakening judgment and controls." This reasoning, while convenient, is hopelessly simplistic and fallacious. In reality, what is central in most criminal acts is a disorder of personality interacting with an external situation brought about by external forces or by the person himself. This disorder can find expression in a number of different forms, which vary from time to time in the same person, and from one individual to another. Crime is only one of these forms. Others, as we have seen, are neurosis, psychosis, addictions, perversions, and all the other forms of psychopathology.

As an example of how a personality disorder can be expressed in different ways in the same person, let us note the case of Jim. This young man of high social, intellectual, and, apparently, moral caliber reacted to mild teasing by an acquaintance by shooting and killing him. A boy in his college dormitory teased Jim one evening. The next day Jim borrowed a car and drove home, ostensibly for some books, but in reality for his gun and ammunition; returning to the dormitory that night, he found the boy who had teased him asleep in his bed. Jim shot and killed the boy. Jim had planned the murder for at least a day, working out detailed accounts of his whereabouts that he could later use for an alibi. During the day and evening before the shooting he conversed with people who knew him intimately and others who knew him casually. In the course of the investigation following discovery of the murder, no one, including the professor of psychology, could recall having noticed any abnormality in Jim. Later it was learned that twice in the previous three years he had had episodes of full-blown psychosis, for each of which he had been committed to a mental hospital for periods of about two months. This murder appeared as an equivalent of the previous psychotic episodes. Apparently in each of these two prior instances there was a reaction of rage of such intensity that it so disrupted his mental state as to produce frank schizophrenic symptoms, disorganizing the ego functions of perception, integration, and mature behavior. The third time it came through as direct hostility, murder, without any such disruption discernible to others. (An excellent book is *The Criminal Mind*, by Philip Roche.)

If this description is correct, then we have progressed a step in detecting the causal chain, while realizing that in this context, as in most, causality is better understood as a network than as a chain. Here strong feelings and motivational forces, pressing for action, come to expression in the overt hostile act. Going a step further, we must ask why the rage and hate were so strong or the forces of control so weak, or both, as to produce on two occasions schizophrenic psychoses and on the third occasion, murder. The answer to this question lies in the particular individual's makeup, in his personality, the essential components of which are his emotional interrelations—his patterns, attitudes, and feelings toward other persons. Jim was hypersensitive and filled with unremitting rage, chiefly from feelings of abysmal inferiority, which, in turn, stemmed from abuse by his father and extreme overprotection by his irritable mother. This rage was usually covered over and controlled, creating the extreme kindness that overlay barely supportable inner tension. When sufficiently increased, this tension, consisting mostly of repressed hostility, disrupted the usual mental processes, twice producing psychotic episodes and then breaking through as naked violence. Possibly one reason it could break through in such action was that in early childhood he was repeatedly subjected to harsh physical punishments, and his father's favorite sport was hunting.

Thus the real pathology, the real mental disorder, consists of disturbed feelings toward others—and also toward self. As we have stressed throughout this book, the pathology in a physically sound, healthy organism is always a pattern of emotional reactions formed in childhood in response to the way the child was treated by other human beings, chiefly by those responsible for the child or close and emotionally important to it. Of course, under powerful enough external pressures, anyone, no matter how good his human relations since birth, can show untoward patterns of reaction, as are widespread in times of stress, strain, and violence such as war. But this military violence is not the essence of behavior that is criminal, which arises from within the personality under ordinary conditions. Criminal behavior is an outcome of personality disorder—it is not caused by neurosis or psychosis or other symptoms of syndromes; it is, like neurosis and psychosis, *itself a form of disorder*. Criminal behavior is but one type of psychopathology and symptom.

The ideal would be to cure all the sufferers from psychosomatic disturbances, phobias and other forms of neurosis, addictions, psychoses, criminal acting out, and every other type of psychopathological symptom. But this is impossible for at least two basic reasons. First, psychiatry is not like surgery—it can only help people to help themselves. If a person does not have a powerful and sustained urge to change himself, psychiatry cannot change him. Second, all of these conditions are for the most part entrenched lifelong personality disorders. Even if the individual has all the will in the world to change, it may be too late, and he may not be curable. Even help for persons who desperately want it is slow and not fully successful in every case, as in cases where the childhood warping was too early, severe, consistent, and prolonged. Usually the criminal type of behavior disorder is not curable, and even if it were, there are not enough psychiatrists available. Nor can there ever possibly be enough psychiatrists for a treatment that involves reopening the development of personalities warped so early in childhood as to eventuate in criminal behavior. To think that a few months or even years in a mental institution will produce any permanent cure in the vast majority of cases is totally unrealistic. Psychiatric treatment for such disorders, in any form available today, is ineffective, unreliable, and impracticable. The fact that sending repeaters back to jail does not help them or change their behavior does not mean that sending them to a psychiatrist or mental hospital will achieve the desired effect, however much this is a gesture in a more rational, humane direction.

What, then, can be done? Let us look first at our present system. The jails are full to overflowing, crime is increasing, and the extraordinarily high rate of recidivism shows that something fundamental must be wrong. Perhaps one basic fallacy lies in the concept of *punishment* for wrongdoing. This notion permeates the thinking of our society, and yet the jails show more often than not that its effect on criminals is the opposite from the intent. Punishment and incarceration have long been questioned as the best ways, first, to protect society, and second, to help the criminal. But while new approaches to the problem are sought, we must still strive to make the present system work as effectively and justly as possible. This requires as a basic minimum that we agree on the definitions of certain key terms. Without sharpness of definition, terminology can only lead to confusion in reasoning, psychiatric and legal opinions, charges to the jury, and outcome. But most psychiatric terms are broad and loosely used. There is a lack of uniformity in definitions of diagnostic labels, and often inadequate objective evidence is offered for the diagnosis.

The District of Columbia Court of Appeals (in *Carter vs. United States*) stated:

> Unexplained medical labels–schizophrenia, paranoia, psychosis, neurosis, psychopathology–are not enough. Description and explanation of the origin, development and manifestations of the alleged disease are the chief functions of the expert witness . . . the material from which his opinion is fashioned and the reasoning by which he progresses from his material to his conclusion . . . the explanation of the disease and its dynamics, that is, how it occurred, developed and affected the mental and emotional processes of the defendant . . . not the mere expression of a conclusion. The ultimate inferences . . . of cause and effect, are for the trier of the facts.

Eventual agreement as to definitions of terms rests upon a sound base of understanding. This must include an understanding of the emotional forces behind the phenomenon that the term is meant to describe. Understanding of these emotional forces is contributed to by modern psychodynamics. The following is a brief dynamic discussion of a number of terms that are commonly used and misused in considerations of criminal behavior and its relationship to the law.

Insanity, the key term in the plea of "not guilty by reason of insanity," is generally considered in the field of psychiatry to be a legal term, not a psychiatric one. Probably among psychiatrists there is general agreement that it designates a disturbed condition of thinking, feeling, and behavior of such kind and degree that the person is unable to comprehend reality because of illusions, delusions, and hallucinations, unable to manage his own life as a free member of society, and therefore must be committed–voluntarily or involuntarily–to a mental hospital. (Borderline conditions present special problems regarding committment.)

The term "insanity" which is used to describe such a state of mind, has the same meaning to the psychiatrist as it does to the general public, to whom an insane person is one who is "crazy," "out of his mind." The insane person is one whose behavior is so remote from reason and reality that we cannot talk and communicate with him in an ordinary and reasonable fashion. This usual meaning of insanity is termed by the psychiatrist "psychosis."

Psychosis can be defined psychiatrically in a somewhat more technical way, which would be consonant with the dynamic psychiatrist's view of the mind and its operation. Psychosis is understood as partial or complete disruption of the functions of the ego. One may, for example, have strong sexual or hostile impulses from his id, but if his superego (which includes his conscience) is strong in maintaining his standards, and his ego is strong in its powers of judgment, reason, control and in its directing of thinking and behavior, then he may use these forces in a constructive way. If his superego reactions are too strong, he may feel so guilty about these id impulses that he becomes depressed. If he is too dependent to live up to superego ideals of, say, adult independence, he may feel inadequate, frightened of life, inferior, and, therefore, through the fight–flight reaction, enraged. This hostility may cause guilt, or it may, if repressed by the superego, cause neurotic or psychosomatic symptoms. (See chart in Chapter 7.) On the other hand, it may be denied and excused, as in cases of paranoid projection, wherein the individual suffers under the delusion that it is not he who is hostile, but that other persons are persecuting him. In this latter case, the person's perception of reality is grossly distorted to fit his emotional needs: and this distortion of the sense of reality is usually the key to psychoses. The ego function of perception is thus disordered. In summary, then, we see how under emotional pressures from the id and superego or both, and usually also from the outside world, the ego functions may be more or less disordered. When they are grossly deranged and especially when perception, judgment, control, and sense of reality are distorted, the condition is described as psychosis.

It is clear that emotional forces, especially hostility, which is our primary concern and the most constant factor in psychopathology, can affect the ego in many ways, depending upon the balance of forces from id, superego, and environment. Psychosis is one of these ways, but it is one form only in the whole range of mental and emotional disorders, as we have discussed and have diagrammed (chart in Chapter 7).

In psychosis many or all of the functions grouped together as ego are severely impaired or distorted: (1) Consciousness may be impaired or entirely suspended, the person having no memory whatever of what took place during his psychotic episode. (2) Perception of internal feelings and external reality may be distorted in almost every imaginable way and to extreme degree. The person may believe that he has a disease or deformity (hypochondria), or that small creatures are crawling about under his skin. Or, his delusions may be about the external world, particularly about people, as in those of persecution, already mentioned. If guilt, a reaction of the superego, is of certain form and strength, or if hostility from the id is directed against the self, psychotic depression may occur. The sufferer may feel himself to be guilty of the most heinous sins and crimes, and worthy only of punishment and death, which he may try to inflict upon himself. One of the more shocking experiences of my residency in psychiatry occurred in making my first rounds early one morning on the most disturbed male ward. On one bed lay a middle-aged man whose testicles hung outside of his scrotum, a mutiliation he had just accomplished on himself. Gross distortion of reality is familiar to the psychiatrist as illusions, delusions, hallucinations. The psychotic may not know the date, time, or place, or he may mistake them, in which case he would be described as being *disoriented.* (3) Memory, reason, judgment, and other powers of integration may be deranged. (4) Control may be weakened to any degree, releasing any and every impulse, such as the sexual, the infantile–dependent, and the hostile; and there may be loss of sphincter control (with smearing and eating of feces). (5) Capacity to relate to others with healthy and friendly feelings and identifications may be disordered or lost almost completely so that no communication with others is possible (alienation, isolation, partial or total). Where id and superego forces are powerful enough relative to the ego, the ego functions may be totally disrupted, and the person seems to us completely confused, incoherent, and withdrawn.

The balance of forces in the personality varies greatly from one individual to another. A thoroughly healthy personality is not common—that is, a person with no overly strong antisocial forces in his id, with a superego that has been formed of loving childhood relations and identifications with his parents and with a current life situation well within the limits to which such a reasonable and mature person can adjust with a moderate degree of happiness. It is also obvious that there are many pathological dynamics with even more numerous outcomes, and that the outcome in criminal behavior is very different from the outcome as psychosomatic symptoms, neurosis, or psychosis. Combinations of one or more of these outcomes are usual (e.g., criminals have neuroses, perversions, and psychosomatic symptoms), but the most *prominent symptoms* are usually recognizable as a diagnosable condition.

A superego that permits or encourages criminal acting out, as a parent encouraged it in childhood, is in that part a criminal superego and conscience. An ego that accepts and acts out hostile impulses that are unchecked by the superego is a criminal ego. It is disordered in a criminal way, but very differently from an ego that is deranged in its functions in a psychotic fashion. The mark of criminality, as we discussed in Chapter 8, is the ego's (and superego's) acceptance and acting out of hostile impulses that society considers antisocial, immoral, and criminal; and this is biologically anti-human. This ego, unlike the psychotic ego, may be strong and effective in all of its functions, as in the case of an outstandingly successful criminal who fully accepts his criminality.

It is not uncommon to see persons with circumscribed psychotic areas in their egos that serve the criminal drives; common ones are hostility displaced to society and paranoid trends. The latter involve paranoid delusions of being threatened by certain persons or groups, which justify using all the other unimpaired powers of the ego to attack them in the delusion of defending oneself.

Criminality is a disorder. Psychosis is a disorder. Both may combine in a person in various ways and degrees. But they are two totally different and distinct disorders. The term "insanity" makes sense only when used in its usual meaning of psychosis.

The term *mental health* is not easy to define and no one psychiatric definition is universally agreed upon. Descriptively it is a state in which a person is in reasonable harmony internally with himself and externally with his environment; this includes, in Freud's phrase, the ability to love and to work (and to play). More dynamically—that is, more in terms of the emotional forces that shape personality—it is *emotional maturity* combined with *adjustment*. Adjustment means harmony with the self and the environment. This equilibrium is dynamic; for example, a person may not be satisfied with his skills or with the environment, but he is satisfactorily adapted to his efforts to improve both. A regressed schizophrenic, for example, who is entirely helpless and dependent in a mental hospital, may reach a degree of adaptation on this level (of total withdrawal and regression to the behavior of a parasitic baby), but this is not a mature adjustment and is therefore not mental health.

As we have said, maturity and mental health have been tersely defined as the ability to enjoy working and loving in good balance with socially acceptable recreation (i.e., play). Maturity is the end result of the development of the fetus and baby from parasitic dependence upon the mother into an adult who is able to meet the dependent needs of spouse, child, and society responsibly and lovingly. The baby needs care and love to survive–it is completely dependent and needy of love; as it reaches awareness, it senses its smallness and weakness with consequent feelings of insecurity, anxiety, and inferiority, and often competitiveness in reaction to these feelings.

The drives of the child's id are to grow and develop; but this is achieved healthfully only in a setting of good human relations with the parents, who keep good feelings between the child and themselves. Then the child, out of love for and identification with the loving, understanding, and respecting parents, forms a superego that is loving, understanding, and respectful of itself and of others. With good relations during early childhood, the child's ego is free to develop its own interests, activities, and functions. Characteristic of disturbance in a child are the falling off of grades in school and worsening of relations with other persons. If the environment remains suitable, we have a person with a well-functioning ego, impelled by mature drives from his id, with a superego that is approving and supporting and in harmony with the rest of the personality. The mature adult can meet the needs of his family and his society by being relatively independent, responsible, and giving of love and work.

Mental disorder is a broad term covering every deviation from mental health, that is, from maturity combined with adjustment. This disorder may be primarily internal, in which case the deviations arise from within the personality. Or, the disorder may be chiefly external or *reactive*, as when a mature person is subject to excessive environmental pressures (as in time of war). Under great enough stress even the strongest personality may develop symptoms and may break down.

Mental is itself a term of mixed meanings. It is sometimes used to refer only to the intellect, as in *mental retardation*. It is often employed, however, to mean psychotic, as for example when a person suffers from severe anxiety, and he and his family want to be reassured that this is "nothing mental." But "mental" is also used very broadly to cover every manifestation of the life of the mind. In this connection *mind* means everything, conscious or unconscious, that it is possible to experience subjectively—thoughts, feelings. These things are primarily interpersonal and intrapersonal. Mind comprises all the forces of id and superego as the ego tries to harmonize them with each other and with reality. Thus, we could not experience psychologically, mentally, subjectively, consciously, the manufacture of additional white cells for our blood when we have an infection—this is *sub*psychological and not an emotional force, that is, not a motivation for the behavior of the organism as a unit.

Mental defect is also a very broad and imprecise term carrying different meanings. It is sometimes employed to mean only an intellectual deficiency, such as retardation; or, less frequently, it refers to a specific deficiency, such as a reading disability. It is not usually applied to neurotic symptoms (e.g., stage fright). It is rarely used in psychiatry and cannot be considered a psychiatric term of any established meaning. As used popularly and legally it may mean any deviation from mental health, intellectual or motivational. Used in this way it is applicable to almost everyone, since, as we have said, in this sense few if any persons enjoy perfect mental health.

Mental disease, some maintain, means a condition identical with or closely similar to what we know as organic disease, such as measles, cancer, heart disease, and the like. Dynamically, all the mental disorders do indeed have the characteristics of the physical diseases, but the popular connotation established by this association is apt to be misleading. Everyone understands that the body can, in response to infection, generate malaise and fever. Probably few, however, realize that mistreatment of a child can be internalized and lead to the formation of a harsh and rejecting superego. This, in turn, would generate in the id a reaction of hostility, which is projected and experienced by the child and later the adult as phobias or paranoid projections. A person with pervasive inferiority feelings and under powerful pressure of hostility may be as allergic to slights as an asthmatic is to ragweed pollen. Thus the processes of psychological pathology are the same as of bodily pathology, and the psychological disorders are true diseases.

In organic medicine we became accustomed to thinking of *disease entities* for which there is more or less specific treatment, medical or surgical. At present, however, in organic medicine, attention is focused less on entities than on *disease processes*. Psychologically, we deal with just such processes, disorders in the development of the total personality, often from birth. Tranquilizers may mollify tension and anxiety, but unlike the antibiotics for bacterial infections, they do not touch the basic cause. Psychodynamic therapy seeks causes and other elements whereby the pathways to emotional development are reopened. It is a matter of outgrowning old childhood emotional patterns that interfere with adult living and forming new, more mature ones. In the overwhelming majority of cases there is a deep-seated chronic personality disorder behind the symptoms, so that quick results are often temporary palliation and not removal of the cause. Perhaps in time drugs may be found that affect therapeutically some causal elements in certain emotional conditions as suggested by recent biochemical studies of psychotic depressions and schizophrenias.

Psychodynamics means, most simply, the interplay of *emotional forces*, that is, feelings, motivations, and reactions.

The term *paranoia* is used to refer to a psychosis presenting delusions of persecution of a rather clearly defined type, well rationalized and defended by the individual. These systematized delusions generally involve a more or less circumscribed portion of the personality although they tend to spread out, involving more and more. In this state of mind there may or may not be deterioration, the illness having essentially a chronic course and often remaining unchanged for years.

Masochism is a term that has come to have the broad meaning of acting unconsciously in ways that are injurious, even destructive, to the self. What looks at first like an external force beyond control or like a natural error of judgment, may be seen to repeat itself in a person's life over and over and assume an unmistakable pattern of behavior. This self-injuring trend seems regularly to consist primarily of hostility taken out unknowingly upon the self although there may also be other mechanisms operating.

Guilt may be an intermediate step in masochistic behavior. For example, the individual may feel so guilty and deserving of punishment that he actually courts it, directly or subtly. Guilt comes most often, but not exclusively, from hostility, or at least it is most often closely associated with it. For example, if a man ruins his marriage and deeply hurts his wife and children by having extramarital affairs, it is not necessarily the sexual relationships that make him guilty, but rather it is apt to be the hostility and injury to his wife and children that give rise to the guilt. Another mechanism is seen in the adult who was rejected as a child and therefore feels that because his own parents did not value him, he must be worthless and not deserving of success. Usually beneath this reaction, however, is a burning resentment for the feelings of rejection, with or without much guilt. The fact is that intense hostility is apt to rebound, injuring the self as well as others.

Self-injury can take any number of forms—having repeated major automobile accidents or accidents in sports or the home, making a bad marriage, subtly wrecking a good marriage or promising career, losing one's savings by gambling, antagonizing people, drinking, taking drugs, acting out criminally and being punished, ambitious striving beyond one's capacities, and every other kind of self-torment and self-defeat. Whether hostility is always taken out in some part on the self is not known. Perhaps there are completely criminal characters who were so mistreated and so trained in childhood that they can vent hostility upon others freely and without contrary conscience reactions. Such persons are generally considered to be monsters because they have no conflict over destructiveness and sadism to their own species.

History abounds with examples of mass masochism, which are reminiscent of the lemmings stampeding into the sea to their own death: Athens and Sparta destroying each other, almost welcoming Roman conquest as a relief from internecine strife; the Hundred Years War; and after it, the Wars of the Roses, that "indefatigable suicide" of the Anglo-Norman nobility. This masochism is not a fully solved problem, but usually at bottom it is a reflection back upon the individual, directly or through guilt, of his own hostility to others.

Personality disorder is a broad term used in at least two ways, one of which has a clear-cut psychodynamic meaning. Descriptively, it is used in psychiatry as roughly equivalent to "character disorder" in contrast with the terms "neurosis" or "psychosis." For example, a man is in all observable ways mature, loving, and responsible, but he has a fear of heights which he keeps secret. He is said to have a normal, healthy personality but to suffer from a neurosis, a phobia—meaning in this connection an area of psychopathology that is circumscribed. Dynamically it turns out that he has intense sibling rivalry because of his parents' preference for a younger brother. He reacted with excessive competitiveness and ambitions, symbolized by climbing the heights of success, but fraught with so much hostility and guilt toward others seen as rivals, on the pattern of his brother, that it produced the phobia, although the latter is well controlled and covered over by the healthy parts of his ego and superego. Psychodynamically, personality disorder refers to the underlying disorder, however circumscribed it may be in the development of the total personality. In this example it would be the hostile, guilty, excessively competitive dynamics. In this sense, every type of mental and emotional symptom (except organic and purely intellectual impairments, which are excluded from discussion in this book) is a manifestation of some area and degree of personality disorder.

Character disorder is a form of personality disorder in which what is usually and vaguely called a "good character" is deficient; that is, the individual fails to live up to the generally accepted standards of stability, responsibility, honesty, loyalty, and the like, which are necessary for civilized social living. Often he is too dominated by desires for immediate pleasure to be fully reliable and responsible. However, character disorder is too commonly used to designate any personality in which the psychopathology appears in the way of living instead of in symptoms (e.g., a series of marriages and divorces, making and losing money, etc.). Many alcoholics are clearly character disorders.

Personality means, psychodynamically, the makeup of a person's id, superego, and ego, that is, each individual's accustomed ways of thinking, feeling, reacting, and behaving. Each individual's environment is in part happenstance and in part what he consciously and unconsciously makes it. The makeup and accustomed functioning of the personality is predominantly a result of the emotional patterns formed in early childhood. It is these early influences that are internalized as superego and which favor or warp proper maturing of the id and the ego.

Sociopath is a diagnostic term. It means an individual in whom the disorder of personality is not much repressed. In such a person, for example, hostility is not expressed in psychosomatic or neurotic symptoms; instead, the hostility and much of the childhood emotional pattern that generates it is "acted out" in the person's behavior. If the hostility is strong and unrepressed, the condition has criminal elements in it; if not, then the person is more a nuisance to others and usually also to himself. He may be regarded merely as an eccentric. He may have a life pattern of an endless series of marriages and divorces, making and losing money, unconsciously getting himself discharged from jobs, getting in and out of scrapes with the law, and, in a variety of other ways, acting out a disordered childhood pattern of human relations and social maladjustment. Thus *sociopathic personality disturbance* is used to refer to individuals whose childhood emotional patterns distort their satisfactory conformance to social, cultural, and ethical standards, making them pathological in their social behavior. The term "sociopath" or "psychopath" generally is used to refer to an individual who is not readily classifiable as intellectually defective, neurotic, or psychotic, but whose behavior is characterized by what comes to be recognized as patterns of recurrently episodic impulsivity, irresponsibility, lack of emotional control, and inadequate or unstable educational, marital, occupational, and other social adaptations (i.e., aberrant social behavior), whose thinking, feeling, and behavior are too immature and maladjusted.

Abnormal mental condition is not a technical term but a general expression of the greatest scope, which is used to cover any and all deviations from mental health. But, as is usually the case when the word "mental" is used, this term can also be used more narrowly to mean psychotic. Here too, then, a fear of heights would be an abnormal mental condition in the broad sense, but not necessarily in the narrow. "Abnormal" is itself to some extent a misleading term, for it implies that the normal, in the meaning of average or majority of people, is healthy and that the deviations from this normal mental health are the exceptions, the abnormal. However, as discussed above, full mental health is rare. The abnormal, then, is in fact the condition that obtains among the majority. Thus to be useful in a specific situation, as in a court of law, the term "abnormal mental condition" must be sharply defined. Most people use the term "normal" to mean healthy, but often confuse it with an implication of average.

Some deviation from mental and emotional health and adjustment will be found in every defendant because it is present in nearly every person (and therefore in the lawyers, judge, and every member of the jury). Some relationship of deviation to criminal acting out is also almost inevitable, since nearly everything a person does is the expression in action to some degree of most or all of his motivations. It is particularly true that most of a person's psychopathological motivations (from his disordered childhood emotional patterns) enter into his pathological behavior. If a person committed a criminal act, it would be rare for it not to be, at least in part, an expression of his psychopathology. Hence, it is a foregone conclusion that, in every criminal case, psychopathology will be found, and that this, more in some cases, less in others, will be related to the criminal behavior.

Schizophrenic reaction is one of the relatively few basic psychological ways of reacting to emotional stress. The schizophrenic withdraws emotionally from relations with other persons and becomes much preoccupied with his own fantasies. The feelings that produce the fantasies usually give them a bizarre, dreamlike quality, which also is evident in the individual's thinking and behavior. Many or most people have schizophrenic reactions of at least a very mild degree at times when, under certain kinds of stress, they react by withdrawing emotionally. If this type of withdrawal is strong in a person, it may be recognized as an important trend in his makeup. Such a person may, however, be productive and successful and able to maintain a good family life. He may then be called *schizoid*—the most characteristic feature of which, besides a certain bizarreness of thinking, is the feeling that life lacks resonance and responsiveness. An emotionally healthy person may experience something like it if he awakens unable to shake loose from a particularly vivid absorbing dream, before he "has his coffee or shower." If the reaction is still stronger, it may be diagnosed as *ambulatory schizophrenia*. In the extreme the individual may withdraw so completely that he has little or no emotional contact with anyone, and his fantasies include gross distortions of reality such as illusions, delusions, and hallucinations. The person lives in a world of dreams, which he experiences as reality or which predominate over reality. In this extreme, his reality sense may be so warped that he is readily seen to be psychotic. Such a state of schizophrenia may be acute, episodic, self-limited, and sometimes brief; or it may be chronic and lifelong. So far as questions of insanity are concerned, the condition is significant only quantitatively, that is, only if it is so severe that the individual is psychotic.

* * * *

Official disposition of those convicted of crimes against the prevailing social order has, through the ages, taken six main forms: (1) elimination from society by execution; (2) separation from society by banishment (Russia's Siberia and England's colonies in America, (e.g., Georgia); (3) segregation or incarceration for specified periods (such as those that carry the offender through the period of youthful crime into a later age when criminal impulses are apt to be weaker and controls stronger; (4) punishment; (5) closely related to punishment, deterrence of the person from repetition of his criminal act, and of others from committing such acts; (6) rehabilitation (which, for reasons discussed above, has thus far been predictably ineffective).

Since criminal acting out is a form of personality disorder, it is folly to think of treatment in the ordinary terms of medical treatment, such as antibiotics for pneumonia. Rather it is a question of whether the condition can be influenced at all, and, if so, to what extent; and whether punishment by law would be an effective procedure as treatment, as a deterrent to the offender and others, and as a protection for society.

Thus Jim, the young man mentioned at the beginning of this chapter was committed as permanently and incurably dangerous because his hostility had produced two psychotic episodes and then the irrational, senseless murder of an attractive, able, promising young man. After two years the family requested that a new examination and evaluation of Jim be made in the hopes that he could be discharged into society. The problem in such a case becomes one of prognosis: Will Jim's experience of the last two years in a hospital for the criminally insane prove an adequate and permanent deterrent to him or have any effect at all? The basic question is: Will his personality disorder again generate enough hostility for some sort of episode, and, if so, what form will it take? Will it disrupt his ego functions to produce psychosis, or, with these functions relatively intact, will it again break through nakedly as murder of another innocent victim? Jim was discharged into society after two years, obtained an academic position in a small college, and has lived without incident that we know of for the past five years. He is enraged because some people who know his history do not completely trust him. At least one excellent psychiatrist thinks this reaction is severe enough to be termed "paranoid," and that he lives in an ambulatory paranoid state. Certain of the problems in the present system of dealing with criminals are fundamental. For example, it is the essence of democracy that everyone be considered equal before the law. This, of course, precludes recognition of individual differences. However, if a man snatches a purse, no rational disposition can be made without knowing his major motivations for this act, its relation to his personality, to his accustomed feelings, thinking, and behavior. Only with this knowledge can it be predicted with any confidence what his future behavior will be like, and whether it will be influenced by punishment or other procedures.

At one extreme the purse-snatching may be an isolated reactive bit of behavior in response to unusual physical or emotional strains. That such a combination of pressures will recur with this intensity may be unlikely. If the man's personality is mostly sound, he probably will not repeat the act. At the other extreme we have the confirmed, possibly compulsive purse-snatcher. His behavior in this respect is probably not influenceable by punishment or psychiatric treatment. In both of these examples the behavior is the result of emotional disorder but not of psychosis. In the first case there is no great need to protect society, but in the second there is. A third possibility is that the man is actually psychotic, perhaps schizophrenic. For practical and reasonable disposition it is essential to have a usable *psychodynamic diagnosis* in each individual case.

In regard to the emotional disorder, if a person commits an act in a florid, unmistakable psychotic state in which he has delusions and hallucinations, that is clear-cut. If the act is not committed in a psychotic state, then it is usually the result of an emotional disorder which, as we have stated, is a manifestation of a personality disorder. This arouses our sympathy for the man who commits the act, but that should not impair our primary obligation of protecting society. If a man has typhoid fever or smallpox, he has our full sympathy and should have the best medical treatment available, but the doctor's first duty is to protect society by quarantining the carrier of the contagion. For the protection of society it makes little difference whether criminals are thought of as bad or as sick, although the dynamics of the deed and the personality may be of great importance for disposition.

As we have reiterated, almost everyone has some form of personality disorder, but often it emerges in psychosomatic, neurotic, or other symptoms and not in directly hostile, criminal acting out—a useful new label would be "pathological hostile acting out." To say that the new criminal is not responsible for his acts because of how his childhood has shaped his personality is, for the most part, true; but this is true of *everyone*—none of us are completely and entirely responsible for how we are. All our personalities, with their heterogeneous traits, have been shaped in large degree by our childhood emotional reactions to those who reared us and were close to us. We have all been helped or warped in our growth toward maturity. Nevertheless, the more mature and responsible people, who have better personal relations and are better socialized, must protect themselves against the more infantile, warped, and hostile personalities. To do this is the prime function of the judicial system.

13 Hostility and Politics

In most . . . human beings . . . the need for support from an authority of some sort is so compelling that their world begins to totter if that authority is threatened.

Sigmund Freud

Nothing hurt [Martin] more than that man could attempt no way to solve problems except through violence. He gave his life in search of a more excellent way, a more effective way, a creative rather than a destructive way. We intend to go on in search of that way.

Coretta Scott King

For my own part I would as soon be descended from that heroic little monkey who braved his dreaded enemy in order to save the life of his keeper, or from that old baboon, who descending from the mountains, carried away in triumph his young comrade from a crowd of astonished dogs—as from a savage who delights to torture his enemies, offers up bloody sacrifices, practices infanticide without remorse, treats his wives like slaves, knows no decency, and is haunted by the grossest superstitions.

Charles Darwin, *The Descent of Man*

The population is a reservoir of conscious and unconscious hostility. Counterbalancing this threat to survival are morality, ethics, and law, which are expressions of the mature forces of cooperation upon which society is based and without which life in communities would be impossible. Demagogues rise to power chiefly by organizing and manipulating the latent hostility in the body politic, usually in the name of some worthy cause as a rationalization. Hence they so often begin with little lies, twists of the truth, and other corruptions of law, morality, and ethics—the dikes against the ever present sea of hostility—seeking to make little cracks that will widen to let through the latent elements of violence and permit criminal and criminoid action to be expressed eventually with little hindrance. Our central concern here is not with specific political actions and beliefs but only with the personal, emotional forces that influence and often determine an individual's political feelings. Because of its very nature, because of the freedom it provides, democracy is always threatened by tyranny, by the risk that the reservoir of pathological hostility in the population will be organized and directed by a skillful demagogue in the name of some appealing rationalizations.

The deepest sources of political attitudes lie in childhood. In general, adults repeat in their social and political experience the pattern of family government that they knew in childhood. Otto Klineberg did a fascinating survey, "Tensions Affecting International Understanding," for the Social Science Research Council. Among other findings Klineberg reported, during the Third Reich, authoritarian homes in Germany produced authoritarian (Nazi) adults, whereas anti-authoritarian homes produced democratic (anti-Nazi) adults. Many other sociological and anthropological studies have since sketched much the same pattern. Given the considerable amount of evidence that has been collected by researchers, we are safe in saying that democracy, as most of us consciously desire it to be, requires first and foremost the existence of basically democratic homes. This means homes wherein each member of the family has his individuality respected and his voice heard, and the children are reared without chronic arousal of their fight–flight reactions to make them violence-prone, sadistic adults.

Looking more closely, there are four fundamental problems that must be met in the course of family development. These are: (1) the child's attractions to and rivalries with brothers and sisters (or, if an only child, with other children); (2) the child's attractions to and rivalries with parents; (3) the child's adaptation to its dependent position in the custody of adults; and (4) the child's adaptation to the parents' position of power over him. The potential tyranny in these last two areas has already been discussed, in Chapters 5 and 6. Let us, therefore, turn to how political feelings may be affected by the adult's childhood experience of sibling rivalry and the parental relationship.

It is likely that the child's emotional problem of adapting to brothers and sisters is the root of later demands for equality among grown men and women. Children want equality of treatment from their parents and are much upset and angered by favoritism, and this feeling forms a foundation for the adult's desire for social, political, and economic equality. At the same time, the pathology of rivalry with brothers and sisters may provide the nucleus for pathology in an individual's later view of social equality. If one child is grossly favored over another, he may turn into a social being who expects, wishes, and demands that he himself or his small group be favored over other persons or other groups in society. Conversely, children who have been rejected often mature into adults who gravitate to the fringes of society, feeling that because they had not been accepted even by their own parents, they are unworthy of acceptance by their society. Many of them continues to yearn as intensely for love and acceptance as they did in childhood. Relentlessly they seek it, but, inexorably following their childhood pattern, they never achieve it, and continue their pattern of feeling unworthy and unacceptable.

It is probably in the child's relationship to its parents that the hierarchical pattern for all societies has its roots. One reason why democracy has been so constantly threatened from without as well as from within may be the despotism that is still exerted within so many homes. Children who come from families in which this is not true will not accept such a society; they say with Abraham Lincoln, "I would not be a master as I would not be a slave."

The basic problem arising out of the parental relationship that has political implications has to do with the adult still aggressively seeking to gain the power that he wished to have as a child so that he could be as strong as his parents. Perhaps this is most clearly seen in the relationship of a boy to his father. To the small child, the parents appear enormously big and powerful. Wishing to be like them, the child tries in many ways to be big and powerful also. If he develops well, if his parents understand and help him with this rivalry as with his sibling rivalry, he will solve these problems and eventually, as an adult, achieve a mature identification. But such childhood attitudes as dependence, submissiveness, and guilt, persisting strongly, make many adults continue to feel anxious and weak. Consequently they struggle, as it were, to be like the parent, not the child, in their relations with others. What they attempt to do is establish a predominant position for themselves with little regard for the realities and needs of other people. Unresolved relations to the father and the mother thus can become an important enemy of democracy and an aid to regimentation and dictatorship. For the child learns to think only in terms of what he knows—to be like his parents, strong masters, or, like himself, a helpless slave.

These family problems of childhood and the type of solution found by the child form one important factor in the individual's later social and political reactions and motivations. But other childhood motivations also are important, persisting as they do within the adult and shaping his views and behavior far more than his reason guesses. Indeed, *rationalization, not reason, rules the world.*

If we look at an individual like Hitler we see an example of the relationship between individual dynamics and group (in this case, national) dynamics. He was born in Austria in a town near the German border in 1889, when his father was 52 and his mother 29. He had a half brother (seven years older) and a half sister (six years older), both of whom had been born to his father's second wife, who died of tuberculosis. The father's third wife, Klara (Adolph's mother), had been a maid in the inn where he and his second wife lived. She had probably been his mistress for a number of years, and may in fact have been his niece. She was a devout Catholic, a meticulously clean housekeeper, and a woman of very little formal education.

Klara Hitler's first three children were born in rapid succession, and all died of natural causes within weeks of the birth of the third. Adolph was born during the year following these deaths. In the face of the compound tragedy of having three children die within a year, Klara was probably exceedingly anxious over the possibility of losing her fourth child. If so, she would have tended to be overprotective toward Adolph, who was sickly at birth. As Gertrud M. Kurth* has noted:

> It seems quite likely that, in what may have been a kind of panicky tension, Klara handled the infant at the breast in a manner that transmitted to the baby a threat of being overwhelmed . . . . Clearly, such maternal behavior is bound to interfere with the development of the infant's and the toddler's ego functions, specifically with the development of individuation and autonomy. Concomitantly, the child's ability to develop viable and ego-syntonic identifications and durable object relations is severely undermined. In fact, it is legitimate to say that the mother who stunts her child's development by forcing him to remain a baby for too long virtually "kills" some of the child's indispensable functions.

Hitler's father was a chunky, authoritarian customs inspector. During Adolph's childhood and youth, the often brutal father was locked in an intense struggle with his son. The battle was waged over the

*From "Hitler's Two Germanies, a Sidelight on Nationalism," Gertrude M. Kurth. In *Psychoanalysis and The Social Sciences,* edited by G. Roheim, 1973. International Universities Press, Inc., New York.

man's constant attempts to assert his dominance over the boy. Young Adolph was, in part, tempted to yield and become submissive to his father, but another part of his makeup panicked at this possibility and felt that his identity and integrity as a person would be swallowed up and destroyed if he yielded. The notion of submission became intolerable to him, and as a result he fought against it with all his psychic resources of defense. Typically, like every child, he saw only the two possible outcomes that he grew up experiencing: either submit and be destroyed psychologically, which was unthinkable, or else identify with the aggressor, that is, himself be the dominating one and thereby defend against being dominated. Most of this conflict raged within the boy unconsciously.

It is quite possible that Hitler's "hypothetical cases" of Viennese family life, which are described in *Mein Kampf*, are in fact thinly camouflaged accounts of his own experiences. If this is indeed the case, and there is considerable evidence supporting this notion, then the passages in *Mein Kampf* offer us a revealing picture of Adolph Hitler's family life during childhood. Here is an excerpt:*

> So, from their earliest days, the young children become familiar with misery. But things end badly indeed when the man from the very start goes his own way and the wife, for the sake of her children, stands up against him. Quarreling and nagging set in, and in the same measure in which the husband becomes estranged from his wife, he becomes familiar with alcohol. Now he is drunk every Saturday, and in her instinct of self-preservation for herself and her children, the wife fights for the few pennies which she wrangles from him, and frequently her sole opportunity is on his way from the factory to the saloon. When he finally comes home on Sunday or Monday night, drunk and brutal, but always without a last cent and penny, then God have mercy on the scenes which follow. I witnessed all of this personally in hundreds of scenes and at the beginning with disgust and indignation; but later I began to grasp the tragic side and to understand the deeper reasons for their misery.

Again from *Mein Kampf* we have this passage:*

> Now let us imagine the following: In a basement apartment of two stuffy rooms lives a worker's family of seven people. Among

*From *Mein Kampf* by Adolph Hitler, translated by Ralph Manheim. Copyright 1943 and © renewed 1971 by Houghton Mifflin Company. Reprinted by permission of Houghton Mifflin Company.

> the five children there is a boy, let us say, of three. This is the age at which a child becomes conscious of his first impressions. In many intelligent people, traces of these early memories are found even in old age. The smallness and the over-crowding of the rooms do not create favorable conditons. Quarreling and nagging often arise because of this. In such circumstances people do not live with one another, but on top of one another. Every argument, even the most unimportant, which in a larger apartment would take care of itself for the reason that one could step aside, leads to a never-ending, disgusting quarrel. Among the children this does not usually matter; they often quarrel under such circumstances and forget completely and quickly. But when the parents fight almost daily, their brutality leaves nothing to the imagination; then the results of such visual education must slowly but inevitably become apparent in the little ones. Those who are not familiar with such conditions can hardly imagine the results, especially when the mutual differences express themselves in the form of brutal attacks on the part of the father towards the mother or to assaults due to drunkenness. The poor little boy, at the age of six, senses things which would make even a grown up person shudder.

This also implies a conflict in the child, Adolf, between identifying with the beaten mother or the brutal father. The sanction for violence is transmitted by the child's repeatedly witnessing the violence between the parents.

When Adolph was eight years old, the family moved to a new town, at least in part for the purpose of gaining better educational opportunities for the boy. Here the school was attached to a Benedictine monastery. Already we can see the young boy's fascination with the idea of domination. He was intrigued by the black-robed monks and particularly taken with the abbot ruling over his flock with absolute authority. The church ritual and ecclesiastical music delighted him, and he took singing lessons and joined the church choir. In *Mein Kampf* he says: "Again and again I enjoyed the best possibility of intoxicating myself with the solemn splendor of the dazzling festivals of the church." Later he wrote that "it seemed to me perfectly natural to regard the Abbot as the highest and most desirable ideal, just as my father regarded the village priest as his ideal." His fantasy life seemed to center around ways of joining the community of monks and eventually becoming the all-powerful abbot. It is noteworthy that one of the abbots had his coat of arms displayed on the church, and it prominently contained a swastika.

Adolph's conflicts with his father persisted, and the boy more and more reacted to the threat of the older man's domination with fear, rage, and a drive to dominate others. (As usual, the bullied child bullies others; the child who has grown up knowing only cruel treatment treats others cruelly.) By the time he was 11, he had developed many difficulties in social and academic adjustment. A teacher remembers the boy at 12 as "definitely gifted, but only in a one-sided way, for he was lacking in self-control, and to say the least he was regarded as argumentative, willful, arrogant and bad-tempered, and he was notoriously incapable of submitting to school discipline." Adolph became interested in reading and constantly poured over military accounts, which he found in popular magazines, of the Franco-Prussion War of 1870–1871. He then discovered Karl May, who wrote fictional pieces about the "Redskins" of the American Wild West. These stories appeared every few months and featured as a hero Old Shatterhand, an American cowboy who specialized in slaughtering Indians. This grandios hero justified his butchering by his own innate infallibility and by his claims that the Redskins were an inferior race. When all the Redskins were done away with, Old Shatterhand moved to Persia and slaughtered Arabs. (Years later, when the Nazi armies invaded Russia, Hitler sometimes referred to the Russians as Redskins.)

When Adolph was 13 years old, his father died of a lung hemorrhage. He wrote in *Mein Kampf* that this event "plunged us all into the depths of despair." Although he became the male head of the family, there was little visible evidence of any permanent change in the boy. He continued to have difficulties at school and gained a reputation for baiting teachers and quarreling with students. Even though his father was now dead, and thus the threat of domination was removed, Adolph's pattern of response to that conflict continued unabated, for it was by now a deeply ingrained feature of his personality, a set part of his childhood emotional pattern.

By the time he was 15, his teachers had apparently had enough of this troublesome boy, and he was expelled from school. His mother then arranged for him to attend a school in another town and to live in a boarding house. Although his academic work was poor, he managed to receive a certificate that his work was completed. However, this did not entitle him to proceed to higher education. The night that he received this certificate he went out to celebrate, and after getting drunk he passed out on the road. A milkman woke him the next morning, and he had a complete amnesia for the previous night. The certificate was gone, and he had to apply for a copy. When he went to pick up the duplicate certificate, the school principal called him in and showed him the original, which was torn into four pieces and covered with brown stains. Apparently he had used it as toilet paper when he had gotten drunk. Nothing could more clearly have expressed his total contempt for school and authority. Years later he wrote that he considered most teachers to be mad and poor influences on their pupils. And even as der Fuhrer, he is reported to have passed flatus unceasingly. We cannot be sure if this has a psychosomatic meaning, but it is of interest in this connection.

As is usually the case in conditioning experiences, the pattern of reaction established in childhood toward a parent spreads to other people and situations involving authority and power. Young Adolph's fear and rage in the face of the threatened domination by his father came to characterize all his later experiences. When he went to Vienna for the first time, he became intrigued with the social democratic party. However, when he was informed as a workman that he *must* join a trades union (which was a socialist body), his favorable disposition toward the party changed radically. The notion of being forced to do anything was abhorrent to him, and he refused to join on those grounds alone. With ever increasing violence he argued that he would under no circumstances yield to the demands of the socialists. Finally he was told that he must join the union or leave the job. If he refused both these alternatives, he was assured of being thrown off the scaffolding. In *Mein Kampf* he reports that he gave way to terrorism and left his job.

Combined with this abhorrence of what he felt as being dominated was, as we have said, Hitler's powerful drive to dominate others, which was probably in part defense against being dominated by his father through identification with him (i.e., "identification with the aggressor"). One key aspect of Hitler's fascination with the past military glories of Germany and the violent destruction of "inferior races," which developed early and intensified during adulthood, was his fantasy of being stronger and more powerful than his hated father. He seems to have made a connection between his father and Austria. He detested the Hapsburg monarchy that ruled Austria and catered to such "inferior races" as the Czechs, Slavs, Bohemians, and Hungarians. He longed for the day when Austria could be reunited with Germany so the Austrians of Germanic background would again be supreme rather than only another minority group in Austria. Symbolically, Germany's triumph over undeserving and inferior races probably represented his own victory over his father. Of course, he himself was born Austrian and not German. For him, being German probably meant achieving identification with the strong, brutal father.

It would also represent his own victory over himself, that is, over the weak submissive part of himself that wanted to submit to his father's domination. He hated this aspect of himself, this weakness, and he detested anything or anyone that reminded him of it. Many books have recently appeared detailing Hitler's personality, and it seems likely that part of this weakness may have consisted also of his underlying overattachment to his mother and his failure to mature out of it, partly because of fear of his father. Since, lacking adequate information, it is not our goal to diagnose his precise dynamics, we will only note that some of the resulting hostility that grew out of his sense of weakness was directed against himself. Hitler's masochism and sadism are dramatically revealed in his orders to his generals near the end of the war to stand and fight even in the face of certain disaster. Chronicles of the war report how, for example, German soldiers were forced to die on the near bank of a river when they could easily have retreated to the other side, which could have been defended. But Hitler forbade retreat. To the very end, even when defeat was clearly in sight, Hitler's orders were always to yield no ground but to fight to the death, to the very last man. This entailed needless slaughter and suffering. But for Hitler negotiation was unthinkable, just as it had never been possible for him as a child with his father.

In analyzing Hitler's character, Robert Payne had this to say:*

> If he resembled anyone at all [we note that he was not so different dynamically from others we have sketched in this book], it was Dostoevsky's ill-tempered "underground man" . . . . His strength lay in the fact that he was totally alienated; it was all one to him whether he conquered the world or shot himself in the mouth . . . . What Hitler was committed to was his own rage, his own destructive

*From *The Life and Death of Adolph Hitler* by Robert Payne: © 1973 by Robert Payne, Excerpted by permission of Holt, Rinehart and Winston.

fury . . . it seems unbelievable a single man could cause such havoc. [We note that a single man only detonated a population ready for him.] What he sought to do, what he very nearly succeeded in doing, was to dominate the entire world and reshape it according to his own desires, as though the world had been created for his pleasure . . . . There was madness in him almost from the beginning. His mind was a distorted mirror in which he saw himself as a vast imperial figure, overshadowing the world, the supreme judge and executioner, the destined master who had come to cleanse the world of its iniquities. His ferocious hatreds fed on mythologies, which he only half believed, and he had no deep affection for the Germans, who became the willing instruments of his self-serving will to power. In his dreams he saw himself as one marked by destiny, protected by a divine providence, but destiny and providence have their own mythologies. Because he lived, 40 million people died, most of them in agony, and as though this were not enough, he spent his last days giving orders for the destruction of Germany, devoutly hoping no German would be left alive to mourn over their defeats. "They are not worthy of me," he said. Such was his ultimate verdict on the people who had obeyed him as blindly as the children obeyed the Pied Piper of Hamelin.

Here, of course, lies the sociological key. It was not Hitler alone, it was the pathologically hostile child within the millions of his followers who identified with his dynamics that created the national tyranny and sadism. Because of how atrociously so many children are raised, there are always many of them—youths and adults—filled with "irrational, pathological hostility," ready and even eager to follow such a leader.

Winston Churchill wrote in *The Gathering Storm:**

After the end of the World War of 1914 there was a deep conviction and almost universal hope that peace would reign in the world. This heart's desire of all the peoples could easily have been gained by steadfastness in righteous convictions, and by reasonable common sense and prudence . . . [but] the peoples, transported by their sufferings and by the mass teachings with which they had been inspired, stood around in scores of millions to demand that retribution should be exacted to the full . . . . no one in great

*From *The Gathering Storm* by Winston S. Churchill. Copyright renewed 1976 by Lady Spencer-Churchill, Lady Audley and Lady Soames. Reprinted by permission of Houghton Mifflin Company.

authority had the wit, ascendancy, or detachment from public folly to declare these fundamental, brutal facts to the electorates; nor would anyone have been believed if he had. History will characterize all these transactions as insane . . . .

Thus, both in Europe and in Asia, conditions were swiftly created by the victorious Allies which, in the name of peace, cleared the way for the renewal of war . . . . the final safeguard of a long peace was cast away. The crimes of the vanquished find their background and their explanation, though not, of course, their pardon, in the follies of the victors. Without these follies crime would have found neither temptation nor opportunity.

Thereafter mighty forces were adrift; the void was open and into that void after a pause there strode a maniac of ferocious genius, the repository and expression of the most virulent hatreds that have ever corroded the human breast—Corporal Hitler.

Crimes were committed by the Germans, under the Hitlerite domination to which they allowed themselves to be subjected, which find no equal in scale and wickedness with any that have darkened the human record.

It is my purpose, as one who lived and acted in these days,first to show how easily the tragedy of the Second World War could have been prevented; how the malice of the wicked was reinforced by the weakness of the virtuous . . . .

The following capsule seems worth quoting here also, especially as it was by an interested layman, Albert Einstein,* and not a psychiatrist, or sociologist or politician:

The Germans have been trained in hard work and made to learn many things, but they also have been drilled in slavish submission, military routine and brutality . . . . then came inflation and depression, with everyone living under fear and tension. Hitler appeared, a man with limited intellectual abilities and unfit for any useful work, bursting with envy and bitterness against all whom circumstance and nature had favored over him. Sprung from the lower middle class, he had just enough class conceit to hate even the working class which was struggling for greater equality in living

*Excerpts from *Albert Einstein, The Human Side: New Glimpses from his Archives,* selected and edited by Helen Dukas and Banesh Hoffmann. (Copyright ©1979 by the Estate of Albert Einstein), published by Princeton University Press, pp. 18–112. Reprinted by permission of Princeton University Press.

standards. But it was the culture and education which had been denied him forever that he hated most of all. In his desperate ambition for power he discovered that his speeches, confused and pervaded with hate as they were, received wild acclaim from those whose situation and orientation resembled his own. He picked up this human flotsam on the streets and in the taverns and organized them around himself. This is the way he launched his political career.

But what really qualified him for leadership was his bitter hatred of everything foreign and, in particular, his loathing of a defenseless minority, the German Jews. Their intellectual sensitivity left him uneasy and he considered it, with some justification as, un-German.

Incessant tirades against these two "enemies" won him the support of the masses to whom he promised glorious triumphs and a golden age. He shrewdly exploited for his own purposes the centuries-old German taste for drill, command, blind obedience and cruelty. Thus he became the *Fuehrer.*

Money flowed plentifully into his coffers, not least from the propertied classes who saw in him a tool for preventing the social and economic liberation of the people which had its beginning under the Weimar Republic. He played up to the people with the kind of romantic, pseudo-patriotic phrasemongering to which they had become accustomed in the period before the World War, and with the fraud about the alleged superiority of the "Aryan" or "Nordic" race, a myth invented by the anti-Semites to further their sinister purposes. His disjointed personality makes it impossible to know to what degree he might actually have believed in the nonsense which he kept on dispensing. Those, however, who rallied around him or who came to the surface through the Nazi wave were for the most part hardened cynics fully aware of the falsehood of their unscrupulous methods. (Dukas and Hoffman)

Probably the intensity of Hitler's conflict over domination versus submission and sadism versus masochism contributed much to his genius for sensing power in politics. It was doubtless a large element in his spellbinding oratory, for he aroused a response by the power of his own passions. To shed some light on this feature of Hitler's personality, we can look briefly at the case of a young woman who believed she had telepathic powers. In a way, she was partly right, in the sense that she was so keyed up by intense emotions that she could discern the faintest cues, which the more tranquil would miss. Her ego could barely control her feelings and she was constantly in a hypersensitive state. The emotional intensity, threatening her ego with psychotic breakdown, kept her hyperacute and stretched to the very extreme of intuitiveness. In like manner, Hitler was keyed to the highest pitch short of emotional collapse. He could just barely restrain his egoistic and sadistic drives to dominate and control others. The intensity of his own feelings, conveyed through his skilled, demagogic speeches, evoked a resonance in all those with similar emotional dynamics in their makeup. These people, of course, developed their dynamics just as Hitler did—that is, by the way they were treated by their mothers and fathers. The dynamics were sufficiently similar to unite all persons with these dynamics (dread and denial of weakness and submissiveness, drive for power, sadism, and basic masochism).

Here the question suggests itself: What are the relationships between national characteristics, such as authoritarianism, and child-rearing practices and family life? Further: What are the relationships between social and economic conditions and an individual's psychological orientation and response to experience? Child-rearing practices, that is, the specific ways in which members of the family interact and satisfy (or thwart) instinctual needs, are at once an expression of and a determinant of the behavior and personality traits of the individual members of the society and of the character of the culture. The relationship between the way people think, feel, and behave and the character of their culture arises out of the way they adapt to specific situations. Thus it is always a matter of the dynamics of the personalities of the leader and his followers, including the national and racial traditions and ideals that are a part of their makeup, interacting with the current, external situations and pressures. Hitler at another time, say that of Frederick the Great, might have had few followers. But the German trauma of defeat following 1918 created a special set of circumstances. Gertrud M. Kurth* believes that the enormous deprivations that the Germans had to endure during and immediately following World War I played an essential role in the people's compliance with Hitler's wishes and demands (and we have quoted Churchill's view of this).

> The shortage of supplies vital for survival—food, fuel and the like—was severe enough to cause extensive suffering and regressive anxiety.

*From "Hitler's Two Germanies,a Sidelight on Nationalism," Gertrude M. Kurth. In *Psychoanalysis and The Social Sciences,* edited by G. Roheim, 1973. International Universities Press, Inc., New York.

However, the Inflation of the early 1920s and the Depression of the early 1930s, entailing unemployment and poverty, brought the additional shortage of emotional supplies such as self-esteem and self-confidence. In other words, *it was this unique combination of economic and social crises that made it possible for Hitler to activate in the German people the same unconscious conflicts as motivated him.* [Italics by L. J. S.]

When Hitler was asked how he could possibly put into effect such a program as he envisioned, he replied: "No problem–*the kind of men* we want will flock to us from all over Europe." It was this kind of men that made Hitler and Nazism possible.

As one single example, the story of the destructiveness and ultimate self-destruction of Adolph Hitler and Nazi Germany provides a vivid illustration, and caution, that politics and political feeling cannot be considered apart from the concerns of psychodynamics. Politics serves as an expression not only of an individual's immediate estimate of what he wants for his welfare, but often also of his entire personality makeup. What a person wants for himself, how strongly he wants it, how much he considers the well-being of others, whether or not he would actually sacrifice others for his own goals, how far he will go with his hostilities to achieve his ends, how clearly he sees that his own well-being is intimately tied to his society's well-being–all these factors depend upon the *kind of person* he is. And this, of course, results from his childhood emotional pattern. There is a dynamics of political feeling that reflects the dynamics of the personality.

It is likely that when Hitler became master of Germany, he felt an identification with his hostile violent father. But no one can escape his childhood emotional pattern. Perhaps then the world came to represent his father. He attacked it and the outcome was, inevitably, what it would have been if, as a child, he had attacked his father directly–defeat and punishment. This probably was a result of his inescapable masochism. At the height of his triumphs and power, when Rommel had swept North Africa and Italy was an ally and intrinsic part of the Axis, it took no military strategist to see that Hitler's army was unopposed if Hitler linked with Japan; then, at the height of her power after winning the Indian Ocean, with the United States not a belligerent, he could have won the war. But at this point of triumph, at the beginning of winter, against the advice of the German General Staff, against all reason, he insisted on attacking Russia.

At about this time a friend with whom I was discussing the war remarked: "Don't worry, Hitler must lose. The psychological forces against him are too strong." I thought my friend meant the psychological forces of the free world. Now I wonder if he meant the unconscious masochism in Hitler himself, and in many of his followers. For could Hitler have survived his childhood without psychosis if he did not have some love from his mother, and must this love not have formed in him some conscience, however rudimentary? Would this not have created an element of guilt? And would this guilt not have contributed to his masochism? Did not the overwhelming majority of his followers have similar dynamics? Had not the remaining Catholicism and the effects of Luther, Goethe, and Beethoven left some inescapable conscience in that people and culture? If my friend meant psychological forces in people throughout the world, he was doubtless correct. I think the major cause of this worldwide hostility to Hitler was fear and hatred of the naked, monstrous egotism and sadism for which he stood, from murdering and plundering the Jews and other eastern European minorities to the sacrificing of whole armies of the German Wehrmacht. He carried human hostility so far, especially in as cultured a country as Germany, as to cause a reaction of fear and revulsion throughout the world, even in those who were themselves hostile, egocentric, even criminal. Hitler's raw id was just too much to tolerate, coming out so nakedly as to threaten our very concept of humanness. If he could be that much of a beast, could not anyone? He threatened our own humanness, and he had to be destroyed: unconditional surrender was the only way. The naked beast within Hitler lent him fascination for the world initially, but ended in uniting the world psychologically against him.

* * * *

Permission for American Nazis to rally and march is strongly supported by the American Civil Liberties Union on the basis of freedom of speech.

Because there are only about 1500 Nazi party members in the United States today, the substantive issue is not of immediate urgency. Reading the arguments pro and con, however, one is struck by the preoccupation with abstract concepts and intellectual opinions to the almost complete neglect of what is surely a central concern, namely, the emotional element. We recognize this emotional basis in sports, where cheerleaders have become an intrinsic fixture, trying to whip up sufficiently strong feelings to influence the vigor of the teams. The main issue in marches and rallies is not to influence reason but to stir up feelings and emotions, as every demagogue knows. What emotions? Chiefly, hostility.

The potential for hostile impulses, feelings, and behavior is within every individual. We have laws against assault and against murder, as well as laws against plotting such violence. But the greater danger to the rule of law in society comes from *inciting* to assault or murder. Is it not ironic that we have laws against inciting to violence when the violence is unorganized, but we protect violence by law when it is organized? Freedom of speech is a foundation of democracy, but there is something wrong when its guarantees are used to support an evil against which our country and the world expended more than 60 million lives in World War II. The assurance of "inalienable rights," "life, liberty and the pursuit of happiness," is also a cornerstone of democracy. Are we using one basic right–freedom of speech–to threaten an even more elemental right, to life, liberty, and the pursuit of happiness? The avowed purpose of the Nazi rallies is robbery and murder.

How can this hostility of man to man, group to group, the essential evil of the human race, be allowed to incite recognized crimes and not be forbidden by law, not to mention being forbidden by the Judeo-Christian religion and ethic? Should the law not recognize more clearly and explicitly the incitement of hostile feelings, emotions, and motivations as crime that is no less criminal just because it is perpetrated by a so-called religion, such as some cults, or labeled "political" by its members?

Emotion is accepted in courts of law as motive (e.g., crimes of "passion") and so is "incitement" (e.g., to riot), but the law has not really faced such emotions and motivations squarely nor dealt with them directly. If it did, we would have no such heated and confused arguments over a clear-cut issue each time the Nazi Party or other advocates of organized violence sought a permit to rally. If existing laws do not protect a minority group in our society, then obviously we need new laws .

Sometimes political feelings result from very specific relationships to parents and siblings, whereas in other cases they are derived from more general emotional dynamics. In either instance, of course, we are discussing only the personal, that is idiosyncratic, element in political feelings and not the normal and expectable reactions to real pressure, frustration, and injustice in society. This is hard to grasp, and therefore everyone's view of political reality is so readily colored and distorted by his emotions. Here especially the intellect and grasp of reality are the slaves of the emotions.

Nazism could happen again, in any nation—if the socioeconomic, political, historical, philosophical, psychological, and other conditions acted to mobilize the impulses to violence and sadism in a sufficient number of the population; leaders whose overintense personal dynamics fitted this situation would inevitably arise. Let us not forget, however, that the dynamics of personality interacting with the conditions of the times make not only Hitlers but such constructive, pro-human leaders as Thomas Jefferson, Andrew Jackson, and Abraham Lincoln. Little is known of the childhood emotional patterns of these great Americans, but they are worth brief mention at least as an indicator from which we can attempt to draw correct conclusions from even such inadequate data.

Political feelings arising from specific relationships in the family are exemplified by two brothers, Ted and Bill. The boys had a colorless, submissive mother and a strict, dominating father whose word was law in the household. As a child, Ted, who was two years older than his brother, found that his best *modus vivendi* with his father was an unquestioning obedience, which obviated all conflict with him. As an adult Ted fully accepted his father's unbending religious orthodoxy, his authoritarian political views and party affiliation, his rigid conventionality. What rebellion he had against the paternal molding was so effectively repressed that no signs of it were discernible. Politically then, Ted became the completely obedient follower, a dupe for the demagogue and the power-hungry. Here was a man conditioned to regimentation, afraid of equality and democratic expression.

Not so the two-years-younger brother. Bill conformed, but only outwardly. A little beneath the surface seethed his rebellion until, just after adolescence, it finally emerged. Bill was slightly preferred over Ted by his mother and given more emotional support by her. This gave him the security to accept his rebellion against his father while keeping a surface peace. He left home and swung to the opposite sides from his father on all major issues. He defied convention with drinking and sexual excess, turning openly against his father's church, and jumped all the way to the opposite side of the political fence, joining noisy protest groups where he could speak and act out his revolt.

Here, then, are two sons of the same family who develop political feelings and identifications that are extreme opposites. But in both boys there are underlying personality factors that are reactions to the same parent. Why these reactions assume different forms is a matter of the specific quantitative differences in all the emotional influences on each of the brothers. In this case the younger brother was slightly preferred over Ted by his mother, and clearly preferred over his father; he was given more emotional support by her, as well as receiving a certain indulgence from his father. All this gave him the security to rebel.

Another example of a specific relationship contributing to political feelings is that of Nancy, a young girl whose mother was one of those forceful widows who take hold of a business on the husband's death and drive on to outstanding financial success, while continuing at the same time to dominate the family. Neglected by her mother, and even resented by her as an interference with her career, Nancy was entrusted to a martinet of a governess, who did not hesitate to beat the little girl into submission. Probably only a good relationship to a younger brother as a fellow sufferer saved Nancy from a psychotic breakdown as an adult. As it was, when she grew up she "spread" her feelings of hostility against her mother to include all wealthy people and all successful business people. Politically she became what her mother's friends called "a traitor to her class." Various attempts were made by Nancy's family to blame her seditious political attitudes on the girl's leftist teachers and the radical students whom she had befriended in college. However, external elements actually played a very minor role in her particular political activities. On the contrary, it was her hostility and rebellion toward her mother and governess that drove her into identifying with radicals in college, and not vice versa. She influenced them more than they influenced her.

In contrast to Nancy, we see individuals in whom external events evoke repressions and regressions. Hugh sought help allegedly because of stomach trouble and sleeplessness. He was a young man of high ideals who entered politics in an effort to break a corrupt machine. The fight involved many men who were out only for themselves and had little interest in the good of their party, and less, or none, in the welfare of their constituency. Hugh found that to accomplish anything at all he had to work and cooperate with many a criminoid and even criminal character. He was infuriated by them to the point of losing his appetite for food and ability to relax and sleep. He was mature enough to have a true interest in others, but not mature enough or secure enough in his own identity or sense of independence to have the strength to stand alone and use all he learned for socially constructive ends. Overly indulged in his own childhood, Hugh had tendencies to act for his own advantage regardless of others, even to the extent of being criminoid himself. If his associates had themselves been mature and working primarily for the public good, he probably would have identified with them, taken them as models, and gradually grown to that stature. But corrupt as they were, he was torn between his childish reward-seeking pattern and his avowed mature drives toward the good of others.

In all the vignettes sketched above, political feelings arose, as we have said, out of emotional relationships within the family that were quite specific. We now look at an example of political feelings deriving from more *general* emotional dynamics. Glen, a recently married young man, has just embarked upon his career. He is a kindly person with good feelings for most people, but a streak of prejudice against those less fortunate than himself. In analysis it soon appears that Glen represses and is quite unconscious of pathologically intense envy of those who have more money and more elaborate homes than he has. His feelings are quite unreasonable because he cannot expect at his young age the income of those who are much older and more experienced. However, the infantile motivations do not respect such realities of time. The unconscious, as Freud said, is timeless. The child wants what it wants at the moment it wants it. Glen is not even vaguely conscious of his hostility, born of envy, toward the older men who are his benefactors; he acts in a friendly way to his superiors at work because he likes them and they like him, and he is grateful for their attention and help. Also he fears they might otherwise fire him or in some other way damage his career. So he ingratiates himself with them and projects his hostility onto those who are less well off than he is.

In them he sees the envious competition that he dares not face in himself (which derived mostly from his sibling envy of a preferred older brother), and he fears that they will take away what he has, although it is actually he who wishes to take from those who have more than he himself has. It does not occur to him that in reality he is closer to the young men in his firm than to his seniors. In a parallel pattern his political feelings develop: he distrusts the poor, the foreign, the have-nots, and the underdogs, and casts his arguments and votes only to aid the successful to be more successful. He represses his envious hostility toward the haves and identifies with them, turning his hostility on the have-nots.

A similar mechanism is encountered in some self-made men. One who came originally for advice about his daughter showed a typical pattern. Although this man wore expensive tailor-made suits, although a chauffeur waited outside for him, although his honors were many and distinguished, he saw himself in his mind's eye as still a poverty-stricken immigrant laborer slaving at a menial job. His envy of those successful people who were now his friends was as intense and competitive as it had been when he was at the bottom of the ladder. But of none of this was he aware; he repressed it out of shame and guilt and the practical need for their approval and help. The hostility thus engendered found its outlet only against those—the poor and needy—who reminded him of his one-time inferiority, of the things he could not stand in himself. Of course this is not the pattern of all self-made men. To be sure, many are especially understanding and generous toward those who started with them but did not rise so far. But there are also those who never outgrow the childhood feelings of inferiority and poverty ingrained in their souls, an outcome that can be due to socioeconomic and also personal family reasons. The man we have just mentioned never outgrew the grinding poverty in which he was reared, and into this situation played his complaining, somewhat paranoid father and his own position of neglected youngest child of eight children. The poverty acted directly but also, and most strongly, through its effects upon the personalities and interpersonal relations in the family, especially through the overworked, ever striving, always frustrated and complaining father.

A rather different mechanism was seen in a man who was the somewhat neglected middle child of a large family. Ross felt he had to compete for any love and attention he might get. Being rather deprived and unwanted, he felt an inferiority that he masked with a great show of amiability. As a businessman Ross continued to strive unremittingly for love, prestige, and a feeling of belonging, changing his views and attitudes to suit his associates. Inevitably this pattern was reflected in his politics. While Ross was a struggling apartment dweller in the city, he identified with the underdog, but when he moved to a fashionable suburb, he unhesitatingly switched his identification and affiliations in efforts to find acceptance (real or imagined) with his advantaged neighbors.

Here are two complementary examples of other outcomes of domination in childhood. Larry was a brilliant but unfulfilled man who had grown up an only child, much dominated by his mother and grandmother. He recalled several times how, when his grandmother wanted his grandfather to do something and the grandfather did not immediately comply but said he would do it later, the old woman would give him a terrible tongue-lashing. Larry became a frightened little boy, always feeling that he must comply and repress all rebellion against his grandmother and his equally strong-willed mother. He thus lived in constant fear and guilt, and, as a defense, developed an exaggerated need to be very good and very obedient in order to assure himself of the love of his mother and grandmother and avoid punishment by them. So great was this need and also his training to show no anger or even feel it, that he could not bear any violence, even in a motion picture.

When Larry came for help, he was oppressed by a feeling that he must work all the time—a "workaholic." He was unable to take even a single day off, not because of a great interest in his work, but because of his anxiety and sense of obligation. Often he felt as though his mother and grandmother were standing over him telling him that he must work, work, work. Even the wishes of his wife for a vacation could not help him chase this ghost, this mother-grandmother imago. Larry's behavior in areas other than his work was excessively passive. He was in no way active politically except in his dreams. In this arena he often projected the power conflict onto the political scene and identified and sympathized with the downtrodden, whom he saw as himself in childhood seeking freedom from oppression.

An almost opposite case was that of Ralph, a man whose effort to solve the same problem was made by identifying with the oppressor. He projected his mother's domination onto those who were in political power and identified with them. His own submissiveness was projected onto the underdog, whom he felt he must conquer as he himself had been conquered. Ralph feared that if he did not hold complete control, others might try to run his life just as his mother had done. In other words, he saw the world as he did in childhood—

either dominate or be dominated. Ralph dared not cease to dominate lest he become the one who was dominated. This is typical. Most people see the world in the narrow restricted confines of their childhood relations to parents and siblings, in which they had to be on one side or the other, missing the many alternatives.

These examples are meant to illustrate how the underlying dynamics of personality can influence or even determine a person's political feelings and attitudes. No attempt has been made to survey the various specific and general emotional mechanisms. Our attention has been confined to political *feelings*, to the importance of the emotional factors involved with no reference to any actual facts of political life. Of course not all political feelings are entirely emotional; people try to react, usually for their self-interest, to the rational and realistic elements in politics. But the point of this is that most political feelings do have some unconscious "rationalized" emotional components. Hence the dictum to avoid arguments by never discussing politics or religion, into which unconscious emotional elements generally enter.

Projection, that is, unconsciously denying motivations in oneself by experiencing them as though they were in others, is counteracted by reality sense, reenforced by experience and knowledge. Groups and nations are hard to know realistically, and thus there is little corrective for immature, emotionally dictated attitudes. Therefore, as we have noted previously, many can imagine a foreign nation or an unknown or simply unfamiliar group as having all sorts of characteristics and motives, projected from one's own unconscious impulses, with little appreciation of the members as actual persons.

In the following, the projected hostility was directed not to another human being or group but to a stereotyped notion of an animal. Bob, a man with very high standards, had a terrible quarrel with his wife one evening, with much rage aroused in both. He retired and dreamed that two snakes were whirling around together, menacingly. Then one of the snakes came threateningly toward the dreamer, tongue darting and tail rattling; Bob tried to step on it but failed in a clumsy fashion. After telling this dream, Bob went on to say that snakes were dangerous, venomous, and deadly, and that one must be sure to destroy them. It occurred to him, however, that the snakes in the dream represented his anger of the night before, concerning which he felt much shame and guilt. Bob thought that it was awful to fight this way with his wife, and that some of the things that he attempted to say to her, but fortunately did not, were really vicious. In regard to his clumsiness in stepping on the snake in the dream, he thought of his difficulty in actually doing anything like that in reality (just as he could not strike or even verbally injure anyone, especially his wife, even if he were threatened).

These few associations (amplified by many supporting ones) will suffice to illustrate the central mechanism of the dream. Bob goes to bed distressed and critical of himself because of the fight with his wife. In the dream he handles this sleep-disturbing stimulus by saying: "No, it is not my wife and myself fighting, it is only two snakes. It is not *my* impulses or hers that are dangerous, venomous, deadly and vicious; it is snakes that are that way." But part of Bob's hostility projected onto the snakes comes toward him, and he seeks to defend himself by stepping on it. Thus by projecting his own vicious impulses onto the snakes and turning them against himself, he justifies his hostility to them and his impulse to destroy them.

Obviously his prejudice against snakes is shared by many people. The fact is that most snakes are friends of man. Most species are easily domesticated; in fact, some people who know snakes even keep them as pets (See C. Pope, *Snakes Alive.*) Further, they perform functions helpful to man in the ecological balance of the environment. The idea is unrealistic that all snakes are deadly and must be destroyed. This is a stereotype not unlike the ones formed and maintained about alien and minority groups. These prejudices also arise through illusions and projections that obfuscate reality, making it difficult to discriminate between what is and what is not really dangerous.

Another example of how hostility and projection are intimately tied to feelings of prejudice is provided by Jane, an attractive spinster who was strictly raised in a puritanical home. Now, at age 40, Jane is approached by a rather glamorous man who is mostly intrigued by her substantial bank account. He sets about seducing her and soon succeeds. At the outset of their sexual affair Jane begins to dream of herself as covered with dirt. However, she manages to repress her guilt, shame, and self-reproach that formed this dream. According to the standards by which she was raised (her superego), Jane has reasonable cause to feel she is doing something dirty.

Before long, however, this feeling of her own dirtiness is projected in her dreams onto other persons. Now it is no longer she but rather others who are dirty. These others appear in her dreams as members of minority groups, and soon this comes out as open prejudice in her conscious life. She develops an intense hatred of almost all minority groups because of this recently developed notion that they (not she) are dirty. Clearly, Jane is deeply enraged at herself for behaving in a way that so overtly contradicts her puritanical training and conscience, but all this hostility is turned outward onto others in the form of prejudice against members of minority groups.

From the foregoing discussion it seems obvious that prejudice is not simply an artifact of our social or political organization. It can also be a deep-seated psychological phenomenon that is rooted in childhood and persists neurotically, psychotically, and criminally when normal development to emotional maturity is warped. Prejudice is a symptom often based on the dynamics of hostility, egotism, pride, status, and the needs to be loved and valued. In addition to these narcissistic components of the personality, fear and insecurity also give rise to feelings and attitudes of prejudice. Essentially whatever generates hostility in children is a potential source of prejudice because this is one of the manifold forms that hostility can take.

In the political sphere feelings of prejudice often take the form of extreme emotional leftism or rightism. The dynamics are frequently as follows. The emotional rightist projects his feelings of inferiority and his hostilities upon the underdog. Hence he sees the underdog as representing that which he denies in himself. The underdog, then, represents to the emotional rightest all that is to be rejected, despised, and feared. The emotional leftist, on the other hand, through his own feelings of inferiority, identifies with the underdog, and projects his egotism, needs for power, and hostility onto the top dog. Thus the top dog, with whom he does not identify, tends to represent the rejected impulses within himself. While he envies the top dog, he also feels oppressed by him and therefore directs his hostility toward him. The childhood emotional pattern is usually not far to seek.

These closely related but antithetical mechanisms are represented in two typical dream characters. In emotional rightists the dream figures, which of course differ widely in details, all seem to show the same basic mechanism. Here is one such dream: A poor old creature is working hard and has with him a poorly paid underdog assistant who is of little help. The rightist's associations with these figures have to do with his efforts to identify with those who have wealth, fame, and prestige. The dreamer goes in for expensive women, automobiles, and houses, and he generally looks down upon those who are poor and belong to minority groups. It soon appears from his associations, however, that he fights off a tendency to identify with the underdogs whom he represents in his dreams. He actually feels inferior to those with wealth, power, and position but denies this to himself in his efforts to feel that he is one of them. In so doing the rightist projects his inferiority feelings upon the less fortunate and the minorities, and feels that they want to take away what he has. He also thinks that they are envious and hostile toward him, which may well be true, for there is often some kernel of truth on which a delusion is based. But by this projection he denies his own envy and hostility toward those who seem to him to have more wealth and prestige than himself. In addition, he asserts his superiority, power, and hostility toward those he sees as being beneath him. Since childhood this man, an emotional rightist, has always been fearsome and angry lest others get something more or better than he. Although well-situated, he lives in fear that he will become the poor old downtrodden creature of the dream.

The opposite mechanism is that of the emotional leftist. In the dreams of one such man, he is only a menial assistant working hard and getting little in return, while an older figure is sitting back doing nothing but being waited upon. Sometimes the older man is in the process of enjoying a sumptuous meal. Here the dreamer attributes to the older man all the gratifications that he himself wants, while his own lot is seen as that of the menial assistant who works basely for the older man and is exploited by him. The leftist denies his own wishes for power, prestige, wealth, and self-indulgence at the expense of others and projects these desires onto the older man: he also projects his hostilities onto the older man and feels abused, depreciated, and taken advantage of by him.

These considerations suggest why revolutions usually change so little but leave the same old abuses in only slightly different form.

The ideal situation is for each individual to be so mature that he understands his own motivations and those of others realistically and has humanitarian feeling not only for himself and his family, but for all people. In this way, he would be relatively freed from projections and stereotypes. This is the emotional essence of democracy, as it is of Judeo-Christian morality, and shows why such democracy and morality are so difficult to achieve. The psychodynamic mechanisms involved in determining the direction and form of political-emotional feelings are of great significance. But the basic problem is the hostility, the most sinister symptom of psychopathology, the force that warps the grasp of reality, impairs identification and fellow feeling, and prevents the shaping of societies without extensive cruelty and destruction.

Twenty years as psychiatric consultant to a coeducational residential college led me to at least two fundamental conclusions: First, the problems of the students were by no means the light little, inconsequential ones that some anticipated, but rather they were distressingly severe and were only, in latent form, the serious emotional disorders that would explode later when they were under the pressures of adult life; second, a knowledge of one's own psychodynamics is an illuminating experience of invaluable help in living—hardly a new discovery, but only confirmation of the wisdom of the ancient Greeks. Socrates said, "An unexamined life is not worth living," and the Oracle advised, "Know thyself." Knowing one's own psychodynamics deepens the understanding of others, enriches life, and is a protection for oneself. It should most certainly be made a basic part of a liberal education.

14
Hostility Begins at Home

The regal and parental tyrant differ only in the extent of their dominions, and the number of their slaves.

Samuel Johnson

Children and subjects . . . are much seldomer in the wrong than parents and kings.

Chesterfield

None deserve so well of the world as good parents. There is no task so unselfish, so necessarily without return, though the heart is well rewarded, as the nurture of the children who are to make the world for one another when we are gone . . . . over the unborn our power is that of God, and our responsibility like His toward us. As we acquit ourselves toward them, so let Him deal with us.

Bellamy, *Looking Backward*

With some oversimplification and schematization, we can say that every individual is motivated simultaneously by two sets of forces operating, as it were, on two levels: the conscious and reasonable, and the unconscious and irrational. The conscious and reasonable forces are in general the more mature; the irrational forces are essentially residues of those reactions of childhood that, disturbed in development, furnish the source for neuroses, psychoses, psychosomatic illness, and violence as crime and war. Mature love can be counted among the rational needs and drives of man. Hostility cannot be counted as rational except as self-defense.

Throughout this book we have stressed the point that hostility (whatever else it may turn out to be) is part of a basic biological adaptive mechanism—automatically to meet threats, irritations, and frustrations by withdrawing from them or destroying them. When hostility is generated from persisting warped childhood emotional patterns with their handicaps, causing threats and frustrations, and hostility is misused for immature goals and resorted to in place of mature understanding and cooperation, it becomes a disordered adaptive mechanism, which is transmitted by contact from parents to children, from generation to generation, and is preventable only by cutting through this process of transmission.

The statistics on violence in the home are discouraging. A study by Murray Strauss and Richard Gelles, (1980) estimates that eight million Americans are attacked each year by members of their own families. In a random sampling of 2,143 family members, they discovered that almost 40 percent of all homicides are *within* the family. Twenty percent of police officers murdered each year are killed answering domestic violence calls. Further, 16 of every one hundred couples have a violent fight involving physical abuse at least once a year, and four out of every one hundred wives are seriously beaten by their husbands. Sibling relationships are equally violent: more than a third of all brothers and sisters severely attack each other, many using guns and knives. Nearly ten percent of American youngsters assault their own parents. In turn, three out of every one hundred children are kicked, beaten or punched by their parents each year.

This is a central challenge to the family and, by extension, to society. Ideally, the best approach is to reduce or eliminate hostility in all parents. Unfortunately, since parents are still so much the children they themselves once were, this is impossible to achieve in any one generation. To be realistic and practical we must settle for the slower pathway of diminishing hostility as much as possible, sublimating the rest, and striving constantly to replace hatred and anger with responsible love and kindness. This is the same as the therapeutic process in the individual, where successful treatment means getting the patient securely on the way out of unconscious rage and toward emotional development.

Insight into the appalling importance of early influences (during 0 to 6) upon the developing emotional life has always been known to folk wisdom, to writers and artists. The following description of Somerset Maugham's early life (in *Somerset and All the Maughams*) will illustrate:

> In September 1877, when Willie was nearly four years old, his three elder brothers were sent [from Paris] to boarding school in England, at Dover College, and the gap in age that divided them became wider still. During the next few years, except for the holidays, Willie had his mother and her love all to himself. I suppose that this was one of the most important periods in his long life, for though he was to write only a little about it in his reminiscences, his early boyhood and his mother's illness and her death had a profound effect on his character which endured to his own death. Her love, her protection, her physical beauty, her comfortable apartment [in Paris], and her elegant pattern of living—all were suddenly torn away from him and replaced soon after by an environment [in England] so alien and bleak and so lacking in affection that it scarred his mind forever. But there were still a few years of happiness before that terrible day came.

In this chapter we noted some of the most common sources of hostile behavior that often occur in the child-parent relationship. Then, in the following chapter, we will take a look at the problem of reducing hostility in the adult personality.

A key word to good upbringing is *balance*. An excess of attention may be almost as bad as too little. Too great urging of the child toward growth can hurt the development and be as unhealthy as too much babying. The child must be allowed, perhaps encouraged gently, but certainly not forced, to grow up into being a mature interdependent adult. It must be accepted and respected as an individual who is a member of the family group. Emotional development unfolds from infancy in a setting of good loving interpersonal relationships to form the mature patterns of parental and social adaptation. Disturbances in the main lines of development, which, as we have seen, form the chief sources of hostility, are: (1) persistent and excessive childish dependence; (2) insatiable needs to be loved; (3) extreme demands for prestige motivated by envy and rivalry; (4) a disordered conscience; and, generally, (5) revenge for hostile or misguided treatment during childhood.

It is always difficult to give practical advice about emotional problems, especially because they assume a unique form in each person. If it were possible to prescribe for the emotions in the same "miracle drug" fashion that we do for the purely physiological ills, we might lump together the following into one antidote for hostility: mature parental love, in which we include understanding and respect for the child's personality, our guideline being "the inevitability of gradualness" in socializing the child and "love them and leave them alone."

The growth of human beings, as of other animals, from conception to maturity, consists very largely in outgrowing the biological dependence upon the parents. The mature adult not only can be relatively independent but must be interdependent. If parents overprotect the child, they impede its growth to self-reliance. If they force the child prematurely into independence and responsibility, they may cause an aversion to these. Interference with this development produces an adult who, however powerful physically and intellectually, feels like a child, still craving protection, the need for which he never outgrew. The underlying need to be dependent usually is in sharp conflict with the desire to be mature, at least in our civilization, causing an inner sense of inferiority and insecurity and a reaction of impotent rage. The individual may try to overcompensate through a lust for power. These emotional dynamics sometimes eventuate in open criminality, even murder. No stable personal relationship or stable society is possible in which individuals who are apparently adult have not sufficiently outgrown their too strong childish dependent love needs. But during the earliest years of life almost total dependence is normal, to be expected, and should not be discouraged.

When the child begins school, its independent relationships with the outside world begin in earnest. How well it adapts to its larger social world will reflect how well it has adapted to family-group life. Trouble signs at this age–including overdependence–should be carefully weighed, and the comments of teachers, counselors, and doctors on this behavior should be considered and guidance sought as to where the child may need help. Children who are overly "bad" (hostile) at this age obviously need help, but children who are excessively "good" may also. The too quiet, overshy child is often warmly welcomed and admired by its overworked teacher, but exaggerated compliance may signal lack of outgoingness and potential future difficulties. As we have stressed, the difference between the healthy and the pathological is a matter of degree–in the emotional life, all is quantitative.

In cases of flagrant misbehavior it is usually well to consult experts without delay. There are many excellent child guidance clinics throughout the country, which can save the well-intentioned parent from much grief later on. Just a few hours of assistance may be all that is necessary at this age to help the parents understand the problem and set them and their child on the right track toward dealing with it.

The child's independence of its family grows in small ways. Its physical skills benefit by encouragement; but the mother whose fear inhibits bicycle riding or tree climbing is no worse a handicap to the child than the demanding father who flings his child into the lake with the cry, "Sink or swim!" Balance between protectiveness and prodding is needed here, just as it is in the child's expanding social life and its whole maturing emotional life. Anything wrong with the child's development from dependence to independence is apt to form a source of hostility.

With the early teens the child's growing independence prepares the individual for maturity. In this prepubertal, 10 to 13 period the child begins showing natural signals of the breakaway that will eventually lead it into the outside world. The way in which criticism of the home, lack of responsibility, failures in affection, lapses in following accepted mores, and even direct hostility are handled at this stage can help stabilize the child's later adolescent explorations of the ways of group life, its relationships with the opposite sex, and its sometimes reckless attempts at premature adulthood. Conversely, harsh parental responses cause reactions in the child that easily create vicious circles of mutual hostility between child and parent.

Basically, though, the core of the child's personality pattern is formed by the time it is about six. If this early care is healthy, it will, from birth to about age six and in ordinary circumstances, have no serious problems in adolescence. If its interpersonal relations during these very early years have not been good, problems had best be watched for.

Emotional conditioning is much less permanent in its effects after these early years (0 to 6), but behavior patterns can still be guided and help obtained, when indicated, in correcting unhealthy infantile patterns. The wise parent, seeking to avoid future hostility because of the carryover of excessive dependent love needs, will avoid thwarting or overindulging these early, very real, inevitable needs of the infant, and aid and assist the equally real strivings toward independence, the infantile seeds of which flower from the pre-teens to early adulthood.

The time for prevention is before dating has become marriage and parenthood, before studies have become career, before peccadilloes have become the interminable maldajustments that make life what it usually is. The time for prevention is before one must *play for keeps.* The roots of emotional problems lie in the years of childhood in disturbed feelings that are natural reactions of the child to how it has been treated. When the person reaches college, one sees these problems as they are manifested in young adulthood. Usually they are in larval form, not yet full-blown as they will become with the struggles and frustrations of adult life and later years. Hence the college age, when the emerging adult is old enough to comprehend them, is an ideal time for insight, although a little late for help and prevention.

* * * *

The young child's needs for love are necessarily intense, the parents' love being its only guarantee of food, care, and protection. Over the years, the child shifts from the receiving end, loved as a baby, to being capable of giving as a parent who puts out responsible love and meets his own offspring's all but inexhaustible needs. Normally this same ability to enjoy giving as a parent carries over from the emotional life to the individual's social and economic life.

Deprivation and overindulgence are two of the common errors of upbringing that disturb the normal development of the child's need for love. As mentioned earlier, if the emotional diet in early childhood is too rich or too poor, then the appetite for love in later life is distorted. True love is a genuine interest in the child's well-being, for its own sake, as well as a respect for its individuality. Spoiling, overattention, excessive demonstrativeness, overindulgence are poor substitutes for this true love. Too great a residue of infantile desires for love cannot be gratified in adult life, and forms a source of constant frustration leading to irritability, a sense of hopelessness and depression, feelings of inferiority and insecurity, and thus constant stimulation of the fight–flight reaction, leading to all sorts of neurotic symptoms including rage and hate.

It sometimes seems quite difficult to welcome a child into this world with real warmth, for it brings with it so many problems—financial worries, caretaking chores, and housekeeping upheavals; but the chief, most vital problem is the strain it puts on those areas of emotional immaturity in each parent and in the parents' relationship to each other. The child's demands for love, care, and attention and the crying when these needs are not met immediately drive infantile parents into rages and lead some parents into striking and even injuring their child. The child itself is not to blame for this stress on the parents, but rather their own weaknesses are. True love for a child can only come from those mature enough to be capable of giving much long-sustained day-in-day-out loving. Certainly every child should be a wanted child. The unwanted child is foredoomed. (How can we get immature parents to raise mature children?)

There is probably no one without some capacity for mature love. The problem facing most of us is not total lack, but rather greater development of what we have. Self-control, consistent giving of oneself, patience, affection, understanding, respect—all these help to develop a mature ability to love a child *for itself* without expecting anything from it in return except proper maturing. The parent-child relationship is one in which it is true that the more you give, the more you get.

Love to be love must encompass both the irksome two o'clock feedings of the baby and the back-talk of the adolescent testing his powers. "Love is not love that alters when it alteration finds."

* * * *

A third powerful source of irrational hostility is found in narcissism—inordinate desires for prestige, vanity, pride, egotism, and egocentricity. Self-love, within normal limits, is only an expression of self-preservation. The very life of a small child depends upon its being highly valued by the parents. But for the adult parent, a genuine, unselfish interest in his child, in other persons, and in responsible, productive accomplishment should be more enjoyable than the egocentric satisfactions natural to the small child. The child's self-centeredness persists to some extent within the mature adult, but the proportion is changed; no longer are rivalry, envy, and narcissism overriding motivations.

Two of the common errors in upbringing that cause excessive drives for narcissism are favoritism and rejection, but anything that wounds the self-esteem can cause exaggerated narcissism as a reaction. If the child's needs for prestige are not properly handled, then his inflated narcissism may persist throughout adult life, and he may become the kind of man of whom Napoleon cynically remarked: "Men will go through Hell itself for a bit of ribbon." Again and again we can observe how little of the interest of some adults lies in the task at hand, and how much it is devoted to using the situation for their vanities. If a child is made to feel that it is the lord of the household, or if one parent sides with it consistently against the other, or if the parents expect it to fulfill their own ambitions, then the child is prone to be fixed in a power pattern and feel in adult life that he must be the best, the preferred one. His own status will be all that matters, and every person will be to him primarily a hated rival, or a means to boosting his own egocentricity, egotism, and "bestism"; and his hostility will be evident in arrogance, insolence, and contempt. On the other hand, the child who is rejected and not sufficiently valued is likely to carry throughout life a sense of inferiority, an injury to his self-regard. In vain efforts to overcome the debility, this child too may fail to outgrow overcompensatory egotism as a motivation. He is doomed to frustration and therefore rage and hate, for all competitors can never be vanquished; childish egotism can never be sated.

The foisting of parental ambitions onto the child is another common source for fixated drives for power, prestige, and bestism in the adult. When a parent tries to force a child toward the kind of success he or she once dreamed of, this pressure in itself usually creates a source of hostility, as rebellion and protest, as hate of rivals, or from frustration of these ingrained compulsive strivings.

There is, to be sure, nothing wrong with healthy ambition, competition, and success, provided it is the reflection of self-reliant, responsible doing, producing, contributing. It is only when it is exaggerated into excessive egotism, hostile personal rivalry, and egocentric childish battles for personal status that it becomes frustrating and antisocial. The distinction between the healthy and the pathological in this regard is not always easy to make today. The welfare of a society depends upon how much its members contribute, but our current standards of material success are based mostly on how much the members can take out in their competition for money and power.

* * * *

A fourth common source of irrational hostility is friction between the individual and his conscience. The conscience should be the internalized result of gradual, reasonable socialization, balancing individual desire with the good of others and of society as a whole. As we have noted, society cannot exist without some control of instinct, especially of each individual's passive-receptive dependence, his vanity, his sex drives, and his hostilities. But how often is the adult conscience little more than the imago of a depriving or overprotecting or threatening parent, whose attitudes and treatment (psychologically and physically) have created feelings that impair rather than help socialization and development?

Physically harsh treatment of the child is rarely anything more than the parent's own fears and hostilities being vented upon the helpless. "I'll teach you to hit people," cries the parent in a rage, striking the child. And that is exactly what he is doing—what a lesson in hostility this turns into: Teaching is accomplished best by example, not precept, and the example here is an enraged adult using physical violence to meet a difficult situation. This provides the child with a model that it is quite sure to follow. If the child were properly reared by its parents, the occasions for severe punishment would occur but rarely, and would be handled by reason, not violence or hostility.

Emotionally harsh treatment is less obvious but equally or more destructive to personality. The inculcation of too high ideals in childhood dooms the adult to incessant, hopeless striving to achieve the unattainable. "A man's reach should exceed his grasp"—yes, but not by so much as to create despair. The piling up in the child of guilt and shame can create a burden that may be borne for life. The discrepancies between behavior and conscience or the existence of an immature conscience usually forms a chronic source of hostility.

The difficulties of a toddler may be those of an experimenter. The vanity and selfishness of the young adolescent may be a stage of growth. The sex interest of the growing youth is not necessarily wickedness but preparation for establishing a mature sexual relationship and for parenthood. *A pura omnia pures*—to the pure all things are pure. The parent must try to see the adult growing in the child, and in so doing attempt to seek a balance in the ideals set before it. If training is forced upon the child too early, too harshly, or too constantly, his spirit can be crushed; if training comes too late, too leniently, or too little, the child may become impulse-ridden, lacking secure, automatic controls. Such an individual is a likely candidate for accepting immature, even criminal behavior. If training is too inflexible, it may result in an adult so rigid that he will break down for lack of adaptability; if it is inconsistent, it can produce constant vacillation and confusion. But if the ideals are those of emotional maturity, then the conscience aids a balanced, harmonious development and good interpersonal relations—and life is, after all, mostly human relations. A good principle in the necessary socialization of the child is to win the child over to harmonious social behavior by the inevitability of gradualness, as we have mentioned, but this requires much patience and maturity in the parents.

* * * *

A fifth common source of hostility is displaced revenge for any and all sorts of mistreatment, deliberate or unintentional, during childhood. Probably parental hostility to the child is the greatest single source of the lifelong hatreds and readiness to violence that we see so widely in adults. The fog of sentiment enshrouding parental love hides much of the immaturity, stupidity, rejection, and abuse to which small children on all levels of society are subjected.

Parents, unknowingly, frequently incite a child to anger and hostile behavior and then punish it for this reaction. Commonly this occurs because of failure to understand the child's nature and development, by causing demands to be made upon the child beyond its capacities. Also the parents create rage by "boxing in" the child, allowing it no "out." For example, a little girl trying to learn to cook damaged a pot. Her mother was angry. The child said, "I'm sorry, I'll get you another one out of my piggy bank." Her mother said, "No, don't do that." She allowed the girl, contrite though she was, no way to make amends, but blocked her attempts at solution and "boxed her in." Another common cause of hostility is the mishandling of the natural rivalries that exist in the child with parents and with brothers and sisters.

Guidance in cooperation is the answer to a fist fight between two young brothers—not another verbal or physical battle between the parent and the children involved. Some thought should also be given to the parent's role in the fight—too often, all unwittingly, it is for the parent's love and attention that the children are really battling. Children who are predominantly hostile are sending out storm signals of the greatest importance; they must be handled with increased understanding rather than force. For the child he once was lives on in the adult, and so do the imagos of those who reared him. The hostile parent tends, *ipso facto,* to make a hostile child. It is unhealthy for a child to grow up hostile and angry, for the hostile child is on its way to becoming a hostile adult, destined for a life of ostracism, loneliness, emotional disorder, and suffering.

Rationalization, not reason, runs the world. What looks like appropriate anger and violence stimulated by real deprivations may be largely rationalization; they are the good reasons but not the real reasons. Hate engendered in children by parental mistreatment seeks excuses for venting itself on others. Since reasons are abundant, we have a world of irrational violence generated by disordered childhood emotional patterns and rationalized by innumerable excuses. Our survival as a nation depends in large part upon preventing ourselves from being chosen as the object for the reservoir of hate generated in our children and in children the world over by the way they are raised.

The key to what is mature as distinct from what is immature lies in the overall contrast between the ideal parents' feelings and behavior toward the baby and very young child and the healthy child's feelings and behavior toward the parents. The young child receives, but the parents must give.

The child at first cooperates only to fill its needs. However, through accepting love and through identification with those who give it love, it learns to give love, to grow into its place in the family unit and to enjoy contributing there. All training should be designed to free the child's potentials for love, cooperation, and responsibility. For maturing is a process of growing from the passive, receptive, dependent (PRD) attitudes and feelings of the child toward the parent into the responsible, productive, independent (RPI) ones of the parent toward the child.

Parents often ask: "Is it all right to give the child a spanking if it is mild?" Such a question is beside the point. The essential is good emotional relationships with the child and a good model of behavior for the child. It is possible for a parent to spank a child but to do it in such a way that the child feels justly treated. It is also possible for a parent never to spank a child, but by tone and manner to create such feelings of shame and guilt as to warp the child's opinion of itself. This child may come to think of itself as an inferior creature, and this, as we have seen, is a prime source of fear, frustration, and hostility. When parents react with vengefulness, it eventually destroys any possibility of a good relationship and will sow seeds in the child of lasting hate, with all its dire consequences for the child later in life and for the society. It must never be forgotten that the child will do much more what the parent *does* than what the parent *says*. The guiding principle is, "Keep good loving feeling with the child."

In this sense *what* is done is of much less importance than *how* it is done. The parent who is able to keep the child's love and friendship and to provide it with a good model for mature behavior has laid the foundation in that child for the capacity to love and be friendly and responsible throughout life. The parent who understands and trusts the course of development, who expects the good rather than the bad, will get it. And the question of spanking will not arise, for it misses the point.

So long as parents have genuine good feelings for their child and respect him or her as a person, there will be a responsive core of healthy good feelings in the child toward them, which will facilitate its maturing and provide it with the underlying capacity for good relationships with others for the rest of its life. Children respond to love and confidence with love and confidence and, through identification with the parents, take over these feelings and attitudes, modeling themselves upon those who cared for them. Children, like pets, *reflect* their home.

Faults of upbringing occur even in families of intelligence, good will, and love, but in these families such faults are apt to be subtle and hard to discern.

She was a quiet, pert, pretty little ten-year-old. Her blonde hair was straight, which I guessed inspired her nickname, "Curly." As she spoke, it became obvious that she was very intelligent. I take patients regardless of youth if they can talk with me as reasonable persons, which means usually no younger than eight.

Curly knit her brows and answered my questions like a serious little adult in a most charming manner. I would have been surprised at her chief complaint if her mother had not informed me of its nature in our initial talk: Curly had much difficulty holding friends.

"Surely," I thought, "she has good relations with her parents and therefore with all adults, or she and I would have not instantly liked each other and gotten on so well. Her trouble must be with her peers."

Without hesitating, Curly told me that her seven-year-old sister "is a pain, a pain in the neck," and when I inquired further, she added, "She's a brat! She's not a human being, she's an animal!" When I eventually met this "monster," she turned out to be a quite delightful little girl. Some hostility in sibling rivalry is inevitable, but what intensified it so in this loving, well-intentioned family?

The question is relevant to the main symptom found often among children, namely, the general difficulty in making friends among their own age group, and more specifically, the problem of being singled out for teasing, being "ganged up on," which is what brought Curly to me. In my experience, there are two chief causes for such difficulties: First, a physical handicap can open a child to peer ridicule. One little girl had a physical illness that confined her to bed while the other children in the neighborhood ran and played together. In grade school her personality was gentle and sweet, but she lagged behind her friends in size and coordination. As so often happens, another girl became the leader of a clique that bullied and teased her. But her parents were so loving and supportive that she sustained the teasing although she suffered under it.

The second cause for difficulty is psychological: If there is a problem with peers, then there is usually a problem with family, often with a sibling. But how could Curly have a problem with such loving, caring parents? This mystery became clear after an early interview in which her mother was included.

Curly had some resentment of her mother but was secure enough in her love to say so. She told me that before leaving home that day, her mother had asked her to take her sister on an errand after school. Curly felt compelled to obey her mother even though she had made other plans, and she felt this was typical—her mother often failed to be aware that Curly had a life of her own, and failed to respect Curly's personality. Then, too, Curly's mother was suddenly away from home a great deal because she had taken a job which she enjoyed and which added needed income to the family. But she had not bothered to explain to Curly why she needed and wanted the job. Once this was out in the open, Curly understood and was more cooperative. It became clear quickly that a major source of her frustration and irritation, and her almost constant anger, was the sense of a lack of empathy from her mother and a lack of respect for Curley's personality. This family operated too much with punishment as a method of child-rearing. For example, Curly's sister had a near accident with an auto when she was riding her bike, and for this her father spanked her. She had awakened his anxieties, and he struck her more to vent his own anger than for the child's good.

When I suggested to Curly near the end of this interview that we had learned so much from her mother's presence that perhaps we should invite her father to sit in on the next visit she became frightened. She finally agreed, but only if her mother were there also. In other words, this child was so afraid of her own loving, devoted father that she dared not talk about their relationship without her mother's protective presence.

This example typifies how problems with peers in general and being teased in particular usually, if not always, trace back to problems of the child within its family, no matter how well hidden these problems may be. Of course those children who take the role of bullies rather than victims are expressing family problems also. All such peer problems usually contain elements of hostility, however hidden and indirect, of one or both parents toward their child, which intensifies the sibling hostilities and thus leads to difficulties in peer relationships. Parental hostility, even though repressed and disguised, is damaging to the child's emotional development to maturity. For security in its good feelings toward others the child must feel deeply that its own parents are "on my side." Then the child can accept the long process of necessary socialization with the "inevitability of gradualness," and temptations for the parent to punish are rare, even nonexistent. Treat the child as a small, weak, tender, sensitive but reasonable adult, and have full respect for him or her as a person, as you would any adult.

It is said that if one is not a socialist in youth, he has no heart; if he is still one in his maturity, then he has no head. Probably most individuals do become more conservative as they get older. This is in part, I think, because they have learned through harsh personal experience the amount of hostility that exists between individuals and groups and nations. They learn the tremendous power of the instincts over the intellect, instincts that dictate the cruelty and suffering of life. They learn that the intellect tends to serve the instinctual life, that people use fine minds for the greatest hostility and selfishness.

They acknowledge the power of the irrational, the emotional forces, the instinctual drives and their warpings of human nature by faulty child-rearing. From all this they gain a respect for convention, law, and conformity to standards of social behavior. They learn this respect because they know that every nation is held together only by tenuous threads and could readily fly apart. They know that this is true also for the world, and that nations strain at the leash, which may snap and let them at their own and each other's throats. They know that hostility enters into the way men and women get along together, use their sexuality, and relate to their children.

They see that society manages to exist at all only through conventions, laws, and a minimal degree of conformity. The knowledge that people are imperfect, hostile, and hypocritical, that they preach proper behavior to others but indulge themselves, only adds to the realization that morality, law, and convention, evolved over many thousands of years, are the only dikes against chaos and destruction.

Love is the indispensable essence. Everyone needs love—enormously and desperately. We cannot go after it without realizing that if we are to get it, others must give it. Love means an unselfish interest in the loved one for that one's own sake, for no ulterior selfish motive. The reward to the parents comes not from exploiting the child in some way during childhood or later, nor from molding it to the parents' wishes. It comes only from the satisfaction of seeing the child develop and live out its life as a healthy and mature human being.

Our jails and hospitals are filled to overflowing, and our courts cannot handle their backlog; and the incidence of delinquency, crime, divorce, alcoholism, and drug abuse are all still rising rapidly. Dozens of "therapies" (estimated at this writing at about 150 identifiable ones) are mushrooming to meet the demands for help of those who suffer emotionally. Why are there all these emotional disorders? The problem is obvious to anyone who recognizes the truth of the old adage: "As the twig is bent, the tree is inclined." We are a forest of inclined trees—all were bent as twigs.

Taking my seat on an airplane for a business trip and having a choice, I selected a window seat on the right, far enough behind the wings to have an unobstructed view. A few minutes after I sat down, a generally attractive young woman sat down on my left with an infant, about three months old, in her arms. As best I could, I helped her get settled. Passengers were still boarding amid noise and confusion. The infant whimpered, and the young mother fished a full baby bottle out of her tote bag, offering it as a pacifier. The child accepted it eagerly, but soon in the midst of the noise swirling up and down the aisle, it began to cry. The mother removed the bottle for a moment and then tried again. This time the baby refused it and began to cry even louder. The mother tried cuddling it, soothing it with soft talk, but the hullabaloo on the plane continued, and the child continued to cry. Again it refused the proffered bottle. The mother suddenly lost patience and slapped the baby hard on its cheek, causing it to cry more loudly, at which the mother delivered another slap. I felt a good slap at the mother's face warming up in my right arm, but I restrained it. Maybe a distraction would break up this battle between mother and child; I started a conversation, asking the baby's age, name, and other general persiflage. After what seemed like hours, the plane taxied into position and took off. The mother's anger at her baby subsided, and the child quieted down gradually. Moral: Some young mothers do not hesitate to get enraged and even physically hit their babies, doing irreparable psychological damage to a child who is too young to comprehend.

Is the above a totally unwarranted generalization? No–it is unfortunately all too common. In shops, supermarkets, department stores, just watch a mother with small children. It is rare not to see her take out some frustration by striking the child. The Mohave Indians believe that any parent who strikes a child is psychotic, but we so take it for granted that we usually do not even notice it. Moral: If exposure of a very young child to hostility, either emotional or physical, can warp its development, then the mother who warps her child's development is the *rule* rather than the exception.

Two weeks after returning from my plane trip I was next door visiting a neighbor, whose 22-year-old daughter was upset. She explained that several months before, the girl had taken a job in a day-care center, providing for children from infancy to age four. The mothers were mainly young and unwed. Such mothers are themselves usually immature, if not emotionally disturbed; they have tried the novelty of motherhood, and found the child an insufferable burden. The child in turn feels the rejection and reacts with anxiety that causes it to cling all the more to its mother. It has "imprinted" the mother in the first few days and weeks after birth, and will accept no substitute. Hence, a vicious circle: The more the child is anxious and clings, the more resentful and rejecting is the unwed, young mother. And the more resentfully she rejects her child, the more anxious and clinging the child becomes. If the social worker tries to talk to such a mother, she will resist, get angry, and take it out on the child.

A beautiful little girl of not quite two years wet her bed, which is not unusual or abnormal at that age. Her mother got angry, and of course the child became unruly and continued wetting. The social worker at the day-care center talked with the mother gently and lovingly about ways to correct the situation, but the mother, like so many others, responded with anger. That night, the little girl's mother rammed a Q-tip into the child's ear, shattering the eardrum. Few injuries are more painful; psychologically, the effects of such an attack by one's own mother may be even worse. Deafness as a result of such an attack may not make as much difficulty as the lifelong emotional warping. My neighbor's daugher saw such situations every day at the day-care center, and the pain of having to witness such brutality and being totally impotent to help disturbed her greatly. Moral: Other animals are better mothers to their young than immature humans, who perpetuate emotional disorder and crime, by abuse of their own children, making the children into neurotics, psychotics, and criminals when they grow up.

15
Fighting the Devil and Seeking the Grail

How can a man be wise if he hate?

Rudyard Kipling

Only the ignorant man becomes angry. The wise man understands.

Indian Wisdom

Look not lo here, lo there . . .
The Kingdom of Heaven is within.

Luke 17:21

Humanity has every reason to place the proclaimers of high moral standards and values above discoverers of objective truth. What humanity owes to personalities like Buddha, Moses and Jesus ranks for me higher than all the achievements of the enquiring and constructive mind . . . . What these blessed men have given us we must guard and try to keep alive with all our strength if humanity is not to lose its dignity, the security of its existence, and its joy in living.

Albert Einstein

Although hostility is a widespread and malignant disease that underlies or is a link in many serious social and personal problems, there are powerful curative forces on the side of mankind in efforts to deal with this tormentor and killer. Innate drives of the human organism provide a biological basis for behavior that is constructive for the individual and the species. Ethics, good will, healthy family life—these are not artificial ideals somehow foisted upon us. On the contrary, they are expressions of our basic potential for maturity. They are the results of adult strength, even as hostility is a signal of frustration and weakness.

Such constructive personal and social forces are strengthened by a tendency toward the evolution of higher forms. We know that phylogenetically there has been progress up the scale from peck orders to true leadership. Civilization itself and what we broadly call "mental development" or "culture" can be seen as part of the evolutionary process, and this process is an aid to the sublimation and control and, we hope, at least partial resolution of man's hostilities.

Man is not equipped to survive naked in the wild, but can only exist in societies, which means the restraints of social behavior and control of the fight–flight response—which means civilization and culture. Increasing clinical and experimental evidence that the thrust toward maturity and cooperation can save us from the more primitive fight–flight reflex bears this out. The problem appears to be one of education and social engineering—how to accomplish on a worldwide scale what is already being done by good parents and by good psychodynamic treatment for individuals.

We have seen how faulty early conditioning produces lifelong deformities of personality, which, in turn, generate hostility. But conditioning is something controllable. This has been proved in experiments and field research with animals and other methods, as summarized in Chapter 18. On a human emotional level, reconditioning is seen daily in psychoanalytic practice. A neurosis is essentially a persisting pattern of a disturbed childhood emotional relationship to parents (and siblings) (especially 0–6). It is essentially a repetition and continuation of this relationship, more or less internalized and more or less transferred to other persons. The patient also "transfers" this relationship to his analyst, each session providing the dynamic therapist with a sort of laboratory sample of the patient's relations to other persons, a sample of his key imagos and reaction patterns. The therapeutic task, then, is to correct these imagos and disordered childhood patterns and thus reopen emotional growth. This may be a slow process, but in suitable cases it is very effective.

Progress toward cure is achieved by exposing the pattern of infantile motivations to the patient's highest powers—to his ego—his reason, reality sense, memory, experience, judgment. In the process the analyst comes to replace the authority of the parents. The tendency of the person being analyzed to put himself in the position of a submissive, dependent child toward the analyst, as he once was toward his parents, is unconscious and automatic. The analyst cannot prevent it, but it is his responsibility to correct and reduce it in favor of the patient's shifting his attitudes and outgrowing his dependence while developing independence and maturity. As the analyst succeeds in exposing and altering disordered childhood feelings, the patient reduces the image of himself as an insecure, guilty child in a world of powerful controlling adults, ceases putting himself emotionally in such a position toward others, and comes to see himself as he is through the eyes of the analyst, as a person with mature powers for work and love and the capacity to enjoy them in a mature fashion in a balanced life.

Whatever the injurious childhood conditioning, the analyst must make repeatedly clear to the patient the *distinction* between the disordered patterns of reaction formed during earliest childhood and the present reality. He must constantly confront the patient with his tendency to react to the treatment situation, to others, and to himself in terms of this early, outmoded, now inappropriate conditioning and these imagos. He must show that what was logical, appropriate behavior when the patient was a child and helpless may be unrealistic and unworkable in the present. In this way the patient can learn to see himself in his adult makeup, with his mature powers and the capacity for pleasure in exercising them. In this way he can learn to see others as they are in reality and not as figures of his childhood.

Analysis frees the ego from the tyranny of fixed, automatic, unconscious, infantile patterns. Understanding these patterns is the first step in this reeducation, and continues as an essential. But insight alone is usually not sufficient. The central technique for correcting the personality fault is transference, that is, the repetition of childhood patterns to the analyst. The infantile is "analyzed out," so to speak, and the mature is freed so that emotional growth can take place through life experience. This is a process of *de*conditioning the disordered infantile and *re*conditioning to the mature and adjusted. This process of cure, of freeing the mind and spirit, we now fortunately understand—but unfortunately, it may take a long time, even many years, to accomplish it.

The means of treatment used by the analyst suggest the growth patterns of the generally healthy in handling their hostilities and in seeking emotional maturity. More than a purely intellectual comprehension of the goals sought and the problems and patterns to be overcome must be achieved by the individual if growth is to occur, as progress from first intellectual glimpses to deepening emotional realization and appreciation accompanies insight.

One question is whether it is possible for an individual to achieve this for himself, by himself. It would seem that the answer is perhaps, but only with great difficulty, for what is unconscious in each individual can rarely if ever be raised to the conscious level solely by his own deliberate efforts. But before this is taken to mean that it is futile to think a man can attempt new emotional growth alone, let us note that the intellect can probably achieve some insight if it knows what to look for. It is possible, therefore, that any man or woman who is seeking, through insight into himself, greater strength, higher goals, and a deeper capacity for mature satisfactions, might find help in consistently educating himself toward these goals and in holding within himself at all times a vision of these ideals. Such a person may then be better prepared to benefit from insight, should it occur, for he will know what to look for in himself and be in a better position to learn from life, literature, and science and to develop his mature powers. This is one cogent reason for books on psychodynamics and their applications. But it would be a most effective start if everyone had help from another in learning accurately his own psychodynamics as part of his education, which should pass on his cultural heritage and prepare him for living.

In what ways and to what extent different persons can help themselves has not yet been sufficiently explored scientifically. A severe warping of the personality will never, in all likelihood, be corrected by reading a book. Nor will those who think they know all about themselves, or those too remote from reality, probably ever be made open to such learning by simple reading. Nevertheless we can realistically hope and expect that much will be gained as some people come to recognize the roots of personal emotional disorders and hence of social disorders, as they come to appreciate what maturity consists of and how indispensable it is for satisfying living, and as they grasp and learn to apply the essential principles of child-rearing. We can anticipate a more insightful and rational and possibly even a slightly less hostile, violent world as this knowledge is clarified and disseminated and gradually filters into our ideology and our practical living.

One of the most important problems that each individual must face in his day-to-day experience is that of achieving a balanced way of life—that is, a life in which the give and the get and the progressive and the regressive, are in equilibrium. The meaning and implications of such a mode of life are significant for enjoyment and for the reduction of hostility.

The logic of a balanced life derives from our knowledge, incomplete though it is at present, of the two opposing directions taken in everyone by his or her motivational forces. Biologically, the progressive forces impel the organism toward mature, productive, responsible, interdependent efforts, making a happy family and a happy society. But the forces grouped as regressive urge the organism to relinquish such responsible, productive, creative effort, and to return to the more passive, receptive dependence of fetal life, infancy, and childhood. Fledglings do not leave the nest until they can fly. Young animals are confused when they must first face life alone without the help of their mothers.

Like biochemical anabolism and catabolism, both tendencies are essential to life. Probably no animal organism can exist in maturity without some independent effort; even forms so completely parasitic that they neither have nor need mouths to nourish themselves nevertheless must expend some nonegocentric energy for reproduction to continue their species. In the higher forms the centrifugal energy output and no re-creation of energy is inconsistent with living. Rest, eating, sleeping, play, and the like are necessary self-indulgences and forms of natural, healthy, necessary regression seen throughout the animal kingdom.

For modern man, especially in times of economic difficulty, life has become largely the art of getting these two opposing forces into balance. This balance involves not only adequate amounts of responsibile, giving work and of play, but also *enjoyment* of both these progressive (RPI—responsible, productive, independent) and regressive (PRD—passive, receptive, dependent) activities. While, socially speaking, we instinctively distrust either extreme—the playboy or the loafer at one end, and the compulsive workaholic at the other—there are many reasons why modern man finds the balanced life difficult to achieve. Even what should be sport or play often becomes respected only as work, and some people apologize for balancing duty with adequate recreation.

Of course much of the reason why individuals get trapped in this sort of attitude stems from inner conflicts. We have all known people who when they worked longed for relaxation—and when they relaxed, felt they should be working. These people seem to have to force themselves to work and force themselves to play. Each tendency, the progressive and the regressive, clashes head-on against the other; the two are never separated so that they can establish a balance and rhythm. Such people can enjoy neither work nor play; they should *enjoy both.*

Sometimes a partly healthy reaction of shame and self-defense against an overindulgent childhood derives a man or woman into compulsive working, fearing that to stop driving himself will cause him to give up entirely; he works too much lest he work not at all (just as we sometimes laugh lest we weep). Frequently guilt and the need for self-punishment are the unconscious motivation for too much or too little work. The virtues of healthy ambition are often lost in the excuses. How frequently is the sleepless struggle for "happiness" mistranslated into dollar terms, only to bring suffering, breakdown, a broken home, ulcers, high blood pressure.

For nature will not be outsmarted. We are born to a certain mold, and our development follows nature's pattern; we grow, mature, and decline according to her laws. The only happiness and power lie in understanding and flowing along with the forces of nature that shape and control us and in whose inexorable grip we are. Personal vanity and pride are ludicrous in the face of the overwhelmingly powerful realities of biology and of the universe, the underlying forces of which made us and use us for their expression. To obstruct their ability to help us make use of our mature powers to love both sexually and socially and to make a harmonious society, is inevitably to pay the price in the whole range of emotional disorders and their consequences.

Thus knowledge has accumulated of the natural course of human emotional development, of what constitutes maturity, and of the inevitable problems that, with appropriate guidance, the child must solve if he is to grow up adequately and to enjoy living out his life in the full expression of his mature, constructive powers, with all that this means to himself, his family, his nation, his species.

To this basic knowledge, all the physiological, biological, and social sciences can contribute. Because of the overlapping of the various fields, interdisciplinary teams should be especially effective. Much more work is crying to be done in this area than is going on at present within the scientific community. Existing scientific societies could well serve this goal by establishing special sections for the investigation of how to grow better human beings. At present more is done to study and achieve the growth of hogs and cattle than of men. Efforts should be made to bring together all scientists who share this interest, as the national societies for cancer and heart disease have done. Individuals might be recruited from our educational system as well as from the various related sciences to serve as researchers in this field. Ideally, a "Manhattan District Project" should be organized for the study of human development and for combating its chief obstruction and danger: man's hostility to man. A great cooperative effort taught us how to make the atom bomb; now we need to learn how *not* to use it. The growing body of knowledge could then be made constructively effective through school, church, and state. If a tiny fraction of what is spent on armaments were spent on studying human destructiveness and human constructiveness, then just as science has reduced for us the terrors of inanimate nature and even of disease, it might show us how to reduce the terrors of that ever threatening disease of hostility within man himself.

Through advances in the physical sciences we are developing an amazing technology of production, distribution, communication, and transportation. We can expect that in time behavioral and social scientists—the economists, political scientists, sociologists, and others—will help us to improve social organization. The power of circumstance is obvious. The stresses, insecurities, anxieties, complexities with which adults struggle to maintain themselves and their families and to establish even a minimally secure place in society influence everyone. But full solution cannot come from increasing improvements in social organization alone, urgently as they are needed, for the most perfect organization consists of people and will not operate maturely unless the individual men and women who constitute it are sufficiently mature. Organization, in fact, should be directed toward achieving the proper development of children and the proper conditions of life for mature adults. The epiorganism always reflects the characteristics of the unit organisms that compose it. Our bodies have the earmarks of our cells; our society has those of the individuals who constitute it.

Our times are marked by a great paradox: man tends to use his enormously increased power over nature much less for his good than for his destruction. Thus, for example, the dream that science might tap the power of the atom has brought us, not rejoicing over new wealth and new security, but fear of total destruction. This paradox springs from the fact that each individual in our society is activated by strong asocial or antisocial motivations as well as by social ones. Survival has become a matter of understanding these two sets of impulses in order to aid the constructive and pro-human, and to reduce the destructive, and anti-human motivations. To seek emotional maturity and thereby secure what is pro-human, is to seek the grail; the devil is the incarnation of evil, and evil is the disordered infantile impulses that generate man's hostility to man.

Hostility can be attacked at its roots: in the rearing of the child and in the reeducation of the adult. It can be banished as smallpox and typhoid have been banished in this country, or at least reduced as tuberculosis has been. Then we will realize the dream of producing mature, constructive men and women so that there may be many of them among us. The ancient war of good against evil, of love against hate, of God against Devil, of democracy against tyranny, is the war of the mature and loving people against the infantile and hostile people. In this struggle lies humanity's most thrilling challenge; in the outcome lies the hope of a desperate world.

Psychodynamically, man's inhumanity to man springs almost entirely from irrational sources. Today the individual cannot meet difficulties by physical attack, and neither can nations. War and tyranny are basically and ultimately irrational. Our survival on this planet is possible only through cooperation, responsibility, productivity, and interdependence. The fight–flight reaction, however indispensable it was in the wild, is now, as a method for solving the complex problems of modern social adjustment among individuals or nations, like trying to repair a fine watch with a hammer.

Hostility should be made universally known for what it is: a neurotic symptom, a symptom of weakness and frustration, a once invaluable primitive animal method of defense in the wild, which now has become mankind's principal enemy and threatens to destroy it. We should know that a Nero and a Hitler are *made, not born,* that evil and violence have their main genesis in the mishandling of the emotions of small children and are therefore preventable perversions.

The problem should be tackled by all the related sciences. It should be pursued at least as widely and energetically as cancer and heart disease. Our best brains should be mobilized and given adequate funds to attack this problem on a national scale. What is already known should be disseminated systematically and as widely as possible to improve the upbringing of our children and thereby the lives of our adults. In the long run our security will not rest with sophisticated computer-controlled weaponry but with a population that is strong, realistic, and resourceful, through its achievement of emotional maturity. The best available information should be made readily accessible through libraries, mass media, schools, churches, and all those who deal with people and particularly with children. Colleges cannot shirk the question of how much responsibility they should assume for the emotional development of their students. Many colleges are now begining to realize that college years for most students are *not* carefree, and that many adolescents experience emotional difficulties that hamper their full intellectual and emotional development. They are also beginning to recognize that the strains and emotional uncertainties associated with adolescent growth and transition to adult life are common to all students no matter how brilliant and emotionally stable. Almost all students could realize themselves more fully with increased insight.

Ideally the greatest single effort of the nation and of the world should be devoted to seeing that its children mature emotionally from the moment of conception. This is the basic answer to man's tendency to torture and destroy himself. The practical difficulties are overwhelmingly immense, but they are not insuperable. They *can* be overcome in the long range if we persevere in our attack on the problem. When they are, peace and brotherhood will be, not sentimental dreams, but practical reality, and man will have saved himself from being a more spectacular biological failure than the dinosaur.

Section III
Additional Supporting Observations

16
The Anthropology of Hostility

Jerome H. Barkow*

Cultural and social anthropologists seldom speak of "hostility." Their vocabulary is one of feuding and raiding, of sorcery and witchcraft, and the ecological correlates of infanticide or the political context of ritualized rebellions. There is hostility behind these and a great many other cultural phenomena, of course, but the anthropologist is a social scientist. His or her concern is with how behavior—hostile or otherwise—maintains or alters social structure; or how the meaning of that behavior forms part of a system of symbols that transcends any lone individual because it is cultural. With the exception of a single subfield (to be discussed later), anthropologists are concerned with group rather than with personality processes. Hostility becomes of interest to anthropologists only when it is expressed, aroused, or controlled either in institutionalized form, or in terms of symbols created not by the individual but by his society as a whole.

Culture has been American anthropology's major contribution to our perception of man. No longer do we automatically ascribe an outsider's differences to his being a "native" or a "foreigner" and therefore biologically inferior to ourselves, at best childlike and at worst, criminal. We appreciate that the apparently strange behavior of others may form part of an understandable and coherent social structure and pattern of meanings. We have learned to accept, for example, that some cultures may scold their gods instead of beseeching them, or expect a man to discipline his sisters' children rather than

*Dr. Barkow is Associate Professor of Anthropology, Department of Sociology and Social Anthropology, Dalhousie University, Halifax, Nova Scotia.

his wife's (wives'). Some cultures create much hostility in the individual, and some little; some may demand that he suppress it, and others offer him channels for its expression.

MALLEABILITY AND HOSTILITY

Anthropology has taught its lesson of the power of culture by stressing the malleability of human behavior. Nowhere has the Freudian stress on the primacy of early learning been more accepted than among anthropologists. Ethnographers often seem to view human beings as passive sponges, absorbing their society's traditions by "enculturation." This emphasis on human flexibility and the importance of culture has led to a debate, among anthropologists, concerning the nature of hostility and aggression.

In their battle against those who would "explain" behavioral diversity by appealing to supposed biological differences between groups, anthropologists have tended to make of culture not merely a shaper but a creator—a creator of human nature. Is aggression necessarily part of our behavior? Some have argued "no," claiming that the few remaining peoples of the world who still make a living by hunting and gathering are neither aggressive nor territorial. The issue is a vital one, for we were hunters and gatherers for most of our existence as a species. Human beings have been around for perhaps one million years; only during the past ten thousand have we become farmers, herders, and high-technology industrialists. If hunters and gatherers are peaceful, the argument goes, then we too must be inherently peaceful. Therefore our wars and hostilities are the products of our civilizations and not the inevitable results of human nature.

This kind of argument can easily confuse interpersonal hostility with organized aggression. Hunting and gathering societies do indeed tend to be peaceful, but, as the human ethologist Irenäus Eibl-Eibesfeldt has pointed out, they have their share of interpersonal hostility. Sibling rivalry is likely to be a human universal; anger, quarrels, and arguments certainly exist everywhere. But the degree and expression of hostility vary enormously from one society to another.

One determinant of a society's aggressiveness is how it makes a living—its ecology. Hunters and gatherers, for example, must live in small, nomadic bands. Large, stationary groups would rapidly exhaust the game and plant foods in any given area. Hunter-gatherer cultures necessarily lack large-scale, organized warfare, since they also lack large-scale social organization and a stored food surplus. The ecology here is a limiting factor on the nature of aggression.

But the ecology can also affect the level of hostility. Food sharing is a must among hunter-gatherers. Not everyone hunts or even gathers every day, and sharing is a necessity. It is also a wise investment on the part of even the best hunter, for he and his family alone would in any case be unable to devour all of a large kill. So, we find that generosity is an important trait of hunter-gatherers and is early taught to the children. At the same time, children have relatively little work to do, and much of their task develops naturally from playing at the work of the adults. Harsh discipline is therefore unnecessary, and hunter-gatherer child-training tends to be quite indulgent. This presumably lowers the amount of frustration and hostility the child experiences. The anger that does arise, however, can be directly expressed. At worst, a quarrel with another is likely to lead to one of the disputants simply changing local bands.

Farmers are in a very different situation. At the level of organized aggression, they are likely to have the scale and resources to permit warfare. Moreover, there stored reserves and stationary wealth attract those who covet them, making war even more likely (at least for defense).

Farming work itself is demanding, monotonous, and tedious. It requires rigid adherence to schedule. Not surprisingly, farmers emphasize obedience in training their children. It seems quite possible that childhood frustration and hostility is stronger among farmers than among, for example, hunter-gatherers. Moreover, a farmer is chained to his farm–to move away is to lose his land and crop. Thus, farmers must learn to get along with one another, at least on the surface. Their anger and hostility are therefore likely to be expressed covertly. As we will see in the Hausa example, discussed below, covert hostility often takes the form of sorcery.

Culture does indeed pattern the nature of aggression and hostility, but it does not do so in a vacuum. Our ecology and technology–and historical patterns and traditions–influence both the extent to which we experience hostility and the manner in which we express it. In one society, the hostility that is a part of our human potential may be exaggerated; in another, it may be minimized. In one, it may be expressed in organized warfare, or ethnocentrically displaced against neighboring peoples who serve as scapegoats; in another society, it may be expressed only in terms of individual against individual, or at the most, kin-group against kin-group. Hostility is a part of human nature, but war and other forms of organized aggression are products of culture and of history, and of all the factors that affect them.

A HAUSA EXAMPLE OF CULTURALLY PATTERNED HOSTILITY

The Hausa of the northern states of Nigeria provide a good example of how culture patterns the expression of hostility. This farming culture strongly emphasizes the careful control of emotional expression, particularly among the aristocracy. Abusing someone publicly is considered quite low-status behavior, whereas physical violence rarely occurs. Come what may, an individual should be calm and good-humored, his voice never raised.

In such a culture, an outsider needs practice merely to recognize a hostile interaction. For example, Hausa greetings are ordinarily lengthy and ritualized. Cutting one short indicates hostility, whereas ignoring one entirely *(yanga)* shows very serious hostility. Most of the time, one greets even an enemy with the same smiling face and polite inquiries one addresses to a friend. There is rarely, on the surface, much sign that anger and hostility exist at all.

Sorcery is the great avenue of hostility, and individuals often have a personal relationship with a particular *mallam* (Moslem scholar and supernatural practitioner). Some may frequent the non-Moslem practitioner or *boka,* who is familiar with the supernatural properties of a wide range of herbs (or who claims to obtain such knowledge from the spirits). The *mallam* can supply protection from the malevolence of others. Amulets with the proper sura of the Quran or (in the case of the *boka*) the appropriate herb negate the hostile intentions of others. So too may *rubutu*—the water resulting from the washing of a wooden prayer board upon which had been written the appropriate sura of the Quran. But the *mallamai* and *bokaye* are said to have offensive as well as defensive powers. Some are believed to be able to drive a client's enemy mad, or to cause him to wander about aimlessly. Some can cause illness or death—or failure in civil service examinations. Though Hausa publicly accept all misfortune as the will of Allah, to be passively accepted, many privately ascribe it to sorcery, to an enemy having a supernatural practitioner more powerful than their own.

The hostility-sorcery system among the Hausa functions effectively. First, it is self-evidently valid to its participants, for the misfortune that is the lot of us all proves (to them) the reality of sorcery. Thus, misfortune need not be mysterious and demoralizing, for it always has an explanation (other than attributing it to Allah). Second, people have ways to protect themselves against the aggression of others and need not feel helpless or defenseless. Third, they are able to act out their hostility without fear of the social sanctions that would punish its overt expression. Thus, individuals are enabled to continue to suppress their hostilities in public.

PSYCHOLOGICAL ANTHROPOLOGY

Off to the side of social and cultural anthropology is psychological anthropology or "culture and personality." This subfield, born in part of the impact of Freudian thought on anthropology, *does* expressly consider hostility per se (rather than limiting itself to more macroscopic forms of organized aggression, such as warfare).

Psychological anthropology is a field so diverse that there is not even a consensus as to whether it is to be called by that term or by its older name, "culture and personality." In its early form, it attempted such feats as portraying subsistence economy as causing childrearing practices, which in turn were thought to give rise to personality dispositions that were directly expressed in cultural institutions. This school of thought was centered around the 1930s Columbia University seminar organized by psychoanalyst Abram Kardiner and anthropologist Ralph Linton. One of the participants in their seminar was Cora Dubois.

Dubois studied the village of Atimelang on the island of Alor, in what is now Indonesia. Using the data she brought back, the Kardiner-Linton seminar addressed itself to the question of why there was so much distrust between the sexes among the Alorese, and why men combined high hostility toward women with high dependence on them. The root cause, the seminar found, was the subsistence economy of Alor. In this society, in which women grew most of the food, infants would be left at home with others while their mothers worked in the field. At the age of five or six, boys would go off to roam with other boys, while the groups of girls would stay closer to their mothers. Mothers and other adults would often tease and frighten young children, then calm them with gifts of food.

The seminar concluded that Alorese cross-sex tension was due to early oral frustration. Men continued to search all their adult lives for a nurturing "mother." Since no woman could meet such needs, unstable, hostility-filled marriages resulted. The seminar noted that men would often call their wives "mother."

This kind of analysis, which considers an entire culture as if it were a single individual and treats social-historical processes as identical to intra-psychic processes, represents a kind of artistic triumph. A great deal of varied data is pieced together to form a consistent whole—a whole at times verified (to the extent possible) by independently analyzed Rorschach tests. But art is not science. Another anthropologist, Hortense Powdermaker, working in Lesu on the island of New Ireland in Melanesia, found that there, too, mothers left infants with others and spent their days in the fields. Yet, the New Ireland personality and cultural institutions were quite different from those of Alor. Impressive as Kardiner-type analyses may be, they fail to be replicable scientific studies.

One of the drawbacks of the Kardiner-Linton approach was that only a single society could be studied at a time. A comparative dimension, as the New Ireland example showed, was missing. In 1953, anthropologist John Whiting and psychologist Irvin Child published a study that was not merely comparative but an actual survey of a comprehensive world sample of societies. They chose variables from five systems of behavior—the oral, anal, sexual, aggressive, and dependence—and based their hypotheses on the idea of "negative fixation." If an individual is severely frustrated during his socialization of any one of these systems, he should be anxiously preoccupied with it in his adult life. As a measure of frustration, they used ethnographic descriptions of child-training systems, rating them in terms of a number of different scales. Theories of illness were their measure of adult "anxious preoccupation." For example, an early weaning in which the nipples are coated with pepper should be associated with a belief that illness is caused orally—by eating or drinking poison, perhaps, or by verbal spells or incantations. Though they were less successful in their predictions with the other behavior systems, those dealing with the effects of early oral frustration were largely confirmed.

The Whiting and Child study gave rise to a sophisticated school of research in which cross-cultural surveys were used to test various aspects of personality theory. Though much of the research was successful, and studies of this kind are still carried out, they suffer from excessive reliance on inference. Actual children are not looked at, for example, and the personality effects of idealized generalizations about child-training techniques are only inferred. Similarly, adult personalities are not studied, their psychodynamics being inferred from cultural institutions (such as theories of disease). Once again, the relationship between cultural traits (e.g., child-training techniques and disease theories) are treated not in terms of a theory of history or sociocultural evolution but in terms of a theory of individual psychodynamics.

Whiting and his co-workers at Harvard therefore mounted a major study in which actual people and actual behavior would be looked at. The comparative aspect was retained by sending six teams of investigators to six different cultures, each armed with carefully prepared data-collection manuals so that their respective research results would be comparable. The focus was on specific categories of behavior in specific settings, rather than on personality dynamics. The study found, for example, that children in cultures with nuclear families tend to be more aggressive than children in nonnuclear societies. It is not clear why this should be so, or what the psychodynamics involved are. Moreover, since "aggression" here means an observed, overt act (as defined in a rating manual), we have no data about the inner feelings of hostility involved.

Where the Whiting school has emphasized child socialization, Melford Spiro of the University of California at San Diego has emphasized adult personality. His concern with why people are motivated to take up the social roles of which their societies are composed is much closer to the "mainstream" of anthropological thought than is that of the Whiting school. Spiro's research on Ifaluk (in the South Pacific) and more recently in Burma has led him to conclude that people fulfill their social roles because by doing so they satisfy their own inner needs.

How do we handle our feelings of hostility? Repressing them may lead to guilt and depression and do no one any good at all, Spiro explains. Instead, our cultures often permit us to gratify them in socially approved and even useful ways. Perhaps I can project and displace my anger against the malevolent spirits that my religion says surround us. Perhaps it is the neighboring ethnic group, or some other enemy, whom I am encouraged to hate. My culture may have an avoidance rule between son-in-law and mother-in-law, so that my hostility toward her never has repercussions (though in this case, it is not really gratified, either). Women's hostility toward male repression may be permitted expression in a yearly ritual-of-reversal holiday, when females are encouraged to dress in men's clothing and to join other women in physically assaulting any man they meet.

In Spiro's terms, these are "culturally constituted defense mechanisms." Socially and personally unacceptable feelings–including but by no means limited to hostility–are displaced, projected, or sublimated in culturally patterned ways. Individuals utilizing these defenses cannot be said to suffer from pathology because their behavior is acceptable, in their social milieu, and they are able to function effectively. Identical defenses and beliefs in an individual of a different culture, of course, might well be pathological.

CONCLUSIONS

Non-Western societies often seem to permit easier management of hostility than does our own. Culturally constituted defenses appear to be more available to non-Westerners than to ourselves. Religion-supported rationalizations, akin to our own former belief that the successfully evil will be punished supernaturally in an afterlife, are widespread. Groups that might incite envy are often walled-off, psychologically encapsulated as a sort of different species, so that those with low social position can accept their place vis-a-vis upper classes or castes. Ethnocentric displacement of hostility to outside groups is both frequent and acceptable among the world's cultures. Guilt about hating those different in race or language or culture appears, outside our own society, to be quite rare. It seems quite possible that strong hostile feelings may be more destructive for us than for many less "liberal" and "sophisticated" peoples.

But this conclusion is perhaps premature, for research continues. The nature of intersocietal warfare remains a topic of major interest in anthropology. The field of psychological anthropology is in the midst of a renaissance, with a recently formed Society for Psychological Anthropology and the journals *Ethos* and *The Journal of Psychological Anthropology* publishing excellent original research and theory papers. Although no general anthropological theory of hostility exists (and why should we expect one?), these journals frequently include careful particularistic studies of the psychodynamics and socialization of hostility and aggression in the various cultures of the world.

BIBLIOGRAPHIC NOTES AND REFERENCES:

For a general introduction to the concept of culture, see Ralph L. Beals, Harry Hoijer, and Alan R. Beals, *Introduction to Anthropology,* 5th ed. (New York: Macmillian Publishing Co., 1977).

For a symposium on the anthropolgical study of war, see Morton H. Fried, Marvin Harris, and Robert Murphy, eds., *War: The Anthropology of Armed Conflict and Aggression* (New York: Natural History Press, 1968). For more recent work along these lines, see Martin H. Nettleship, R. Dale Givens, and Anderson Nettleship, eds., *War, Its Causes and Correlates* (World Anthropology Series, The Hague: Mouton; Chicago: Aldine, 1975); and the rather uneven but often interesting volume of discussions of the topic by the contributors to the previous work: Martin Nettleship, R. Dale Givens, and Anderson Nettleship, eds., *Discussions on War and Human Agression* (World Anthropology Series, The Hague: Mouton; Chicago: Aldine, 1976). But for the reader concerned with how socialization can reduce and control the expression of aggression and hostility, the most important work is Ashley Montagu's reader, *Learning Non-Aggression. The Experience of Non-Literate Societies.* (Oxford: Oxford University Press, 1978). Many of the contributors to this volume emphasize the importance of prolonged and loving mother–infant contact in the child-rearing practices of the nonaggressive peoples they have studied.

For a discussion of aggression in hunting-gathering societies, see Irenäus Eibl-Eibesfeldt, "The Myth of the Aggression-Free Hunter and Gatherer Society," in Ralph L. Holloway, ed., *Primate Aggression, Territoriality, and Xenophobia* (New York: Academic Press, 1974, pp. 435–458).

For an ethnography of one of the world's more aggressive peoples, see Napoleon A. Chagnon, *Yanomamö. The Fierce People,* 2nd ed. (New York: Holt, Rinehart and Winston, 1977).

For an introduction and bibliography to the Hausa of West Africa, see Jerome H. Barkow, "The Hausa," in Richard Weekes, ed., *Muslim Peoples: World Ethnographic Survey* (Westport, Conn.: Greenwood Press, 1978).

A good synthesis of psychological anthropology is Robert A. LeVine's *Culture, Behavior, and Personality* (Chicago: Aldine, 1973). A less personal view of that field is the collection edited by Francis L. K. Hsu, *Psychological Anthropology. New Edition* (Cambridge, Mass.: Schenkman Publishing Co., 1972). The last chapter of that volume, Melford Spiro's "An Overview and a Suggested Reorientation," includes a discussion of his idea of "culturally constituted defense mechanisms." Chapter 12 of that work, by Charles Harrington and John W. M. Whiting, is a good overview of Whiting's school of thought. Readers wanting a closer look at Whiting's older work should see John W. M. Whiting and Irvin L. Child, *Child Training and Personality* (New Haven: Yale University Press, 1953). Those concerned with his more recent approaches should consult Beatrice B. Whiting and

John W. M. Whiting, *Children of Six Cultures. A Psycho-Cultural Analysis* (Cambridge, Mass.: Harvard University Press, 1975).

The work of the Kardiner-Linton seminar is contained in part in Abram Kardiner's *Psychological Frontiers of Society* (New York: Columbia University Press, 1945). Hortense Powdermaker's study is *Life in Lesu* (New York: W. W. Norton and Company, 1938).

For a fascinating study of how envy and the hostility it creates are controlled and expressed by culture, see George M. Foster, "The Anatomy of Envy: A Study in Symbolic Behavior," *Current Anthropology,* 1972, vol. 13, pp. 165–201.

Psychiatric anthropology (transcultural psychiatry) has been omitted from this chapter because its focus on psychopathology makes it more properly a branch of psychiatry than a subfield of anthropology. Readers interested in this area might begin with the CIBA Foundation symposium reader edited by A. V. S. DeReuck, *Transcultural Psychiatry* (London: J. and A. Churchill, 1965).

17 Some Physiological Bases of Psychodynamics

Since human experience is always bound up with the processes occurring in a living organism, the relations between fundamental biological problems and the general problems of philosophy must be regarded as very intimate.

Ralph Lillie

The new world picture does not wipe out the old one, but permits it to stand in its entirety, and merely adds a special condition for it. This special condition involves a certain limitation, but because of this very fact it simplifies the world picture considerably . . . .

Max Planck

EMERGENCE OF PSYCHODYNAMICS

Modern medicine has arisen chiefly from the study of the inner machinery of the human organism. Psychodynamics studies a different aspect of this organism, on a different level, as a unit, noting its behavior, its motivations, its inner drives and tensions, even its hidden feelings and emotional forces—for these determine the course of the organism's life, its joys, its sufferings, and many of its ailments.

Psychodynamics is the science of the motivations of biological organisms. It is the science of the drives that power our bodies, minds, feelings, thoughts, and behavior. Our minds are powered by (1) the biological drives and processes of our bodies and also by (2) our reactions to the circumstances of life to which we must adapt. Thus psychodynamics stands between biology and sociology. It deals with the total personality, with all relevant motivations and determinants of behavior, external as well as internal.

Psychodynamics is a new biological science. It is fundamental to understanding life in general, and particularly human life. It is part of medicine's contribution to biological science and to the understanding of human beings.

As a science of motivation, it is fundamental to understanding all biological organisms: (1) ourselves, our families, our friends, our pets; and (2) cultures, societies, and history. As a medical subject it is fundamental to understanding (3) patients and therefore the proper practice of medicine. Every disease and every disorder occurs in a human being who is tense with emotion. Helping a patient is usually like repairing a car while it is running at 45 miles per hour. For all diseases occur not in static structures, but in feeling, thinking, functioning, intensely motivated organisms. A patient's recovery, to paraphrase Osler, often depends as much upon what is in his mind as upon what is in his body.

One can never get away from psychodynamics, not in drama, literature, art, not even in recreation, or in life in all its forms, for it is the science of man's mental and emotional life.

Once the matter looked rather simple: there were the "crazy people" in the "asylums," and there were the normal people outside, and great stigma attached to the poor sufferers on the inside. With the recognition of Freud's work, the *neurotic* came into the limelight. The neurotic, too, carried a stigma. He was thought of as not mentally normal like the rest of us.

But the study of neurotics produced some revolutionary effects; for "neurosis" was found to take myriad forms. A woman had symptoms of "anxiety hysteria"; she was afraid to be alone and became panicky in crowds or in closed places such as the upper berths on a train. She was able to get herself into a theater, but only if she could sit on the aisle near the rear and feel that she could get out easily. She dreaded riding in subways. However, she had reasonably good relations with her family and friends and held a well-paying, responsible job.

The next woman, although not a "neurotic with anxiety hysteria and phobias," nagged her children, henpecked her husband, and eventually broke up her home with a divorce. Here the neurosis was not in the feelings of anxiety which hampered her freedom of movement but in her behavior toward the members of her own family. Here the neurosis was in her personality and her behavior.

Originally, it was thought that healthy personalities suffered from neuroses as sort of foreign bodies, much as one might have a splinter in one's finger or a shell fragment in an otherwise healthy back—or bacteria in one's throat. However, it came to be recognized that personalities could be neurotic.

Exploring personalities further, it was quickly found that no one is free of inner tensions; no one is free from conflicts; no one is on perfect terms with himself, with his conscience, with his parents, brothers, and sisters, with his wife and children, with his friends and associates. The elements of neuroses, emotional tension and emotional conflict, are in everyone, and these inner tensions and conflicts come out in innumerable forms, not only in specific neurotic symptoms, such as anxieties and phobias, or compulsions, but also in (1) family tensions and divorces, (2) alcoholism and drug addictions, (3) wrecked careers and mismanaged lives, (4) delinquency and crime, and (5) all manner of physical symptoms, in disturbances of the heart and the circulation, disorders of the stomach, asthma, headache, colitis, constipation, dysmenorrhea, and many other "psychosomatic" disorders.

These same forces of inner conflict and tension, which cause so much personal suffering in private lives in the form of psychosis, neurosis, alcoholism, broken homes, accidents, psychosomatic symptoms, and wrecked careers, also play a significant role in social affairs. We see that persons who are driven by infantile emotions can come into positions of power and leadership. We see that great numbers of individuals in a population can join together to make common cause with their tension, conflicts, demands, hates, and violence. We see that the sources of tension within groups and between groups are identical with the sources of tension within individuals and between individuals. The groups may be tiny, they may be social, scientific, educational, political, or of any other type, or they may be great nations. It has become commonplace to speak of a sick nation, a sick Europe, or a sick world. This is a perfectly correct use of the term.

With the triumphs over the infectious diseases, a new type of disorder has arisen on the list of the great enemies of the human body. Heart disease, the allergies, hyperthyroidism, diabetes, arthritis, and the like, are all diseases that more and more have seemed to result in part from the stresses and strains of life.

Many a dread disease stems from the way in which the sufferer lives—and the way a person lives is determined largely by his motivations.

Indeed, even the infectious diseases are often determined mostly by human motivation. For example, the incidence of tuberculosis, which drastically increased in large areas of Europe, and the even higher incidence (in certain areas, at least) of syphilis were aftermaths of World War II, that is, a result of man-made catastrophe, which, in turn, was a result of human motivation. The next great increase in venereal disease followed the use of "the pill" and the age of permissiveness.

Psychodynamics is a branch of biology; it is also fundamental to the social sciences, which deal with the motivations and the behavior of the biological unit man in social groups. It can be a contribution of first importance to civilization.

The nucleus of human motivations consists of the motivations of childhood. Beneath the surface of every adult are the attitudes and the motivations that he had as a child. They are hidden, disguised, and distorted by the front he puts up to the world. The adult can be under-

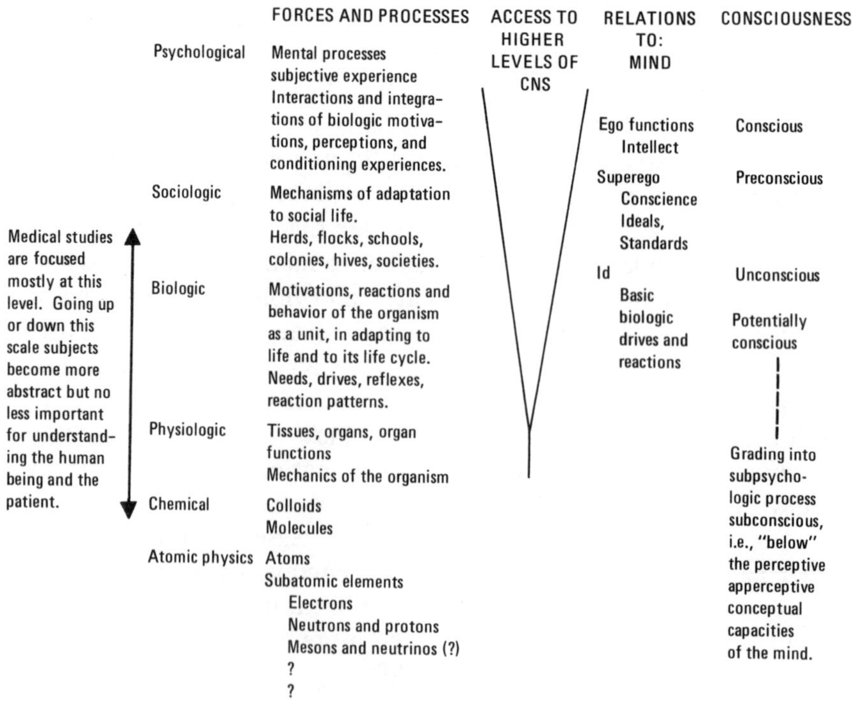

Figure 1

stood only through understanding them. This insight, long the province of the great writers, dramatists, poets, and philosophers and of folk-wisdom, is now becoming a part of the science of psychodynamics.

Psychological capacity depends largely on an individual's own internal emotional makeup. It can be influenced and improved by experience in life, by direct study, and through a personal analysis.

Life experience deepens understanding through (1) observation and (2) personal adventures, joys, and sufferings. Probably only through personal experience can anyone appreciate marriage, children, what illness means in a home, and other deeply moving experiences of life. The key to psychodynamic understanding is simply "emotional honesty."

The concept of "levels" is a valuable one and has been used in many ways:

In the limitless vistas of astronomical space, there is an all but imperceptible mote in the form of a colloidal suspension. This bit of matter is utterly negligible in amount, compared with the universe. All there is of it is on our earth—so far as we know. It persists through constituting what we call life, living protoplasm. Minute though it is, it is also (in our present knowledge) unique, a bit of highly unstable, "watery salt," clinging to a speck in the universe.

One tissue developed by a small part of this colloidal suspension is the brain. And a function of this form of the suspension is what we call mind, and in particular, consciousness.

The consciousness of human beings, as of other animals on our earth, the will, judgment, memory, reason, in short, the conscious "ego," is inconceivably insignificant and impotent, being at the mercy of biological forces from within and of the incomprehensibly vast physical forces of the universe. Figure 2 is an attempt to diagram this.

The body and brain are threatened with injury and destruction at all levels by atomic radiations, bacteria and viruses, pollution, overpopulation, innumerable aberrations of chemistry, diet, climate, and, above all, other human beings.

The cortex of the brain, has evolved over millions of years, despite all the dangers to man. It is this tissue that makes possible the human mind. It is especially valued biologically in the sense that, in starvation, for example, all other tissues are drawn upon first. It is preserved to the last.

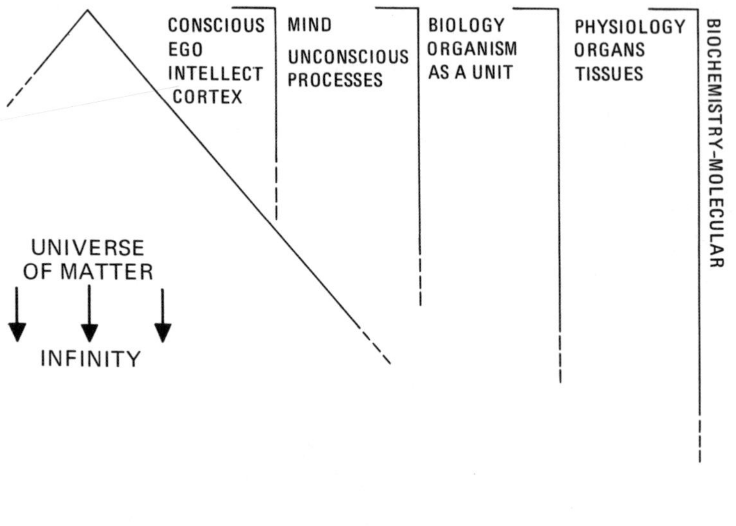

Figure 2

EMOTIONS AND PHYSIOLOGY

Psychodynamics means "the interplay of emotional forces." Our first objective is to grasp the reality of the biological motivations, to see that they are powerful forces that (1) affect the physiological functioning of the organism, and (2) affect our perception, thinking, feelings, and behavior. It is not necessary to enmesh ourselves in fine distinctions and definitions so long as we agree that we are dealing with motivational forces and use the term that seems best to fit the situation we are describing.

Psychodynamics has developed in part from physiology. It rests on the fundamentals of the past—the classic work of Freud, Pavlov, and Cannon, which is as important today as when published. The superego (roughly, the conscience and standards) is the "conditioned" part of our minds—the conditioned reactions accumulated especially during childhood, which so dictate our reactions in adult life.

The first serious systematic study of the physiology of the emotions was by Walter Cannon. On the basis of these studies, Cannon formulated his theory of the "emergency mobilization for fight or flight." The emergency reserves of the body are mobilized, and the whole organism is able in this state of arousal to perform feats far beyond its ordinary capacities. This concept of mobilization for fight or flight as a method of biological reaction and adaptation has turned out to be fundamental in understanding the psychodynamics of much of man's ordinary behavior and also of his personal and social problems.

In sum, the body functions as a biological unit and is constantly adapting. This process is reflected in and achieved by constant fine, sensitive, physiological adjustments which maintain the body's stability or "homeostasis."

EMOTIONAL FORCES CAN AFFECT THE PHYSIOLOGY TO PRODUCE SYMPTOMS

Chronic physiological arousal, either general or partial, or other types of physiological disturbance can represent a failure of adaptation to a stress or threat. In other words, the body's own natural defensive reaction can become so protracted or disordered as to constitute symptoms. This is of importance in our thinking and in our concepts of what we call physical disease, and mental and emotional illness. It shows that the symptoms and disease (at least in one aspect) can consist of the body's defensive reactions against threats to its integrity.

In an acute infection, the body's temperature rises as part of its normal defense against the causative bacteria. It may be, however, that the temperature rises above 106°F and therefore itself becomes a threat to the individual. In any event, the symptoms that we see in many diseases consist largely of defensive reactions of the body.

The body's defensive reactions are much the same for many different irritants and dangers. For example, the temperature rises as a defense against a variety of infections and also in some other conditions. The reaction of inflammation is much the same to a great variety of irritants, including infections. The fight–flight reaction is an element or form of defense against all sorts of dangers; fear and rage are subjective feelings that are also themselves *part* of the organism's reaction to some threat or stress.

Emotional stress is often a factor in disease. Emotional forces play some role in every case in their relationship to the *will to get well.* Eugene O'Neill's *The Straw* depicts the will to live of a young girl in a tuberculosis sanitorium when she feels that she is loved and can look forward to marriage with the man of her heart, and how she becomes depressed and sags toward her death when she feels abandoned by him and by the world.

Emotional forces take the form of self-destructive tendencies, for example, in diabetics who cheat on their diets, in sufferers from tuberculosis or heart disease who drive themselves mercilessly until they break down again, in cases of stomach ulcers, in coronary disease, and in a variety of other conditions, in which the individual fails to arrange his life properly, and flagrantly or subtly brings about his death.

Emotion and motivation must also be reckoned with in considering the *results* of illness, and emotional forces play their part in those invalids who utilize illness in order to justify dependence, to tyrannize over others and otherwise exploit their condition. It is well known, of course, that very many individuals consciously or unconsciously "malinger"; that is, they tend to remain ill in order to utilize their disabilities for the purpose of collecting compensation or insurance or for other reasons.

Chronic Stress Symptoms

If we ask why symptoms caused by emotional stress are so common, we immediately come face to face with vast problems of epidemiology and prevention–problems that have their roots in our social life and in the kinds of adults produced by our present benighted ways of rearing children.

Regardless of class, every man, woman, and child goes through life under a burden of strain and anxiety. Money, power, position make little difference. Most people go through life with some combination of constant fear, like the Timid Soul, or constant anger, like the Terrible Tempered Mr. Bang.

What is the nature of these emotional strains which are so universal in our civilization? Two factors are involved: the stress upon the person, and the person's capacity to meet the stress.

Stresses are both external and internal:

1. *External Stresses.* No matter how stable and mature a person is, he is subjected, from birth, to a variety of external stresses–from nature, from disease, and especially from the hostilities of other human beings in some form. There are always financial insecurity and taxes.

There are wars and danger of wars. There are the atom bomb and pollution and overpopulation.

2. *Internal Stresses.* In addition to "the slings and arrows of outrageous fortune," man is subject to pressures and poisons from within. Generally, these inner stresses derive from the frustrations of conflicting infantile and mature drives.

Man craves what he wanted in infancy and childhood—exclusive love, security, protection, help, praise, esteem, and recognition. Frustration is inevitable, for the world of nature and mankind is not the strong, kind, understanding parent of the child's yearnings. Thus, man harbors cravings that are unsatisfied and forever unsatisfiable.

People are driven by motivations that are partly infantile and partly mature, which, tragically, conflict in varying degrees with the world and with each other. In the adult who is adequately mature emotionally, both the infantile and the mature motivations can blend and can be realizable and enjoyed. The normal adult enjoys both. But almost everyone, strive as he will, feels the stress of frustration, guilt, shame, and inferiority and of chronic anger and anxiety.

Needless to say, most people sustain a combination of internal and external stresses. Moreover, each person is to a considerable extent himself responsible for the external stresses upon him. People tend through their own inner makeups to marry difficult spouses, to keep themselves financially insecure, and so on, quite unconsciously handling their lives in ways that cause them troubles. Constant emotional stress, say anxiety, tends to keep the physiology always aroused for flight or fight.

Yet, a person who is under ceaseless stress usually develops only certain signs and symptoms. Not always is his entire physiology aroused, at least not sufficiently so to produce symptoms. Some parts of the physiology usually respond to the strain more than others. The pulse is too fast, or the blood pressure is elevated, or the stomach action disordered, without other involvements being equally prominent.

There is a difference in the physiological responses to acute, transient stress and to chronic stress. If the danger and the fear continue indefinitely, the organism tends to adapt in some way. The arousal for fight or flight quiets down, but not necessarily evenly and equally. The adaptation is partial, and a partial mobilization may persist. The continuing anxiety may keep the fast pulse, the sweating, or other of the acute responses going, while the remainder return to relative equilibrium. It may also be that the whole physiology returns to relatively normal basal functioning, but, because of the constant stimulus of the anxiety, is kept in a hyperreactive state.

EMOTIONAL FORCES CAN AFFECT THE PHYSIOLOGY TO PRODUCE TISSUE DAMAGE

It is well recognized that prolonged functional reactions can produce structural damage in the tissues concerned. Basically, the distinction between function and structure perhaps resolves itself. However, the distinction is valid as a gross statement on our present level of observation. "You can kill a horse but you can't kill a mule." The horse will allow himself to be driven to death, but the mule will "stubbornly" stop before its heart or other organs are structurally damaged by overexertion.

The illustrious anatomist John Hunter said of his angina, "My life is at the mercy of any rascal who can make me angry."

The knock in an automobile engine may result not from any structural damage in the engine but from the fact that the car is being driven up a steep hill in high gear at too low a speed. But if the car is driven in this way too much, structural change takes place.

Scientific evidence for the effects of stress in producing gross structural damage to the organism derives from a number of sources, the most systematic experimental work on the effects of stress in producing structural pathology being that of Hans Selye.

Suppose you are subjected to prolonged cold or to prolonged ill-treatment. At first there is the alarm reaction, the emergency mobilization for fight or flight, to meet the threat. Then come longer-range efforts to adapt to the strain. If the resistance of body and mind are not sufficiently tough by this time, there ensues some sort of exhaustion and disruption in one or more of the systems of the body.

The mechanisms of adaptation are intricate and delicate. Under too severe and prolonged stress, disorders occur. They occur on all levels, in thinking, feeling, behavior, as psychological symptoms and physiologically, as psychosomatic symptoms. The total individual tries to adapt, but one mechanism may be involved more than another, and under excessive stress one regulating, adaptive mechanism may fail and suffer damage more than another. It is a matter of the make-up of the individual organism, with its specific vulnerabilities, versus the nature and the duration of the stress. The stress can cause damage severe enough to eventuate in death.

Among the diseases that are apparently unsuccessful efforts at adaptation there must be considered: hypertension and renal diseases, periarteritis nodosa, nephritis, rheumatic diseases and eclampsia, "accidental thymus involution," appendicitis and tonsillitis (there being much lymphoid tissue in the appendix and the tonsils), Cushing's syndrome (pituitary hyperfunction), secondary shock, acute gastrointestinal ulcers which develop in conjunction with adrenal hemorrhages after extensive burns, or especially acute infections or intoxications, Addison's disease (destruction of adrenals), and Simmonds' disease (destruction of the pituitary).

Because of the great advances in the control of the infectious diseases, it is now estimated that approximately 50 percent of the total population of the United States will die from one or another of the diseases of adaptation, especially those accompanied by hypertension or arteriosclerosis.

The stage of resistance to the strain or stress may last for years, well into middle age, before the signs of failing adaptation appear physiologically and psychologically.

EMOTIONAL FORCES CAN AFFECT PERCEPTION, THINKING, FEELING, AND BEHAVIOR

When we use the word "disease" we usually lump together both the noxious agent and the body's defensive responses to it. Therefore, we have used the term "emotional stress" in a similar way to include both the threat to the individual and the individual's response to this threat.

As we would expect, the functioning of the brain (like that of any other part) can be disturbed by emotional stress as well as by other agents such as drugs, alcohol, infections, fatigue, extremes of temperature, and the like.

The functions of the brain are as follows:

1. Perception through the senses of the internal urges and feelings and of the outer world.
2. Integrative intellectual processes including thinking and memory.
3. Executive transmission and perception of emotion (feelings, affects).

Perception. Extremes of disordered perception are seen in hallucinations, delusions, and illusions. Misinterpretations (illusions) and hallucinations (perceptions where there is nothing to perceive) can occur through all of the senses, including taste and smell.

Dreams. When we sleep, we all hallucinate; that is, we conjure up visions, dreams that, as long as we sleep, we believe to be reality.

Outlook and Views. When an individual is in high spirits, he tends to see the happier things in life through "rose-colored glasses"; when he is depressed, he tends to note chiefly that which is gloomy and distressing. In the event of an accident, no two witnesses later tell exactly the same story, no matter how honestly they try to describe what they saw.

Behavior. Sometimes a disorder of behavior is the central feature in an emotional disturbance.

One man was in his thirties, handsome, energetic, and able, a pillar of society and possessing warm friends, a fine family, and home life. Yet every so often, perhaps without meaning to do so, he would drink himself out of the picture. A few episodes of drinking sufficed to make him lose his position, which was an excellent one, and drove his wife to consider divorce, in spite of the fact that they had children. When such an episode was over, he would do everthing to repair the damage, usually managing to reestablish himself, and all would go well for a few months or several years. Then he would drink again and perhaps disappear for a week. His friends and family had so much confidence in him that, despite all this, they finally set him up in business for himself. This flourished for nearly a year; then all his fine characteristics, level-headedness, and good judgment notwithstanding, he again gave himself up to drink.

The emotional forces that impel a person to such behavior, even though it be contrary to the rest of his makeup, are exactly the same as those that produce disturbances in perception, thought, and feelings. There is very apt to be much underlying hostility. Another common tendency in these cases is a much-lowered resistance to the flight reaction. Alcohol offers a quick way of escape, and apparently slight emotional pressures are enough in some individuals to make them flee immediately from the world of reality in this way. The individual may have an excellent external life situation but nevertheless be under great internal stress because of conflicts within his own emotional life, inner feelings of inferiority, guilt, frustration, and the like.

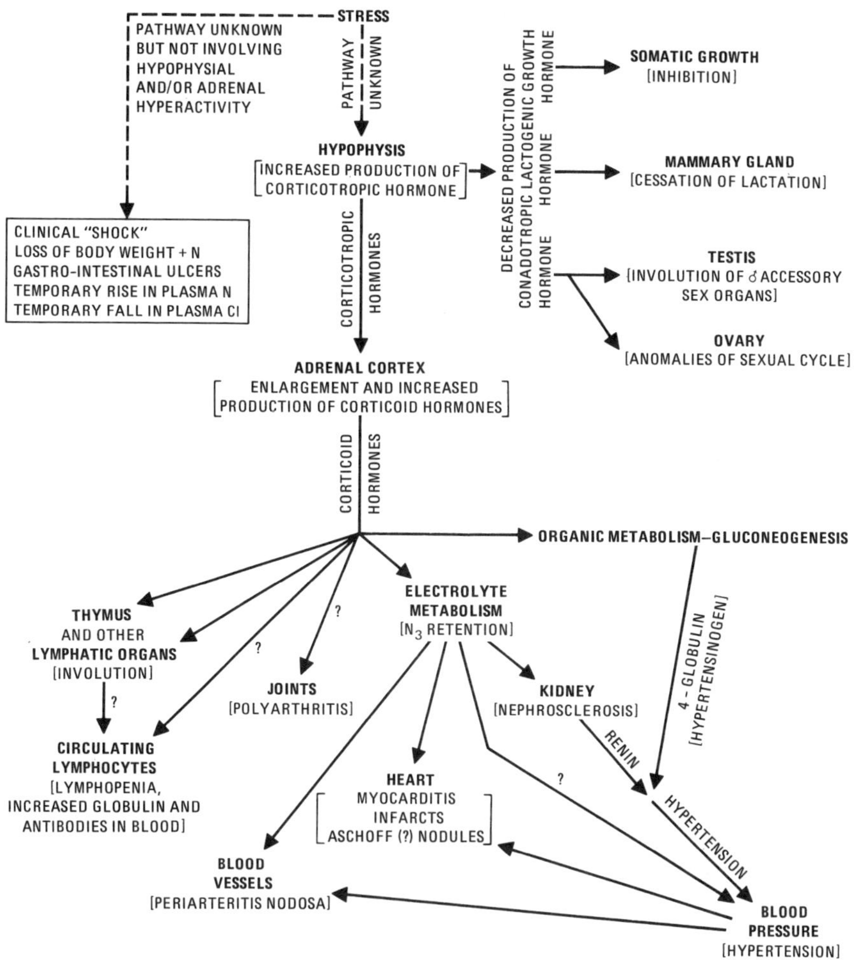

Figure 3

Criminality. Disorders of behavior injure not only the person himself but others. If these injuries are unwitting and unconscious, the condition is "neurotic" in the narrow sense. But if the hostility is more or less consciously accepted by the offender and lived out rather directly, then it is "criminal."

Sociological. Perhaps the most fateful form of behavior disorder is that which, in the general population or in key leaders, directs the decisions of nations and hence the destinies of vast numbers of persons. Historical forces are to a large extent emotional forces. A thoroughgoing understanding of them is probably necessary before any group, just as any individual, will be able to control its destiny rather than, so to speak, have its life lived for it by these unconscious motivations.

We all have motivations and emotions, and internal tensions and problems. If we are able to face the truth, we see something of ourselves in the problems and sufferings of every other human being. "No man is an island," John Donne said. Human sympathy leads to understanding. "The basis of medicine is sympathy and the desire to help others."

Almost any patient who is willing to talk can be "understood" emotionally in terms of the major motivations. For example, an attractive, intelligent young woman, obviously distressed by care and anxiety, related the following complaints:

In the intellectual sphere she told of some confusion and some disturbance of her sense of reality in that at times she had a strange feeling that people were not entirely real.

In her emotions, she felt anxious sometimes to the point of panic, and she often felt severely depressed with a sense of gloom and helplessness and a wish to give up her struggles.

In the area of her physiological functioning, she suffered from nausea and diarrhea, and at times, palpitations.

Fortunately, this young woman's behavior was not grossly disturbed, but only because of a constant supreme effort of will, which was exhausting her. She felt that she was on the verge of breaking down and ceasing to carry out her obligations and responsibilities in life, but she sensed that her only hope lay in forcing herself to carry on in spite of everything. In this she was no doubt correct. Sometimes under emotional pressures a person relinquishes the effort of controlled adult behavior, and the result is a degree of dissolution of part of his personality in which a transient psychosis may develop. Another result is that the individual "regresses," going back to the dependent relationships of childhood. Once these or other effects occur, it may be extremely difficult to get the person back to where he was before. It is as though the mature organized part of the personality, once overwhelmed or weakened, thereby sustains some damage and cannot readily regain command of the emotional forces that have erupted. It is as though a short circuit has occurred in the brain.

What problems did she have? In barest essentials, she was married and had two small children. She had been very carefully and properly brought up under the ever present eye of a strait-laced but kind mother. She was conditioned to be a very proper young woman in all things. However, there arose now in this young woman's life certain difficulties, and it appeared that these difficulties could be resolved satisfactorily through certain compromises with morality. Incredibly, the young woman's mother urged these compromises. From the time of her birth, for nearly 30 years, she had been conditioned to behave in accordance with the highest standards. Now her mother, the very person who had so conditioned her, pushed her to contrary behavior. Thus, her whole "character" was threatened. The girl simply could not believe that her mother was capable of this. All of the girl's standards were shaken. Hence, her feelings of confusion and her sense that people were not quite real. Her mother was not in fact as the patient had thought of her for all these years. Faced with doing something contrary to her strong conscience, she of course felt frightened, guilty, and depressed. In this plight, her physiology responded with mobilization for fight or flight. Hard-pressed emotionally though she was, the healthy part of her mind grasped enough of the reality for her to come for help.

Her ego, with its perception of reality, its judgment, its willpower, its control of behavior, suffered as it was caught between (1) her id desires to solve her life's problems, (2) her superego reactions, shaken as they were by the change in her mother, and (3) the outside world, with which the girl was trying to come to terms in order to make an adjustment for herself and her family. Thus do we all seek to satisfy our primitive animal needs and our standards and consciences in their relationships to each other and to the outside world.

These same emotional forces impel the more mature and the more fortunate to productive and satisfying lives.

SCHEMA OF OPERATION OF EMOTIONAL FORCES

Our exposition thus far has rested upon a number of basic concepts developed by outstanding investigators and their followers. Their work, in turn, rests upon that of eminent forebears of previous generations, such as Claude Bernard, Charcot, and others.

Levels of Integration. A unicellular animal performs all its functions as a single cell. The somewhat larger, but relatively simple, multicellular creatures require some form of coordination and integration of the activities of their cells. In them the nerve net appears. In somewhat higher forms, for instance the earthworm, there is a considerable degree of coordination and integration provided by a well-developed nervous system but with only the bare rudiments of a brain. In the higher biological forms, particularly perhaps when limbs or wings appear, we encounter well-developed brains.

Thus, in the higher mammals the brain not only makes possible the coordination of the body's activities but also integrates these activities with perceptions from the environment and from past training. In the human being it makes possible intricate relationships to an intricate man-made environment as well as highly complex relationships with other human beings.

Automatic Adaptation. The primitive reflexes operate on a low nervous system level; that is, they take place relatively automatically without the participation of those structures in the brain that we consider more highly developed on the evolutionary scale. For example, the peristalsis of the small intestine, or the knee jerk, does not require a brain at all. It is of great help in the organism's adjustment if it is not preoccupied with vegative functionings of the viscera or with purely reflex responses which can be taken care of automatically on "lower levels." The adjustments to the environment, on the other hand, make use of what we call the highest centers of the brain: those concerned with the correlations of perception, thinking, feeling, and behavior. We eat lunch and our viscera digest it while we go about our business.

The brain is the organ par excellence for integrating the activities of the body and for regulating its behavior. With the development of the brain the capacity for adaptation becomes enormously more flexible.

A fundamental principle seems to be that *all modes of adaptation tend to become automatic.* Thus, for example, it is a great effort at first to learn to drive an automobile, but after a while this becomes relatively automatic. The same applies to facility with the piano keyboard or other musical instruments. This is a basic principle in all learning. It probably rests upon the broader principle of conservation of mental energy and the freeing of the mind for other purposes.

Lower centers take over an action and make it automatic so that the higher centers can be free for other tasks of adaptation.

Whatever their origins, all sorts of patterns appear in different biological forms of life. These patterns, in many instances, represent special modes of adaptation; for example, the building of an ant hill or the migration of birds. Man, of course, has his own special methods of adaptation. One of these is the fight–flight reaction, and another is social cooperation. The latter apparently is on the higher biological and evolutionary level of the two methods.

Fight–Flight Reaction. Human history is very largely the story of the struggle of morality, which is an expression of social cooperation, of man's efforts to live in peace together, against the deep-seated automatic fight–flight reaction, and adaptive pattern that served so well in cave and jungle but now, as part of our animal nature, is itself such a threat to civilized social living.

Capacity for Conditioning. An outstanding feature of the human brain is its tremendous capacity for conditioning, which is a form of learning. Every patient who is intensively studied by a psychodynamic psychiatrist demonstrates the finding that the fundamentals of the personality are laid down by the age of approximately six years. If a child comes through even the first three years of life with a well-balanced personality, this provides a healthy nucleus for his emotional reactions for all the rest of his life. It is probable that in those severe psychoses that are of psychological origin there is usually a disturbance in the personality that goes back to an earlier period than the age of three, or even two. Probably harmful emotional influences have affected that child since birth. Of course, if current pressures of

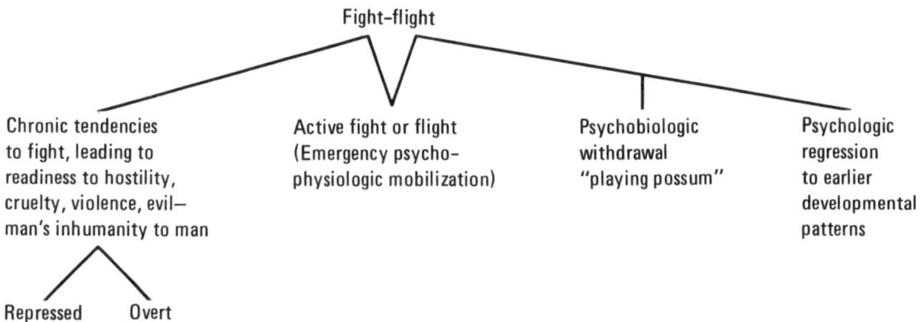

Figure 4

life are severe enough to strike a person's emotional vulnerabilities, the most stable person will break down. These are the *reactive* rather than *internal* cases.

Unrelieved Excitations. To summarize the motivational operation of the human organism, let us resort to a highly oversimplified, schematized diagram. Let us imagine the central nervous system in its role of integrating the whole organism. We do not neglect other methods of coordination and communication within the organism such as those provided by the endocrine system, but we focus here primarily upon the nervous system.

Let us imagine an area in the brain as corresponding to our conscious ego, to that part of us which makes possible perception, thought, feeling, judgment, and memory. This area will be impinged upon by its perceptions of the outside world, both inanimate and animate nature in general, and other human beings in particular. (Think for a moment of the incessant impressions and observations that roll in to your consciousness as endlessly as the waves of the sea.) It will also be impinged upon by the forces of the individual's conditioning and training, by his standards and conscience. Moreover, it feels from within the force of the biological drives, urges, needs, motivations, and reactions. An interplay goes on between all these forces. What a person sees in the outside world stimulates certain biological desires and also certain reactions of standards and conscience. On the other hand, driven by the forces of standards and conscience and by the biological urges, the individual seeks to satisfy these forces in the outside world.

Let us imagine that this whole interplay of forces is a matter of the activity of the nerves of this area of the brain. As we know, the activity of nerves consists of chemical impulses accompanied by electrical charges—"action potentials." Therefore, we are quite justified in visualizing this interplay of forces, which we have described in psychological terms, as essentially going on in a complex chemical-electrical machine.

This machine depends upon the principle of homeostasis and no doubt, on the second law of thermodynamics, to reduce the tensions to a minimum; in other words, if the organism is driven by a biological urge, say hunger, it tries to reduce this tension by finding food and eating. Suppose, however, that the individual is so situated that he is tempted to satisfy his need to eat by stealing food. This arouses a reaction of standards and conscience if he was trained not to steal.

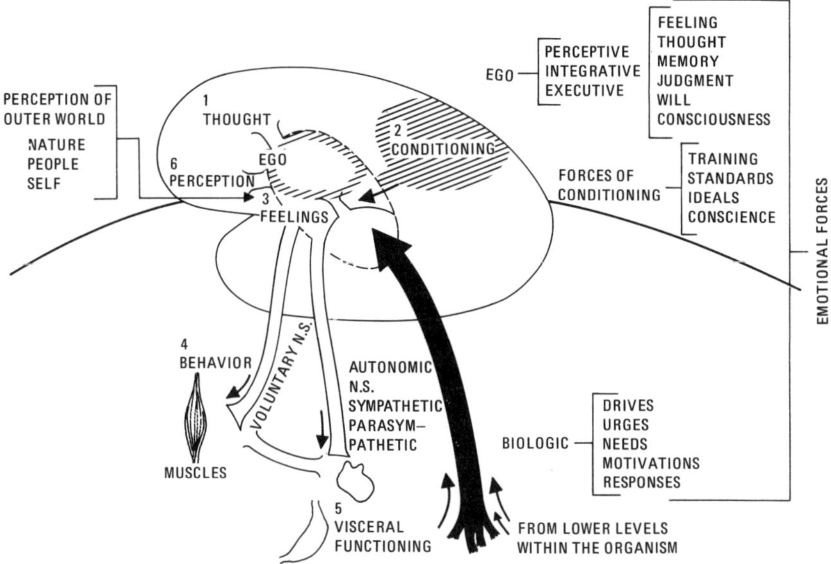

Figure 5

The wish for food is now not drained or satisfied through action but is blocked by conscience. Conflict and emotional tension result.

Let us visualize this tension as nerve activity within the brain, affecting the systems and circuits that have to do with various psychological functions. If the nerve excitation affects one area or system, thought will be affected. If it affects another, it impinges upon those circuits that have to do with the standards, conscience, and judgment of self. Others that are affected have to do with the perception of feelings and mood; still others have to do with sensory perceptions, in relation to the outside world and from within.

Normally, of course, the effect of the excitation is stimulation of the organism to some sort of action or behavior; in other words, it would stimulate the voluntary nervous system and appear in muscular action or inaction. Normally, this would involve adjustments of the viscera to the muscle activity to provide the muscles with the necessary blood supply and nutriment, as well as preparing the organism in brain and muscle to meet the stress of the life situation.

Our schema shows how the various areas of activity can be affected. If it is thought of as similar to a hydrodynamic system (such as water in pipes), then one can easily imagine how excitation in a certain area in the brain, which cannot be drained off in one direction, will endeavor to flow in another direction with appropriate consequences. For example, an individual gets angry but is in a social situation in which he must behave like a gentleman. The anger is checked by his judgment as well as by his training and standards; it does not stimulate his muscular system to activity, but it does not vanish. It is a quantity of excitation; it may be deflected and act as a stimulus to his autonomic nervous system, which activates the viscera, so that he experiences symptoms such as cramps and palpitations of the heart.

Our most intense feelings are directed toward other human beings. This is a point of first importance and one that is not always fully realized. Like mixtures of positive and negative charges of electricity, human beings have the most intense effect upon each other's emotional reactions. Apart from situations of danger before the great impersonal forces of nature, all our usual intense feelings are primarily toward human beings. Our loves, hates, fears, and ambitions must be realized through, and in relation to, other persons in civilized life. Each other human being generates in us some mixture of feelings. This effect is sometimes multiplied in a group, so that an individual will have stage fright before a large audience. In others, it is pleasure that is multiplied. But always our emotions are basically toward human beings.

This is even true of self-preservation in the face of an impersonal danger that threatens one. Here, the human being who is the object of one's strong feelings is oneself. People can love and hate themselves as well as other people. All, or at any rate most, feelings can be turned inward toward a person's own self. Self-love is often obvious in those we call vain; self-hate becomes evident in "masochistic" characters, in an extreme form, in depressions and suicide. The achievement of healthy attitudes toward others and toward oneself is the result of a long process of psychological biological development to emotional maturity.

Even fear of the impersonal forces of nature is very often in large part at its source a fear of people. Men tend to personify the forces of nature, to think of them as sort of personal forces, which can be friendly or hostile but at least are somehow personal.

Even the fear of death itself is very largely psychologically determined. No doubt there is a basic nucleus in this fear that is a part of the instinct for self-preservation, but for the rest the fear varies from person to person, and it varies usually with the person's relationship to his own conscience.

The adult's intense feelings toward others, as well as toward himself and toward nature, all operate according to the patterns of these feelings that were shaped during the earliest years of life. These early years are so important because at this time the child is utterly helpless. His very existence, almost from minute to minute, depends upon his relationship with his mother and other close and responsible human beings. This emotional interplay is usually intense and difficult, even for the adults with their obvious advantages. The child must cope with it from the very beginnings in helplessness and bewilderment. There are personal, biological, and cultural reasons for the intensity of our feelings toward other persons and toward ourselves.

The Riddle of Consciousness. The central riddle in the borderland between neurophysiology and psychology would seem to lie in the phenomenon of consciousness. Everything that we perceive with this consciousness we are able to imagine as reproducible by ourselves through the invention of sufficiently ingenious machines resembling intricate circuits of the approximately 13 billion nerve cells of the outer cortex of the human brain.

In his fascinating *Road to Xanadu*, G. Lowes Dickinson traces the images and ideas of *The Ancient Mariner* to their varied sources in the wide reading of Coleridge, showing how these fragments, hidden away and long since forgotten consciously by the poet, emerged in his mind and were worked into the combination that became the famous poem.

Certainly consciousness is part of a physiological mechanism. It is a sensitive part, readily responsive to changes in blood flow, to chemicals (such as alcohol), to drugs and the like. Perhaps it is itself something like a virtual image, a special point of focus for all of the perceptual impulses in conjunction with the many outgoing ones. The comprehension of the ways of consciousness would seem to require either further information or else a daring new turn of thought.

The analogy of brain, mind, and machine is not one-sided nineteenth century mechanicalism. Science can only strive in humility to describe what it is able to observe and to formulate the basic principles. The fact that it describes phenomena only partially does not mean that it denies other phenomena. For example, we describe the sources of the conscience in conditioning, but this does not deny other sources. We use the analogy of the machine for its immediate use in approaching the riddle of the brain's operation and the riddle of consciousness, with full realization that there is more in the brain and the mind than is yet dreamed of in our current knowledge.

Consciousness marks the boundary between the world of the physical sciences and the world of the psychological sciences. Perhaps one day "the swing of Pleiades, the rift of dawn, the reddening of the rose," or love, or genius, will be reduced to mathematical formulae that convey the interplay of nerve impulses in the brain. But that is not how we would wish to perceive them if we had a free choice, at least not the good things.

There is a machine and its workings, and there are the effects of these workings, which we experience in our consciousness. This is the demarcation between physiology and psychology, between brain and mind.

THE ORGANISM AS A UNIT

Whether it be a work of art or a significant scientific achievement, that which is great and noble comes from the solitary personality.

Albert Einstein

Life, largely the hostility of your fellow men, will beat upon you. So will the diseases and the social turmoils that result from human hostility. Knowledge of men's motives can be of some use in helping you to understand and adapt to this life.

If you have some appreciation of the reality of the emotional forces that motivate you, your family, friends, pets, enemies, and all the animal kingdom, and partly the vegetable, then you have the key to the most wondrous phenomenon in the whole world, the mind of man.

Understanding of man's mind must rest upon sound biological knowledge. Man lives his life as a biological unit and not a collection of parts. To build a concept, then, of man in his complexity, start with a picture of man in his unit.

As soon as an animal, however lowly, comes to consist of a collection of many cells, it loses the classic simplicity of the single-celled amoeba. Even a lowly sea animal, a mere sac of cells, must somehow be organized and coordinated and behave as a unit like the amoeba. In these creatures we see a "nerve net." Through it the cells communicate in their own way, and the whole collection acts as a unit. In a much higher form, the still lowly worm, the network of nerves has a more definite structure, as has the worm itself. Higher forms have brains.

Man's cells, tissues, and organs are concerted into a unison by the nervous system with its master integrator, the brain. Another great system of integration consists of the interrelated chemicals secreted by the endrocrinc glands—pituitary, thyroid, adrenals, sex glands, and others.

Social organizations have been called "epiorganisms," in other words, organisms comparable with biological units but formed out of biological units themselves. Social organizations of all sorts in part increase the freedom of their component units but in part constrain them. Thus the termites, like ants and bees, have highly organized societies, but each individual member is weak and is fixed and rigid in his own patterns of behavior.

As we focus upon the human brain and upon the products of its activity, let us never lose sight of the human being as a single unit organism. The best way to study the activities of the organism, which in man we call "human nature," is by studying the actual behavior of the organism and those reflections of its motivations and reactions that appear in the activity of the brain that we call the "human mind."

In his intrinsic biological nature, the human being is the opposite of the various machines he has created. The machines are built by fitting together carefully constructed parts. Man, however, like the rest of the animal kingdom, starts life in the form of a single unified cell. Gradually, his varied parts differentiate from the original homogeneous whole. The cells specialize, but the organism remains a unit in motivation, reaction, behavior, and spirit, as described in any textbook on embryology.

BASIC BIOLOGICAL FORCES IN THE MIND

We have discussed the power of the emotional forces in the biological organism. Here we review some basic principles of their operation.

The Pleasure Principle. The forces that operate in the minds of all of us are reflections, as we have seen, of basic drives and reactions of the whole biological organism. Various observers have naturally sought the most basic energies that can account for the behavior of biological organisms. Having studied these forces by observing their operation in the mind of man, Freud was early impressed by the "pleasure principle"—that nearly everything a person did was to gain pleasure and to avoid pain. "The reality principle" operated in addition to and more or less in opposition to "the pleasure principle." The infant and young child is dominated by desires for immediate gratification, without taking into account the world of reality and the consequences. One packs a suitcase for a trip although it would be much more pleasurable to set out unencumbered. The reality principle, then, is only a modification of the pleasure–pain principle. It involves foresight—delaying the immediate gratification in order to adapt better to reality, to avoid greater pain later, and eventually to get greater pleasure.

Freud made rough groupings of the "sexual instincts" and the "ego instincts." The former referred to race preservation and were associated with sexual pleasure; the latter had to do with those drives in the individual that were concerned with his own personal self-preservation.

Stability, Economy, and Inertia. Insofar as pleasure consists in the relief and release of accumulated tensions that return the organism to a state of equilibrium, it serves the principle of stability or homeostasis.

Another principle is that of "economy" or "inertia," which is of special importance in connection with learning and conditioning of the human being. In order to adapt to his family and society, each human being must gradually *learn* how to behave. It is a great saving in energy if one learns to do a thing quite automatically and does not have each time to go through an original process of thought and effort. Thus, the "principle of economy" operates in the service of the "principle of stability." It keeps the organism in equilibrium through a saving of energy.

An inevitable result of the "principle of economy" is its corollary, the "principle of inertia," which is perhaps only another aspect of it. Once a person has learned to do a thing automatically (and therefore with little effort), he becomes loathe to relinquish his way of doing it in favor of anything new. It is easier to stay in a rut. The great advantage of energy-saving involves the disadvantage of the loss of flexibility and adaptability. Hence, man's struggles to adapt to the new while still clinging to the old. These principles play a part in the phenomena of fixation and regression. They are the technical psychodynamic expressions of the fact that "as the twig is bent, the tree is inclined."

Surplus Energy. The principle of "surplus energy" helps us to understand the phenomena of growth, play, and sexuality. The energy that goes into growth spills over as play; and after the organism has achieved its full growth, it spills over in the form of a capacity for reproduction and mating and for work. This "progressive" energy, pressing the child to growth, development, and maturity (physical, emotional, and intellectual), and as an adult to mate and work, is opposed by the counterforce of regression to the passive dependent love neediness of childhood. The discharge of energy naturally serves to maintain the individual in homeostatic equilibrium.

Implication for Humanity. Related to the drives toward growing up and the countertendency toward remaining in or returning to childhood patterns or previous states in general, one sees the source of people's needs to be dependent and also of their needs to be independent. Vanity, egotism, and desires for prestige and power (often to deny the feelings of weakness from dependence) are powerful motivations in human life. The hunger for love, as in the child, is equally powerful, as is the drive toward sex, mating, the making of a home, and the rearing of children. Also, the conscience and the whole weight of standards, ideals, and past conditioning are far greater in each individual than he himself realizes.

Can these needs, drives, and reactions all be included in a single simple but comprehensive theory? Freud tried to subsume all of the "instinct theory" of psychoanalysis under the simplified duality of Eros, the tendency of protoplasm to come together as individuals and societies, and Thanatos, the tendency to death, destruction of self and others. Eros (life and love) and Thanatos (death) correspond to the bodily processes of anabolism (building up) and catabolism (tearing down), the two aspects of metabolism. This theory, although having the beauty of simplicity, is so broad as to be a philosophical idea rather than a provable statement.

A cat may look at a king, and we ordinary mortals cannot shirk the attempt to weld the emotional forces into some sort of unified theory. The progressive and regressive tendencies and Cannon's concept of the fight–flight reaction fit together: The progressive tendencies, probably built on an instinct to social cooperation, drive toward maturity, responsibility, productivity, and independence with the capacity to love (RPIL). The regressive trends toward childhood emotional patterns include the fight–flight reaction. The fight part of the reaction seems to account for the hostility and anger in people in all their forms. The flight part manifests itself in part through passive receptive dependent love needs (PRDLn), which are probably the most common source of feelings of inferiority and the opposing reactions of narcissism, egotism, vanity, hubris. Thus we link in theory the two great poles of the emotional life seen in every patient, hostility and dependent love needs.

Unsublimated sexual desire can, it seems, be linked to both the progressive forces toward growth and mature capacities for love, mating, reproduction, and childrearing, as well as to their opposite, regressive wishes, with coitus as a way in which the male gets back close to his mother. What regressive desires coitus serves in women is not clear, but it may also contain similar wishes for a regressive return to being a child; even though the other person is a male, he may be a mother figure to the woman.* There is also a regressive element in narcissism,

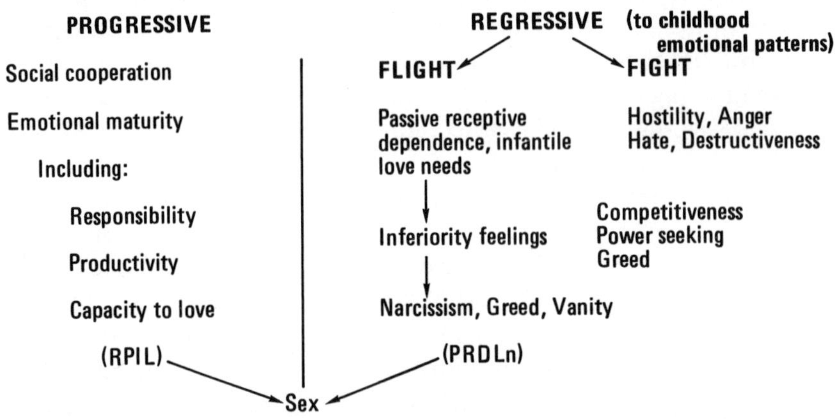

*A superior young woman wrote me 15 years after the end of her analysis and 10 years after her marriage: "I have frequently thought how much my husband is like my mother. Certainly he is incredibly different from my father. I suppose that is why our marriage works so marvelously–as I think I am sufficiently hostile to my father that I could not live with anyone that I saw to be like him. We are all well and happy . . . we are totally happy with our children."

egotism, vanity, pride, greed, competitiveness, and power as part of the flight reaction to the childhood dependent love needs toward mother, whose praise and attention is sought in all of them.

This formulation lacks the beautiful simplicity of Freud's dual theory, but I believe it accounts more directly for what every dynamic therapist observes daily in all his patients. It links all these forces together, even if not in a perfectly unified theory. It turns out to bear a similarity to the oedipus complex.

If the individual has not developed properly, if these needs are unusually strong or unusually in conflict, then the individual is filled with a variety of emotions. Flight is rarely physically possible to an individual in our civilization and overpopulated world. Therefore, his flight usually is by means of psychological regression to childhood patterns of behavior, to adolescence, early childhood, or possibly prenatal stages, and thus to a neurosis or possibly a psychosis. On the other hand, the fight that may be generated tends to come out as anger and hate against his fellow men. The student of psychodynamics has the key to the sources of this hostility of man to man and thereby he has the key, in theory, to prevention. In spite of the obviously enormous difficulties, we now have the knowledge, and there is no course but to continue to attack this central danger to mankind.

Once the basic theory of the atom was discerned, it did not take long to engineer it into the most destructive device known to man—the atom bomb. The formula was $e = mc^2$, representing the transformation of matter into energy. Now we have the basic formula for making responsible adults, functioning as good spouses, parents, and citizens: knowledge of the 0 to 6 that represents the proper rearing of children during that period with love, respect, and understanding. Let us engineer that theory into the production of mature adults who will constitute a strong, mature, peaceful society. It is the only safeguard against humanity destroying itself by overpopulation, pollution, or atomic blast. The task is long and hard, but that is the excitement of the challenge.

18
A Review of Research Literature*

Our knowledge of the effects of experiences and influences upon the young during their earliest years does not depend only upon observations by dynamic therapists in a clinical setting; such effects have also been studied in humans and other animals by a variety of scientific methods. Solveig Wenar has given the author invaluable help by preparing a comprehensive review of much of this work. It appears here at the end of the book, for those who are interested. Because many research studies by different methods all reach a substantially similar result, we accept as established the power of these early experiences and influences (during 0 to 6) on human personality and its disorders.

Solveig and Charles Wenar have written, regarding early influences: "This is a time of ferment. New data are challenging the comprehensiveness (not the validity) of the old model which assumes the primacy of the infant–preschool period in determining subsequent development. A more differentiated question is being asked: what periods are most important for the development of what aspects of human behavior? Whether a satisfactory comprehensive model can be generated within the foreseeable future is doubtful."

The analyst has long been concerned with trauma and its long-range effects and how to correct them, more than with whether trauma is caused by mother, father, sibling, or whatever circumstances.

Today few students of behavior question the concept that early experiences, particularly interpersonal ones, have profound and permanent effects upon animals, including humans. But what is the

*This chapter was prepared in the main by Solveig Wenar, Ph.D.

actual evidence for this? The studies mentioned in this chapter show that a variety of research methods lead to the same conclusion.

Freud opened many more fields of exploration in human psychology than could be cultivated in his lifetime. One of these was the lifelong effects of emotional influences during early childhood. With its relation to the dynamic unconscious it is only now receiving concentrated research attention. The manifold findings are of great importance for the theory of personality, for the etiology of neurosis and all other psychopathology, including irrational hostility. These findings also have practical significance for therapy and prevention and may provide the key to understanding various sociological problems, the most outstanding of which is the infantile, libidinally fixated, hostile behavior with which man threatens man. This chapter offers a representative sample of research findings that are central to the concept of the lasting effects of early influences on adult personality.

Analysts reach their conclusions primarily through work with patients. They see evidence in each patient that symptoms, values, conflicts, and personality characteristics can be traced back to his reactions to his unique constellation of childhood experiences. The details of the whole process are many and involved and have given rise to a vast psychoanalytic literature. The very fact that the data of psychoanalytic observation are confidential, associative, and diffusely bulky makes difficult their study by strict research methodology. For adequate research review, we include other fields related to psychoanalysis. No science stands alone; strength and healthy expansion are derived from interchange with related disciplines. While psychoanalysis has stimulated much of the research in all the behavioral sciences, it still seeks to learn and incorporate what is relevant to it from all sciences. Many problems appear in fresh perspective and can best be solved through other knowledge: for example, through the observations of animal behavior, the psychology of learning and Gestalt psychology, and experimental studies of conditioning and imprinting.

The following review of the literature is organized around some of the hypotheses implicit in the concept of the after-effects of early influences. Eight hypotheses and their implications will be examined in detail in surveying the literature; also, only such discussion of research as is essential to this review is included.

To help clarify the main principles, it is well first to delineate the variables (Siegel, 1956). This is attempted here in the single area of childhood trauma. Comprehension of the after-effects of early influences is essential to an understanding of fixation, regression, introjection, superego, transference, and other psychoanalytic concepts, and of course of mankind's central problem, his hostility to his fellows. Today these concepts and the importance of childhood trauma can be accepted as established regardless of other opinions because they have been checked repeatedly over the past 80 years by the clinical observations of hundreds of analytic therapists, both M.D.'s and Ph.D's, all over the world. These clinical observations stand on their own, but it broadens perspective to review the evidence obtained from other methodologies as exemplified in the following review.

DEFINITIONS, ASSUMPTIONS, AND HYPOTHESES

In formulating a rough working concept, "personality" can be defined as a pattern of basic motivations and reactions. The pattern for each individual is unique although its elements are common to all. The individual pattern represents one of all possible variations in quantity and combination of the basic elements, which are comparatively few. They can be conveniently grouped under the familiar headings of id, superego, and ego. In oversimplified form they are the biological needs, drives, and reactions of the id; the internal representations of identifications and training of the superego; and the defensive, perceptive, integrative, and executive activities of the ego.

Motivation is conceptualized as an inner variable. It prompts overt behavior, also modifications and inhibitions of it. Overt behavior includes verbal responses and all behavior that is in some way observable by others. It is assumed that the behavior caused by any particular motivation is identifiable as such, at least by experienced clinicians. The clinician bases his diagnosis and treatment on his ability to identify his patient's behavior in terms of motivations.

Admittedly, these definitions are general and imprecise and would not suffice for specific research studies (Lindzey, 1958). However, they are adequate for this general survey of the relevant literature.

In the development of personality it appears that two broad classes of variables determine the pattern of motivations. The first of these is the class of inherited variables, including maturational and constitutional factors. The second of these is the class of external variables. In the first of these classes, the maturational factor is the force that impels each individual toward maximal growth and development. It proceeds, within certain variations, according to a biological timetable. Constitutional factors are described in the literature in two senses: (1) to signify inherited or gene-determined potentials, and (2) to signify gene-determined potentials present at birth that are modified by influences in utero and during the birth process. The term is used here in the first sense, while uteral conditions are considered among the external factors. (Whereas many studies indicate that constitutional factors play a considerable role in the development of temperamental and other personality aspects, they are not generally found to have great influence in causing psychopathology, except possibly some psychoses. For this reason they are not of prime relevance in this chapter.)

External factors provide the conditions that determine to what extent and in what respects an individual's genetic and maturational potentials are realized or warped. These factors appear to play an important role in forming personality and to be the critical factor, that is, the one having the greatest weight, in producing the distortions of personality that underlie all familiar forms of psychopathology. We are concerned with the operation and effects of these external influences from the conception of the individual.

In the interest of clarity, the view of personality development to be scrutinized in this chapter is presented in the form of eight hypotheses, each more or less subject to testing.

The first four hypotheses of personality development all bear time relations.

Hypothesis A: The earlier an influence impinges upon the developing personality, the more pervasive and significant are its effects.

Hypothesis B: Exceptions to hypothesis *A* concern functions that are most susceptible to influences during critical periods, which occur most frequently early in life.

Hypothesis C: The fundamental characteristics of the personality are established by the age of approximately six years.

Hypothesis D: Once formed, the personality pattern remains fairly constant throughout life.

The next two hypotheses have to do with relevant influences.

Hypothesis E: Given adequate conditions for physical survival, the most important external influence is the emotional relationship between a child and his parents (or parental substitutes).

Hypothesis F: The most relevant aspects of the child's emotional milieu are parental warmth, parental control in accordance with his needs, and stability in his relationship to his parents.

The final two hypotheses have to do with the effects of relevant influences.

Hypothesis G: To the extent that ideal conditions prevail, maturation proceeds to the fullest and the individual eventually develops a mature personality, becoming a responsible, productive adult of good will.

Hypothesis H: Any deviation from ideal conditions is usually detrimental, and the greater the deviation, the more thwarted the maturation will be, and the more intensive and extensive becomes the pathology of the personality.

METHODOLOGICAL CONSIDERATION

The task of reviewing research involves weighing the evidence against the adequacy of the methods used. To date there is no flawless procedure for the study of the development, consistency, and pathology of a personality during a lifetime (Dennis, 1955; Garn, 1957; Harris, 1960; Martin, 1960). Hence, caution is required in drawing conclusions. Methodological flaws do not necessarily produce unreliable or invalid results, but they do limit the scope of conclusions that can be drawn from them. Whenever similar results are obtained by different investigators using different procedures (with different flaws), and few or no studies contradict these results, the chances that the hypothesis tested is valid are greatly increased. Even conflicting conclusions may yield important clues.

To facilitate the reader's evaluation of the studies to be reported, the advantages and disadvantages of the most common developmental research methods will first be discussed briefly.

The Longitudinal Approach

This method studies the same subjects over a protracted period of time, observing them at frequent intervals in a systematic fashion. It has also been called the prospective method (Bell, 1960). Many advantages derive from the availability of firsthand observations by trained observers during the whole developmental sequence studied. Such observations are often more reliable and more complete, and they offer better comparability of subjects than data from other studies. The longitudinal approach makes possible the direct observation of changes in the personality as they occur, and thereby of factors related to, or causative of, the changes. Thus it offers a unique opportunity for describing effects of different combinations of variables. The method is suitable for predictive studies (Kris, 1957) and for studies of time relations in development. (Saul, 1977).

Kagan and Moss (1963) of the Fels Research Institute point to the value of the longitudinal approach for studying the emergence of "derivative behaviors" and the "sleeper effect." By derivative behaviors is meant the behavior forms occurring at successive phases of development, representing modifications of the original primitive expression of a motivation; for example, verbal sarcasm may be a derivative of early forms of hostile physical aggression. Kagan and Moss state that "adult behavior is a complicated code in which certain responses bear a lawful relation" to early behavioral patterns. This code gives important clues to understanding human development, and it enhances the ability to predict adult reactions from behavior in childhood.

What the Fels group calls the sleeper effect represents delayed results of early environmental influences on the functioning of the personality. As an example, "maternal acceleration" of the child's external development (that is, efforts to push the child ahead) shows the highest correlation with school-age achievement when the measure of maternal acceleration is obtained during the first three years of life. When maternal acceleration is measured at the same time as the child's achievement, the correlations are much lower (cf. Sontag and Kagan, 1963).

The longitudinal studies in the literature are relatively few, their combined number of subjects amounting to only several hundred. The disadvantages are apparent: spans of 20 years or more of work; financing; the long wait for results; the processing of many data; the difficulty of incorporating new scientific findings and techniques; and others. A few research groups have carried out major longitudinal studies in which personality functions are included (Anderson, 1963; Klatskin and Jackson, 1955; Kodlin and Thompson, 1958; Schaefer and Bayley, 1963; Skard et al., 1960).

The Follow-up Approach

The follow-up approach, which is closely related to the longitudinal method, consists in studying adults for whom detailed histories of their childhood are available. Usually the person studying the adult subject is not the same as the one who recorded the data. Typically, the procedure follows these steps: (1) start with a group whose members have some common characteristics; (2) assemble all data available during a given time period; (3) relocate and study anew each of the subjects; (4) look for correspondence between the childhood and the later status of the subject. Often the common feature of the subjects was that they had been observed in child guidance clinics (Frazee, 1953; O'Neal and Robins, 1958, 1959). This choice of subjects has, of course, been determined by its advantages from the researcher's point of view, that is, the particular behavioral problem and the availability of records.

There are evident methodological defects. To begin with, data taken from clinical records not intended for research are generally inadequate (Grinker, 1961). Further, a common criticism of this approach is that it is limited to a population that is characterized by early gross disturbances. While this opinion is generally correct, it carries no great weight; what is important is that the conclusions match the premises. Without a control group, conclusions must be stated as hypotheses subject to subsequent testing by other methods. Control groups need not be "normal"; subjects with different types of early disturbances may serve as control groups, one for the other. Indeed, much interest inheres in comparisons of adaptation among adults who had exhibited different types of disharmony with the environment in childhood.

The Cross-Sectional Approach

This is the follow-up method in reverse. It also starts with a group that has certain common characteristics; but, in contrast to the follow-up method, this procedure traces the development of the subjects back to childhood. An example is the comparison between delinquents and "normals" with respect to the incidence in early life of broken homes, ordinal sibling position, socioeconomic condition, and the like. Considering the difficulties in obtaining unbiased accounts of personality variables in retrospect, it is an advantage, from the point of view of reliability, that only rather gross factors have been isolated by the cross-sectional approach. Both this approach and the follow-up methods have been criticized for their poor techniques of sampling. In this respect they contrast sharply with the longitudinal method, which has been praised for its good sampling and valid data. The merits, however, are more evenly distributed, at least in studies of personality disorders (Bell, 1960).

The cross-sectional method is comparatively easy and quick and therefore useful in the early phases of a research program for the identification of relevant variables and the formulation of hypotheses.

The Experimental Approach

Experimental procedures are variations of a basic model. Subjects known or assumed to be equal in relevant respects are assigned at random to an experimental and a control group. The former is subjected to the influence of the variable under study, and the latter is not, but in all other respects the groups are treated equally. Both groups are measured subsequently, and the effects of the experimental variable are assessed.

Were it not precluded by humanitarian considerations, many questions about human development could be answered by assigning children at random to various types of controlled environments and comparing the different groups at intervals. "How," asks Shakow (1959), "can one study human psychological phenomena scientifically . . . with a minimum of distortions . . . and ethically . . . with a minimum of inevitable trespasses?" Animal experimentation, therefore, is increasingly resorted to in studying emotional development. The subjects have a short life span and are easy to care for, and control groups are readily available.

To generalize from animals to humans requires great scientific caution. Animal experimentation is not a substitute for the understanding of humans, but it nevertheless furnishes excellent models and is a fertile field for developing and testing hypotheses. With respect to the question of the effects of early experience upon adult personality, research with animals is becoming increasingly important as a basis for hypotheses about human behavior. The variables involved are being systematically tested on a large scale; the adult consequences are being more carefully specified and measured. The rat and the monkey are now joined by many other species in the laboratory, and correlations with humans are being evaluated. Direct observation of various species in nature and in approximately natural settings is also casting much light on human behavior (Lorenz, 1935, 1952; Ostow, 1960).

The Cross-Cultural Approach

This approach to the problem of early influences on adult behavior consists of a comparison between different cultures or subcultures. Different cultures may be regarded as experiments in the problem of the nature of human development. They may furnish invaluable information about the ways in which widely varying early experiences affect later personality.

Specific childhood variables are selected and correlated with differences in the adult personality predominating in the different cultures. The uncontrollable variables—geographic, social, political, cultural, genetic, and others—are many. The diversity itself, however, may prove to be fruitful for the understanding of the laws of human behavior. The anthropologist Whiting states: "The advantages of the cross-cultural method are twofold . . . . First, it ensures that findings relate to human behavior in general rather than being bound to a single culture, and second, it increases the range of variation of many of the variables" (Whiting and Child, 1953).

The Reconstructive Approach

Although the cross-sectional method may use reconstructive data, the term has commonly been reserved for the clinical method of psychoanalysis in which adult patients give data about their childhood as they remember it, and in which dreams, associations, feelings, and behavior reveal emotional patterns that can be traced to childhood.

Commonly listed as weaknesses of the method, from a scientific point of view, are the subjective nature of the data, the fallacies of human memory, and the difficulties of obtaining independent data to validate the statements made. The psychoanalytic situation nevertheless has a number of unique advantages that are apt greatly to reduce bias in the data and to offset the weaknesses. First, the verbal communications given in therapeutic sessions that are contaminated by such factors as defensiveness, carelessness, and distortions of memory are less likely to go undetected as such than are the responses given in the questionnaires or in the single interviews on which many research projects rely. It is also probably true that statements made in the psychoanalytic situation are generally less likely to be contaminated. Psychoanalysis can reasonably be expected to reflect more accurately a person's actual subjective feelings and attitudes as well as his otherwise unobservable behavior. Furthermore, as the treatment usually lasts for months or years, the therapist gets to know his patient's personality extremely well and, if he is of a scientific mind, he has many opportunities to make and to check predictions.

The psychoanalyst usually sees a select group of patients in terms of educational and socioeconomic conditions. Admittedly, his research population is restricted. Actually, he should therefore confine his conclusions to the same restricted population. On this point the temptation to err is great, and many fail because of the consistency of the findings. In case after case, without exception, unfortunate early experiences are found to characterize patients with adult dificulties. The rigorous scientist may challenge the psychoanalyst's claim that the former lead to the latter without establishing that persons free of the symptoms are also free of the damaging early experience. The psychoanalyst, however, sees more than simple correlations between childhood and adult disturbances. He can trace, in great detail, patterns of specific disorders in the adult back through the years to specific origins in childhood, which, moreover, not infrequently can be confirmed from other sources. These are only a few points in the evaluation of psychoanalysis as a research tool (cf. Alexander, 1948; Waelder, 1960).

RESEARCH RELEVANT TO HYPOTHESES A AND B

Hypothesis A: The earlier an influence impinges upon the developing personality, the more pervasive and significant are its effects.

Hypothesis B: Exceptions to hypothesis *A* concern functions that are most susceptible to influences during critical periods, which occur most frequently early in life.

In reviewing studies of factors that determine the effects of early experiences upon the behavior of mature animals, King (1958) lists seven important variables: (1) the age of the animal when the early experience occurred; (2) the age of the animal at the time of the test; (3) duration or quantity of the early experience; (4) type or quality of the experience; (5) type of the performance task required by the adult animal; (6) methods for testing persistence of the effects; (7) relation of the experience to the genetic background of the animal. The approach demands that the researcher first try to predict the effects of each of these variables separately, and then try to unravel the interactions between them. King concludes that ". . . until the effects of the seven variables are analyzed further, it is possible to accept only the general hypothesis that early experiences affect later behavior."

Recent systematic studies pose the following questions: (1) Is there a relationship between age and the effect of an influence? (2) If so, is this relationship a monotonic function compatible with *A*? (3) Or is it a more complex function that might fit the critical period of *B*? (4) Does it fit neither hypothesis?

Among many studies under each of the following headings, only those are discussed that dwell specifically on the variable age of the subject at the time of the influence studied.

Imprinting

Imprinting refers to a certain type of study of critical periods in the early development of animals. Its relevance to human development has not been established. Lorenz (1935) introduced the term to designate the infant bird's early ability to recognize and to follow its parent. Psychologists in studying the phenomenon have varied the age of the bird at the time of exposure to its parents and to other objects. These studies have been extended to other animals and to a variety of substitutes for parents, including parents of other species as well as inanimate objects. They invariably show that the age of the imprinted animal at the time of exposure to the object of imprinting is of paramount importance (Frisch, 1957; Gottlieb, 1961; Gray, 1963;

Gray and Howard, 1957; Hess, 1958, 1959a, b, c; Jaynes, 1957; Moltz, 1960). Without exception, imprinting can take place only during a specified time, very early in the animal's life. This period varies from species to species. The results, insofar as they are applicable to hypothesis *B*, are in accordance with it.

Tests of imprinting were initiated at various hours after hatching in neonate chicks. The imprinting object in this study was a green, seven-inch cube, which was presented to the subjects for a 30-minute period. At the age of 10 days, the animals were given a retention test. The results showed that the percentage of animals imprinted declined steadily from 90 percent, one to six hours after hatching, to zero, 54 to 60 hours after hatching. Other studies that have used a finer scale for the time variable find that imprinting often fails to take place in the very first hours of life. Hess (1958) reports that some imprinting occurred immediately after the birth of mallard ducks, but that it was most effectively acquired at about 16 hours after hatching. Many studies on different species give comparable results.

Two explanations have been offered to account for these effects. One holds that the critical period for imprinting is determined by the animal's perceptual development. According to this view, the critical period coincides with the earliest age at which the animal is perceptually capable of recognizing an object and able to remember it. It is a common finding that the older the animal (within the critical period), the more vigorous is its response and the greater its degree of retention. This finding has been considered to support the theory of minimal perceptual development. The second explanation assumes that the end of the critical period corresponds to the age at which the first emotional response occurs (Hess, 1959a,b,c). Moltz (1960), however, reasons that during the early hours of its life—when the animal imprints or becomes aware of a close object in its environment—fear reactions are minimal. This desirable state of freedom from anxiety becomes associated with being near the object. When, later, unfamiliar conditions arouse anxiety, the animal reacts as if the imprinted object is reassuring. To remain close to the object, the animal may have to follow it, as it does with a "following response" as soon as it becomes mobile.

These explanations are of special interest for those who find in them implications for human behavior as well. Gray and Howard (1957), for example, speculate that imprinting may prove to have conditioned those who later become criminals because of formative negative experiences during a few weeks of infantile fearfulness. They also speculate about the influences that may make adopted children wild and incorrigible when taken from institutions to private homes.

Sensory Deprivation and Related Studies

Studies of sensory deprivation illustrate dramatically that even basic perceptual development, rather than being solely maturational, is significantly influenced by early environmental stimulation. For example, Reisen (1960) subjected chimpanzees and kittens to total darkness, varying the duration of the deprivation. He reports chemical and atrophic changes in the retina that were not only pronounced but also irreversible in those cases where the deprivation extended from birth throughout infancy.

Nearer to our interest in personality development are time studies of food deprivation. In Hunt's (1944) study, which is the classic, two hereditarily equal groups of rats were observed; one half of each group was subjected to deprivation, while the other half was used for control purposes. The deprivation consisted of 15 days of very restricted feeding. For one group this started on the twenty-fourth day of life; for the other, it began on the thirty-second day of life. Control animals from both groups were freely fed. Following the experiment, all rats were allowed free feeding for five months, during which time Hunt measured the amount of food hoarded by the now adult animals. The rats that had been part of the 24-day-old group hoarded approximately two and a half times as many pellets as the controls. The rats that had been in the 32-day-old group hoarded approximately the same amount as the controls. These results neatly confirm hypothesis *A*, that the earlier the influence, the more powerfully effective it is.

Handling and Shock

In a contrasting type of study, animals are stimulated either by handling or by electric shock. The shock, usually from a wired floor, is always unpleasant although entirely harmless. Handling consists of holding the animal, stroking it, or otherwise touching it. The handling or, as it is sometimes called, gentling, illustrates a point made earlier in the discussion of the applicability of animal studies to human functioning. What it means to a rat to be handled by human hands is questionable, but experimenters who are particularly fond of rats tend to interpret it as pleasure and comfort, whereas others think it must be dreadful for the rat. Possibly these different feelings and interpretations may in part be responsible for the different results that have been obtained in studies of time factors in handling as related to later behavior.

Gertz (1957) handled rats at various early ages and later tested them for emotionality. As adults the rats failed to show significant differences. Gertz concluded that there is no evidence for either the earliest age or any other critical age at which handling is influential in later behavior. A study by Denenberg and Karas (1959) yielded different results. They tested both rats and mice. One group was handled from age one to age 10 days, another from 11 to 20 days, and a third group from one to 20 days. For each time group there was a corresponding control group. The adults were tested for weight, mortality, and resistance to stress. Results showed that the group handled from first to tenth day survived stresses better than the other two groups. Among the rats, the one-to-twenty group weighed the most and lived the longest. However, the one-to-twenty group of mice had the shortest life span of all the mice.

If the results of these studies are valid, a great many variables need further exploration before the results can be meaningfully compared. For instance, aspects that vary without being controlled in the two studies are duration of periods of handling and the effect variable chosen for adult study; also the differences of species in the second study need further exploration.

In an earlier well-known study, lambs were raised exclusively on a bottle by Scott et al., (1951). He varied the time of initiation and the duration of the bottle feeding, which also involved handling. The adult test consisted in observing the lamb's social behavior in its own flock. All the experimental lambs showed some indifference to the flock and even to their own baby lambs. The timing of the initial period away from the flock made a significant difference; the most profoundly affected lambs never learned to adapt socially to the flock or to relate to its movement. Since the most effective time period was not the earliest but rather an intermediary one, Scott found his results to speak strongly for the existence of a critical period. Meier and Stuart (1959) report concordant findings in their experiments with Siamese kittens (cf. Meyers, 1962).

Two well-designed studies (Brookshire et al., 1961) explored the age at the time of a shock trauma in rats as related to adults' escape learning and shock avoidance.* One of the studies compared adult performance in rats who had been shocked at 20 and 30 days of age, respectively. The other study did a similar comparison on rats shocked at 20 and 120 days of age, respectively.

> With regard to the notion of critical periods our data are essentially negative. We may answer the question of age at time of treatment by comparing experimental groups A (traumatized at one hundred and twenty days of age) and C (traumatized at twenty days of age), since these groups were equated with regard to all other significant variables . . . . In both escape learning and avoidance learning no differences were found. It appears then that age is not an important factor. The hypothesis that infantile traumatic experiences more severely affect an organism was not substantiated in this experiment.

Denenberg and Bell (1960) report a similar study except that mice were used as subjects. Their findings give a possible clue to the variable most responsible for the results of the above studies, namely, the voltage. They varied the age at which different levels of shock (i.e., different voltages) were administered to baby mice. They found that mice shocked during infancy had an easier time mastering avoidance learning as adults if the magnitude of shock had been low. An intense shock, however, produced an interference so that all experimental subjects did more poorly than controls in adult avoidance learning. In terms of the effect of age at shocking, there was some evidence of a critical period at low shock levels (cf. Denenberg, 1963).

Institutionalization and Maternal Separation

In the forties, Goldfarb (1943), Ribble (1943), Spitz (1945), and Spitz and Wolf (1946) published studies documenting the pervasive

---

*Escape learning here means being trained to run across charged flooring to escape further shock. Shock avoidance, or avoidance learning, refers to learning to avoid shock altogether by changing location on signal.

and permanent ill effects of inadequate mothering during early infancy. The impact of these studies was considerable and led to the establishment of a new branch of scientific inquiry, commonly termed maternal deprivation (Glaser and Eisenberg, 1956). Two independent surveys of the literature on maternal deprivation have been published, one by Yarrow (1961), the other by Casler (1961). Both authors comment that the concept of maternal deprivation is a mixed one. Yarrow observes that at least four quite different conditions of abnormal mothering have been included under this heading: institutionalization; separation from a mother or mother substitute; multiple mothering (several persons at the same time or in quick succession); distortions in the nature of mothering in terms of domination, indifference, and the like. A further complication is that few studies have been confined to the main variable under study. Separations, for example, are often a consequence of distorted mother–child relationships; institutionalization often involves multiple mothering; distortions of the normal mother–child relations occur much more frequently in institutions.

A number of other factors compound the complexity of the details. Conditions in institutions vary greatly; without adequate description in these studies, their effects cannot be appraised. Casler observes that reasons for maternal separation from a child similarly cover a wide range. Separation from a loving but physically fragile mother may mean something very different from separation from a neglectful mother. Genetic or constitutional factors may also interact with aspects of mothering. To a higher degree than in the general population, children in institutions are in some way defective at birth, or they are the offspring of parents who are unable to care properly for them, be it for mental, physical, or economic reasons. Page (1955) voices the same thought in his discussion of Spitz's work: "The absence of adequate experimental controls leaves room for doubt. Might it not be that infants kept in institutions for long periods are biologically less favored than infants who are adopted or placed in foster homes after a brief stay in an institution?" Casler suggests that " . . . women in our culture, unless they be unwed mothers, do not ordinarily yield their babies to institutions. Children who are in insstitutions cannot, therefore, be regarded as comprising a random sample from a larger population." One possible effect of the mother's unwed status is a greater intensity of anxiety during pregnancy. That anxiety during pregnancy may have an adverse effect on the offspring is suggested by numerous studies (Ader and Conklin, 1963; Ferreira, 1960; Kaplan and Thompson, 1957; Mintz, 1958; Montagu, 1962; Norris, 1960; Pasamanick et al., 1956; Sontag, 1958, Stott, 1957).

The problems of research design, choice and suitability of measuring instruments, selection of samples, statistical methods, and so forth, enter into the comparisons of studies of maternal deprivation as they do in other comparisons of research work. It is nevertheless possible to make comparisons and draw tentative conclusions on the basis of these studies, particularly with the help of the contributions furnished by Yarrow and Casler.

In studies varying the age factor, the age of six months emerges repeatedly as a crucial period. Spitz and Wolf (1946) and Bowlby (1956) have both observed that it is at approximately six months that the infant first appears capable of distinguishing the mother from other persons. In one of his earlier studies on "affectionless thieves," Bowlby (1944) notes: "In practically all these cases, the separation which appears to have been pathogenic occurred after the age of six months. This suggests that there is a lower age limit before which separation, while perhaps having undesirable affects, does not necessarily produce the particular results we are concerned with here—the affectionless and delinquent character."

Other investigators have explicitly or implicitly (by choice of ages studied) confirmed the importance of the six-months stage (Beres and Obers, 1950; Bridges, 1932; Drever, 1955; Schaeffer, 1958). Schaffer and Callender (1959), investigating effects of early hospitalization, report a related finding:

> Two main syndromes, each associated with a particular age range, have emerged from this study of the effects of hospitalization in infancy. The findings parallel those of Spitz and suggest two developmental stages: a global and a differentiated. The latter, centering around the differentiation of self and environment, appears to be essentially continuous with the adult form, and only when it has been obtained can object relations by specific persons be established. The global stage . . . is quite different and certain life experiences may have quite a distinct meaning according to the developmental phase of the individual. The present study . . . suggests that the crucial factor in hospitalization at

the differentiated stage is maternal deprivation, whereas, at the global stage, it is perceptual deprivation.

Beres and Obers (1950) report that of four cases that showed mental retardation, all were admitted to the institution before six months of age; four children who developed schizophrenia were admitted to the institution at a later age. Despite serious methodological flaws, particularly that the selection of subjects was not random but was biased in a pathological direction, the findings are suggestive in that they confirm a hypothesis that may easily have been derived on the basis of Schaffer's results. This hypothesis might be framed thus: If it is true that institutionalization before the age of six months constitutes perceptual deprivation and after six months maternal deprivation, and if it is true that early institutionalization constitutes an experience significant enough to inflict lasting effects, then institutionalization prior to six months of age might be a factor in causing mental dullness or perceptual distortions, whereas after age six months it would produce interpersonal difficulties.

The first six months having thus been confirmed as a sort of critical period, what then are the relationships of institutionalization and maternal separation to the age of the child after six months? Yarrow (1961) sums up the situation: "Psychoanalytic theories regarding the significance of early experience for later development have often been interpreted as postulating that the younger the organism, the more severe and fixed the effects of an environmental impact." Only limited data are available on human subjects. Ribble (1943) tends to interpret her data on maternal rejection as supporting this point of view. The retrospective studies of Bender (1947, 1954) and Goldfarb (1955) suggest that the younger the child, the more damaging the effects of deprivation and stress. Some animal research supports this hypothesis (Seitz, 1959); other studies do not (Beach and Jaynes, 1954; King, 1958). A more refined hypothesis regarding the significance of the timing of experiences is the critical phase hypothesis. This theory holds that there are points in the developmental cycle during which the organism may be particularly sensitive to certain kinds of events or most vulnerable to specific types of deprivation or stress. Several animal studies (Moltz, 1960; Scott et al., 1951; Tinbergen, 1954) support the general outline of the critical phase hypothesis. It could be added that the studies by Liddell (1961) and

Freedman et al. (1961) also belong in this group. Both used isolation as the experimental variable (with or without extra stress introduced) to study the time factor in the development of relationships with members of the same species. Both studies confirm the hypothesis of a critical period.

Yarrow makes the following key points:

> Although the general consensus in the literature is that maternal separation which occurs before the child is five years of age is likely to be most damaging, the findings are not sufficiently clear to pin-point any one age as being most vulnerable . . . . One might postulate differing vulnerabilities at different periods of development. The developmental level of the child is likely to influence the significance of deprivation for the meaning of a separation experience for him. With regard to separation, the period during which the child is in process of consolidating a relationship with his mother may be an especially vulnerable one. Also significant may be the developmental stage with regard to memory functions. After the point in development at which the child can sustain an image of the mother in her absence and can anticipate her return, the meaning of a brief separation may be less severe than at an earlier developmental period.

Yarrow also suggests that the degree of autonomy the child has achieved, his ability to talk, and other such capacities, may affect the degree of severity that institutionalization or separation imposes on the child.

> There may also be age-linked effects of different types of deprivation. Some animal studies suggest that a minimal level of stimulation may be necessary to produce the biochemical changes for the development of the underlying stress structures. Deprivation in certain sensory modalities may be more significant at one age than at another . . . social deprivation may be most damaging during the earliest period of the development of social responses.

Unfortunately there are almost no data available on the effect of institutionalization and separation at different ages, systematically varied. A publication of the World Health Organization (1964) offers further pertinent discussion on maternal deprivation and its effects.

Distortions in Mother–Child Relationship

There have been numerous studies of mother–child interaction, but few have explored the effect of certain patterns of mothering at different ages of development.

Studies by a group conducting research on animals are relevant to the present topic (Ader et al., 1960). These authors found that rats were more susceptible to ulcer if they were separated from their mothers at 15 days of age rather than at 21 days. Another study has more of the character of distortions in mother–child relations in that the conditions consisted of interruption in the mother–child interaction. These interruptions consisted of one-half hour to five and one-quarter hour periods in which the mother was not present. Two sets of experimental and control groups were used. One set was submitted to the interruption during the first 10 days of life and the second set during the second 10 days of life. The results showed that animals of the former group were significantly more resistant to gastric ulcers than animals experiencing the same interruption during the later period.

Some authors distinguish an autistic phase of development in human beings. During this period of time the newborn child is not yet psychologically very different from his prenatal state. This is followed by a symbiotic phase beginning at about three months (Mahler et al., 1959). It may be, however, that one or two weeks after normal birth, the infant begins to relate to the mother. This may well be the beginning of imprinting for the human young, and there may be serious consequences if the child becomes ready to relate to and attach himself to his mother and is prevented from doing so.

To summarize the material reviewed under hypotheses *A* and *B*: drastically withholding food from experimental animals and depriving others of sensory stimuli gave results compatible with hypothesis *A* (the earlier the influence, the greater its effects); and studies of imprinting have yielded results supporting hypothesis *B* (there are critical periods of special vulnerability). Handling of animals and moderate shock sometimes supported hypothesis *B*, but negative findings were not uncommon. Institutionalization and separation of human children from their mothers showed the first six months as a critical period that affected later social development. Studies of mother–child relationships reported that the first year was critical for the development of psychosomatic traits. Whenever critical periods were found (hypothesis *B*), these occurred early in life (cf. Meyers, 1962).

Hypothesis *A* (the earlier the influence, the greater its effects) is the general concept; hypothesis *B* (there are critical periods of special vulnerability) is a refinement. It might be that the closer an influence on the personality coincides in time with the early emergence of the function affected by the influence, the more pervasive are its effects. The greatest effect will ensue if an influence impinges upon a function just as it is becoming established. This formulation encompasses both *A* and *B*. Results compatible with either of these seem also to be compatible with this formulation. It also would relate to the idea of specific emotional vulnerabilities (Saul, 1979b).

RESEARCH RELEVANT TO HYPOTHESES C AND D

Hypothesis C: The fundamental characteristics of the personality are established by the age of approximately six years.

Hypothesis D: Once formed, the personality pattern remains fairly constant throughout life.

By "fundamental characteristics" of the personality is meant the main basic motivations. "Personality pattern" refers to the individual constellation or patterning of these motivations.

The longitudinal approach has great advantages for testing these hypotheses. A careful study using this method was done by the Fels Research Institute. Originated and directed by Sontag, the Fels group during its more than 40 years of operation has studied a variety of developmental variables. Of special relevance to hypotheses *C* and *D* is a project reported by Kagan and Moss (1960, 1963) on the stability of certain behavior over a period of time. In addition to the constancy or stability of motivations or, as the authors express it, "motive-related behavior," the study also investigated sources of anxiety, defensive responses, and modes of personal interaction from earliest childhood through young adulthood. The specific variables measured were passivity and dependency, aggression, achievement and recognition, heterosexuality and sexual identification, tendencies to withdraw, and maternal treatment of the child.

The Fels investigators defined motives as a variable intervening between an identifiable class of stimuli (incentives), on the one hand, and overt goal-directed responses, on the other. The desire for recognition from the social environment; naturalness and affection from friends, parents, and love objects; mastery of attack; sexual stimulation; co-activity with peers; and perception of a state of injury or anxeity in others (aggression) are the major motivational systems studied in the present research. The investigators concentrated their efforts on quantifying overt goal responses, and in most cases avoided placing themselves in the position of assessing motive strength.

The subjects were 89 white middle-class children who, with their parents, had been enrolled in the Fels longitudinal program from birth during the period 1929 to 1939, and who continued the contact with the Institute until early adulthood or longer. The data in childhood were collected in interviews with the subject and with the mother, by observations of them in their homes and in school, by school grades, and by a variety of tests. The childhood period was divided into four parts: birth to three, three to six, six to 10, and 10 to 14 years. On the basis of the data, each subject was rated on 48 variables for each of the four age periods. To illustrate the nature of these variables, it may be noted that in the area of aggression some of the variables were "aggression to mother," "physical aggression to peers," "indirect aggression to peers," "behavioral disorganization," "conformity," "competitiveness," and the like. The data for assessment during adult life were obtained by interviews and by extensive testing. Ratings of test results were organized into the same categories as the childhood data except for maternal treatment and physical fear. The numerical data thus consisted of the ratings of 48 variables for each of four time periods.

In summarizing their conclusions, the authors found that the most consistent finding of the entire study was that much of the behavior exhibited during the age period six to 10, and some during the age period three to six, provided moderately good predictors of theoretically related behavior during early adulthood. Passive withdrawal from dreaded situations, dependency on family or love objects, ease of arousal to anger, involvement in intellectual tasks, and the pattern of sexual behavior in adulthood were related to the child's behavioral disposition during the early years. These results thus give strong support to the concept that the adult personality begins to take form during early childhood. The Fels investigators sum up their findings this way:

> However, the degree of continuity of a class of responses was intimately dependent upon its congruency with traditional sex role values. The differential stability of dependency, aggression, and sexuality for males and females emphasizes the importance of cultural roles in determining both behavior change and stability.
>
> Passivity and dependency are subjected to cultural disapproval for men; aggression and sexuality are disproportionately punished for women. School-age passivity and dependency were related to adult withdrawal and dependent behavior for women but not for men. School-age aggression and preadolescent heterosexual behavior predicted corresponding adult dependencies for men but not for women.
>
> Intellectual mastery . . . which was rewarded for both sexes, showed continuity for both males and females from the early school years through adulthood. Social class membership is an additional variable relevant for particular sex role values. Certain behaviors (e.g., interest in art and music) would be more acceptable to middle class than to lower class males, and vocational aspirations are, of course, highly dependent upon social class position. Thus knowledge of the sex and social class of a child allows one to make an unusually large number of predictions about his future interests, goals, vocational choice, and dependent, aggressive, sexual, and mastery behaviors.

Further studies should uncover variables other than social class and sexual traits, that effect changes in behavior. In this way, the accuracy of the predictions that can be made on the basis of childhood behavior will increase.

As mentioned, the Fels group did not measure motives, which they defined as intervening variables not directly measurable. They dealt instead with what they termed motive-related behavior. The variables classified under each main heading in the Fels material appear to fit well with accepted definitions of motives in the psychoanalytic sense. It can therefore be concluded that the findings reported by the Fels group on the whole confirm the constancy hypothesis on selected aspects of aggressivity, passivity, dependency, involvement in intellectual tasks, social ambitiousness, and patterns of sexual behavior and identification.

During the years from six to 10, the child exhibits behavior that is significantly related to his behavior as an adult. With some variables this also held true for the second age period, from three to six years. For instance, the sex-role content of boy's play during ages three to six was predictive of their adult sexual interest. Competitiveness and involvement in grossly mechanical motor and aggressive games during the preschool years were sensitive indicators of sex-role behavior 20 years later. Choice of vocation was also roughly predictable from the activities of children three to six years old. Another motive established very early in both sexes was social anxiety.

> Inhibition and tension with peers during early school years was predictive of social anxiety in adulthood for both sexes. For boys, the continuity of this anxiety was traceable to the first three years of life. Inhibited and nonspontaneous approach to strangers during the first three years was significantly associated with social anxiety in adulthood. For girls, the same relationship was not established until age ten.

As mentioned, most of the significant variables were stabilized by six to 10 years of age; the behavior shown by then made it possible to offer fairly reliable predictions of a similar adult pattern. It should be noted that behavior that establishes this high coefficient of stability between childhood and maturity does not emerge suddenly at the age when it becomes significantly evident. It grows steadily, especially from the three-to-six period. In almost all cases there are high correlations between ages three to six and between the latter and the ten-to-fourteen period.

Tuddenham (1959) reports a more dynamically oriented follow-up of constancy in personality. At the early part of the study his subjects were teen-agers for whom extensive personality ratings were available. Nineteen years later he had them rated again. He then correlated the two ratings on each variable to estimate stability of the variables. The results differed for the sexes in that, for example, the aggressive ratings were more constant for men, and the desire for social prestige topped the list for women. That the subjects were adolescents when they were first tested detracts from the value of the study; however, it is noteworthy that the results agree very closely with those of the Fels group.

Another follow-up study (O'Neal and Robins, 1959) compared the rate of adult deviance among those who, as patients in child guidance clinics, had been "runners away" with those who had committed other offenses. As adults those who ran away had far higher rates of arrests and incarceration, of divorce, and of the diagnosis of sociopathic personality. The data give little information about precisely what personality variables in childhood are related to adult functioning. No doubt the nature of the data made difficult the task of determining variables. There are, of course, many reasons for running away, for arrest, divorce, and other deviations; but one may safely generalize that there was continuity of maladaptation (cf. Gesell and Thompson, 1941; Gregory, 1958; Kuhlen and Thompson, 1963; McKinnon, 1942; Mussen et al., 1963; Neilon, 1948).

In summary, although not all variables measured by these studies showed childhood-to-adulthood continuity, the bulk of the data do support hypotheses *C* and *D*. Thus, certain functions of personality are definitely formed in early childhood, and certain social and cultural traits and maladjustments tend to remain constant in the personality. Of course, this does not mean that alterations cannot take place through inner growth and development, from remedial experiences in living, and as a result of treatment.

RESEARCH RELEVANT TO HYPOTHESES E AND F

Hypothesis E: Given adequate conditions for physical survival, the most important external influence is the emotional relationship between a child and his parents (or parental substitutes).

Hypothesis F: The most relevant aspects of the child's emotional milieu are parental warmth, parental control in accordance with his needs, and stability in his relationship to his parents.

Rigorous scientific evidence, as opposed to clinical observation, that bears down upon the above two hypotheses is scanty. Our discussion will therefore have to be fairly brief and speculative.

Studies of imprinting have relevance to hypotheses *E* and *F*. In simplest terms imprinting means the formation of an attachment. This attachment is normally to the mother. If the young animal is removed from the mother during the critical period, it still can attach itself to substitutes, even inanimate ones. If no substitute is provided, the young animal may die. Liddell (1961) separated one of twin kids from a mother goat. The one died, while the other twin, left with its mother, thrived. In another experiment a litter of puppies is left in a field with the mother and kept from any contact whatever with humans. If the puppies are so kept for 14 weeks, they permanently lose their capacity to become attached to human beings (Lorenz, 1952). Ducklings and goslings separated from their mother during the critical period attached themselves to Lorenz if he squatted as they followed him; but if he stood, they then attached themselves to his boots only.

When normal imprinting is disrupted, the animal's capacity to attach itself and relate to its own species is disordered, as are many of its physiological functions.

It is characteristic of psychotic children that they are unable to establish attachments to anyone. It is not known whether this is a result of some form of mistreatment or gross neglect during the period when infants are normally helplessly dependent on their mothers, or whether this arises from some other cause. Spitz, in addition to his writings (1945, 1951, 1954, 1955, 1965; Spitz and Wolf, 1946), made a film showing that children separated from their mothers at five months and placed in foundling homes where they had excellent physical care but no love developed severe depressions and physical disorders, a considerable number ending in death. Bowlby (1944, 1956, 1957, 1958, 1960a,b, 1961; Bowlby et al., 1956; Bowlby and Cantab, 1953), who has studied the reactions of infants and young children to separation from their mothers, distinguished three states: protest, despair, and withdrawal. These results likewise demonstrate the vital importance of the natural biological need for a mother and the dire, irreversible effects that one would reasonably expect to find when such a necessity is withheld or otherwise interfered with.

The fact that the helplessly dependent infant is biologically conditioned to such completely symbiotic attachments leads parents, whose biological instincts may have become attenuated or perverted, to treat their young in ways that are injurious to them. Their infants may be made to become too dependent, may be coldly neglected, may be abused by threats and punitive dicipline, or may be exploited in other ways that are directly or inferentially observed by psychoanalysts. It seems likely that a healthy attachment, responded to by love and disciplinary guidance, may perhaps determine the difference between neurosis and psychosis.

Harlow's experiments are now famous (1959a,b; Harlow and Harlow, 1962; Harlow and Zimmerman, 1959; Seay et al., 1962). Baby monkeys who were separated from their mothers were exposed in a small enclosure to a nearly vertical roll of chicken wire with a milk-yielding nipple protruding from the center. Next to it was another roll, identical except for being covered with terry-cloth toweling. Given a choice, each baby monkey clung to the latter cloth-covered roll. Varying the nipple showed that it played no part in the choice. In another experiment, baby monkeys who were separated from their mothers and apparently handled very little by humans, were frightened by a mechanical face with flashing lights for eyes and grossly flapping parts. A baby monkey with no previous cloth "mother" ran as far as it could from this contraption and buried its face in its hands; but a baby monkey accustomed to a cloth "mother" rushed to it and clung to it. All of these baby monkeys showed severe disorders when they became adults: they were unable to relate to other monkeys or to the group, and their sex lives were deranged. When attentions of normal males were forced upon the unwilling females, the latter turned out to be sterile, only four out of 46 becoming pregnant. Here the profound permanent effects of early maternal deprivation are dramatically demonstrated.

This type of study is a step toward achieving a detailed evaluation of hypothesis F, concerned with the most important elements in mothering for the child. It shows that sensory comfort in a "mother" is more important to the baby monkey than the feeding function, but that the properties of being alive and belonging to the same species are immensely more important than the sensory comfort alone. What particular aspects of the natural mother are crucial still remain to be established.

Perhaps the three best-known principles of learning theory are those of frequency, primacy, and motivation. All seem to combine to make it likely that the parent's (or substitute's) influence on the small child is very great. The parent is usually the child's first or primary contact; the parent, usually the mother, is the most frequent one in the early years; and the parent is the one whose approval the child is most highly motivated to obtain. Under the combined impact of these three principles, the child can be expected to learn very well what the parent teaches him. What the parent teaches him is done partly consciously, in terms of skills and controls, and partly unconsciously and involuntarily, in terms of emotional interrelations. Moreover, the child tends to be like the parent, to take over his attitudes and feelings, to identify with him. The parents may, of course, not be the only influence on the child's learning and so ultimately on his personality. Siblings and other significant persons can also be important, but the parent appears to be the most important influence.

RESEARCH RELEVANT TO HYPOTHESES G AND H

Hypothesis G: To the extent that ideal conditions prevail, maturation proceeds to the fullest, and the individual eventually develops a mature personality; that is, he becomes a responsible, productive adult of good will.

Hyposthesis H: Any deviation from ideal conditions is necessarily detrimental, and the greater the deviation, the more thwarted the maturation will be and the more intensive and extensive becomes the pathology of the personality.

Traditionally there has always been a relative lack of interest within the field of personality study in what makes people healthy as compared to what makes people sick or maladjusted. Recent trends have shown a modification of this attitude. Considering first the dimension of warmth versus hostility, the publication by Bayley and Schaefer (1960) on the results of the Berkeley Growth Study is relevant. They found that early warmth and affection in mothers are associated with calm, happy, cooperative behavior in boys at most of the preadolescent age levels. For girls, the correlation between early maternal affection and friendly cooperative behavior tends to decrease with age. It is curious that the strongest relationship between maternal warmth and friendly behavior in girls occurs at the age when the same relationship is smallest in boys. There were no data on the influence of fathers on later behavior. A different pattern emerges when the mother's behavior is assessed during the child's adolescent period. These data show that hostile mothers have unhappy and hostile daughters and sons.

Slocum and Stone (1958), in a study of factors associated with family affection patterns, gave a questionnaire to more than two thousand teen-agers in order to determine possible relationships between the subjects' perception of affection in their families and present behavioral variables. No striking relationships were found except that, on the whole, more benefits were shown to come from living in affectionate families than in ones where warmth is low. With respect to the autonomy–control variable, the findings appear even more consistent. Tsumori and Inage (1958) interviewed and observed mothers and children. They found that infants tend to show better development under permissive mothers who are in frequent contact with their infants than under autocratic mothers (cf. Hernstein, 1963). Of course, mothers showing different attitudes on strictness and frequency of contact may also have differed in other respects. However, the fact that alternative causation is possible does not detract from the significance of the relationship demonstrated between strictness and permissiveness and favorableness of development. Peck (1958) and Peck and Havighurst (1960) compared four dimensions of family interaction—consistency, democracy, mutal trust, and parental severity—with six dimensions of children's personality—ego strength, superego strength, willing social conformity, spontaneity, friendliness, and a hostility-guilt conflict. The results showed ego strength to be significantly correlated with stable and consistent family life in which there is mutual trust and approval between parents and child. Superego strength was related to ego strength and was associated with the same family factors but was not associated with severely autocratic rearing. Friendliness and spontaneity seem to arise from a lenient, democratic family atmosphere. The importance of stability and consistency was also reported by Scarpitti et al.(1960), who found that boys originally selected as "good boys" in an area where the delinquency rate was high were found to continue to be good after several years, in terms of both their self-concept and their attitudes to parents and school. What particularly characterized the environment of these boys was a stable home life with few moves and few divorces or other destructive influences.

Baldwin et al. (1945) showed a very clear relationship between democratic child-rearing attitudes in the parents and psychological health in the offspring. Similarly, Watson (1957) found that greater freedom in the parental discipline was clearly associated with more initiative and independence, socialization and cooperation, less inner hostility and more friendliness, and a higher level of spontaneity and originality.

Thus, there is remarkable concordance among the studies in support of hypothesis *G*. Research relevant to hypothesis *H* (concerning the effects of various deviations from ideal conditions) is too extensive to be covered adequately. Only a small sample of studies can be considered here. As an aid in organizing the presentation, Schaefer's circumplex model of maternal behavior will be utilized. Its two perpendicular diameters consist of love–hostility and autonomy–control (approximately, permissiveness–domination). Other dimensions can be described in terms of their relation to these two. For instance, indifference falls in the quadrant bordered by permissiveness and hostility; overprotectiveness falls in the quadrant limited by warmth and domination. The following parental influences will be discussed: parental rejection, overdomination, indifference or underdomination, overindulgence, and overprotection. Inconsistency will be treated separately.

Parental Rejection

Studies of maternal separation, which have been conducted with institutionalized children, may be grouped under rejection. As noted earlier, many investigators have reported extensive detrimental effects (Bowlby, 1957, 1960a, 1961; Bowlby et al., 1956; Bowlby and Cantab, 1953; Dennis and Najarian, 1957; Goldfarb, 1943, 1955; Maas, 1963; Spitz and Wolf, 1946). Bender's (1947) general conclusion is representative: "We found that children who had been emotionally deprived (usually by hospitalization) in the first several years showed personality damage beyond repair."

A great many studies of existing (not disrupted) parent–child relationships yield results that show that parental rejection without actual separation is also a strong determinant in the behavior of the child. Some investigators (Baldwin et al., 1945; Radke, 1946) found that rejection in childhood leads either to shy and submissive qualities in the child or to aggressive, quarrelsome traits. These and other effects have been confirmed by Levy (1943). Redl and Wineman (1951) found that children who experienced extreme rejection and abuse show fear and anxiety, low frustration tolerance, irresponsibility, panic in novel situations, and great difficulty in reacting to failures. Symonds (1949) found rejected children to be fearful, hostile, overaggressive, and exhibiting antisocial behavior such as lying and stealing. Lewis (1955) found a particularly strong relationship between parental rejection and unsocialized aggression in the child. The findings of Redl and Wineman concerning difficulties in handling novel situations have been confirmed by Shirley (1942) and Heathers (1954). Peck (1958) found hostility and guilt in children to be associated with an unloving atmosphere in the home. Glueck and Glueck (1950) found, as have many others, that a high percentage of juvenile delinquents come from homes lacking in parental warmth. A growing number of studies emphasize the importance of the father (Baker and Holzworth, 1961; Chess and Whitbread, 1978; Fries, 1977; Gaddini, 1976; Hamilton, 1977; Heath, 1976; Hjelholt, 1958; Hoffman, 1960; Kramer, 1978; Leichty, 1960; Mussen and Distler, 1960; Payne and Mussen, 1956; Ross and Biller, 1978; Sears et al., 1957; Vogel, 1960).

Baker and Holzworth (1961) and Sears et al. (1957) have also shown that there is a close relationship between hostility in the parents and aggression in the child. They have made particularly careful separate analyses of girls and boys in relation to the father and mother separately. Quantitative factors, of course, enter into whether a child responds with shyness and timidity or with overaggressiveness, or in other ways.

Overdomination

A great deal of research has been devoted to the results of domination. In terms of the child's behavior, it commonly leads to the constellation of shyness, submissiveness, dependency, difficulty in establishing friendships, self-consciousness, and dependability (Baldwin, 1948; Radke, 1946; Symonds, 1949). Mussen and Kagan (1958) demonstrated the submissiveness and conformity in an actual experimental situation. Using 27 male college students, they first elicited TAT stories from them and then observed them individually in the Asch conformity situation. The results showed that a greater proportion of extreme conformists rather than independents perceived their parents as harsh, punitive, restrictive, and rejecting. It is suggested that tendencies to conformity are manifestations of basic personality structure and are influenced by early parent–child relations. Lewis (1955) found that strict and constraining parental behavior led to inhibited, neurotic behavior in the children seen in a clinic. Similarly, Peck (1958) found a hostility-guilt complex in the children of severely autocratic and disapproving parents.

In contrast to these studies, other investigations show positive relationships between severity of strictness and aggressive, controlling behavior in the child. Bayley and Schafer (1960) report that controlling mothers have sons who are rude, irritable, impulsive, and independent. In an experimental situation in which he allowed male college students to give him electro shocks, Hokanson (1961) found that the frequency of shocking was related to reported severity of punishment by parents during early life. In the same vein, Madoff (1959) reports that mothers of delinquent children are more primitive, more controlling, and more authoritarian than mothers of a group of control subjects. Bandura (1959) compared the family relations and child training practices of 30 aggressive and 30 withdrawn boys. Parents of the inhibited boys were shown consistently to deny the child an overt outlet for aggressive and dependent behavior. On the other hand, the parents of aggressive boys would not allow aggressive acts toward themselves but encouraged and reinforced aggression outside of the home. Another difference between these two types of parents was in their disciplinary methods, the former using guilt to enforce obedience and the latter directly punitive dicipline.

Most studies of parent–child relationships of children or adults who are mentally disturbed, alcoholic, or criminal report some combination of rejection and untoward discipline (Abbe, 1958; Andrey, 1960; Becker et al., 1959; Bethell, 1958; Brody, 1958; Cameron and Margaret, 1951; Caplan, 1961; Cline and Wangrow, 1959, 1970; Davits, 1958; Edel, 1962; Epstein and Westley, 1960; Finney, 1961; Frankel, 1959; Haley, 1960; Havighurst, 1963; Jenkins, 1960; Kagan, 1958; Kohn, 1963; Mohr, 1940; Monkman, 1958; Mussen, 1960; Palter, 1960; Pascal and Jenkins, 1960; Pringle et al., 1958; Pulver, 1959; Reiner and Kaufman, 1959; Rosenthal et al., 1959; Sears et al., 1957; Slater, 1962; Sontag, 1952, 1955; Thompson, 1955; Wenar et al., 1962; Winder and Rau, 1962).

The opposite poles from rejection and overdomination may be considered to be warmth and permissiveness or autonomy. These two have already been discussed under hypothesis *G*. Three additional parental attitudes occupy intermediate positions in the circumplex model: the detached or underdominating parent, the overprotective parent, and the overvaluing parent. The first of these belongs in the quadrant bordered by hostility and autonomy; the second two belong in the opposite quadrant bordered by warmth and control.

Indifference or Underdomination

Insufficient control may be a manifestation of passive rejection and have undertones of neglect, but this is not always true. Bayley and Schafer (1960) found some detached, ignoring mothers to have reserved, timid, polite sons, while Ausubel (1958), Levy (1943), and Cameron (1947) found a quite different clinical picture. The mothers studied by Bayley and Schafer seem to be more indifferent, negative, and colder than those described by Ausubel. This, as well as other differences, may account for the differences in the children.

Overindulgence

According to Ausubel (1958) the overindulged child may be very much like the underdominated child. However, he is more used to dealing with adults and will modulate his behavior to obtain what he wants from them as well as their approval. His relationship with his peers is precarious, partly because he has not learned to compromise with their need satisfactions. Few studies have been done on the overindulged child. On the circumplex of parental behavior, overindulgence would be closer to warmth than to control. Extrapolating from the findings of the effects of warmth on the one hand and overdominance on the other, one would expect the indulged child to be considerably better off than the overprotected child, who more closely resembles the overdominated child.

Overprotection

Levy (1943) and Radke (1946) both describe overprotected children as lacking in skill, apprehensive, shy, anxious, and submissive. Ausubel adds that they are unable to defend their rights, are fearful, and tend to withdraw from peer relationships to the company of parents and adults. In novel situations or under stress, they feel and act inadequate (Shirley, 1942). It may be noted that in the descriptions of the overindulged and the overprotected child, there are no references to hostility, although clinical experience clearly shows that the overprotection and overindulgence produce attitudes and feelings that cause a strong sense of inferiority, making frustration inevitable; both the sense of inferiority and frustration produce hostility (Saul, 1979a).

Inconsistency

In the study by Peck (1958) stability and consistency in the family life were found to be significantly correlated with ego strength in the child. In a similar vein Scarpitti et al. (1960) found, as mentioned, that the boys who stood out as "good" in an area with high delinquency, characteristically had very stable home environments. Inconsistency in parental attitudes has frequently also been held to be one of the determining factors in the etiology of schizophrenia (Bateson et al., 1958; Haley, 1960; Reichard and Tillman, 1950). Eels (1960) has reported disturbances in animals as a reaction to inconsistent treatment.

Most studies support hypotheses *G* and *H;* that is, the more parental attitudes are characterized by love, warmth, permissive and democratic discipline, stability, tolerance, and security, the more emotionally healthy and well-adjusted is the child. Conversely, deviations from these ideal conditions result in various maladaptive attitudes on the part of the child and in failures and warpings of development that constitute and produce psychopathology, including man's hostility to man.

All the studies of the effects of early influences of all kinds upon the young expand our knowledge of psychodynamics and thereby are useful for treatment and prevention. Judd Marmor (1979) has summarized the effective elements in analytic treatment. Others have written about these elements (Frank, 1976; Masserman, 1979; Strupp, 1976), but Marmor's summary seems so excellent that his main points are listed here:

1. First and most important, the transference–countertransference relationship between patient and therapist, all the fully conscious as well as the unconscious feelings and attitudes, including "therapeutic alliance" and rapport.
2. Release of emotional tension, including catharsis.
3. Insight.
4. Operant conditioning, including "the corrective emotional experience."
5. Suggestion, usually unconscious, through the tolerant helping attitude of the analyst.
6. Identification with the mature parts of the analyst.

7. Reality testing and "working through."
8. Genuine interest in the patient by the mature therapist.
9. "Participant observation" of the patient by the therapist.
10. The very careful, dynamically and thoroughly understood setting of a termination date to counteract unhealthy dependence and show confidence in the patient's capacity to live independently.

In sum, it seems unmistakable that the varied evidence supports the essential validity of the eight hypotheses described above and of the clinical formulation that the child he once was lives on in every adult. The long-range challenge to the behavioral sciences is to make a better world through avoiding the abuses in child-rearing, which make men of cruelty and violence instead of mature adults of good will.

Epilogue

Man may be excused for feeling some pride at having risen, though not through his own exertions, to the very summit of the organic scale; and the fact of his having thus risen, instead of having been aboriginally placed there, may give him hope for a still higher destiny . . .

Charles Darwin, *The Descent of Man*

Human life is in essence tragic. This has been known since the dawn of history and was stated repeatedly by the ancient Greeks. But exploration of the reasons for the tragic quality of life did not advance until Freud's discovery of the dynamic unconscious.

The psychiatrist sees aspects of the human tragedy in every patient, as well as in the mental and emotional suffering endured throughout most if not all lives. Tragedy seems to be intrinsic to a certain core of psychodynamics, which is universal and which can be condensed as follows (bypassing momentarily the personal histories and external socioeconomics).

Inevitable conflict, and therefore frustration, exist in everyone. The broadest conflict is between the progressive and the regressive sets of forces in the personality. On the one hand are those of growth and development, both physical and emotional; the *progressive* thrusts toward maturity, which include responsibility, productivity, and relative independence, (RPI); the capacity to love; and a well-developed sense of reality. These probably reflect the instinct, or at least the trend, toward social cooperation that is seen throughout the animal kingdom (Allee, 1951).

On the other hand, there are the *regressive* urges to return to previous ages and stages ("I must get away from it all"), which include the child's passivity, receptivity, needs for love, and dependence upon parents or substitutes (PRD), and the child's primitive tendency to react to every threat, frustration, or irritation with the fight–flight reaction.

We expect the relatively mature person to cope with both his own problems and the problems of those who might look to him for leadership with realism, good will, and reason rather than with emotion, especially hostility. Abraham Lincoln and Thomas Jefferson are examples of such a personality.

What we see in most people, however, is a mix of highly emotional reactions to every threat, frustration, and irritation. These reactions are revealed upon examination as either *flight* (escape) or *fight* attempts to destroy. Usually, neither flight nor fight can be carried out because humans do not live by the same primitive, automatic, instincual responses as do mammals in a state of nature. Societies demand certain controls of behavior that more or less forbid physical escape or destruction. Therefore, most flight is attempted psychologically, by regression to earlier patterns of feeling, thinking, and behavior, such as those of adolescence or of middle or early childhood. Such flight is usually manifested by neurotic symptoms. If flight regresses to so early a period as conception to age two or three, it may be evidenced by psychotic symptoms. (Our discussion is strictly limited to the physically and chemically intact, healthy organism, free of brain, endocrine, or other damage.)

These regressive reactions of thinking, feeling, and behaving cause both frustration and a sense of inferiority: frustration because adults cannot gratify the childhood desires that live on in them, and inferiority because these childhood attitudes and desires make adults feel like children in a world they see as more mature. These inferiority feelings hurt the self-esteem and usually exaggerate the reactive narcissism, i.e., the needs for self-regard, esteem, pride, vanity, praise, and competitiveness, which is why extreme egotism and hostility are so often linked. And the fight-flight reaction to both generally creates rage, which, with or without accompanying guilt (of which hostility is the major source), causes masochism. This in turn makes misery instead of happiness for the individual's brief span of life on earth and thereby brings more frustration and inferiority feelings. If this vicious cycle intensifies the emotional forces beyond the control and reason (of the conscious realistic ego), then breakdown occurs, usually as violence or psychosis, or both.

Thus, fight and flight together produce all forms of psychopathology, from simple anxiety and the other neuroses, through all the depressions, addictions, and all forms of acting out, including masochism, sadism, murder, and every kind of crime and psychosis (whatever organic elements may also be present). The other great drive is sex. It can "carry" or serve as a drain or pathway of expression for all motivations and is readily disordered by them, as in rape instead of love, perversion instead of loving coitus, and all other disorders of the sexual function.

These basic psychodynamics, in all the quantitative variations that occur in the interplay of these emotional forces, underlie all the manifestations of psychopathology seen in each particular patient, who is unique in his dynamics and psychopathology. In some degree of balance or imbalance, every person has these nuclear psychodynamics. This basic interplay of powerful emotional forces operates not only inside everyone but also between all individual humans as they come into relationships with each other. Thus we see joy, misery, hate, and hostility develop in marriages and also between groups and nations.

We are confronted daily with reports of crime and horror in the news media—ubiquitous vandalizing, smashing of mailboxes, the rape and murder of a nine-year-old girl, the possibility of a third world war. No wonder that even so great and good a man as Freud could write to his friend, the Rev. Otto Pfister, "Most people are trash," or that one frequently hears the remark, "People are no damn good." What is all this evil, really?

First, man's hostility to man is humanity's central problem. What are the sources of this hostility? All the evidence points to one all-important source: people are hostile to others out of revenge for the way they themselves have been treated. Specifically, individuals who were badly treated during early childhood, especially between birth and the age of six or seven (0 to 6), have been left with an unconscious pattern of revenge. However, they no longer take it out on those who perpetrated their mistreatment; rather, they displace it and vent it for life against whomever is available. This is usually done regardless of age or sex. It is even carried out against animals, inanimate objects, or whatever can serve as a recipient of this vengeful hostility. "Most people are no damn good," translates into "Underneath, most people are weak, hostile children, venting hostility as revenge for how they were mistreated in early life, particularly from 0 to 6."

Why do most people not mature adequately? The reason seems to be mistreatment by omission or commission during their 0 to 6 period on the part of parents or substitutes. Why do parents, either knowingly or unwittingly, mistreat their children? Mostly because of how they were raised by thier own parents. They take out their revenge against their parents on their own helpless children. Knowing this, can we improve childraising? Of course—eventually. Many diverse and encouraging attempts are already being made. The task will take centuries, but it is not insurmountable. It is the special responsibility of psychiatrists to know enough psychodynamics to understand and contribute what they can in order to make a better life for all humans.

There must be some truth to the Quaker idea that there is "that of God" in everyone. However, it shines through in few. *Homo sapiens* is perhaps still an unsocialized animal. He does not live with others easily in organized societies. The child lives on in every adult. If this child within is too young and too disturbed emotionally, then it can disorder the maturity of the adult with all kinds of mental and emotional aberrations, including every variety of hostile and criminal behavior. To live in society, external controls are required. Yet such control exercised by a few over many takes a toll—some freedom is traded off for a degree of security. Such sacrifice of intellectual or other freedoms would not be necessary if children were reared with love, respect, and sympathetic understanding, which would socialize them with minimum control. They would in turn react to their parents and other humans throughout life with the same sympathetic understanding, respect, and love accorded to them during their earliest years, especially up to age six or seven.

Life is tragic because people are hostile. The task of reducing hostility, although difficult, is possible through proper childrearing. Not only our happiness but our survival depends on accomplishing this.

Selected Bibliography

Abbe, A. E. (1958): Maternal attitudes toward children and their relationship to the diagnostic category of the child, *J. Genet. Psychol.* 92:167-173.

Abrahamsen, D. (1973): *The Murdering Mind.* New York: Harper & Row.

—— (1970): *Our Violent Society.* New York: Funk & Wagnalls.

—— (1960): *The Psychology of Crime.* New York: Columbia University Press.

Ackerman, N. W. (1956): Disturbances of mothering and criteria for treatment, *Amer. J. Orthopsychiat.* 26:252-263.

Ader, R., and Conklin, P. M. (1963): Handling of pregnant rats: Effects on emotionality of their offspring, *Science* 142:411-412.

Ader, R., Beels, C. C., and Tatum, R. (1960): Social factors, affection emotionality and resistance to disease in animals. 2. Susceptibility to gastric ulceration as a function of interruptions and the time at which they occur. *J. Comp. Psysiol. Psychol.* 53:455-458.

Adler, A. (1924): *The Practice and Theory of Individual Psychology.* New York: Harcourt, Brace and Jovanovich.

Adler, G. (1972): Prison treatment: Past, present and future, *Psychiat. Opinion* 9:6-10.

Adorno, T. W., Frenkel-Brunswick, W., et al. (1950): *The Authoritarian Personality.* New York: Harper & Row.

Aichhorn, A. (1964): *Delinquency and Child Guidance: Selected Papers*, ed. by O. Fleishman, P. Kramer, and H. Ross. New York: International Universities Press.

—— (1935): *Wayward Youth.* New York: Viking.

Alexander, F. (1961): *The Scope of Psychoanalysis.* New York: Basic Books.

—— (1960): *The Western Mind in Transition.* New York: Random House.

—— (1950): *Psychosomatic Medicine.* New York: W. W. Norton.

—— (1948): *Fundamentals of Psychoanalysis.* New York: W. W. Norton.

—— (1930): The neurotic character, *Int. J. Psycho-Anal.* 2:293.

Alexander, F., and French, T. (1942): *Psychoanalytic Therapy.* New York: Ronald Press.

Alexander, F., and Healy, W. (1935): *Roots of Crime: Psychoanalytic Studies*. New York: Alfred A. Knopf.

Alexander, F., and Ross, H. (1952): *Dynamic Psychiatry*. Chicago: University of Chicago Press.

Alexander, F., and Selesnick, S. (1966): *The History of Psychiatry*. New York: Harper & Row.

Allee, W. C. (1951): *Cooperation Among Animals*. New York: Schuman.

Allen, M. A. (1972): A cross-cultural study of aggression and crime, *J. Cross-Cult. Psychol.* 3:259–271.

Alpert, A. (1959): Reversibility of pathological fixations associated with maternal deprivation in infancy, in *The Psychoanalytic Study of the Child* 14:169–185. New York: International Universities Press.

Altman, C. H. (1958): Relation between maternal attitudes and child's personality structure, *Am. J. Orthopsychiat.* 28:160–169.

Alvarez, A. (1970): *The Savage God, A Study of Suicide*. New York: Random House.

Amanat, E., and Eble, S. (1973): Marriage role conflicts and child psychopathology, *Adolescence* 8:575–588.

Anderson, J. E. (1963): *Experience and Behavior in Early Childhood and the Adjustment of the Same Persons as Adults*. Minneapolis: University of Minnesota, Institute of Child Development.

Anderson, R. E. (1968): Where's Dad? Paternal deprivation and delinquency, *Arch. Gen. Psychiat.* 18:641–649.

Andrey, R. G. (1960): *Delinquency and Parental Pathology*. London: Metheun.

Anthony, E. J., and Benedek, T., eds. (1970): *Parenthood: Its Psychology and Psychopathology*. Boston: Little, Brown.

Arendt, H. (1970): *On Violence*. New York: Harcourt, Brace and Jovanovich.

Ausubel, D. P. (1958): *Theory and Problems of Child Development*. New York: Grune & Stratton.

Bach-y-Rita, G., and Veno, A. (1974): Habitual violence: a profile of 62 men, *Am. J. Psychiat.* 131:1015–1017.

Bach-y-Rita, G., Lion, J. R., Climent, C. E., and Ervin, F. R. (1971): Episodic dyscontrol: A study of 130 violent patients, *Am. J. Psychiat.* 127:1473–1478.

Bacon, M. K., Barry, H., and Child, I. L. (1963): A cross-cultural study of correlates of crime, *J. Abnorm. Soc. Psychol.* 66:291–300.

Baker, J. W., and Holzworth, A. (1961): Social histories of successful and unsuccessful children, *Child Dev.* 32:135–149.

Baldwin, A. L. (1948): Socialization and the parent–child relationship, *Child Dev.* 19:127–136.

Baldwin, A. L., Kalhorn, J., and Breese, F. H. (1945): Patterns of parent behavior, *Psychol. Monogr.* 58, No. 268.

Bandura, A., and Walters, R. H. (1963): *Social Learning and Personality Development*. New York: Holt, Rinehart and Winston.

—— (1959): *Adolescent Aggression*. New York: Ronald.

—— (1958): Dependency conflicts in aggressive delinquents, *J. Soc. Issues* 14: 52–65.

Bastiaans, J. (1972): General comments on the role of aggression in human psychopathology, *Psychother. Psychosom.* 20:300–311.

Bateson, G., Jackson, D. Haley, J., and Weakland, J. (1958): Toward a theory of schizophrenia, *Behav. Sci.* 1:251–264.

Bayley, N., and Schafer, E. S. (1960): Maternal behavior and personality development data from the Berkely Growth Study, *Psychiat, Res. Rep.* 13:155–175.

Beach, F. A., and Jaynes, J. (1954): Effects of early experience upon the behavior of animals, *Psychol. Bull.* 51:239–263.

Beck, M. W. (1971): Abortion: The mental health consequences of unwantedness, in *Abortion, Changing Views and Practice*, ed. by R. B. Sloane. New York: Grune & Stratton.

Becker, W. C., Peterson, D. R., Hellmer, L. A., Shoemaker, D. J., and Quay, H. C. (1959): Factors in parental behavior and personality as related to problem behavior in children, *J. Consult. Psychol.* 23:107–118.

Bell, R. Q. (1960): Retrospective and prospective views on early personality development, *Merrill-Palmer Quart. Behav. Dev.* 6:131–144.

Bender, L. (1963): Genesis of hostility in children, *Psychoanal. Rev.* 50:95–102.

—— (1956): *A Dynamic Psychopathology of Childhood*. Springfield, Ill.,: Charles C. Thomas.

—— (1954): Infants reared in institutions: Permanently handicapped, *Bull. Child Welf. League Am.* 24:1–4.

—— (1953): *Aggression, Hostility and Anxiety*. Philadelphia: Saunders.

—— (1948): Genesis of hostility in children, *Am. J. Psychiat.* 105:241–245.

—— (1947): Psychopathic behavior disorders in children, in *Handbook of Correctional Psychology*, ed. by R. M. Lindner and R. V. Seliger. New York: Philosophical Library.

Benedict, R. (1934): *Patterns of Culture*. Boston, Houghton Mifflin.

Benjamin, J. (1961): The innate and experiential in child development, in *Lectures on Experimental Psychiatry*, ed. by H. W. Brosin, Pittsburgh: University of Pittsburgh Press.

Beres, D. (1958): Vicissitudes of superego functions and superego precursors in childhood, in *The Psychoanalytic Study of the Child* 13. New York: International Universities Press.

Beres, D., and Obers, S. J. (1950): The effects of extreme deprivation in infancy on psychic structure in adolescence: A study in ego development, in *The Psychoanalytic Study of the Child* 5. New York: International Universities Press.

Berkowitz, L. (1969): *Roots of Aggression: A Re-examination of the Frustration-Aggression Hypothesis*. New York: Atherton Press.

—— (1962): *Aggression: A Social Psychological Analysis*. New York: McGraw-Hill.

—— (1960): Some factors affecting the reduction of overt hostility, *J. Abnorm. Soc. Psychol.* 60:14–21.

Bethell, M. F. (1958): Restriction and habits in children, *Z. Kinderpsychiat.* 25:264–269.

Bird, B. (1957): A consideration of the etiology of prejudice, *J. Am. Psychoanal. Assn.* 5:490–513.

Boisvert, M. J. (1972): The battered-child syndrome, *Soc. Casework* 53:475–480.

Bowlby, J. (1961): Childhood mourning and its implication for psychiatry, *Am. J. Psychiat.* 118:481–498.

—— (1960a): Separation anxiety, *Int. J. Psycho-Anal.* 41:89–113.

—— (1960b): Ethology and the development of object relations, *Int. J. Psycho-Anal.* 41:313–317.

—— (1958): The nature of the child's tie to his mother, *Int. J. Psycho-Anal.* 39:350–373.

—— (1957): An ethologic approach to research in child development, *Br. J. Med. Psychol.* 30:230–240.

—— (1956): Mother–child separation, in *Mental Health and Infant Development*, ed. by K. Soddy. New York: Basic Books.

—— (1944): Forty-four juvenile thieves, *Int. J. Psycho-Anal.* 25:1–57.

Bowlby, J., and Cantab, J. (1953): Some pathological processes set in train by early mother–child separation, *J. Ment. Sci.* 94:265–272.

Bowlby, J., Ainsworth, M., Boston, M., and Rosenbluth, D. (1956): The effects of mother–child separation: A follow-up study, *Br. J. Med. Psychol.* 39: 211–247.

Bramson, L., and Goethals, G. W., eds. (1964): *War: Studies from Psychology, Sociology and Anthropology*. New York: Basic Books.

Bridges, K. (1932): Emotional development in early infancy, *Child Dev.* 3: 324–341.

Brody, S. (1958): Signs of disturbance in the first year of life, *Am. J. Orthopsychiat.* 28:362–367.

Bromberg, W. (1948): Dynamic aspects of psychopathic personality, *Psychoanal. Quart.* 17:48–70.

Bronson, W. (1969): Stable patterns of behavior: The significance of enduring orientations for personality development, in *Minnesota Symposia on Child Psychology*, 2. Minneapolis: University of Minnesota Press.

—— (1966): Central orientations: A study of behavior organization from childhood to adolescence, *Child Dev.* 37:125–155.

Brookshire, K. H., Littman, R. A., and Stewart, C. N. (1961): Residua of shock-trauma in the white rat: A three factor theory, *Psychol. Monogr.* 75. No. 514.

Brosin, H. W. (1967): Human aggression in psychiatric perspective, in *Aggression and Defense–Neural Mechanisms and Social Patterns (Brain Function)* 5, ed. by C. D. Clemente and D. B. Lindsley. Berkeley and Los Angeles: University of California Press.

—— (1960): Evolution and understanding diseases of the mind, in *Evolution after Darwin* 2, ed. by S. Tax. Chicago: University of Chicago Press.

Brown, D. (1970): *Bury My Heart at Wounded Knee*. New York: Holt, Rinehart & Winston.

Brown, W. J., and Palmer, A. (1975): A preliminary study of schizophrenic women who murdered their children, *Hosp. Community Psychiat.* 26 (2): 71-72.

Buss, A. H. (1961): *Psychology of Aggression.* New York: Wiley.

Button, A. (1973): Some antecendents of felonious and delinquent behavior, *J. Clin. Child Psychol.* 2:35-37.

Bychowski, G. (1968): *Evil in Man: The Anatomy of Hate and Violence.* New York: Grune & Stratton.

—— (1967): Psychopathology of aggression and violence, *Bull. N. Y. Acad. Med.* 43:300-309.

—— (1966): Patterns of anger, in *The Psychoanalytic Study of the Child* 21: 172-192. New York: International Universities Press.

—— (1958): Struggle against the introjects, *Int. J. Psycho-Anal.* 39:182.

Bylinsky, G. (1973): Violence, *Fortune*, January, 135-146.

Cameron, N. (1947): *The Psychology of Behavior Disorders: A Biosocial Interpretation.* Boston: Houghton Mifflin.

Cameron, N., and Margaret, A. (1951): *Behavior Pathology.* Cambridge, Mass.: Riverside Press.

Cannon, W. B. (1939): *The Wisdom of the Body.* New York: Norton.

—— (1929): *Bodily Changes in Fear, Hunger, Pain, and Rage.* New York: Appleton.

Caplan, G., ed. (1961): *Prevention of Mental Disorders in Children: Initial Explorations.* New York: Basic Books.

Carrighar, S. (1965): *Wild Heritage.* Boston: Houghton Mifflin.

Carthy, J. D., and Ebling, F. J., eds. (1964): *The Natural History of Aggression.* New York: Academic Press.

Casler, L. (1961): Maternal deprivation: A critical review of the literature, *Monogr. Soc. Res. Child Dev.* 24, Serial No. 80.

Chess, S. and Whitbread, J. (1978): *Daughters: From Infancy to Independence.* New York: Doubleday.

Child, C. (1924): *The Psychological Foundation of Behavior.* New York: Macmillan.

Clark, L. D. (1962): A comparative view of aggressive behavior, *Am. J. Psychiat.* 119:336-341.

Cline, V. B., and Wangrow, A. S. (1970): Female criminals: Their personal, familial, and social backgrounds: The relation of these to the diagnosis of sociopathy and hysteria, *Arch. Gen. Psychiat.* 23:554-558.

—— (1959): Life history correlates of delinquent and psychopathic behavior, *J. Clin. Psychol.* 15:266-270.

Cohen, F. J., ed. (1957): *Youth and Crime.* New York: International Universities Press.

Cohen, F. S. (1956): The relationship between delusional thinking and hostility—A case study, *Psychiat. Quart.* 30:115.

Comfort, A. (1950): *Authority and Delinquency in the Modern State.* London: Routledge & Kegan Paul.

Corning, P. A., and Corning, C. H. (1972): Toward a general theory of violent aggression, *Soc. Sci. Inf.* 11:7–35.

Craft, M. (1965): *Ten Studies into Psychopathic Personalities.* Bristol, England: Wright.

Curran, W., and Harding, T. (1977): The law and mental health: Harmonizing objectives, *International Digest of Health Legislation.* Albany, N.Y.: World Health Organization Publications.

Daniels, D. N., Gilula, M. F., and Ochberg, F. M., eds. (1970): *Violence and the Struggle for Existence.* Boston: Little, Brown.

Daniels, G. E. (1971): Approaches to a biological basis of human behavior, *Dis. Nerv. Syst.* 32:227–239.

—— (1956): Comprehensive medicine, in *Changing Concepts of Psychoanalytic Medicine*, ed. by S. Rado and G. E. Daniels. New York: Grune & Stratton.

Darwin, C. R. (1965): *The Expression of Emotions in Man and Animals.* Chicago: University of Chicago Press.

Davits, J. R. (1958): Contributions of research with children to a theory of maladjustment, *Child Dev.* 29:3–7.

De Hartog, J. (1971): *The Peaceable Kingdom.* New York: Atheneum.

DeJong, H. H. (1945): *Experimental Catatonia.* Baltimore: Williams & Wilkins.

Denenberg, V. H. (1963): Early experience and emotional development, *Sci. Am.* 131:227–228.

Denenberg, V. H., and Bell, R. W. (1960): Critical period for the effects of infantile experience on adult learning. *Science* 131:227–228.

Denenberg, V. H., and Karas, C. G. (1959): Effects of differential infantile handling upon weight gain and mortality in the rat and mouse, *Science* 130:629–630.

Dennis, W. (1955): Scientific models for the investigation of child development, in *Psychopathology of Childhood*, ed. by P. Hock and J. Zubin. New York: Grune & Stratton.

Dennis, W., and Najarian, P. (1957): Infant development under environmental handicap, *Psychol. Monogr.* 71.

De Rosis, H. A. (1971): Violence: Where does it begin? *Fam. Coordinator* 20: 355–362.

DiTullio, B. (1969a): The relationship between mental illness and criminal behavior, *Monogr. Crim. Law Educ. Res. Cent.* 3:37–52.

—— (1969b): The causes of criminality, *Monogr. Crim. Law Educ. Res. Cent.* 3:53–70.

—— (1969c): Criminogenesis, *Monogr. Crim. Law Educ. Res. Cent.* 3:119–146.

Dollard, J., et al. (1939): *Frustration and Aggression.* New Haven, Conn.: Yale University Press.

Donnelly, J. (1964): Aspects of the psychodynamics of the psychopath, *Am. J. Psychiat.* 120:1149–1153.

Drever, J. (1955): The concept of early learning, *Trans. N.Y. Acad. Sci.* 17: 463–469.

Du Bos, R. (1968): *Man, Medicine and Environment.* New York: Praeger.

—— (1968): *So Human an Animal.* New York: Scribner's.

—— (1965): *Man Adapting*. New Haven, Conn.: Yale University Press.

Dukas, H., and Hoffmann, B. (1979): *Albert Einstein, The Human Side*. Princeton, N.J.: Princeton University Press.

Duncan, G. M., Frazier, S. H., Litin, E.M., Johnson, A.M., and Varron, A. (1958): Etiological factors in first-degree murder, *J.A.M.A.* 168:1755–1758.

Edel, R. (1962): A study of the relationship between certain overt behavior difficulties in children and covert areas of personality in their mothers, *Dissertation Abstr.* 23:1780–1781.

Eels, J. F. (1960): Inconsistency of early handling and its effect upon emotionality in the rat, *Dissertation Abstr.* 21:1259.

Eibl-Eibesfeldt, I. (1972): *Love and Hate: The Natural History of Behavior Patterns*, translated by G. Strachan. New York: Holt, Rinehart & Winston.

Eisner, V. (1969): *The Delinquency Label: The Epidemiology of Juvenile Delinquency*. New York: Random House.

Eissler, K. R., ed. (1949): *Searchlights on Delinquency*. New York: International Universities Press.

Engel, G. L. (1977): The need for a new medical model: A challenge for biomedicine, *Science* 196 (4286) :129–136.

—— (1975): Psychological aspects of gastrointestinal disorders, in *American Handbook of Psychiatry* 4, ed. by S. Arieti. New York: Basic Books. 653–692.

—— (1971): Attachment behavior, object relations and the dynamic-economic points of view; critical review of Bowlby's *Attachment and Loss, Int. J. Psycho-Anal.* 52(2):183–196.

—— (1968): The psychoanalytic approach to psychosomatic medicine, in *Modern Psychoanalysis, New Directions and Perspectives*, ed. by J. Marmor. New York: Basic Books, 251–273.

English, O. S., and Pearson, G. H. J. (1955): *Emotional Problems of Living*. New York: Norton.

Epstein, N. B., and Westley, W. A. (1960): Parental interaction as related to the emotional health of children, *Soc. Problems* 8:87–92.

Erikson, E. (1969): *Childhood and Society*, 2nd ed. New York: W. W. Norton.

—— (1965): Psychoanalysis and ongoing history: Problems of identity, hatred and violence, *Am. J. Psychiat.* 122:241–250.

—— (1959): *Identity and the Life Cycle*. New York: International Universities Press.

Fawcett, J., ed. (1971): *Dynamics of Violence*. Chicago: American Medical Association.

Feldhusen, J. F., Thurston, J. R., and Benning, J. J. (1971): Studying aggressive children through responses to frustrating situations, *Child Study J.* 2:1–17.

Fenby, T. P. (1972): The work of the National Society for the Prevention of Cruelty to Children (N.S.P.C.C.), *Int. J. Offender Ther. Comp. Criminol.* 16: 201–205.

Ferenczi, S. (1950): *Stages in the Development of the Sense of Reality in Sex or Psychoanalysis*. New York: Basic Books.

Ferreira, A. J. (1960): The pregnant woman's emotional attitude and its reflection on the newborn, *Am. J. Orthopsychiat.* 30:553–561.

Feshbach, N. D. (1971): The effects of violence in childhood, *J. Clin. Child Psychol.* 2:28–31.

Feshbach, S. (1971): Dynamics and morality of violence and aggression: Some psychological considerations, *Am. Psychol.* 26:281–292.

Fine, R. (1972): The stress of peace, in *The Emotional Stress of War, Violence, and Peace*, ed. by R. S. Parker. Pittsburgh: Stanwix House.

Finney, J. C. (1961): Some maternal influences on children's personality and character, *Genet. Psychol. Monogr.* 63:199–278.

Fisher, R. D., ed. (1964): *International Conflict and Behavioral Science*. New York: Basic Books.

Fleming, P., and Ricks, D. F. (1970): Emotions of children before schizophrenia and before character disorder, in *Life History Research in Psychopathology* 1, ed. by M. Roff and D. F. Ricks. Minneapolis: University of Minnesota Press.

Forer, L. G. (1972): The rights of children, *Young Children* 27:332–339.

Frank, J. (1976): Restoration of morale and behavior change in *What Makes Behavior Change Possible*? ed. by A. Burton. New York: Brunner-Mazel, 73–95.

Frankel, R. V. (1959): *A Review of Research on Parent Influences on Child Personality*. New York: Family Service Association of America.

Frazee, H. E. (1953): Children who later become schizophrenic, *Smith Coll. Stud. Soc. Work* 23:125–149.

Freedman, D. G., King, J. A., and Elliot, O. (1961): Critical period in the social development of dogs, *Science* 133:1016–1017.

Freeman, D. (1964): Human aggression in anthropological perspective, in *The Natural History of Aggression*, ed. by J. D. Carthy and F. J. Ebling. New York: Academic Press.

French, T. M. (1970a): *Psychoanalytic Interpretations*. Chicago: Quadrangle Books.

—— (1970b): *Selected Papers*. Chicago: Quadrangle Books.

—— (1939): Social conflict and psychic conflict. *Am. J. Soc.* 44:922.

Freud, A. (1949): Aggression in relation to emotional development: Normal and pathological, in *The Psychoanalytic Study of the Child* 3 and 4. New York: International Universities Press.

Freud, A., and Burlingham, D. (1943): *War and Children*. New York: International Universities Press.

Freud, S. (1949): An outline of psychoanalysis, *Standard Edition* 23.

—— (1930): Civilization and its discontents, *Standard Edition* 21.

—— (1922): Some neurotic mechanisms in jealousy, paranoia, and homosexuality, *Standard Edition* 18.

—— (1921): Group psychology and analysis of the ego, *Standard Edition* 18.

—— (1916): Introductory lectures on psychoanalysis, *Standard Edition* 16.

—— (1912): Totem and taboo, *Standard Edition* 13.

Fried, E. (1956): Ego strengthening aspects of hostility, *Am. J. Orthopsychiat.* 26:179–187.

Fries, M. (1977): Longitudinal study: prenatal period to parenthood, *J. Am. Psychoanal. Assn.* 25(1):115–140.

—— (1953): Problems of early development, in *The Psychoanalytic Study of the Child* 8. New York: International Universities Press.

Frisch, O. (1957): Mit einer purpurreiher verheiratet (Married to a purple heron), *Z. Tierpsychol.* 14:233-237.

Fromm, E. (1973): Man would as soon flee as fight, *Psychol. Today* 7:35–39.

Gaddini, E. (1976): Discussion of the role of family life in child development: On 'father formation' in early child development, *International J. of Psycho-Anal.* 57(4):397–403.

Galvin, J. (1956): Some dynamics of delinquent girls, *J. Nerv. Ment. Dis.* 123: 292–295.

Ganth, W. H., ed. (1958): *Physiological Basis of Psychiatry*. Springfield, Ill.: Charles C. Thomas.

Garn, S. (1957): Research in human growth, *Hum. Biol.* 29:1–11.

Gertz, B. (1957): The effect of handling at various age levels on emotional behavior in adult rats, *J. Comp. Physiol. Psychol.* 50:613–616.

Gesell, A., and Thompson, H. (1941): Twins T and C from infancy to adolescence: A biogenetic study of individual differences by the method of cotwin control, *Genet. Psychol. Monogr.* 24:3–121.

Gibbens, T. C. N. (1961): Trends in juvenile delinquency, *World Health Organization Public Health Paper 5*. Albany, N.Y.: WHO Publications.

Gillespie, W. H. (1971): Aggression and instinct theory, *Int. J. Psycho-Anal.* 52:155–160.

Gilula, M. F., and Daniels, D. N. (1969): Violence and man's struggle to adapt, *Science* 164:396–405.

Glaser, K., and Eisenberg, L. (1956): Maternal deprivation, *Pediatrics* 18:626–642.

Glover, E. (1960): *Roots of Crime*. New York: International Universities Press.

—— (1956): Psychoanalysis and criminology, *Int. J. Psycho-Anal.* 37:311–317.

Glueck, B. C., Jr. (1956): Psychodynamic patterns in the sexual offender: Mechanisms of conscience formation, in *Changing Concepts of Psychoanalytic Medicine*, ed. by S. Rado and G. E. Daniels. New York: Grune & Stratton.

Glueck, S., and Glueck, E. (1950): *Unraveling Juvenile Delinquency*. Cambridge, Mass.: Harvard University Press.

Goldfarb, W. (1955): Emotional and intellectual consequences of psychological deprivation in infancy: A revaluation, in *Psychopathology of Childhood*, ed. by P. H. Hock and J. Zubin. New York: Grune & Stratton.

—— (1943): Infant rearing and problem behavior, *Am. J. Orthopsychiat.* 13: 249–265.

Goldston, I. (1971): Psychiatry for the millions, in *Techniques of Therapy*, ed. by J. Masserman. New York: Grune & Stratton.

Goodall, J. (1971): *In The Shadow of Man*. Boston: Houghton Mifflin.

Gossop, M., and Royx, A. (1977): Hostility, crime and drug dependence, *Br. J. Psychiat.* 130:272–278.

—— (1976): Hostility in drug dependent individuals: Its relation to specific drugs, and oral or intravenous use, *Br. J. Psychiat.* 128:188–193.

Gottlieb, G. (1961): Developmental age as a baseline for determination of the critical period in imprinting, *J. Comp. Physiol. Psychol.* 54:422–427.

Gray, P. H. (1963): Checklist of papers since 1951 dealing with imprinting in birds, *Psychol. Rec.* 13:445–454.

—— (1958): Theory and evidence of imprinting in human infants, *J. Psychol.* 48:155–156.

Gray, P. H., and Howard, K. I. (1957): Specific recognition of humans in imprinted ducks, *Percept. Mot. Skills* 7:301–304.

Greenacre, P. (1971): *Emotional Growth*, 2 vols. New York: International Universities Press.

—— (1960): Considerations regarding the parent-infant relationship, *Int. J. Psycho-Anal.* 41:571–584.

Greenberg, H. R., and Blank, R. H. (1970): Murder and self-destruction by a twelve-year-old boy, *Adolescence* 5:391–396.

Greenberg, N. H. (1962): Studies of psychosomatic differentiation during infancy, a longitudinal anterospective approach for the study of development during infancy, *Arch. Gen. Psychiat.* 7:389–406.

Gregory, I. (1958): An analysis of familial data on psychiatric patients, *Br. J. Prev. Soc. Med.* 12:42.

Grier, W., and Cobbs, P. (1968): *Black Rage*. New York: Basic Books.

Grinker, R. R. (1971): What is the cause of violence? in *Dynamics of Violence*, ed. by J. Fawcett. Chicago: American Medical Association.

Grinker, R. R., et al. (1961): *The Phenomena of Depressions*. New York: Hoeber.

Guntrip, H. (1971): *Psychoanalytic Theory, Therapy, and the Self*. New York: Basic Books.

—— (1961): *Personality Structure and Human Interaction*. New York: International Universities Press.

Haley, J. (1960): Direct study of child-parent interactions, observation of the family of the schizophrenic, *Am. J. Orthopsychiat.* 30:460–467.

Halleck, S. L. (1967): *Psychiatry and the Dilemmas of Crime: A Study of Causes, Punishment and Treatment*. New York: Hoeber Medical Division., Harper & Row.

Hallowell, A. I. (1960): Self, society and culture in phylogenetic perspective, in *Evolution after Darwin* 2, ed. by S. Tax. Chicago: University of Chicago Press.

Hamburg, D. A. (1974): Ethological perspectives on human aggressive behavior, in *Ethology and Psychiatry*, ed. by N. F. White. Toronto: University of Toronto Press.

—— (1963): Emotions in the perspective of human evolution, in *Expression of the Emotions in Man*, ed. by P. D. Knapp. New York: International Universities Press.

Hamilton, M. (1977): *Father's Influence on Children*. Chicago: Nelson-Hall.

Harlow, H. F. (1966): Learning to love, *Am. Sci.* 54:244–272.

—— (1960): Primary affectional patterns in primates, *Am. J. Orthopsychiat.* 30:676–684.

—— (1959a): Love in infant monkeys, *Sci. Am.* 200:68–74.

—— (1959b): The development of learning in the rhesus monkey, *Am. Sci.* 47:459–479.

Harlow, H. F., and Harlow, M. (1962): The effect of rearing conditions on behavior, *Bull. Menninger Clin.* 26:213–224.

Harlow, H. F., and Zimmerman, R. R. (1959): Affectional responses in the infant monkey, *Science* 130:421–432.

Harris, D. B. (1960): Conceptual and methodological developments in parent–child research, *Child Dev.* 31:817–822.

Hartmann, H. (1958): *Ego Psychology and the Problem of Adaptation.* New York: International Universities Press.

Hartmann, H., Kris, E., and Lowenstein, R. M. (1949): Notes on the theory of aggression, in *The Psychoanalytic Study of the Child* 3:9–36. New York: International Universities Press.

Haskins, C. (1953): *Of Societies and Men.* New York: W. W. Norton.

Havens, L. L. (1972): Youth, violence, and the nature of family life, *Psychiat. Ann.* 2:18–29.

Havighurst, R. J. (1963): Psychological roots of moral development: Discussion, *Cathol. Psychol. Rec.* 1:35–44.

Heath, D. H. (1976): Competent fathers: their personalities and marriages, *Human Development* 19(1):26–39.

Heathers, G. (1954): The adjustment of two-year-olds in a novel social situation, *Child Dev.* 25:147–158.

Heimann, P., and Valenstein, A. F. (1972): The psychoanalytical concept of aggression: An integrated summary, *Int. J. Psycho-Anal.* 53:31–35.

Helfer, R. E., and Kempe, C. H. (1968): *The Battered Child.* Chicago: University of Chicago Press.

Henderson, S., et al. (1977): An assessment of hostility in a population of adolescents, *Arch. Gen. Psychiat.* 34(6):706–714.

Henry, J. (1971): *Pathways to Madness.* New York: Random House.

Hernstein, M. I. (1963): Behavioral Correlates of breast–bottle regimes under varying parent–infant relationships, *Monogr. Soc. Res. Child Dev.* 28, No. 88.

Herrick, C. J. (1956): *The Evolution of Human Nature.* Austin: University of Texas Press.

Hess, E. H. (1959a): The relationship between imprinting and motivation, in *Nebraska Symposium on Motivation,* ed. by M. R. Jones. Lincoln: University of Nebraska Press.

—— (1959b): Two conditions limiting critical age for imprinting, *J. Comp. Physiol. Psychol.* 52:515–518.

—— (1959c): Imprinting, an effect of early experience, *Science* 130:133–141.

—— (1958): "Imprinting" in animals, *Sci. Am.* 198:81–90.

Hinkle, L. E., Christenson, W. N., Kane, F. D., Osteld, A., Thetford, W. N. and Wolff, H. G. (1958): An investigation of the relation between life experience, personality characteristics, and general susceptibility to illness, *Psychosom. Med.* 20:278–295.

Hjelholt, G. (1958): The neglected parent, *Nord. Psychol.* 10:179–184.

Hoffman, M. L. (1960): Power assertion by the parent and its impact on the child, *Child Dev.* 31:129–143.

Hokanson, J. E. (1961): The effects of guilt arousal and severity of discipline on adult aggressive behavior, *J. Clin. Psychol.* 17:29–32.

Holinger, P. (1977): Suicide in adolescence, *Am. J. Psychiat.* 134(12):1433–1434.

Hough, R. (1970): *Captain Bligh and Mr. Christian.* New York: E. P. Dutton.

Hunt, J. M., ed. (1944): *Personality and the Behavior Disorders* 1 and 2. New York: Ronald.

Ikemi, Y. (1972): A psychosomatic approach to aggressive patients, *Psychosomatics* 13:155–157.

Ilfeld, F. W. (1969): Overview of the causes and prevention of violence, *Arch. Gen. Psychiat.* 20:675–689.

Jaynes, J. (1957): Imprinting: the interaction of learned and innate behavior. 2. The critical period, *J. Comp. Physiol. Psychol.* 50:6–10.

Jenkins, R. M. (1960): The psychopathic or antisocial personality, *J. Nerv. Ment. Dis.* 131:318–334.

Johnson, A. M. (1969): *Experience, Affect, and Behavior: Psychoanalytic Explorations of Doctor Adelaide McFayden Johnson,* ed. by D. B. Robinson. Chicago: University of Chicago Press.

Johnson, A. M., and Szurek, S. A. (1954): Etiology of antisocial behavior in delinquents and psychopaths, *J. A. M. A.* 154:184–187.

—— (1952): The genesis of antisocial acting out in children and adults, *Psychoanal. Quart.* 21:323–343.

Jones, E. (1952): *The Life and Work of Sigmund Freud* 1. New York: Basic Books.

Kagan, J. (1972): Motives and development, *J. Soc. Psychol.* 22:51–66.

—— (1958): Socialization of aggression and the perception of parents in fantasy, *Child Dev.* 29:311–320.

Kagan, J., and Moss, H. A. (1963): *Birth to Maturity: A Study in Psychological Development.* New York: John Wiley.

—— (1960): The stability of passive and dependent behavior from childhood to adulthood, *Child Dev.* 31:577–591.

Kahn, E. (1959): Fear, hostility, reality, *Am. J. Psychiat.* 115:1002–1005.

Kalogerakis, M. G. (1971): Homicide in adolescents: Fantasy and deed, in *Dynamics of Violence.* ed. by J. Fawcett. Chicago: American Medical Association.

Kaplan, A. R., and Thompson, W. R. (1957): Influence of prenatal anxiety on emotionality in young rats, *Science* 126:73–74.

Kempe, C.H., and Helfer, R. E., eds. (1972): *Helping the Battered Child and His Family.* Philadelphia: Lippincott.

Kempe, C. H., Silverman, F. N., Steele, B. F., Droegemuller, W., and Silver, H. K. (1962): The battered-child syndrom, *J. A. M. A.* 181:17–24.

Keniston, K. (1970): Violence: Sadism and cataclysm, in *Violence in America,* ed. by T. Rose. New York: Random House.

Kestemberg, E., rptr. (1972): Panel: The role of aggression in child analysis, *Int. J. Psycho-Anal.* 53:321–323.

King, J. A. (1958): Parameters relevant to determining the effect of early experience upon the adult behavior of animals, *Psychol. Bull.* 55:46–58.

Klatskin, E., and Jackson, E. B. (1955): Methodology of the Yale rooming-in project on parent–child relationship, *Am. J. Orthopsychiat.* 25:373–397.

Klineberg, O. (1950): Tensions affecting international understanding, *Soc. Serv. Res. Coun. N. Y. Bull.* 62.

Kodlin, D., and Thompson, D. J. (1958): An appraisal of the longitudinal approach in studies of growth and development, *Monogr. Soc. Res. Child Dev.* 23, No. 1.

Kogan, K. L., and Wimberger, H. C. (1971): Behavior transactions between disturbed children and their mothers, *Psychol. Rep.* 28:395–404.

Kohn, M. D. (1963): Social class and parent–child relationships: An interpretation, *Am. J. Sociol.* 68:471–480.

Kolb, L. C. (1971): Violence and aggression—An overview, in *Dynamics of Violence,* ed. by J. Fawcett. Chicago: American Medical Association.

Kramer, S., chairman (1978): Role of father in preoedipal years: a panel report, *J. of Amer. Psychoanal. Assn.* 28(1):143–162.

Kris, M. (1957): The use of prediction in a longitudinal study, in *The Psychoanalytic Study of the Child* 12:175–189. New York: International Universities Press.

Kuhlen, R. G., and Thompson, G. G. (1963): *Psychological Studies of Human Development.* New York: Appleton.

Kurth, G. M. (1947): Hitler's two Germanies; a sidelight on nationalism, in *Psychoanalysis and the Social Sciences,* ed. by G. Roheim. New York: International Universities Press.

—— (1947): The Jew and Adolph Hitler, *Psychoanal. Quart.* 16:11–32.

Lampl-DeGroot, J. (1958): Psychoanalysis and its relation to certain other fields of natural science, *Int. J. Psycho-Anal.* 40:169–179.

—— (1949): Neurotics, delinquents and ideal formation, in *Searchlights on Delinquency,* ed. by K. Eissler. New York: International Universities Press.

Langer, W. C. (1972): *The Mind of Adolph Hitler—The Secret Wartime Report.* New York: Basic Books.

Langner, H. (1971): The making of a murderer, *Am. J. Psychiat.* 127:950–953.

Laury, G. V., and Meerloo, J. A. (1967): Mental cruelty and child abuse, *Psychiat. Quart. Suppl.* 41:203–254.

Leakey, R., and Lewin, R. (1977): *Origins.* New York: E. P. Dutton.

Leichty, M. M. (1960): The effect of father absence during early childhood upon the oedipal situation as reflected in young adults, *Merrill-Palmer Quart.* 6:212–217.

Lesse, S. (1958): Psychodynamic relationships between degree of anxiety and other clinical symptoms, *J. Nerv. Ment. Dis.* 127:124–130.

Lester, D. (1971): Suicide: Aggression or hostility? *Crisis Intervention* 3:10–14.

Levine, S. (1962): The effects of experience on adult behavior, in *Experimental Foundations of Clinical Psychology,* ed. by A. J. Bachrach. New York: Basic Books.

—— (1957): Infantile experiences and resistance to physiological stress, *Science* 126:405.

Levy, D. (1943): *Maternal Overprotection.* New York: Columbia University Press.

Lewis, H. (1955): Unsatisfactory parents and psychological disorder in their children, *Eugenics Rev.* 47:153–162.

Liddell, H. (1961): Sheep, in *Lectures on Experimental Psychiatry,* ed. by H.W. Brosin. Pittsburgh: University of Pittsburgh Press.

—— (1958): A biological basis for psychopathology, in *Problems of Addiction and Habituation,* ed. by P. H. Hoch and J. Zubin. New York: Grune & Stratton.

—— (1956): *Emotional Hazards in Animals and Man.* Springfield, Ill.: Charles C. Thomas.

Lindzey, G., ed. (1958): *Assessment of Human Motives.* New York: Holt. Rinehart and Winston.

Livson, N, and Peskin, H. (1967): Prediction of adult psychological health in a longitudinal study, *J. Abnorm. Psychol.* 72:509–518.

Loewenstein, R. M., ed. (1953): *Drives, Affects, Behavior.* New York: International Universities Press.

Lorenz, K. (1966): *On Aggression.* New York: Harcourt, Brace and Jovanovich.

—— (1952): *King Solomon's Ring.* New York: Crowell.

—— (1935): Der kimpan in der unwelt des vogels, *J. Ornithol.* 83:137–273, 289–413.

Maas, H. S. (1963): Long term effects of early childhood separation and group care, *Vita Humana* 6:34–56.

Macfarlane, J. W. (1964): Perspectives on personality consistency and change from the Guidance Study, *Vita Humana* 7:115–126.

—— (1963): From infancy to adulthood, *Childhood Educ.* 39:336–342.

Madison, P. (1961): *Freud's Concept of Repression and Defense, Its Theoretical and Observational Language.* Minneapolis: University of Minnesota Press.

Madoff, J. M. (1959): The attitudes of mothers of juvenile delinquents toward child rearing, *J. Consult. Psychol.* 23:518–520.

Madow, L. (1972): *Anger.* New York: Scribner's.

Mahler, M. S. (1968): *On Human Symbiosis and the Vicissitudes of Individuation* 1. New York: International Universities Press.

—— (1963): Thoughts about development and individuation, in *The Psychoanalytic Study of the Child,* 18:307–324. New York: International Universities Press.

Mahler, M. S., and Furer, M. (1962): Certain aspects of the separation-individuation phase, *Psychoanal. Quart.* 32:1–14.

Mahler, M. S., and La Perriere, K. (1965): Mother–child interaction during separation-individuation, *Psychoanal. Quart.* 34:483–498.

Mahler, M. S., Furer, M., and Settlage, C. F. (1959): Severe emotional disturbance in childhood: Psychosis, in *American Handbook of Psychiatry. New* York: Basic Books, 816–839.

Mandelbaum, G., and Mandelbaum, A. (1957): *Philosophic Problems.* New York: Macmillan.

Mark, V. J., and Ervin, F. (1970): *Violence and the Brain.* New York: Harper & Row.

Marmor, J. (1979): Change in psychoanalytic treatment, *J. Am. Acad. Psychoanal.* 7(3):345–357.

Martin, W. E. (1960): Conceptual and methodological developments in parent-child research, *Child Dev.* 31:123–126.

Masserman, J. (1979): Threescore and thirteen tangential therapies, in *Current Psychiatric Therapies* 18, ed. by J. Masserman. New York: Grune & Stratton.

—— (1961): *Principles of Dynamic Psychiatry.* Philadelphia: Saunders.

Masserman, J., and Schwab, J., eds. (1972): *Man for Humanity, On Concordance vs. Discord in Human Behavior.* Springfield, Ill.: Charles C. Thomas.

May, A., Kahn, J., and Cronholm, B. (1971): Mental health of adolescents and young persons, *World Health Organization Public Health Paper 1.* Albany, N. Y.: WHO Publications.

May, R. (1972): *Power and Innocence: A Search for the Sources of Violence.* New York: W. W. Norton.

McCord, W., McCord, J., and Howard, A. (1961): Familial correlates of aggression in non-delinquent children, *J. Abnorm. Soc. Psychol.* 62:79–93.

McCord, W., McCord, J., and Zola, I. K.'(1959): *Origins of Crime.* New York: Columbia University Press.

McCranie, E. J. (1971): Depression, anxiety and hostility, *Psychiat. Quart.* 45: 117–133.

McDevitt, J., and Settlage, C., eds. (1971): *Separation-Individuation.* New York: International Universities Press.

McKinnon, K. M. (1942): *Consistency and Change in Behavior Manifestations as Observed in a Group of Sixteen Children During a Five-year Period.* New York: Teachers College Bur. of Publ., Columbia University.

McNeil, E. B. (1959): Psychology and aggression, *J. Conflict Resolution* 3:195–203.

Mead, M. (1964): *Continuities in Cultural Evolution.* New Haven, Conn.: Yale University Press.

—— (1957): Changing patterns of parent–child culture, *Int. J. Psycho-Anal.* 38: 369–378.

—— (1949): *Male and Female.* New York: William Morrow.

—— (1935): *Sex and Temperament in Three Primitive Societies.* New York: William Morrow.

Mednick, S. A., and Schulsinger, F. (1970): Factors related to breakdown in children at high risk for schizophrenia, in *Life History Research in Psychopathology* 1., ed. by M. Roff and D. F. Ricks. Minneapolis: University of Minnesota Press.

Megargee, E. I., Hokanson, J. E., eds (1970): *The Dynamics of Aggression: Individual, Group, and International Analyses.* New York: Harper & Row.

Meier, G. W., and Stuart, J. L. (1959): Effects of handling on the physical and behavioral development of siamese kittens, *Psychol. Rep.* 5:497–501.

Menninger, R. W., and Modlin, H. C. (1971): Individual violence: Prevention in the violence-threatening patient, in *Dynamics of Violence,* ed. by J. Fawcett. Chicago: American Medical Association.

Meyers, W. J. (1962): Critical period for the facilitation of exploratory behavior by infantile experience, *J. Comp. Physiol. Psychol.* 50:1099–1101.

Milgram, S. (1973): *Obedience to Authority: An Experimental View.* New York: Harper & Row.

Mintz, B., ed. (1958): *Environmental Influences on Prenatal Development.* Chicago : University of Chicago Press.

Mohr, G. J. (1940): Influence of mothers' attitudes on mental health, *J. Pediatrics* 16:641.

Moltz, H. (1960): Imprinting: Empirical basis and theoretical significance, *Psychol. Bull.* 57:291-314.

Monkman, J. A. (1958): The relationship between children's adjustment and parental acceptance, *Dissertation Abstr.* 19:1117-1118.

Montagu, A. (1978): *Learning Non-Aggression: The Experience of Non-Literate Societies.* Oxford, England: Oxford University Press.

—— (1976): *The Nature of Human Aggression.* Oxford, England: Oxford University Press.

Montagu, M. F. A. (1962): *Prenatal Influences.* Springfield, Ill.: Charles C. Thomas.

Morris, H. H., Jr., et al. (1956): Aggressive behavior disorders of children: A follow-up study, *Am. J. Psychiat.* 112:991-997.

Morrison, J. R., and Stewart, M. A. (1971): A family study of the hyperactive child syndrome, *Bio. Psychiat.* 3:189-195.

Moss, H. A., and Kagan, J. (1964): Report on personality consistency and change from the Fels Longitudinal Study, *Vita Humana* 7:127-139.

Moyer, K. E. (1971): *The Physiology of Hostility.* Chicago: Markham.

Muslin, H. L., and Pieper, W. J. (1971): On the ego restraint of violence, in *Dynamics of Violence,* ed. by J. Fawcett. Chicago: American Medical Association.

Mussen, P. H. (1960): Developmental psychology Effects of parental behavior and attitudes on child personality and behavior, *Ann. Rev. Psychol.* 11:439-478.

Mussen, P. H., Conger, J. J., and Kagan J. J. (1963): *Child Development and Personality,* 2nd ed. New York: Harper & Row.

Mussen, P. H., and Distler, L. (1960): Child rearing antecedents of masculine identification in kindergarten boys, *Child Dev.* 31:89-100.

Mussen, P. H., and Kagan, J. (1958): Group conformity and perception of parents, *Child Dev.* 29:57-60.

Naka, S., Abe, K., and Sizuki, H. (1965): Childhood behavior characteristics of the parents in certain behavior problems of children, *Acta Paedopsychiat.* 32: 11-16.

Neel, J. V., and Schull, W. J. (1954): *Human Heredity.* Chicago: University of Chicago Press.

Neilon, P. (1948): Shirley's babies after fifteen years: A personality study, *J. Genet. Psychol.* 73:175-186.

Nelson, S. D. (1974): Nature/nurture revisited: A review of the biological bases of conflict, *J. Conflict Resolution* 18:285-335.

Norris, A. S. (1960): Prenatal factors in intellectual and emotional development, *J. A. M. A.* 172:413-416.

Offer, D. (1971): Coping with aggression among normal adolescent boys, in *Dynamics of Violence,* ed. by J. Fawcett. Chicago: American Medical Association.

O'Neal, P., and Robins, L. N. (1959): The adult prognosis for runaway children, *Am. J. Orthopsychiat.* 29:752–761.

—— (1958): Childhood patterns predictive of adult schizophrenia, *Am. J. Psychiat.* 115:385–391.

O'Neill, D. (1958): Stress and disease: A review of principles, *Br. Med. J.* 5091: 285–287.

Ostow, M. (1971): Parents' hostility to their children, *Israel Ann. Psychiat. Rel. Disc.* 8:3–21.

—— (1960): Psychoanalysis and ethology, *J. Am. Psychoanal. Assn.* 8:526–534.

Page, J. D. (1959): Review of *Depression*, ed. by P. H. Hoch and J. Zubin, *Psycol. Bull.* 52:354.

Palter, G. H. (1960): A study of the relationship between the child's pattern of adjustment and the mother–child interaction, *Dissertation Abstr.* 20:4723.

Parens, H. (1970): Inner sustainment: Metapsychological considerations, *Psychoanal. Quart.* 39:223–239.

Parens, H., and Saul, L. J. (1971): *Dependence in Man.* New York: International Universities Press.

Parker, R. S., ed. (1972): *The Emotional Stress of War, Violence, and Peace.* Pittsburgh: Stanwix House.

Pasamanick, B., Rogers, M. E., and Lilienfeld, A. M. (1956): Pregnancy experience and development of behavior disorder in children, *Am. J. Psychiat.* 112:613–618.

Pascal, G. R., and Jenkins, W. O. (1960): A study of the early environment of workhouse inmates (alcoholics) and its relationship to adult behavior, *Quart. J. Alcoholism* 21:40–50.

Pavlov, I. P. (1927): *Conditioned Reflexes.* New York: Oxford Press.

Payne, D. E., and Mussen, P. H. (1956): Parent–child relations and father identification among adolescent boys, *J. Abnorm. Soc. Psychol.* 52:358–362.

Payne, R. (1973): *The Life and Death of Adolph Hitler.* New York: Praeger.

Pearson, G. H. J. (1939): The chronically aggressive child, *Psychoanal. Rev.* 26: 485–525.

Peck, R. F. (1958): Family patterns correlated with adolescent personality structure, *J. Abnorm. Soc. Psychol.* 57:347–350.

Peck, F. F., and Havighurst, R. J. (1960): *The Psychology of Character Development.* New York: Wiley.

Pemberton, D. A., and Benady, D. R. (1973): Consciously rejected children, *Br. J. Psychiat.* 123:575–578.

Pokorny, A. D. (1962): Background factors in schizophrenia, *J. Nerv. Ment. Dis.* 134:84–87.

Pope, C. (1940): *Snakes Alive.* New York: Viking Press.

Prescott, E., and Jones, E. (1972): *The "Politics" of Day Care.* Washington, D.C.: National Association for the Education of Young Children.

Pringle, M. L., Kollner, E., and Bossio, V. (1958): A study of deprived children, *Vita Humana* 1:65–92.

Pulver, U. (1959): Mutter irritierbarer sanglinge (Mothers of irritable infants), *Schweiz. Z. Psychol. Anwend.* 18:133–143.

Radke, M. J. (1946): The relation of parental authority to children's behavior and attitudes, *Univ. of Minnesota Child Welfare Monogr.* 22.

Rado, S. (1956): *Psychoanalysis of Behavior.* New York: Grune & Stratton.

Rangell, L. (1972): Aggression, Oedipus and historical perspective, *Int. J. Psycho-Anal.* 52:3–11.

Rank, B. (1949): Aggression, in *The Psychoanalytic Study of the Child,* 3:43–48. New York: International Universities Press.

Rappaport, J. R. (1967): *The Clinical Evaluation of the Dangerousness of the Mentally Ill.* Springfield, Ill.: Charles C. Thomas.

Redl, F., and Wineman, D. (1951): *Children Who Hate: The Disorganization and Breakdown of Behavior Concepts.* Glencoe, Ill.: Free Press.

Reichard, S., and Tillman, C. (1950): Patterns of child-parent relationship in schizophrenia, *Psychiatry* 13:247–257.

Reiner, B., and Kaufman, L. (1959): *Character Disorders in Parents of Delinquents.* New York: Family Service Association of America.

Reisen, A. H. (1960): Brain and behavior: Effects of stimulus deprivation on the development and atrophy of the visual sensory system, *Am. J. Orthopsychiat.* 30:23–26.

Resnick, P. J. (1969): Child murder by parents: A psychiatric review of filicide, *Am. J. Psychiat.* 126:325–334.

Rheingold, H. L. (1973): To rear a child, *Am. Psychol.* 28:42–46.

Ribble, M. (1943): *Rights of Infants.* New York: Columbia University Press.

Rice, E., Ekdahl, M., and Miller, L. (1971): *Children of Mentally Ill Parents.* New York: Behavioral Publ.

Richette, L. A. (1970): *Throwaway Children.* New York: Dell.

Ricks, D. F., and Berry, J. C. (1970): Family and symptom patterns that precede schizophrenia, in *Life History Research in Psychopathology* 1, ed. by M. Roff and D. F. Ricks. Minneapolis: University of Minnesota Press.

Robbins, P. R. (1969): Personality and psychosomatic illness: A selective review of research, *Genet. Psychol. Monogr.* 80:51–90.

Robertson, J. (1962): Mothering as an influence on early development, in *The Psychoanalytic Study of the Child* 17. New York: International Universities Press.

Robins, L. N. (1966): *Deviant Children Grown Up: A Sociological and Psychiatric Study of Sociopathic Personality.* Baltimore: Williams & Wilkins.

Roche, P. Q. (1959): *The Criminal Mind: A Study of Communication between Criminal Law and Psychiatry.* New York: Grove Press.

Roff, M., Mink, W., and Hinrichs, G. (1966): *Developmental Abnormal Psychology.* New York: Holt, Rinehart & Winston.

Roff, M., and Ricks, D. F., eds. (1970): *Life History Research in Psychopathology* 1. Minneapolis: University of Minnesota Press.

Roff, M., Robins, L. N., and Pollack, M., eds. (1972): *Life History Research in Psychopathology* 2. Minneapolis: University of Minnesota Press.

Rosenthal, M. J., Finkelstein, M., Ni, E., and Robertson, R. E. (1959): A study of mother–child relationships in the emotional disorders of children, *Genet. Psychol. Monogr.* 60:63–116.

Ross, J. and Biller, H. (1978): Role of fathers in parenting needs rethinking, *Psychiatric News* 13(16):34–35.

Rothe, M. (1972): Human violence as viewed from the psychiatric clinic, *Am. J. Psychiat.* 128:1043–1056.

Rothenberg, A. (1971): On anger, *Am. J. Psychiat.* 128:454–460.

Russell, D. H. (1965): A study of juvenile murderers, *J. Offender Ther.* 3:55–86.

Rutter, M. (1970): Psycho-social disorders in childhood and their outcome in adult life, *J. R. Coll. Physicians London* 4:211–218.

Rutter, M., Korn, S., and Birch, H. G. (1963): Genetic and environmental factors in the development of "primary reaction patterns," *Br. J. Soc. Clin. Psychol.* 2:161–173.

Salzman, C., et al. (1976): Marijuana and hostility in a small-group setting, *Am. J. Psychiat.* 133(9):1029–1033.

Salzman, L., and Masserman, J., eds. (1962): *Modern Concepts of Psychoanalysis.* New York: Philosophical Library.

Sanford, N. (1971): Dehumanization and collective destructiveness, *Int. J. Group Tensions* 1:26–41.

Sargent, D. (1962): Children who kill: A family conspiracy, *Soc. Work* 7:35–42.

Satten, J., Menninger, K., Rosen, I., and Mayman, M. (1960): Murder without apparent motive: a study in personality disorganization, *Am. J. Psychiat.* 117:48–53.

Saul, L. J. (1980): *The Childhood Emotional Pattern and Psychodynamic Therapy.* New York: Van Nostrand Reinhold.

—— (1979a): *The Childhood Emotional Pattern and Maturity.* New York: Van Nostrand Reinhold.

—— (1979b): *The Childhood Emotional Pattern in Marriage.* New York: Van Nostrand Reinhold.

—— (1977): *The Childhood Emotional Pattern and Corey Jones.* New York: Van Nostrand Reinhold.

—— (1976): *The Childhood Emotional Pattern: The Key to Personality, Its Disorders and Therapy.* New York: Van Nostrand Reinhold.

—— (1976): A psychoanalytic view of hostility: Its genesis, treatment and implications for society, *Humanitas* 12(2):171–182.

—— (1965a): Criminal acting out and psychopathology, in *Crime, Law and Corrections,* ed. by R. Slovenko. Springfield, Ill,: Charles C. Thomas.

—— (1965b): Hostility, in *Crime, Law, and Corrections,* ed. by R. Slovenko. Springfield, Ill.: Charles C. Thomas.

—— (1961): Some psychological bases of war and peace, *Comp. Psychiat.* 2:134–139.

—— (1951): Inferiority feelings and hostility, *Am. J. Psychiat.* 108:120–122.

—— (1944): Physiological effects of emotional tension, in *Personality and Behavior Disorders* 1. New York: Ronald Press.

Saul, L. J., and Lyons, J. W. (1952): Acute neurotic reactions, in *The Impact of Freudian Psychiatry,* ed. by F. Alexander and H. Ross. Chicago: University of Chicago Press.

Saul, L. J., and Sheppard, E. (1958): An approach to the ego functions, *Psychoanal. Quart.* 27:237–246.

—— (1956): An attempt to quantify emotional forces using manifest dreams, *J. Am. Psychoanal. Assn.* 4:486.

Saul, L. J., Sheppard, E., Selby, D., Lhamon, W., Sachs, D., and Master, R. (1954): The quantification of hostility in dreams with reference to essential hypertension, *Science* 110:382.

Scarpitti, F. R., Murray, E., Dinitz, S., and Reckless, W. C. (1960): The "good" boy in a high delinquency area: Four years later, *Am. Sociol. Rev.* 25:555–558.

Schafer, E. S., and Bayley, N. (1963): Maternal behavior, child behavior, and their intercorrelations from infancy through adolescence, *Monogr. Soc. Res. Child Dev.* 28; No. 871.

Schaeffer, H. R. (1958): Objective observations of personality development in early infancy, *Br. J. Med. Psychol.* 31:174–183.

Schaeffer, H. R., and Callender, W. M. (1959): Psychologic effects of hospitalization in infancy, *Pediatrics* 24:528–539.

Scharr, J. H. (1963): Violence in juvenile gangs, *Am. J. Orthopsychiat.* 33:29–37.

Schoeck, H. (1966): *Envy, A Theory of Social Behavior.* New York: Harcourt, Brace and Jovanovich.

Schonecke, O. W., Schuffel, W., Schafer, N., and Winter, K. (1972): Assessment of hostility in patients with functional cardiac complaints, *Psychother. Psychosom.* 20:272–281.

Schuffel, W., and Schonecke, O. W. (1972): Assessment of hostility in the course of psychosomatic treatment of three patients with functional disorders, *Psychother. Psychosom.* 20:282–293.

Schur, N. (1966): *The Id and the Regulatory Principles of Mental Functioning.* J. Am. Psychoanal. Assn. Monogr. Ser. No 4.

Scott, J. P. (1962): Critical periods in behavior development, *Science* 138:949–958.

—— (1958): *Aggression.* Chicago: University of Chicago Press.

Scott, J. P., Fredericson, E., and Fuller, J. L. (1951): Experimental exploration of the critical period hypothesis, *Personality* 1:162–183.

Searles, H. F. (1956): The psychodynamics of vengefulness, *Psychiatry* 19:31–39.

Sears, R. R., Maccoby, E. E., and Levine, J. (1957): *Patterns of Child Rearing.* New York: Harper & Row.

Seay, B., Hansen, E., and Harlow, H. F. (1962): Mother–infant separation in monkeys, *J. Child Psychol. Psychiat.* 3:123–132.

Seitz, P. F. D. (1959): Infantile experience and adult behavior in animal subjects. 2. Age of separation from the mother and adult behavior in the cat, *Psychosom. Med.* 21:353–378.

Seyle, H. (1979): *The Stress of My Life.* New York: Van Nostrand Reinhold.

—— (1976): *The Stress of Life.* New York: McGraw-Hill.

—— (1957): Stress and psychiatry, *Am. J. Psychiat.* 113:423–427.

—— (1947): The general adaptation syndrome and diseases of adaptation, in *Textbook of Endocrinology.* Montreal: Montreal University Press.

Shakow, D. (1959): Research in child development: A case illustration of the psychologist's dilemma, *Am. J. Orthopsychiat.* 29:45–59.

Sharma, S. L. (1965): Personality and crime, *Res. J. Philos. Soc. Sci.* 2:150–158.

Shirley, M. M. (1942): Children's adjustment to a strange situation, *J. Abnorm. Soc. Psychol.* 37:201–217.

Shneidman, E. (1976): An overview of suicide, *Psychiat. Ann.* 6(11):9–121.

Siegel, I. E. (1956): The need for conceptualization in research on child development, *Child Dev.* 27:241–252.

Silver, H. K., and Kempe, C. H. (1959): Problem of parental criminal neglect and severe physical abuse of children, *J. Dis. Child* 95:528.

Silver, L. B., Dublin, C. C., and Lourie, R. S. (1969): Does violence breed violence? Contributions from a study of the child abuse syndrom, *Am. J. Psychiat. 126:* 404–407.

Skard, A. G., Inhelder, B., Noelting, G., Murphy, L. B., and Thomae, H. (1960): Longitudinal research in personality development, in *Perspectives in Personality Research,* ed. by H. P. David and J. C. B. Brengelmann. New York: Springer.

Slater, P. E. (1962): Parental behavior and the personality of the child, *J Genet. Psychol.* 101:53–68.

Slocum, W., and Stone, C. L. (1958): Factors associated with family affection patterns, *Coordinator* 7:21–25.

Solomon, G. F. (1970): Psychodynamic aspects of aggression, hostility, and violence, in *Violence and the Struggle for Existence,* ed. by D. N. Daniels, M. F. Gilula, and F. M. Ochberg. Boston: Little, Brown.

Sontag, L. W. (1958): Maternal anxiety during pregnancy and fetal behavior. Alternations in intelligence quotient in relation to personality variations, in *Physical and Behavioral Growth,* 26th Ross Pediatric Conference. Columbus, Ohio: Ross Laboratories.

—— (1955): Psychodynamics of child delinquency—Further contributions, *Am. J. Orthopsychiat.* 25:254–261.

—— (1952): A differential study of psychopathic behavior in infants and children, *Am. J. Orthopsychiat.* 22:223–228.

Sontag, L. W., and Kagan, J. (1963): The emergence of intellectual achievement motives, *Am. J. Orthopsychiat.* 33:532–535.

Spiegel, J. P. (1968): Psychosocial factors in riots—Old and new, *Am. J. Psychiat.* 125:281–285.

Spitz, R. A. (1965): *The First Year of Life: A Psychoanalytic Study of Normal and Deviant Development of Object Relations.* New York: International Universities Press.

—— (1955): The influence of the mother-child relationship and its disturbances, in *Mental Health and Infant Development* 1, ed. by K. Soddy. New York: Basic Books.

—— (1954): Infantile depression and the general adaptation syndrome, in *Depression,* ed. by P. H. Hoch and J. Zubin. New York: Grune & Stratton.

—— (1951): The psychogenic diseases in infancy: An attempt at their etiological classification, in *The Psychoanalytic Study of the Child* 6. New York: International Universities Press.

—— (1945): Hospitalism: An inquiry into the genesis of psychiatric conditions in early childhood, in *The Psychoanalytic Study of the Child* 1. New York: International Universities Press.

Spitz, R. A., and Wolf, K. (1946): Anaclitic depression, in *The Psychoanalytic Study of the Child* 2. New York: International Universities Press.

Stegenga, J. A. (1972): Personal aggressiveness and war, *Int. J. Group Tensions* 2:22–36.

Steiner, L. R. (1960): *Understanding Juvenile Delinquency.* Philadelphia: Chilton.

Sternbach, O. (1975): Aggression, the death drive and the problem of sadomasochism, *Int. J. Psycho-Anal.* 56(3):321–334.

Sterne, R. S. (1964): *Delinquent Conduct and Broken Homes: A Study of 1,050 Boys.* New Haven, Conn.: College & Univ. Press.

Steward, L., and Livson, N. (1966): Smoking and rebelliousness: A longitudinal study from childhood to maturity, *J. Consult. Psychol.* 30:325–329.

Stoller, R. (1974): Hostility and mystery in perversion, *Int. J. Psycho-Anal.* 55(3): 425–438.

Stone, L. Reflections on the psychoanalytic concept of aggression, *Psychoanal. Quart.* 40:195–244.

Storr, A. (1972): *Human Destructiveness.* New York: Basic Books.

—— (1968): *Human Aggression.* New York: Atheneum.

Stott, D. H. (1957): Physical and mental handicaps following disturbed pregnancy, *Lancet* 1:1006–1012.

Strauss, M. and Gelles, R. (1980): *Behind Closed Doors: Violence in the American Family.* New York: Doubleday.

Strupp, H. (1976): The nature of the therapeutic influence and its basic ingredients, in *What Makes Behavior Change Possible?* ed. by A. Burton. New York: Brunner-Mazel, 96–112.

Suttie, I. D. (1952): *The Origins of Love and Hate.* New York: Julian Press.

Symonds, M. (1976): Psychodynamics of aggression in women, *Am. J. Psychoanal.* 36(3):195–210.

Symonds, P. M. (1949): *The Dynamics of Parent–Child Relationships.* New York: Teachers College Bur. Publ., Columbia University.

Szasz, T. S. (1947): The role of hostility in the pathogenesis of peptic ulcer, *Psychosom. Med.* 9:331–336.

Tartar, R., et al. (1975): Social role orientation and pathological factors in suicide attempts of varying lethality, *J. Community Psycho.* 3(3):295–299.

Textor, R. B. (1967): *A Cross-Cultural Summary.* New Haven, Conn.: Human Resources Area Files Press.

Thompson, W. R. (1955): Early environment—Its importance for later behavior, in *Psychopathology of Childhood,* ed. by P. H. Hoch and J. Zubin. New York: Grune & Stratton.

Thorne, F. (1959): The etiology of sociopathic reactions, *Am. J. Psychother.* 13:319–330.

Tinbergen, N. (1968): On war and peace in animals and man, *Science* 160:1411–1418.

—— (1963): *Social Behavior in Animals.* New York: John Wiley.

—— (1954): Psychology and ethology as supplementary parts of a science of behavior, in *Group Processes,* ed. by B. Schaffner. New York: Josiah Macy, Jr. Foundation.

Toch, H. H. (1969): *Violent Men: An Inquiry into the Psychology of Violence.* Chicago: Aldine.

Tolor, H., Warren, M., and Weinrich, H. M. (1971): Relation between parental interpersonal styles and their children's psychological distance, *Psychol. Rep.* 29:1263-1275.

Tsumori, M., and Inage, N. (1958): Maternal attitude and its relationship to infant development. *Japan J. Educ. Psychol.* 5:208-218.

Tuddenham, R. D. (1959): The constancy of personality ratings over two decades, *Genet. Psychol. Monogr.* 60:3-29.

Turnbull, C. M. (1973): *The Mountain People.* New York: Simon & Schuster.

Usdin, G., ed. (1972): *Perspectives on Violence.* New York: Brunner/Mazel.

Vogel, E. F. (1960): The marital relationship of parents of emotionally disturbed children: polarization and isolation, *Psychiatry* 23:1-12.

Waelder, R. (1960): *Basic Theory of Psychoanalysis.* New York: International Universities Press, 3-35.

Waring, M., and Ricks, D. F. (1965): Family patterns of children who became adult schizophrenics, *J. Nerv. Ment. Dis.* 140:351-364.

Washburn, A. H. (1959): Annual report to the board of the Child Research Council. (Unpublished)

Washburn, S. L. (1966): Conflict in primate society, in *Conflict in Society,* ed. by A. De Reuck and J. Knight. Boston: Little, Brown.

—— ed. (1963): Behavior in human evolution, in *Classification and Human Evolution.* (Viking Fund Publications in Anthropology, No. 37.) New York: Wenner-Grenn Foundation for Anthropological Research.

—— (1961): *Social Life and Early Man.* Chicago: Aldine.

Washburn, S. L., and Hamburg, D. A. (1968): Aggressive behavior in Old World monkeys and apes, in *Primates: Studies in Adaptation and Variability,* ed. by P. C. Jay. New York: Holt, Rinehart and Winston.

Wasserman, L. H., ed. (1959): *Individual and Family Dynamics.* New York: Grune & Stratton.

Watson, G. (1957): Some personality differences in children related to strict or passive dicipline, *J. Psychol.* 44:227-249.

Weissman, M., Fox, K. and Klerman, G. L. (1973): Hostility and depression associated with suicide attempts, *Am. J. Psychiat.* 130:450-455.

Wenar, C., Handlon, M. W., and Garner, A. M. (1962): *Origins of Psychosomatic and Emotional Disorders.* New York: Hoeber.

Whithorn, J. C. (1956): Stress and emotional health, *Am. J. Psychiat.* 112:773-781.

Whiting, B. B. (1965): Sex identity conflict and physical violence: A comparative study, *Am. Anthropology* 67:123-140.

—— ed. (1963): *Six Cultures: Studies in Child Rearing.* New York: John Wiley.

Whiting, J. W. M., and Child, I. L. (1953): *Child Training and Personality.* New Haven, Conn.: Yale University Press.

Whiting, J. W. M., Chasdi, E. H., Antonovsky, H. F., and Avril, B. C. (1966): The learning of values, in *People of Rimrock: A Study of Values in Five Cultures,* ed. by E. Z. Vogt and E. M. Albert. Cambridge, Mass.: Harvard University Press.

Wilkerson, D., and Cox, C. (1967): *Parents on Trial: Why Kids Go Wrong–or Right.* New York: Hawthorne Books.

Wilson, D. (1951): *My Six Convicts.* New York: Holt, Rinehart and Winston.

Winder, C. L., and Rau, L. (1962): Parental attitudes associated with social deviance in preadolescent boys, *J. Abnorm. Soc. Psychol.* 64:418–424.

Winnick, H. Z., Moses, R., and Ostow, M., eds. (1973): *Psychological Bases of War.* New York: Quadrangle Books.

Wolf, S. (1963): Life stress and patterns of disease, in *The Psychological Basis of Medical Practice,* ed. by H. Lief, V. Lief, and N. Lief. New York: Hoeber Medical Division, Harper & Row.

Wolff, H. G. (1968): *Stress and Disease,* 2nd ed. Revised and ed. by D. Wolf and H. Goodell. Springfield, Ill.: Charles C. Thomas.

—— (1960): The mind-body relationships, in *An Outline of Man's Knowledge.* New York: Doubleday.

Wolfgang, M. E. (1970): Violence and human behavior, in *Psychology and the Problems of Society,* ed, by F. F. Korten, S. W. Cook, and J. I. Lacey. Washington, D. C.: American Psychological Association.

Wolfgang, M. E., and Ferracuti, F. (1967): *The Subculture of Violence.* London: Tavistock.

Wolman, B. B. (1972): Human belligerence, *Int. J. Group Tensions* 2:48–66.

—— (1971): The empty bucket, *Int. J. Group Tensions* 1:5–25.

Woods, R. L. (1947): *World of Dreams.* New York: Random House.

World Health Organization (1977): Child mental health and psychosocial development, *WHO Technical Rep. Series 613.*

—— (1968): Prevention of suicide, *WHO Publ. Health Papers 35.*

—— (1964): Deprivation of maternal care: A reassessment of its effects, *WHO Publ. Health Papers 14.*

Yarrow, L. J. (1961): Maternal deprivation: Toward an empirical and conceptual re-evaluation, *Psychol. Bull.* 58:459–490;

Zegans, L. S. (1973): Philosophical antecedents to modern theories of human aggressive instinct, *Psychonal. Quart.* 42:239–266.

Zilboorg, G. (1968): *The Psychology of the Criminal Act and Punishment* (Issac Ray Lectures, 1954). Westport, Conn.: Greenwood Press.

Index